THE
SUPERFUN
TIMES
Vegan Holiday
COOKBOOK

THE SUPERFUN TIMES

Vegan Holiday

COOKBOOK

· ENTERTAINING ·
FOR ABSOLUTELY EVERY OCCASION

ISA CHANDRA MOSKOWITZ

*Photographs by Vanessa Rees
and Joshua Foo*

LITTLE, BROWN AND COMPANY

NEW YORK BOSTON LONDON

Little, Brown and Company
Hachette Book Group
1290 Avenue of the Americas, New York, NY 10104
littlebrown.com

First Edition: November 2016

Little, Brown and Company is a division of Hachette Book Group, Inc. The Little,
Brown name and logo are trademarks of Hachette Book Group, Inc.

The publisher is not responsible for websites (or their content)
that are not owned by the publisher.

The Hachette Speakers Bureau provides a wide range
of authors for speaking events. To find out more, go to hachettespeakersbureau.com
or call (866) 376-6591.

Photographs on the following pages are by Joshua Foo: vi, 171, 172, 187, 252, 290, 295,
325, 334, 337, 340, 347, 348, 352, 361, 362, 367, 371, 378, 383, 384, 393, 398,
402, 412, 418. All other photographs are by Vanessa Rees.

ISBN 978-0-316-22189-4
LCCN 2016941207

10 9 8 7 6 5 4 3 2 1

WOR

Interior design and hand-lettering by Laura Palese

Printed in the United States of America

To John McDevitt,
CAT DAD

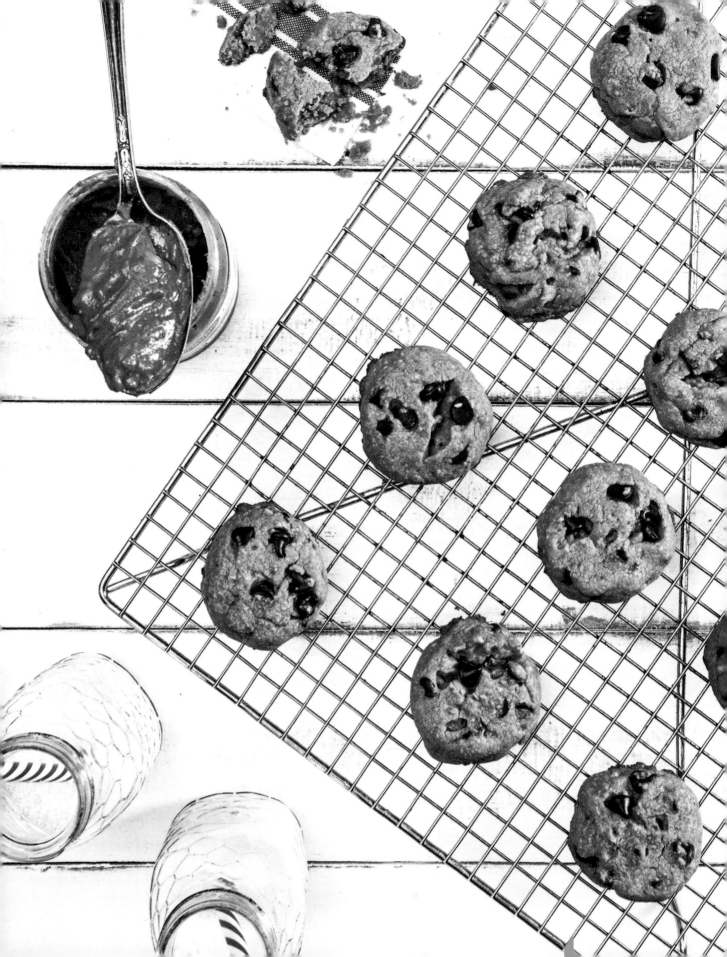

CONTENTS

Introduction

Entertaining for Absolutely Every Occasion 2

THE
SUPERFUN
TIMES
Vegan Holiday
COOKBOOK

Introduction

ENTERTAINING *for* ABSOLUTELY EVERY OCCASION

◆ LET'S GET THE PARTY STARTED! ◆

The reason I wrote this book is simple: I love to cook for holidays and special occasions. *Every* holiday. Even holidays I didn't grow up celebrating and even occasions that I don't especially believe in. Any excuse to bring people together around food is good enough for me. Everyone needs a reason to take a break from normalcy. We have an innate primal urge to celebrate. I am sure there are studies about it from Neanderthal days. If not, there should be.

I also wrote this book for everyone who's ever asked what to serve to the vegans in their lives that is more than just salad. And for every vegan who has ever wondered what to serve to their family at Thanksgiving that would knock their turkey socks off. This book is full of crowd pleasers. Food that is familiar to the occasion, with a fun vegan translation. Food that will bring everyone together.

But this isn't your average entertaining book, where you pull it out once a year and the rest of the time it's being used to press tofu. I want it to be your best friend, sitting on the counter, gossiping with you as you cook along. Here's how to use it.

◆ MENU PLANNING ◆

I didn't set the chapters up as formal menus because I find that limiting. Instead, you should look at each holiday section as a little cook-zine celebrating what makes that day or part of the year special. This way, you have a lot more recipes for each occasion and the ability to pick and choose what you'd like to serve. Of course, I do give a little guidance on what works well together. But menu planning can be as simple or as daring as you like!

On the simple end, for a nice dinner, just choose a few dishes from a chapter, say, a soup, a salad, an entrée, and a dessert. Boom, done. If you need help deciding, ask your favorite people for their favorite dishes or ingredients or type of cuisine, and get inspired from there.

Maybe you're looking for a finger-foods party, in which case just pick a bunch of apps. You don't have to stick to the chapter of a particular holiday. You can certainly mix and match, pulling, say, an hors d'oeuvre from the Oscars section into your Easter spread. There's no reason not to! Maybe you want Smokin' Hot Dates at your New Year's or on Halloween. Maybe you want lasagna, for, hmm, let's see, everything? Simply browse the index organized by "meal type" and see what piques your interest. Speaking of which...

✦ ANYTIME MEALS ✦

Guess what? You can cook any of these holiday recipes anytime and just call them lunch or dinner. Although I wouldn't suggest serving Zomberoni Pizza Faces (page 314) anytime other than Halloween (unless you really want to), you can certainly serve Curry Pork Fried Rice (page 86) for dinner or just enjoy scones (page 192) on any old Sunday.

When it comes down to it, you can treat this like a regular cookbook. Serve the hors d'oeuvres at your friend's baby shower, make jelly doughnuts just because you can, throw together a veggieful salad with your farmers' market ingredients, and of course make a potato salad every day of the week just because.

✦ ENTERTAINING HIGHS & LOWS ✦

When I see magazine articles promising "Tips for stress-free entertaining!" I laugh to myself and hope that the article inside is about ordering in, or maybe a party where you're serving only hummus. I hate to break it to you, but it can be *stressful* to entertain. That's why right around Thanksgiving you actually see couples in yoga pants arguing right in front of the red Russian kale at the market, completely blocking your access.

But stress isn't a reason not to do things. And to help you along, here are a few tips to make things easier. And also keep in mind: not everything has to be perfect. I like my lasagna a little burnt sometimes. It's food. Have fun!

✦ A WORD ABOUT DRINKS ✦

Books have limited space and I didn't want to fill this one with fluff. There are a few drink recipes here and there, but I figure, why waste space with *another* margarita recipe? Those recipes are easy enough to find by looking at AllRecipes.com or Epicurious.com and picking the highest-rated one.

✦ OTHER OCCASIONS ✦

I hope that this book gets you through other occasions as well as the ones listed here! For birthday celebrations, use any of the cupcake recipes (but maybe garnish with sprinkles instead). For baby showers, use the new mom's favorite ingredients in hors d'oeuvres. For Diwali, serve those samosas and curries! There's a world of food in this book—cook from it to make every event special to you!

HOSTING TIPS
for the HOPELESS

1 Find out if there are any guests with allergies (real or imagined). If the "ingredient swaps" in this book don't offer the solution you're looking for, then be sure to research online. If there are too many special requests and your casserole is becoming a Rubik's Cube of allergens, choose a different dish. But remember, not everything has to please everyone; just make sure there are options. Don't give up on your seitan in cashew cream because of only one guest.

2 Once you've got that down, plan the menu two weeks in advance. I know that's like a *looong* time. And I don't mean to actually start cooking anything. I just mean, familiarize yourself with the recipes. See if any specialty shopping needs to be done. Maybe you can order that truffle oil online, or perhaps you'll swing by the Asian market for that curry powder on your way home from work. Which brings me to my next point.

3 Read through the recipes and see that you'll have everything you need. You don't want to have all of your veggies chopped and then have to improvise on that 9-by-13-inch casserole. Or what if you only have one springform pan and two different recipes need it? Horror of horrors! Planning well in advance will allow you to buy as needed, or borrow from friends, or maybe persuade yourself to try another dish altogether.

4 Follow the "Make Ahead" rules on page 6 like they're a religion.

5 Make sure that the day of the event you've got time to shower, get dressed up all nice, and do any of the things that make you feel good! Once you've done that, you can reheat the casseroles, take the plastic wrap off the salads, fill up those punch bowls, and do it all looking flawless and fabulous.

6 Have snacks ready! I personally don't think that pretzels from the store are a great pregame snack, even if they have Paul Newman on them. Chips and stuff are nice to supplement, but have an hors d'oeuvre or two (like a finger food and a dip) at the ready when guests arrive *hangry*.

MAKE AHEAD

Generally, I spread prep for a big holiday across four days. It's a life saver to have your beans cooked, your cashews soaked, your tofu pressed, and your seitan made days ahead.

4 DAYS AHEAD   Soak and cook beans, soak cashews, make pastry crusts, shop for specialty dry ingredients

3 DAYS AHEAD   Make sauces, dressings, marinades, seitan; prepare grains that need to be cold or part of another recipe (for instance, rice for fried rice or veggie burgers, quinoa for a chilled salad)

1 OR 2 DAYS AHEAD   Make desserts (cheesecakes, brownies, cookies, pies), prep vegetables for main dishes that need to be made the day of, cook soups or stews, cook items that reheat easily (like roasts, lasagna, casseroles), reserve garnishes for next day

DAY OF   Prepare salads, reheat main dishes and casseroles, heat up soups, finish up any main dishes

Note: Once you soak cashews overnight, remove from water, store in an airtight container, and use within 2 days.

SETTING *the* HOLIDAY TABLE *(or Not)*

Remember in the '90s when no one had chairs (had they been confiscated by the government?) and everyone was always sitting around on pillows with big mugs of coffee? Yeah, well, most of my events look like that. For some dinners, it's nice to give everyone a little napkin ring, neatly stacked plates, and their silverware in the right order (whatever that is!). But honestly, do most people have room for ten at their dinner table? If you do, cool. No need to read on. You have probably already written your own holiday cookbook. But if you're like me and you've got a couch, some upholstered ottomans, and a bunch of pillows that are too expensive and look like Dr. Seuss creatures, then this should help.

You don't always have to entertain around a table! It's okay to have everyone sitting around the living room in various states. Yeah, don't put your great-grandma on a beanbag chair, you big jerk, but you can use common sense. My only advice is not to be so casual about it that you're unprepared. Make sure there is seating for everyone, be it a chair, a pillow, or a rocking horse.

ALLERGY SUBSTITUTIONS

If you have my other cookbooks, these are already familiar. If not, here are a few of my favorite subs!

Gluten Gluten can be found in the darndest places! Always check labeling for hidden ingredients. These are some of the most common gluten hangouts and what I do to replace them.

SOY SAUCE: Use gluten-free tamari. San-J is my favorite brand, and it's widely available. In fact, I never even use soy sauce now since it's easy and delicious to keep tamari on hand.

BREAD CRUMBS: For fine, dry bread crumbs, unsalted gluten-free pretzels work wonders, but they can be expensive. An affordable alternative is Chex-type cereals in either rice or corn varieties. To make the bread crumbs, finely grind the cereal or pretzel pieces in a blender until they're in tiny, almost powdery, crumbs.

ROUX: To thicken curries, stews, and even mac and cheese, I love to use chickpea flour in place of all-purpose. It works wonderfully and gives a nice toasty flavor, too!

PASTA: Easy enough! There are zillions of gluten-free pastas on the market. Sometimes I use it just because I like it. My favorite varieties are quinoa and rice pastas.

COOKIES AND SCONES: Other baked goods can get more complicated, but for cookies and scones, it's pretty simple. I use certified gluten-free oats. Grind the oats into a flour and then measure. I usually need a bit more flour than the recipe calls for; say, a tablespoon or two extra per cup of flour. For everything else, just read online reviews for the best baking mixes and purchase them that way.

Nuts Okay, so we've got tree-nut allergies, and we've got nut and seed allergies, and we've got peanut allergies. Life for cookbook authors can get complicated fast when trying to accommodate! Here are a few of my favorite swaps for all different sorts of no-nuts-allowed occasions.

PEANUTS: If the diner doesn't have a tree-nut allergy, use cashews. If your guest does, then sesame seeds make a nice treat in savory dishes, even if the texture will be different.

PEANUT BUTTER: Sunbutter (which is sunflower seed butter) makes a great replacement. Although, in baked goods, it sometimes turns the dough green. Maybe that would be fun? If your guest doesn't have a tree-nut allergy, then almond butter is a great alternative.

CASHEWS: As far as the recipes in this book go, cashews are probably the biggest bummer because of all the cashew cream recipes. My heart bleeds for you, it truly does! But listen, a few of my testers had cashew allergies and they had happy results using sunflower seeds instead. In Thai and Indian dishes, coconut milk is a fantastic alternative as well.

Soy I hope that I've provided enough soy-free recipes to keep you entertained for years. But if you're looking to replace soy sauce, there are soy-free miso pastes that you can blend with water. Just make sure that it's still good, thick, and salty, and not too watered down. You can then use it anywhere in place of soy sauce, even in seitan!

EQUIPMENT

(OR WHY YOU DON'T ABSOLUTELY NEED A MILLION DIFFERENT TART PANS BUT YOU CAN GET THEM IF YOU WANT TO)

I tried my darndest to make these recipes with pots and pans and utensils that you already have hanging around. While I don't call for any super-specific one-task tools (no avocado slicer here!), there might be a few things you should add to your equipment checklist. And since it is entertaining, why not grab a few cute mini tart pans or cookie cutters just to make things extra special?

WHIP IT!

If you purchase a whipped cream canister and some chargers, you can make your own whipped cream effortlessly! Just blend together a can of full-fat pure coconut milk and 1 tablespoon agave. Fill, chill, charge, and squirt!

SMOKE IT!

You don't need a stovetop smoker to smoke at home, although they are really awesome. A stainless steel pot fitted with a steamer basket works just great! Simply line the bottom of the pan with aluminum foil and fill with the soaked wood chips. Place the items to smoke in the lightly greased steamer basket and smoke on low.

PRESS IT!

Pressing tofu helps it soak up marinade more easily, and gives it a firmer texture. Wrap the tofu in a paper towel, then a kitchen towel. Rest a heavy pan on it or a cookbook (not this one!), then add a couple cans of beans so the weight is even. Flip after a half hour and press the other side. It's ready!

POWER TOOLS

- Blender
- Immersion blender
- Large food processor
- Hand mixer

BASICS

- Large wooden cutting board
- Chef's knife
- Thin metal spatula
- Slanted wooden spatula
- Potato masher (big and small)
- Tongs
- Peelers
- Slotted spoon
- Ladle
- Microplane grater
- Pasta spoon

STOVETOP & OVEN

- Large cast iron pan
- 2-quart stainless steel saucepot
- 4-quart stainless steel soup pot
- 8-quart stainless steel pot or Dutch oven
- A few 9-by-13-inch ceramic casseroles
- Cast iron grill pan
- Steamer, stovetop or electric

BAKING

- 2 large rimmed baking sheets
- 8-inch square metal baking pan
- 9-by-13-inch metal baking pan
- 8-inch springform pan
- Jelly roll pan
- Parchment paper
- A million mixing bowls
- Dry measuring cups, stainless steel, with strong handles

- Bundt pan
- 8-by-4-inch loaf pan
- Muffin tins
- Large wooden spoon for mixing batters
- Measuring spoons that fit in spice jars
- Baking sheets
- Mesh sifter
- Ice cream scooper
- Cooling racks

FOR SERVING

- Ceramic serving bowls (vintage is great, and cheap!)
- A million large serving spoons
- Smaller ceramic bowls for sauces and sides
- Big ceramic serving trays (white is always pretty)
- Trivets and pretty towels for placing warm things on the table
- Gravy boats
- Pretty napkins

NICE-TO-HAVES

- Vitamix, Blendtec, or other high-speed blender—so you can skip the cashew soaking step in so many of these recipes!
- Standing mixer
- Mini Bundt pan
- Small loaf pan
- Pastry bags with small and big tips
- Funny-shaped ice cube trays
- Whipped cream canister
- Stovetop smoker
- Lots of shapes of cookie cutter
- Lots of mini tart pans

1
NEW YEAR'S

What better way to start a
HOLIDAY COOKBOOK
than with a celebration of the
NEW YEAR?

WHETHER IT'S AN intimate evening in with friends and family, or a full-on party with champagne popping and booty shaking, your evening is ready to rock with these recipes.

The next morning, you're celebrating (or sweeping away) the year you just left behind, and saying hello to the first sunrise (or afternoon) of the first day of a brand-spankin' new year. There's never been a better time to become the best dang vegan cook in the world. Have a vegan brunch!

It really doesn't matter when you roll out of bed. Brunch gives you a luxurious window of time, spanning breakfast and lunch all in one convenient portmanteau. Keep it casual and spontaneous, inviting over whomever you feel like on the spur of the moment, or plan ahead with things you can make beforehand and have very little to do on the day of. Either way, a lavish and fun brunch does not need to be complicated.

The recipes here can be served together or on their own, but they all include foods that have been considered symbols of prosperity throughout history. From fruit like oranges and apples to savory components like greens and beans, I've got your good luck covered. Now it's your job to share that with your friends and family. Eat deliciously and prosper!

TEMPEH SAUSAGE–
STUFFED MUSHROOMS

FOR THE TEMPEH:

3 tablespoons tamari or soy sauce

1 tablespoon olive oil

1 tablespoon balsamic vinegar

1 (8-ounce) package tempeh, crumbled

FOR THE MUSHROOMS:

1 pound cremini mushrooms

2 tablespoons olive oil, plus more for drizzling

1 small yellow onion, diced very small

1 red bell pepper, seeded and diced very small

2 garlic cloves, minced

1 teaspoon fennel seeds, crushed

½ teaspoon dried thyme

Freshly ground black pepper

½ cup plain bread crumbs

¼ cup water, plus additional as needed

Salt

½ cup chopped scallions

Tempeh makes for a succulent and meaty filling in these classy little mushroom caps, loaded with yummy sausage herbs and spices, like fennel seed and pepper. Yeah, they're an hors d'oeuvre, but they're pretty filling! They are really nice at room temp, too, so don't worry about serving them right away.

MAKE THE TEMPEH: In a medium mixing bowl, whisk together the tamari, olive oil, and balsamic vinegar. Add the crumbled tempeh and set aside to marinate for at least 1 hour.

MAKE THE MUSHROOMS: Remove the stems from the mushrooms and set the caps aside. Roughly chop the stems and set aside to be used in the stuffing later on.

Preheat a large, heavy-bottomed pan (preferably cast iron) over medium-high heat. Add 1 tablespoon of the oil and sauté the onion and bell pepper until softened, 5 to 7 minutes. Add the garlic, fennel, thyme, and a few grinds of black pepper; cook until fragrant, about 30 seconds.

Back to the tempeh. All of the marinade should be absorbed into the tempeh. It's okay if a little is left, but don't add it to the pan—just lift the tempeh out.

Add the tempeh to the pan along with the remaining 1 tablespoon olive oil and cook until browned, about 10 minutes, stirring frequently. Add the bread crumbs and stir to coat. Cook until the bread crumbs are toasted and a few shades darker, about 2 minutes.

Add the chopped mushroom stems and the water and cook until the mushrooms release their moisture and the mixture holds together when pressed, about 5 minutes. Add additional water by the tablespoon as needed; the mixture should not be too dry. Taste and adjust for salt and pepper. Fold in the scallions and set aside to cool slightly.

Preheat the oven to 350°F. Lightly grease a large rimmed baking sheet with olive oil and sprinkle with a little salt. The salt goes a long way to making sure the mushrooms aren't bland.

Spoon the filling into the mushroom caps so that it rises above the rim by about ¾ inch. Place the mushrooms on the baking sheet and drizzle each with a little olive oil. Bake until the mushrooms are tender and browned, 20 to 25 minutes. Serve warm or at room temperature.

Roasted Vegetable
BANH MI

FOR THE PICKLES:

1 slender 10-inch daikon radish

2 large carrots

1 cup rice vinegar

½ cup sugar

2 tablespoons salt

FOR THE VEGETABLES:

1 pound eggplant, cut crosswise into not-quite-½-inch slices

1 pound zucchini, cut diagonally into ¼-inch ovals

2 large portobello mushroom caps, cut into ½-inch slices

3 tablespoons refined coconut oil, melted

½ teaspoon salt

¼ teaspoon Chinese five-spice powder

FOR THE SPICY MAYO:

½ cup vegan mayo, purchased or homemade (page 67)

2 tablespoons sriracha

FOR THE SANDWICHES:

3 French baguettes

Fresh mint leaves

Fresh cilantro leaves

Perhaps the best way to decide what to eat on New Year's Eve is simply by listening to your taste buds. And most of the time, but especially late at night, my taste buds are screaming "Banh mi!" This version uses roasted vegetables to play with all the traditional components. The eggplant becomes lush and creamy when roasted, similar to pâté. The portobello is meaty and succulent. And the zucchini is just being its delicious self. Of course there are all the flavors that we love in a banh mi—spicy mayo, bright pickles, and plenty of fresh herbs. Tonight's gonna be a good night! Serve these sandwiches as entrees with the Jicama-Avocado Salad (page 16), or slice them up into sixths for perfectly portioned hors d'oeuvres.

MAKE THE PICKLES: Peel the daikon and carrots and slice into long, thin matchsticks no thicker than ¼ inch. You can use a mandoline for this or take your time with a chef's knife. Toss the daikon and carrot matchsticks together and pack them into a clean, dry 1-pint glass jar or bowl.

In a small saucepan, combine the vinegar, sugar, and salt and bring to a gentle simmer over medium heat. Simmer for 2 minutes. Stir to dissolve the sugar and salt and then pour the liquid over the vegetables in the jar. Cover the jar tightly and chill for at least 30 minutes before using.

MAKE THE VEGETABLES: Preheat the oven to 400°F.

Line two large rimmed baking sheets with parchment and coat lightly with nonstick cooking spray. Lay out the eggplant slices in a flat layer on one sheet and the zucchini and mushrooms on the other. Drizzle each sheet with 1½ tablespoons coconut oil, ¼ teaspoon salt, and ⅛ teaspoon Chinese five-spice powder. Toss the vegetables gently to coat, then spread them out again in a single layer and lightly coat them with nonstick cooking spray. Roast the veggies for 10 minutes, flip them, spray the eggplant again, and rotate the pans. Continue to roast until the vegetables are tender, another 8 to 10 minutes.

MAKE THE SPICY MAYO: Put the mayo in a small bowl and stir in the sriracha to combine.

ASSEMBLE THE SANDWICHES: Cut the baguettes crosswise into fourths or fifths and then halve them horizontally. Lightly toast the bread and then slather the bottom slices with the spicy mayo. Layer the roasted eggplant, mushrooms, and zucchini over the mayo, top with the pickles, fresh mint and cilantro, and the baguette top. Serve warm.

SERVES

6

JICAMA-AVOCADO
SALAD

with Grapes

TOTAL
20 MINUTES
ACTIVE
20 MINUTES

FOR THE DRESSING:

2 tablespoons chopped shallot

¼ cup fresh lime juice

2 tablespoons grapeseed oil

1 tablespoon mellow white miso

1 tablespoon sriracha

1 teaspoon sugar

FOR THE SALAD:

4 cups loosely packed baby greens

1½ cups small-diced jicama

1 avocado, pitted, peeled, and diced small

1 cup halved purple or red grapes

¼ cup (loosely packed) roughly chopped fresh mint

½ cup roughly chopped roasted salted peanuts

6 small fresh cilantro sprigs, for garnish

This is the most prosperous salad there is, and its unexpected flavors are also fabulously yummy together. If round is a symbol of good fortune, then expect everything to go exactly how you want it this year. And a salad couldn't get any more fun: Jicama is crisp and crunchy, grapes are fruity and juicy, and avocado is, of course, creamy and dreamy. Mint, peanuts, and cilantro lend a refreshing Vietnamese flair that everyone will be talking about all year.

MAKE THE DRESSING: Combine the shallot, lime juice, grapeseed oil, miso, sriracha, and sugar in a blender and puree until very smooth. Chill in an airtight container until ready to use.

MAKE THE SALAD: In a large bowl, toss the greens, jicama, avocado, grapes, and mint with the dressing. Divide the salad among six bowls. Some of the grapes and jicama will have fallen to the bottom of the large mixing bowl, so scatter them evenly over the top of the greens. Top each serving with some peanuts and garnish with a cilantro sprig. Serve!

CHICKEE-STYLE SEITAN

MAKES

2

POUNDS

TOTAL
1 HOUR 15 MINUTES
ACTIVE
15 MINUTES

FOR THE BROTH:

8 cups vegetable broth, purchased or homemade (page 203)

6 garlic cloves, peeled and smashed with the flat side of a knife

2 bay leaves

FOR THE SEITAN:

2 cups vital wheat gluten

¼ cup nutritional yeast

¼ cup chickpea flour

2 teaspoons onion powder

1 teaspoon dried sage

¼ teaspoon salt

1¼ cups vegetable broth, purchased or homemade (page 203)

¼ cup tamari or soy sauce

2 teaspoons olive oil

This seitan is so easy and versatile! Yes, I created it to replace chicken in recipes (who would eat a chicken?), but it's perfect for wherever you need a meaty texture and you need it *now*.

MAKE THE BROTH: Fill a stockpot with the broth, smashed garlic cloves, and bay leaves, cover, and bring to a boil over medium-high heat.

MAKE THE SEITAN: In the meantime, mix the vital wheat gluten, nutritional yeast, chickpea flour, onion powder, sage, and salt in a large bowl. Make a well in the center and add the broth, tamari, and olive oil. Mix with a fork and then use your hands to knead for about 3 minutes, until it's a firm dough and everything looks well incorporated. Divide into eight even pieces. An easy way to do this is to divide the dough in half, then divide those halves in half, and then divide *those* halves in half. Ta-da! Eight pieces. Stretch each piece into a cutlet, pressing the cutlet into the counter to smooth the surface. Let rest until the broth mixture has come to a full boil.

Once the broth is boiling, lower the heat to a simmer. This is important: The broth should not be at a rolling boil or you risk the seitan getting waterlogged (aka turning into brains). Add the cutlets and partially cover the pot so that steam can escape. Let simmer for 45 minutes, turning occasionally. Make sure to keep an eye on the heat, because it may start to boil again, in which case just turn it down a notch to keep at a slow, steady simmer.

When the seitan is done, you can let it cool right in the broth or remove a portion to use right away. Once cooled, store the seitan in a tightly covered container, submerged in its broth.

Smokin' Hot
DATES

MAKES
36
DATES

TOTAL
1 HOUR 30 MINUTES
ACTIVE
20 MINUTES

1 cup slivered almonds

2 tablespoons refined coconut oil

½ cup warm water

¼ cup seeded chipotle peppers in adobo sauce (see Tip, page 61)

1 tablespoon fresh lemon juice

½ teaspoon salt

18 Medjool dates, pitted and cut in half crosswise

Here's a neat little spin on fruit and cheese. A smoky almond filling is piped into sweet dates to create an explosion of flavor. These are tiny little things that come together easily and pack a big punch. You'll need a pastry bag fitted with a little metal piping tip, so don't forget to add "become a person with a pastry bag" to your list of New Year's resolutions.

Bring a small saucepan of water to a boil over high heat. Add the almonds and boil them for 30 minutes. Drain the almonds and transfer them to a food processor fitted with a metal blade. While the almonds are still hot, add the coconut oil so that it melts. Add the water, chipotles, lemon juice, and salt and blend until relatively smooth. Almonds tend to not get totally smooth, so a little bumpiness is totally acceptable.

Transfer the almond cheese mixture to a sealed container and refrigerate for 20 minutes or so.

Prepare a pastry bag with a small metal tip. Transfer the almond cheese to the pastry bag. Pipe some of the cheese into the opening of each date, letting it mound up about ¼ inch outside the edge of the opening. Arrange the dates on a flat plate, sitting up with the cheese at the top, and serve.

MAKES
16
CRAB CAKES

TOTAL
1 HOUR 30 MINUTES
ACTIVE
30 MINUTES

Black-Eyed Pea & Zucchini
CRAB CAKES

FOR THE RÉMOULADE:

2 tablespoons vegan mayo, purchased or homemade (page 67)

1 tablespoon Dijon mustard

1 tablespoon Tabasco hot sauce

2 teaspoons capers

FOR THE BREADING:

¾ cup bread crumbs

1 teaspoon Old Bay Seasoning

1 teaspoon onion powder

Freshly ground black pepper

FOR THE CAKES:

1 (15-ounce) can black-eyed peas, rinsed and drained, or 1½ cups cooked black-eyed peas

1½ cups shredded zucchini (about 1 average-size zuke)

¼ cup very finely chopped red bell pepper

1 cup bread crumbs

3 tablespoons vegan mayo, purchased or homemade (page 67)

2 tablespoons fresh lemon juice

1 tablespoon kelp granules or finely ground nori (optional)

2 teaspoons Old Bay Seasoning

2 teaspoons onion powder

Salt

Freshly ground black pepper

Olive oil, for frying

Baby arugula leaves, for garnish

Lemon wedges, for garnish

Shredded zucchini creates that flakiness you expect from a crab cake, and black-eyed peas provide just the right crumbly density. Old Bay Seasoning gives them the seal of authenticity. How fishy you want to get is up to you—if you are craving those oceanic notes, add a little kelp powder or crushed nori. These cakes can do double duty: They work great as a cocktail party appetizer, but they're equally at home for your New Year's Day brunch.

MAKE THE RÉMOULADE: Simply mix everything together in a bowl! Cover and refrigerate until ready to serve.

MAKE THE BREADING: In a shallow bowl combine the bread crumbs, Old Bay, onion powder, and a few grinds of black pepper. Set aside.

MAKE THE CAKES: In a food processor, pulse the black-eyed peas until mashed but not pureed—the peas should still be recognizable. Transfer them to a large mixing bowl. Add the shredded zucchini, bell pepper, bread crumbs, mayo, lemon juice, kelp or nori (if using), Old Bay, onion powder, and salt and pepper to taste. Mix everything together until the zucchini releases its moisture and the mixture holds together well. Refrigerate for about 30 minutes.

To make the patties, take a scoop of batter in your hands and form it into a sphere the size of a golf ball. Gently press the ball into a disk about 1½ inches in diameter. Toss it in the breading to coat. If the breading isn't sticking, moisten the patty a bit with water on your fingertips.

Preheat a large nonstick skillet (preferably cast iron) over medium heat. Add a thin layer of olive oil to the pan. In batches, cook the crab cakes until golden brown, about 4 minutes per side. Keep the crab cakes warm on a plate tented with aluminum foil until ready to serve.

Scatter some arugula over the crab cakes and serve with the rémoulade and lemon wedges.

LACY CRÊPES

MAKES

6

CRÊPES

TOTAL
1 HOUR
ACTIVE
30 MINUTES

1 cup unsweetened almond milk (or your favorite nondairy milk)

1 tablespoon ground golden flaxseed

1½ cups all-purpose flour

1 tablespoon sugar

1 teaspoon salt

1 cup club soda

2 tablespoons canola oil

Refined coconut oil, for the pan

Tips

This recipe is suited even for crêpe-shy beginners. But if you're really nervous about throwing caution to the wind on the very first day of the year, do a test run a few days before.

If you're feeling really fancy and you have some leftover champagne from New Year's Eve, you can use it to replace the club soda in this recipe. It's all about the bubbles.

You can cook the crêpes up to 3 days in advance. When they have cooled completely, stack them between sheets of parchment or wax paper and store them in a large zip-top bag in the refrigerator. To reheat, preheat a large pan over medium heat and warm each crêpe in the pan for 30 seconds on each side.

Good morning! Crêpes make a great start to a fabulous year. Even if nothing else goes right for the next 364 days, at least you've accomplished one thing: You've mastered crêpes. (And that's more than you can say for anyone else!) These crêpes are delicate and buttery, with perfectly crisped curly edges, just right for sweet or savory fillings. The ingredients are deceptively simple, but they produce the most beautiful crêpes. The secret to the butteriness is the coconut oil in the pan, so don't skimp there; use a healthy dab for each crêpe. This recipe doubles and triples well, so you'll be all set for a small, intimate gathering or a big old bash.

In a blender, whiz together the milk and flaxseed on high speed for a minute or so, until the mixture is frothy and the flaxseeds are just tiny specks. Add the flour, sugar, salt, club soda, and canola oil and pulse a few times to mix the flour in. Once it is relatively mixed, blend on high speed until very smooth, scraping down the sides of the blender jar with a spatula to make sure everything is well combined.

Place the blender jar in the refrigerator and let the batter rest for 30 minutes.

Heat a large nonstick skillet over medium-high heat. The pan is ready when a few drops of water flicked onto the surface sizzle.

Put a tablespoon or so of coconut oil in the pan and let it melt. Ladle about ½ cup of the batter in the center of the pan. Spread the batter very thinly by lifting and tilting the pan, or by using the back of the ladle.

Cook until the top of the crêpe is dry, the center is bubbling, and the edges are lightly browned and crinkly and are pulling away from the sides of the pan, usually about 2 minutes. Gently run a spatula under the crêpe to loosen it, then carefully flip it and cook on the other side for 30 seconds. Slide the crêpe onto a dinner plate and tent it with aluminum foil. Repeat with the remaining crêpes (you should end up with six total), stacking them as you go. The crêpes are now ready to fill, fold, and serve.

DO I NEED A
CRÊPE PAN?

I suppose "need" is an extreme word. The answer is no.
And if you are an average person with a time-consuming job and a
few hobbies, not looking to start a crêperie in Paris or
Portland, then the answer is *really* no.

If you already have a crêpe pan, disregard the next few paragraphs and go on with your life (most likely the business plan you are creating for your crêperie—you already know what you're doing). Otherwise, read on.

The most important factor for cooking crêpes is that your pan be nonstick. Now, I'm not judging you. (Yes, I am.) Maybe your nonstick pan is Teflon, or maybe it's cast iron. (I hope it's cast iron!) Whatever the case, it has to be *completely* and *fabulously* and *flawlessly* nonstick. So: no stainless steel, no enamel, no "I'm not sure, but I think I made pancakes in it once." Once you've determined that it's non-stick, you are most of the way to success.

The second most important factor is that your pan be large! A 12-inch pan is ideal. It should leave enough room to get your spatula underneath the edges of the crêpe without much effort.

Other tools of the trade:

THIN, FLEXIBLE SPATULA: You need your spatula to be a state-of-the-art, aerodynamic, modern marvel of technology and engineering. Or, just, you know, that super old but so dependable metal one with the rooster on the handle that you stole from your grandma. Either way, it has to be very, very thin and very, very flexible, to slide under the crêpe like a ninja.

BLENDER: You do not need a high-speed, million-dollar model. A regular old blender works wonders by pumping little air bubbles into your crêpe, and that's how they get lacy. It's also just really convenient to use and makes cleanup NBD.

CINNAMON-APPLE
CRÊPES

MAKES
6
CRÊPES

TOTAL
30 MINUTES
ACTIVE
20 MINUTES

2 tablespoons refined coconut oil

5 large Granny Smith apples, peeled and cut into ¼-inch slices

1 tablespoon cornstarch

1 cup cold water

½ cup lightly packed brown sugar

¾ teaspoon ground cinnamon

Salt

1 recipe Lacy Crêpes (page 22)

Powdered sugar

Maybe your New Year desires are more sweet than savory? You can't go wrong starting the year with apples. Here, a fragrant pie-like filling will have your kitchen smelling like a bakery and will turn your guests' hearts into big juicy apples.

Heat a large pan over medium heat. Heat the coconut oil until melted, then add the apples and sauté until tender but still firm and releasing juice, 5 to 7 minutes.

In the meantime, whisk the cornstarch into the water until dissolved; set aside.

When the apples are ready, add the brown sugar and cinnamon and stir to coat the apples. Add the cornstarch mixture and a pinch of salt and stir well. Turn the heat up and cook, keeping a close eye on the apples, until the mixture is hot and thickened, about 5 minutes. Turn off the heat and cover the pan to keep it warm until ready to serve.

To assemble the crêpes, spoon a line of filling down the center of each crêpe. Fold both sides over and dust with powdered sugar. Serve!

HOPPIN' JOHN
BOWL

FOR THE RED-HOT TAHINI:

½ cup tahini

⅓ cup Buffalo hot sauce
(like Frank's Red Hot)

¼ cup water (plus more as needed)

2 tablespoons nutritional yeast

1 garlic clove, peeled

FOR THE TOMATO-PARSLEY SALAD:

2 cups diced tomatoes

1 cup finely sliced scallions

⅓ cup finely chopped fresh parsley

2 tablespoons red wine vinegar

Pinch salt

Several pinches freshly ground
black pepper

FOR THE HOPPIN' JOHN:

2 tablespoons olive oil

1 onion, thinly sliced

1 green bell pepper, seeded and cut
into thin strips

2 celery stalks, thinly sliced

Salt

¼ cup sliced garlic

½ teaspoon dried oregano

½ teaspoon crushed red pepper flakes

1 pound collard greens, tough stems
removed, leaves torn into 2-inch
pieces

¼ cup vegetable broth, purchased or
homemade (page 203), or water

½ teaspoon liquid smoke

1 (15-ounce) can black-eyed peas,
rinsed and drained, or 1½ cups
cooked black-eyed peas

¼ cup thinly sliced scallions, for
garnish

I'll be honest: Before the internet, I didn't know that unless you eat black-eyed peas on New Year's Day, you're financially doomed *for the whole year.* Specifically, you should eat them in a traditional New Orleans dish called hoppin' John. The beans represent coins and the greens represent cash, so this recipe is all about getting your rent (or mortgage, or Airbnb) paid all year long. And I bet if you make them yourself instead of eating them straight out of a can, then your year will be even better. Serve over rice, if you like.

MAKE THE RED-HOT TAHINI: Simply mix everything up in a little blender until smooth. Add water by the tablespoon to thin as needed. Taste for salt and spiciness.

MAKE THE TOMATO-PARSLEY SALAD: Toss all ingredients together in a medium mixing bowl. Taste for pepper and vinegar.

MAKE THE HOPPIN' JOHN: Preheat a large, heavy-bottomed pan (preferably cast iron) over medium-high heat. Heat 1 tablespoon of the olive oil and sauté the onion, green pepper, and celery with a pinch of salt until translucent, 3 to 5 minutes. Push the vegetables to one side and add the garlic to the cleared spot in the pan. Drizzle the remaining 1 tablespoon olive oil over the garlic and sauté until the garlic is lightly browned and very fragrant, about 2 minutes.

Add the oregano and red pepper flakes and toss the garlic together with the rest of the veggies. Add the collards, broth, and liquid smoke and toss to coat. Lower the heat to medium, cover the pan, and let the collards cook down for about 10 minutes, stirring occasionally.

When the collards are tender, add the black-eyed peas to heat through. Taste and adjust for salt and seasoning. Ladle into bowls, top with the salad, drizzle with some tahini, garnish with the scallions, and serve!

BAGELS And NOX

with Wild Mushroom Caviar

FOR THE WHITE BEAN CREAM CHEE:

2 (15-ounce) cans navy or great northern beans, rinsed and drained, or 3 cups cooked beans

¼ cup refined coconut oil, melted

2 tablespoons fresh lemon juice

1 tablespoon olive oil

2 teaspoons champagne vinegar or apple cider vinegar

2 teaspoons onion powder

½ teaspoon salt

FOR THE WILD MUSHROOM CAVIAR:

¼ nori sheet

1 garlic clove, peeled

1 ounce dried wild mushrooms, soaked in hot water until tender

2 tablespoons capers

2 tablespoons tamari or soy sauce

1 tablespoon olive oil

1 teaspoon fresh lemon juice

¼ teaspoon salt

Freshly ground black pepper

FOR THE NOX (SMOKED TOMATO):

16 (¼- to ½-inch) tomato slices

Sea salt

FOR SERVING:

8 bagels, split in half

Maldon or other flaky salt

Finely chopped fresh chives

Freshly ground black pepper

Bagels are the circle of life, so of course you should start the year off with one (or two, or three tops if you're so, so hungry). Here, a thick, creamy white bean spread stands in for traditional cream cheese—and dare I say I love it even more? Instead of lox, a smoky tomato sits on top. And, for the ultimate decadence, I like to serve these bagels with wild mushroom caviar—it's luxurious and salty with a slight taste of the sea thanks to a little nori. It's so completely fun and easy to pull off even for just a casual little get-together with some coffee and friends.

MAKE THE CREAM CHEE: In a food processor fitted with the metal blade, combine all the cream chee ingredients and blend until thick and smooth. Transfer to a covered container and chill for at least 30 minutes.

MAKE THE WILD MUSHROOM CAVIAR: Clean the food processor and the metal blade. Pulse the nori until it's finely chopped. Add the garlic and pulse. Add the drained mushrooms, capers, tamari, olive oil, lemon juice, salt, and a few grinds of pepper and pulse until the mushrooms are minced. Be careful not to puree; it should have a lot of texture. Transfer the mixture to a bowl, taste, and adjust for salt, pepper, and seasoning. Cover the bowl and refrigerate until ready to use.

MAKE THE NOX: Set up your stovetop smoker, lightly oiling the grill. Depending on the size of your smoker, you may need to smoke the tomatoes in two or three batches. Arrange the tomato slices in a single layer, sprinkle with a little sea salt, and smoke for 10 minutes. They will be juicy and softened. Transfer the tomatoes to a plate. These are best when prepared close to serving time.

ASSEMBLE: Enjoy these open-faced. Spread a big scoop of white bean cream chee on each bagel half, top with a smoked tomato slice, sprinkle with flaky salt, and place a tablespoon of wild mushroom caviar on the tomato. Sprinkle with chopped chives and finish with a little more black pepper.

Tip *For the most authentic "lox-like" flavor, you can go all out and smoke tomatoes for this recipe. But an easier option is to just sprinkle some smoked salt on each raw tomato—this will give you a fresher, lighter flavor. You can order fine-ground smoked salt online or make a trip to that specialty olive oil/salt shop that you've been afraid of.*

BAGEL BAR

This recipe is plenty of fun, but don't stop there! Build a bagel bar with really *really* *REALLY* simple ingredients.

CONFETTI PEPPERS: Dice red, yellow, and green bell peppers real tiny.

SPROUTS: Get some pretty alfalfa sprouts. They can be like New Year's streamers!

NUTS: Toast 'em or don't. Pecans or walnuts sprinkled over cream chee is yum.

HUMMUS: Ain't no shame in your hummus game! Try my Edamame-Mint Hummus (page 152) or Roasted Carrot Hummus (page 312).

AVOCADO: Slice it up and spread it on, with a little truffle oil and some coarse salt.

OLIVES: Visit the olive bar and pick out the prettiest and fanciest specimens you can find.

NUT BUTTERS: Almond or cashew or hazelnut-chocolate...you can't go wrong with an assortment of nut butters at your bagel bar (or by your bedside).

JELLIES AND JAMS: To go with those nut butters! Choose really fancy ones because it's New Year's. Like, I don't know, "apricot-passionberry." If you want to make them yourself, you'll need a different cookbook.

CREAM CHEE DREAMS

Plain cream chee is satisfying on its own, but why not add some fun mix-ins for your bagel bar? Here are a few ideas to get the party started. Simply transfer the cream chee to a bowl after blending and use a spatula to mix in your choice of goodies.

SUNDRIED TOMATO: ½ cup finely chopped oil-packed sundried tomatoes

OLIVE: ¾ cup of your favorite olives, thinly sliced—try kalamatas, the ones stuffed with pimientos, or a mix!

FRESH HERBS: ¼ cup chopped dill, ¼ cup chopped parsley, and 2 tablespoons fresh chopped basil

SCALLION: 1 cup finely sliced scallions, white and light green parts only

VEGETABLE: ¼ cup each minced carrot, cucumber, and red bell pepper

BACON: ¾ cup chopped shiitake bacon (page 145) or your favorite vegan bacon

SEITAN *And* WAFFLES

with Pomegranate Syrup

FOR THE POMEGRANATE SYRUP:

1 cup pure maple syrup

¼ cup pomegranate molasses

Fresh pomegranate seeds, for garnish

FOR THE WAFFLES:

1 tablespoon cornstarch

2 cups unsweetened almond milk (or your favorite nondairy milk)

1 tablespoon apple cider vinegar

2 cups all-purpose flour

3 tablespoons sugar

1 tablespoon baking powder

½ teaspoon salt

⅓ cup water

2 tablespoons canola oil

1 teaspoon pure vanilla extract

FOR THE SEITAN:

3 tablespoons all-purpose flour

2 tablespoons cornstarch

1 cup water

1 cup plain bread crumbs

2 teaspoons dried thyme

1 teaspoon salt

Freshly ground black pepper

½ recipe Chickee-Style Seitan (page 18) or 1 pound store-bought equivalent

Vegetable oil, for frying

For most of my life, I didn't get the appeal of chicken and waffles. But one day I decided to cave to societal pressure and enjoy a juicy, savory fried hunk of something over a carby, crispy something else, covered in sticky sweetness. Even though it made no sense, I was won over. This version is made fancy-shmancy with pomegranate syrup, and sprinkled with a few pomegranate seeds for even more good luck.

MAKE THE POMEGRANATE SYRUP: Simply mix the syrup and pomegranate molasses together in a measuring cup, yay! Set aside, along with the pomegranate seeds.

MAKE THE WAFFLES: In a 2-cup (or larger) measuring cup, use a fork to vigorously whisk the cornstarch into about half of the milk, until fully dissolved. Add the remaining milk and the vinegar and set aside.

Combine the flour, sugar, baking powder, and salt in a large mixing bowl. Make a well in the center.

Add the milk mixture to the flour along with the water, oil, and vanilla. Mix until the batter is relatively smooth. A few lumps are A-OK.

Preheat the waffle iron and let the batter rest for at least 10 minutes. Cook the waffles according to the waffle iron directions, coating the waffle iron liberally with nonstick cooking spray before each waffle is made. Set the waffles aside while you make the chicken.

MAKE THE SEITAN: Have ready a few layers of paper towels (or brown paper bags) for absorbing the oil after frying.

I recommend breading the seitan before starting to heat the oil—that way you don't have to worry about overheating the oil while you bread the seitan. You'll be frying in two batches.

You'll need a wide bowl for the batter and a big plate for the breading. In the bowl, whisk together the flour, cornstarch, and water. Mix vigorously until thick and smooth. On the plate, mix together the bread crumbs, thyme, salt, and a few grinds of black pepper.

Recipe Continues

You can simmer the seitan up to 3 days ahead of time. Refrigerate it in its broth in a sealed container or zip-top bag. The waffles can be made up to 1 week ahead. Freeze them in a plastic zip-bag and simply toast them when ready to eat.

The homemade seitan makes double what you'll need for this recipe, but since you're making it, why not make some extra for the week? It's really great grilled for salads or sandwiches.

NOW LET'S GET BREADING! Cut each piece of seitan on the bias into four long, wing-like pieces. With one hand, dip each seitan slice into the wet batter, letting the excess drip off. Transfer the seitan to the breading plate and use the other hand to sprinkle a handful of bread crumbs over the seitan to coat it completely. Make sure you use one hand for the wet batter and the other for the dry batter, or you'll end up with mitten hands. Set each breaded seitan slice on another big plate.

NOW LET'S FRY! Preheat a large cast iron skillet over medium heat. Once hot, pour in about ½ inch oil. Wait about a minute, then test the oil by throwing in a pinch of bread crumbs. If it sizzles and bubbles without smoking, you know it's ready. If it burns or smokes quickly, lower the heat. If it just sits there doing not much of anything, raise the heat.

Without crowding the pan, fry half of the seitan until golden brown on both sides, 2 to 3 minutes total. Transfer to paper towels to drain the oil, and then do the next batch.

To serve, place a few pieces of seitan over a waffle. Garnish with pomegranate seeds and serve with plenty of syrup.

Ginger-Chocolate-Banana
MINI LOAVES

3 very ripe bananas

⅓ cup refined coconut oil

½ cup brown sugar

½ cup granulated sugar

⅓ cup unsweetened applesauce

2 tablespoons unsweetened almond milk (or your favorite nondairy milk)

1 tablespoon pure vanilla extract

1 tablespoon Microplaned fresh ginger (see Tip)

2 cups all-purpose flour

½ teaspoon baking soda

½ teaspoon salt

¾ cup mini chocolate chips

Make banana bread even more special with fresh ginger and chocolate chips. These loaves taste delish warm out of the oven, but the ginger is even more pronounced if you let them cool a bit, so these are a wonderful make-ahead treat. I love mini chocolate chips here because they disperse so nicely in a mini loaf, but if you use the regular size no one will be mad atcha.

Preheat the oven to 350°F. Grease an 8-compartment mini loaf pan.

In a small bowl, mash the bananas very well with a small masher or a strong fork, until no large chunks are left.

In a large mixing bowl cream together the coconut oil and sugars. Mix in the mashed bananas, applesauce, milk, vanilla, and ginger.

Add 1 cup of the flour, along with the baking soda and salt, and stir to mix, being careful not to overmix. Add the remaining 1 cup flour and the chocolate chips and stir to combine. Again, be careful to mix only until the dry ingredients are moistened.

Scoop equal amounts of the batter into the compartments of the mini loaf pan. Bake until the tops are lightly browned and feel firm if you tap them, 35 to 38 minutes.

Once cool enough to handle, transfer to wire racks to cool completely.

Tips

Serving suggestion! You can totally just devour this in whole-loaf form, but you can also serve thin slices with strawberries and whipped cream (or not).

Of course you can make these as muffins if you like! Just bake for 20 to 22 minutes. Or you can make a standard 8-by-4-inch loaf, baked for 50 minutes. It's also a fun and forgiving batter to experiment with in any funky-shaped pan you like, so if you have mini Bundt pans or Yoda-head mini pans, now is the time to use them.

Grating the ginger with a Microplane, which is a very, very fine grater, yields almost a puree. If you don't have a Microplane, you can simply mince the ginger very finely, almost to a paste.

ORANGE-PECAN
STICKY BUNS

FOR THE DOUGH:

2¼ teaspoons active dry yeast (one 0.75-ounce packet)

½ cup lukewarm water

⅓ cup granulated sugar

¾ cup unsweetened almond milk (or your favorite nondairy milk), at room temperature

⅓ cup canola oil

1 tablespoon grated orange zest

¾ teaspoon salt

3½ to 4 cups all-purpose flour

FOR THE TOPPING:

¾ cup brown sugar

3 tablespoons agave

2 tablespoons fresh orange juice

1 teaspoon grated orange zest

½ cup chopped pecans

FOR THE FILLING:

½ cup brown sugar

1 tablespoon ground cinnamon

1 tablespoon grated orange zest

FOR THE ASSEMBLY:

¼ cup refined coconut oil

Looking for a sticky-sweet start to the year? These buns are just what the doctor ordered. Or was it the baker? I get confused. In any case, a sticky bun is the luckiest of treats, with its cinnamony swirls representing infinity, spiked with orange—long thought to be the luckiest fruit. Cake is a New Year's tradition in just about every culture. Hand out the buns to your guests in order of age, youngest first, to ensure fortune-filled days ahead.

MAKE THE DOUGH: In a large bowl, combine the yeast, water, and 1 teaspoon of the sugar; whisk until it starts to foam, then let sit in a warm spot for a few minutes. Once the yeast has bloomed and the water is foamy, add the milk, oil, orange zest, salt, and 2 cups of the flour and mix until combined. Add the rest of the flour, ½ cup at a time, until the dough is smooth and not sticky.

Turn out the dough onto a clean, lightly floured surface and knead until smooth and elastic, about 5 minutes, adding a little more flour if it gets sticky. Coat the bowl generously with nonstick cooking spray and put the dough back in, then cover with a towel or plastic wrap. Place in a warm spot in your kitchen for an hour or so, or until doubled in size.

MAKE THE TOPPING AND FILLING: While the dough is rising, make the topping and filling.

For the topping, grease a 9-by-13-inch baking pan. Combine the brown sugar, agave, orange juice, and orange zest in a bowl and scatter the mixture evenly in the bottom of the greased pan. Sprinkle the pecans on top.

For the filling, mix the brown sugar, cinnamon, and orange zest in a bowl and set aside.

ASSEMBLE: When the dough has risen, turn it out onto a floured surface, flour the top of the dough, then roll and stretch it out into a rectangle approximately 12 by 18 inches. Spread the filling over the rectangle, all the way to the edges, then dot with little pieces of coconut oil.

Roll up the rectangle, starting on one long side and working slowly to make sure it's even and tight. Wet your fingers to seal the seam. Position the roll, seam-side down, on your work surface and cut it into 12 slices, then place each slice in the prepared pan, right over the topping. Cover with a towel and let rise again for 45 to 60 minutes.

Preheat the oven to 375°F.

When the rolls have risen, bake until puffy and golden brown, 18 to 22 minutes. Immediately turn out the rolls onto a cookie sheet lined with parchment paper, and enjoy!

MIMOSAS
CLASSIC TO EXOTIC

At its heart, a mimosa is a simple mingling of sparkling wine and citrus.
But you don't have to stop there. With citrus in season all winter long, try one or all of these
special mimosas. You can let guests mix their own if you'd like to leave out
a bottle of bubbly and a few pitchers of different citrus blends. You don't have to spend a
fortune on fancy champagne either. Prosecco and Cava are both great-tasting,
less expensive options that will do the trick.

Grapefruit Mimosas

In a pitcher, mix equal parts grapefruit juice (pink grapefruits are the prettiest) and sparkling wine, adding 1 tablespoon agave for each 1 cup grapefruit juice. Pour into chilled flute glasses and garnish with grapefruit slices.

Jalapeño-Lime Mimosas

In a saucepan, mix 1 cup boiling water with 1 cup sugar and stir to dissolve. Seed and slice 3 jalapeños and mix them into the warm sugar water. Let the mixture cool. Add 4 cups water and 1 cup fresh lime juice. Pour equal parts mixture and bubbly into chilled flute glasses.

Orange-Ginger Mimosas

In a blender, combine 4 cups fresh orange juice with a 1-inch chunk of peeled fresh ginger. Blend to combine. Add 4 cups sparkling wine. Pour into chilled flute glasses and garnish with orange slices.

Blood Orange Mimosas

This is the simplest take on a classic mimosa. In a pitcher, mix equal parts fresh blood orange juice and sparkling wine. Pour into chilled flute glasses and garnish with blood orange slices.

2
SUPER BOWL

SOMEHOW, SOMETIME IN JANUARY

I become the number one

FOOTBALL FAN.

I DON'T QUITE GET to the face-painting level, but really, for me even bothering to know who's playing during the regular season is a huge deal. But come Super Bowl time, I pick out the team I want to win, usually based on how cool their uniforms are, or maybe if there's a super cute player. I keep up on what the halftime show will be and stay up to speed on all the hype that is leading up to it. And I plan. Boy, do I plan. The menu, that is.

Super Bowl is the time of year to eat like Guy Fieri: with wild abandon. Out come the hot sauce, the creamy dips, the bready breads, the cheeseburger everything, and nothing is safe from nacho sauce.

I always invite a bunch of friends over, and we keep changing the channel to the puppy bowl. You know, a bunch of existential emo adults, discussing yoga and alternative energy and bike lanes and poetry. All while stuffing our faces with nachos and sandwiches that topple over and drip down our wrists and into our laps. Sorry, America!

Even if you aren't going to turn on the TV at all, ever, these are all great recipes for fun and casual entertaining. So, go ahead—call some friends and take a few huge bites anytime of the year.

BUFFALO CHICKPEA
PITAS

FOR THE CHICKPEAS:

1 (15-ounce) can chickpeas, rinsed and drained, or 1½ cups cooked chickpeas

¼ cup Buffalo-style hot sauce

2 tablespoons vegan mayo, purchased or homemade (page 61)

2 tablespoons tahini or extra mayo

Salt

FOR THE RANCH DRESSING:

¾ cup vegan mayo, purchased or homemade (page 61)

2 tablespoons finely chopped fresh parsley

2 tablespoons finely chopped fresh dill

2 tablespoons finely chopped fresh chives

1½ teaspoons onion powder

½ teaspoon garlic powder

½ teaspoon lemon pepper

FOR THE ASSEMBLY:

16 mini pitas

Buffalo-style hot sauce

1 celery rib, thinly sliced

Thinly sliced fresh chives

This is such an easy way to capture the essence of Buffalo wings. A spicy, tangy chickpea salad, a cooling dollop of ranch, and fresh crunchy celery—all in one little bite that won't leave your fingers greasy! Oh, and everything takes maybe 20 minutes to put together.

MAKE THE CHICKPEAS: In a mixing bowl, use an avocado masher or a strong fork to mash the chickpeas well. They should retain some of their texture and not appear pureed. A few whole ones left are okay.

Mix in the hot sauce, mayo, and tahini and give it a few more mashes. Taste and add salt if needed, although it should be salty enough with the hot sauce and mayo.

MAKE THE RANCH: Just mix all the ranch ingredients together in a little bowl!

ASSEMBLE: Place a tablespoon or so of chickpea salad on each pita. Add a dash of hot sauce if desired. Top with a dollop of ranch. Garnish with a few slices of celery and a piece of chive. Serve!

BUFFALO CAULIFLOWER

FOR THE CAULIFLOWER:

½ cup plus 2 tablespoons all-purpose flour

2 tablespoons cornstarch

1 cup cold water

1½ cups bread crumbs

1½ teaspoons dried rosemary, crushed with your fingers

1 teaspoon salt

3 tablespoons olive oil

1 large head cauliflower, cut into 2-inch florets

FOR THE SAUCE:

¾ cup Buffalo-style hot sauce

2 tablespoons refined coconut oil, melted

FOR SERVING:

Lettuce leaves, for lining the serving dish (optional)

Thinly sliced fresh chives or chopped fresh parsley

1 recipe ranch dressing (page 41)

Handful carrot sticks

Handful celery sticks

Tip

This is not a make-ahead dish, so prepare it as close to serving time as possible, lest it get too soggy. Not to say that I've never enjoyed a soggy cauliflower wing in my day. If you'd like, you can line your serving dish with some lettuce leaves. It's cute—and it sops up hot sauce.

By the time January rolls around, the only thing that seems to be in season is hot sauce. You've got wings on the brain. Everything you look at becomes a wing and you just want to pour hot sauce all over it. But before you dip your cat in ranch dressing, try these cauliflower wings! While this is not an original idea (just search Pinterest for "Buffalo Cauliflower" to see how everyone and your mom invented it), I do love this method. The cauliflower is breaded and baked instead of fried, lending it a deep roasted flavor that is seriously sensuous when mingled with the hot, tangy sauce.

Put out some crunchy carrots and celery and a saucer of creamy ranch to cool down the whole affair, and game day has never tasted so fine.

MAKE THE CAULIFLOWER: Preheat the oven to 450°F. Line a large rimmed baking sheet with parchment paper, coat the parchment with nonstick cooking spray, and set aside.

You'll need a large bowl for the batter and a big rimmed plate for the breading. Combine the flour and cornstarch in the bowl. Add about half of the water and stir vigorously with a fork to dissolve. Add the rest of the water, and stir to incorporate. On the plate, mix the bread crumbs, rosemary, and salt. Drizzle in the oil and use your fingertips to mix it up well.

Now we will set up an assembly line to dip the cauli. From left to right, line up the cauliflower, the batter mixture, the bread crumbs mixture, and lastly the prepared baking sheet.

Dip each cauliflower floret into the batter, letting the excess drip off. Transfer the floret to the breading plate and use your other (dry) hand to toss and coat the floret, pressing the bread crumbs into the crevices of the floret. Make sure to coat the floret completely. Transfer each coated floret to the baking sheet, making a single layer.

Bake for 10 minutes. Flip the florets and bake for another 5 to 7 minutes. The florets should be varying shades of brown and crisp. Taste one to check for doneness—it should be tender but still have some bite.

MAKE THE SAUCE: While the cauliflower is roasting, mix the hot sauce and melted oil in a bowl and set aside.

SERVE: While the cauliflower is still warm, use a large slotted spoon to dip each piece in the hot sauce, drip off the excess, and place on a serving plate (lined with lettuce leaves if you like). Sprinkle with the chives. Put out a bowl of ranch equipped with a spoon, and some carrot and celery sticks. Serve as soon as possible for yummiest results.

RUSTIC
PIZZA DOUGH

MAKES
ENOUGH DOUGH FOR

2

PIZZAS

TOTAL
2 HOURS
(for rising)
ACTIVE
20 MINUTES

1 cup warm water

1 tablespoon sugar

2¼ teaspoons active dry yeast (one 0.75-ounce packet)

2 tablespoons olive oil

2 to 2½ cups bread flour

1 teaspoon salt

½ cup medium-grind cornmeal

Tips

Bread flour is a newer pantry ingredient for me. Usually I use all-purpose for, well, all purposes, because it's always on hand in my kitchen, and probably yours, too. But I love the crusty chewiness that higher-protein bread flour gives flatbread, so if it's not an ingredient you usually keep on hand, give it a shot and see what you think! The difference might be just enough to convince you to keep it around for emergency pizzas. That being said, all-purpose flour will work fine in this recipe.

I knead bread in a standing mixer these days, but of course, you can knead by hand! It will take a lot longer, naturally.

I'm a Brooklyn girl, so of course I love that thin-crust wafery pizza dough. But I find it really hard to replicate in a normal oven or on the grill. When I moved out of NYC, I found that most pizza shops out of the state couldn't really get it right either. And eventually I came to a conclusion: That's okay! There are other kinds of pizza doughs that are different but still completely wonderful. Thus my rustic pizza dough was born. It's a thicker, chewier pizza dough, with a little texture from cornmeal. I find that it's not fussy at all, and if you don't plan on spending the rest of your life perfecting Brooklyn-style pizza crusts that everyone is going to judge you for, then this is the way to go. It's also really sturdy and perfect for the grill.

Combine the water and sugar in the bowl of a standing mixer fitted with the dough hook. Sprinkle in the yeast and let sit for 5 minutes to bloom.

Mix in the olive oil, then add 1 cup of the flour and the salt. Mix on low until well incorporated, then turn up the speed to medium and mix for 3 minutes.

Add another ½ cup flour and the cornmeal and mix well, starting on low and then switching to medium speed. Then add another ½ cup flour, again starting on low and switching to medium. Knead on medium for about 5 minutes. You may occasionally have to turn off the machine and get in there with your hands if the dough starts climbing up the hook. It should become smooth and elastic and slightly tacky.

At this point, start incorporating flour by the tablespoon, with the mixer running. When it starts to seem dry, stop adding flour. This could be anywhere from ¼ to ½ cup additional flour. Knead again on medium until it is elastic and easy to stretch, about 8 more minutes.

Meanwhile, generously oil a large mixing bowl. The dough will double in size, so make sure you have enough room. Form the dough into a ball and place it in the bowl, tossing it around to coat with oil. Cover the bowl with plastic wrap and put it in a warm place. Let the dough rise until it doubles in size, about 1 hour.

Punch down the dough and split it into two even balls. It's now ready to use! To save it for later, place each ball in a zip-top bag with enough room left for expanding, because even if stored in the refrigerator, it will still rise.

BBQ NACHOS

FOR THE PICO DE GALLO:

1 pound vine-ripened tomatoes, diced small

½ cup chopped fresh cilantro

1 small white onion, finely chopped

2 jalapeños, seeded and finely chopped

1 tablespoon fresh lime juice

½ teaspoon salt

Freshly ground black pepper

FOR THE BBQ LENTILS:

2 tablespoons olive oil

1 small yellow onion, diced tiny

1 green bell pepper, seeded and diced tiny

3 garlic cloves, minced

Salt

½ teaspoon ground cumin

2 (15-ounce) cans lentils, rinsed and drained, or 3 cups cooked lentils

½ cup ketchup

1 tablespoon liquid smoke

1 tablespoon brown sugar

All anyone really wants for every meal is nachos. I'm not sure why there is ever another item on any menu or another recipe in any cookbook. Here are some nachos and we are done. This version has BBQ lentils that are broken down to resemble ground meat. On top there's a creamy queso and a fresh salsa. This pico de gallo is as simple as it gets, but that's the beauty of pico! I like to remove all the seeds from the peppers so I can add more fruity pepper flavor without increasing the heat. And that's all you really need for smoky, meaty, creamy nacho heaven! Of course you can keep building and customize to your heart's content, with diced avocado, sliced jalapeños or olives, and sautéed seitan, or you can make it even beanier with some black beans. If you'd like an even simpler option, use the recipe for Swirly Pizza Cheese (page 267) instead of the queso.

MAKE THE PICO DE GALLO: Put the diced tomatoes in a colander in the sink and let them drain for 20 minutes or so. Give the colander a shake every now and again. You don't want to lose all of the liquid, but you don't want your pico to be watery, either.

Transfer the tomatoes to a bowl and add the cilantro, onion, jalapeños, lime juice, salt, and a few grinds of black pepper. Toss to combine everything well. Taste and adjust for salt and seasoning. Transfer the pico to a tightly sealed container and refrigerate for at least 30 minutes before serving so that the flavors can marry.

MAKE THE BBQ LENTILS: Preheat a large skillet over medium-high heat. Heat the oil, then sauté the onion, bell pepper, and garlic with a pinch of salt until lightly browned, about 5 minutes. Add the cumin and toss for a few seconds to coat.

Lower the heat to medium and add the lentils and a few splashes of water. Use a spatula to mix the lentils and vegetables and mash the lentils a bit, until the mixture holds together and resembles ground meat. If your spatula isn't strong enough to accomplish this, just use a fork.

Cook for about 5 minutes, adding splashes of water as necessary if the mixture appears dry. Add the ketchup, liquid smoke, and brown sugar and heat through. Taste and adjust for salt and seasoning. Keep warm until ready to serve.

FOR THE QUESO:

¾ cup raw cashews, soaked in water for at least 2 hours and drained

1¼ cups vegetable broth, purchased or homemade (page 203)

2 tablespoons fresh lemon juice

1 tablespoon mellow white miso

3 tablespoons nutritional yeast flakes

2 garlic cloves, peeled

2 teaspoons ground cumin

½ teaspoon ground turmeric

¼ teaspoon salt

2 teaspoons vegetable oil

1 small yellow onion, diced small

2 jalapeños, seeded and chopped

FOR THE ASSEMBLY:

1 large bag restaurant-style tortilla chips

Finely sliced scallions

MAKE THE QUESO: In a blender, combine the cashews, vegetable broth, lemon juice, miso, nutritional yeast, garlic, cumin, turmeric, and salt. Puree until completely smooth; this can take up to 5 minutes depending on the strength of your machine. Periodically stop the machine to prevent it from overheating, and scrape down the sides of the blender jar with a rubber spatula to make sure you get everything.

Preheat a 2-quart saucepot over low heat. Heat the oil, then sauté the onion and jalapeños with a pinch of salt just until soft, about 3 minutes. Add the blended cashew mixture and turn the heat up to medium. Cook, using an angled wooden spoon to stir occasionally, until the queso is hot and thickened, about 10 minutes. Keep warm until ready to serve.

ASSEMBLE: Assemble the nachos as close to serving time as possible. It works best in a 9-by-13-inch casserole dish, where people can either reach in with their hands or use a big serving spoon to grab a bunch for their own plates.

In the casserole, make a single layer of chips. Spoon on half of the lentil mixture and drizzle half of the queso over. Repeat the process with another layer of chips, lentils, and queso. Finish with some of the pico and the scallions. Offer additional pico on the side if guests would like to spoon some more over any chips that may have been missed.

 Tip

You can make both the BBQ lentils and queso up to 3 days in advance and store them in separate sealed containers in the refrigerator. Gently reheat them on the stovetop or in the microwave with a few splashes of water before serving.

CHEESEBURGER PIZZA

MAKES

2

PIZZAS

TOTAL
1 HOUR 15 MINUTES
ACTIVE
1 HOUR

FOR THE AGRODOLCE:

1 tablespoon olive oil

1 large yellow onion, diced medium

3 garlic cloves, minced

3 tablespoons brown sugar

1 (24-ounce) can crushed tomatoes with basil

3 tablespoons red wine vinegar

¼ teaspoon ground cinnamon

1 teaspoon salt

Freshly ground black pepper

Crushed red pepper flakes

FOR THE TEMPEH BURGER CRUMBLES:

2 (8-ounce) packages tempeh

3 tablespoons tamari or soy sauce

2 tablespoons olive oil

1 tablespoon liquid smoke

Salt

FOR THE ASSEMBLY:

1 recipe Rustic Pizza Dough (page 43)

Cornmeal, for dusting the pan

1 recipe Swirly Pizza Cheese (page 267)

1 cup sliced dill pickles

½ cup very tiny diced white onion

2 cups shredded romaine lettuce

Crushed red pepper flakes

Tip

There's no shame in buying premade pizza crusts. You're making everything else from scratch—what more do people want from you?

Imagine: A cheeseburger and a pizza meet on Tinder and the rest is history! I really wanted to get that authentic cheeseburgeriness into this pie but still have it retain its pizza integrity. That meant creating a red sauce that wasn't quite ketchup (because *ewww*) but had a ketchup-like quality. I immediately thought of agrodolce, which is basically an Italian sweet and sour tomato sauce. The meaty smokiness of the burger comes from tempeh crumbles, which are a cinch to make. And then the cheese is kept simple: a cashew cream with a few basic ingredients and some miso for its umami qualities. It's all pulled together with chopped pickles and onion on top and, of course, fresh lettuce. All in all, it's a surprisingly classy recipe for something called Cheeseburger Pizza. Your guests are going to be talking about it forever!

MAKE THE AGRODOLCE: Preheat a medium saucepot over medium-low heat. Heat the oil, then add the onion and cover the pot. Cook the onion, uncovering the pot occasionally to stir, for 10 minutes. You're steaming the onion so that it gets very juicy. Now, remove the cover and turn the heat up to medium-high. Let the onion brown for 5 minutes. Add the garlic and stir for about 30 seconds.

Add the brown sugar and cook for about 5 minutes, so that the sugar gets melty, dark, and smooth. Stir pretty consistently so it doesn't burn.

Add the crushed tomatoes, vinegar, cinnamon, salt, a few grinds of black pepper, and a pinch of crushed red pepper flakes and cook, uncovered, for about 20 minutes. It takes that much time for the sauce to thicken and the flavors to develop. Taste and adjust for salt and seasoning and set aside.

MAKE THE TEMPEH BURGER CRUMBLES: In a small sauté pan, crumble the tempeh and add enough water to almost cover it, along with the tamari. Turn the heat to high, cover the pan, and steam the tempeh until most of the water is absorbed, about 15 minutes. Drain the remaining water and add the oil. Brown the tempeh, stirring occasionally, for about 10 minutes. Add the liquid smoke and salt to taste. Toss for a few more minutes to blend the flavors. Now it's ready for your pizza. Set aside until ready to use.

ASSEMBLE THE PIZZAS: Preheat the oven to 500°F. Roll out the dough into a 16-inch circle. Lightly dust a pizza pan (preferably) or an unrimmed baking sheet with cornmeal. Spread some sauce over the dough, leaving about an inch of crust around the edges. Sprinkle on the tempeh crumbles. Swirl on the pizza cheese. Bake until the sauce is thickened and the crust is browned, about 12 minutes.

Remove from the oven and top with pickles, onion, lettuce, and red pepper flakes. Slice and serve!

GRILLED
WEDGE SALAD
with Maple-Mustard Dressing & Smoky Pecans

FOR THE MAPLE-MUSTARD DRESSING:

¼ cup spicy brown mustard

¼ cup pure maple syrup

¼ cup canola oil

2 tablespoons apple cider vinegar

1 teaspoon salt

Freshly ground black pepper

FOR THE SMOKY PECANS:

1 cup pecan halves

2 tablespoons tamari or soy sauce

1 teaspoon liquid smoke

1 teaspoon olive oil

FOR THE ROMAINE:

3 romaine hearts

Olive oil, for brushing

Salt

Freshly ground black pepper

FOR SERVING:

1 cup halved cherry tomatoes

1 cup thinly sliced cucumbers

Freshly ground black pepper

This wedge salad rolls its eyes at traditional ranch and says, "You know what, I like maple-mustard dressing better." And you will see why. The lettuce here is grilled and charred, and tastes wonderfully caramelly when smothered in the sweet, tangy dressing. Some easy-to-make pecans add a salty, smoky touch. This is so good that no one will wonder why you are serving a salad at a Super Bowl party! This salad is best served while the romaine is still warm, so grill it as close to serving time as possible.

MAKE THE MAPLE-MUSTARD DRESSING: Combine the mustard, maple syrup, oil, vinegar, salt, and a few grinds of black pepper in a blender and whiz until smooth, which should take only about 30 seconds. Set aside until ready to use.

MAKE THE SMOKY PECANS: Toast the pecans in a dry pan over medium-high heat for 5 minutes. Turn off the heat, add the tamari, liquid smoke, and oil, and toss to coat. Let the pecans sit in the pan for a minute or so for the liquid to evaporate a bit, then transfer to a plate to cool completely.

GRILL THE ROMAINE: Preheat a grill or grill pan over medium heat. Cut each romaine heart in half lengthwise. Brush with olive oil and a sprinkle of salt and pepper.

Lightly coat the grill or grill pan with cooking spray. When hot, place the romaine, cut-side down, on the grill or in the pan. Depending on the pan, it could take 2 to 3 minutes for grill marks to appear. You will probably have to do this in batches if using a grill pan on your stovetop.

SERVE: For each serving, place a warm romaine heart, grilled-side up, on a plate. Scatter tomatoes and cucumbers over it. Drizzle on the dressing and garnish with the pecans. Finish with freshly ground black pepper and serve!

MAKES

4

CUPS

TOTAL
1 HOUR
ACTIVE
20 MINUTES

WARM
ARTICHOKE DIP

¼ cup bread crumbs

2 teaspoons olive oil

2 garlic cloves, peeled

1 cup vegetable broth, purchased or homemade (page 203)

½ cup raw cashews, soaked in water for at least 2 hours and drained

1 (15-ounce) can navy beans, rinsed and drained, or 1½ cups cooked navy beans

3 tablespoons nutritional yeast flakes

1 tablespoon fresh lemon juice

1 (10-ounce) jar artichokes, drained and roughly chopped

½ cup finely chopped fresh chives

¼ teaspoon salt

Crusty bread, for serving

——— *Tip* ———

A 6-inch round casserole dish is great for dips, so get one if you don't have one already! If you absolutely refuse, an 8-inch square casserole works, too.

Just the mention of warm artichoke dip sends people into a frenzy. Serve it with big hunks of crusty bread and let guests dip a big serving spoon through the bread crumb topping to reveal the creamy, rich dip inside. Extra points if you serve this while the dip is still steaming. I like to use a jar of artichoke hearts here, the kind packed in water, not oil, because I think they taste the best. You can also use 1½ cups of frozen artichoke hearts that have been thawed.

Preheat the oven to 350°F. Lightly grease a 6-inch round casserole dish.

In a small bowl, mix the bread crumbs and olive oil and set aside.

In a blender, pulse the garlic cloves to chop them up a bit. Add the vegetable broth and cashews. Puree until completely smooth; this can take up to 5 minutes depending on the strength of your machine. Periodically stop the machine to keep it from overheating, and scrape down the sides of the blender jar with a rubber spatula to make sure you get everything. Add the navy beans, yeast, and lemon juice and blend again until smooth.

Transfer the mixture to a medium mixing bowl, stir in the artichokes and chives, and season with the salt. Transfer the mixture to the prepared baking dish and sprinkle with the bread crumb mixture.

Bake for 40 minutes. The dip should be browned and bubbly. If the bread crumbs have not browned sufficiently, you can broil it briefly, but be sure to keep a close eye on it and check every 30 seconds or so. Serve warm with crusty bread.

RUNZAS

FOR THE DOUGH:

½ cup water, at room temperature

½ cup sugar

4½ teaspoons active dry yeast (two 0.75-ounce packages)

4½ cups all-purpose flour

1 teaspoon salt

½ cup unsweetened almond milk (or your favorite nondairy milk), at room temperature

½ cup unsweetened plain nondairy yogurt, at room temperature

⅓ cup refined coconut oil, melted

FOR THE FILLING:

4 tablespoons olive oil

1 large onion, finely chopped

¾ teaspoon salt, plus a pinch

1 pound seitan, very finely chopped

3 cups sauerkraut

2 tablespoons tomato paste

Freshly ground black pepper

Nebraska loves its runzas almost as much as it loves its football! When I moved to the state, I immediately set about trying to make a vegan version. Every culture has its meat-filled-dough thing, be it empanadas, calzone, pork buns, or pierogi. And of course every meat-filled-dough thing has its own unique characteristics and nuance. And from region to region, or even family to family, there is always a way that it has to be. According to most native Nebraskans, a runza has to be a doughy white bun, shaped like a hoagie. And it has to be stuffed with meat, onion, and cabbage, and not much else.

These vegan runzas contain a savory, toothsome filling, with a little bite and tang from the sauerkraut and lots of meaty flavor, all stuffed into a billowy, doughy bun that you will want to sink your teeth into again and again and again. This recipe makes eight *really* big stuffed buns, but assuming you are serving them as part of a large spread, you can cut them in half, or even in four pieces, to make sure every guest gets a substantial bite.

MAKE THE DOUGH: Combine the water and 1 tablespoon of the sugar in the bowl of a standing mixer fitted with the dough hook. Sprinkle in the yeast and let it sit for 5 minutes to bloom.

Add 1¾ cups of the flour, the rest of the sugar, and the salt and mix until well incorporated.

Add the almond milk, yogurt, and coconut oil and mix until smooth.

Add the remaining 2¾ cups flour in roughly ½-cup batches, beating until smooth after each addition.

When all the flour has been added and a stiff dough has formed, knead on medium until it is very smooth and elastic, about 5 minutes more.

Meanwhile, generously oil a large mixing bowl. The dough will double in size, so make sure you have enough room. Form the dough into a ball and place it in the bowl, tossing it around to coat with oil. Cover the bowl with plastic wrap and put it in a warm place. Let the dough rise until doubled in size, about 1 hour.

MAKE THE FILLING: While the dough is rising, preheat a large pan (preferably cast iron) over medium-high heat. Add 2 tablespoons of the oil. When the oil is hot, sauté the onion with a pinch of salt until nicely browned, about 7 minutes. Add the seitan and the remaining 2 tablespoons oil and sauté until the seitan is browned, about 7 more minutes. In the meantime, drain the sauerkraut, pressing it into a fine-mesh strainer, until most of the moisture is drained.

Recipe Continues

Stir in the sauerkraut, tomato paste, remaining ¾ teaspoon salt, and lots of freshly ground black pepper. Cook for 5 minutes, adding more oil if necessary to prevent sticking. Taste and adjust for salt and pepper.

ASSEMBLE: Preheat the oven to 350°F. Have a greased rimmed baking sheet at the ready.

Once the dough has risen, punch it down and divide it into eight equal pieces. One piece at a time, stretch the dough into an 8-by-6-inch rectangle. Spoon a scant ½ cup filling in a line down the center of the rectangle, leaving 1½ inches of empty dough on all sides. Fold the short ends over first, and then fold the top and bottom, sort of like a burrito. But pinch the edges and smooth them out so that it's more bun than burrito.

Place the filled buns on the baking sheet with the folded parts tucked under, and bake until lightly golden and firm, 20 to 25 minutes. Serve warm.

BLACK BEAN *And* OLIVE DIP

MAKES

3

CUPS

TOTAL
1 HOUR
ACTIVE
30 MINUTES

1 tablespoon olive oil

1 small yellow onion, diced medium

2 jalapeños, seeded and diced

2 garlic cloves, minced

½ cup chopped black olives

1 medium tomato, chopped

2 teaspoons ground cumin

2 teaspoons chili powder

Freshly ground black pepper

1 (25-ounce) can black beans, undrained

¼ teaspoon salt

1 tablespoon fresh lime juice

1 avocado, pitted, peeled, and diced

Chopped fresh cilantro, for garnish

Tortilla chips, for serving

This mouthwateringly savory black bean dip is made even more flavorful with olives. Even though I created it to be made conveniently with canned beans, everything tastes wonderfully fresh and zesty thanks to the tomato, cilantro, and lime. A little avocado scattered across the top? Sure, that never hurts.

Preheat a large, heavy-bottomed pan (preferably cast iron) over medium-high heat. Heat the oil, then sauté the onion and jalapeños until lightly brown, 5 to 7 minutes. Add the garlic and cook until fragrant, about 30 seconds. Add the olives and tomato and cook until the tomato gets saucy, about 5 minutes.

Stir in the cumin, chili powder, and a few grinds of black pepper, then add the beans with their liquid. Warm the beans for a few minutes, then mash all the ingredients with a small masher or a fork directly in the pan, and cook until the liquid reduces and thickens, 7 to 10 minutes. Turn the heat off and set the mixture aside to cool and thicken a little more.

Once the dip has cooled, taste and adjust for salt and stir in the lime juice. Transfer to a serving bowl, cover tightly with plastic wrap, and refrigerate to chill completely. When ready to serve, scatter the avocado over the top and garnish with cilantro. Serve with tortilla chips.

Sour Cream & Onion
POTATO SKINS

5 pounds russet potatoes

Olive oil

Salt

Freshly ground black pepper

1 recipe So Very Sour Cream
(page 368), for serving

½ cup finely chopped fresh chives,
for garnish

Tip

Save the scooped-out potatoes for mashed potatoes or maybe a pureed potato soup?

You probably don't need much convincing to eat a potato skin straight out of the oven. Wearing nothing but your skivvies, holding a little salt shaker. That sounds about right. But add a cool, creamy, tangy dip to their little shells and hooo-boy. They're completely irresistible! The potato skins are wonderful while warm, but they are also really nice at room temperature, so don't worry too much about their serving temp. So long as the sour cream is nice and cold when you fill them, they can be kept out for a few hours—not that there's any chance they'll last that long.

The sour cream is a really simple blend of cashews and coconut milk, for creaminess and body, coconut oil to hold its beautiful shape, and lemon juice for tang, along with a few seasonings. It needs a couple of hours to set, so make it a day ahead to play it safe.

Preheat the oven to 425°F.

Pierce the potatoes all over with a fork and wrap each in aluminum foil. Place the potatoes directly on an oven rack and bake until easily pierced with a steak knife. Depending on the size of the potatoes, it could take from 45 minutes to an hour. Use tongs to transfer the potatoes to a cooling rack and let sit until cool enough to handle, about 15 minutes.

Unwrap the potatoes and cut in half lengthwise. Use a spoon to scoop out most of the potato flesh, leaving about ¼ inch of the potato on the skin.

Set the oven to broil. Lightly coat a rimmed baking sheet with nonstick cooking spray. Drizzle the insides of each potato with a little olive oil and rub it around with your fingers. Sprinkle on a little salt and freshly ground black pepper.

Place the potatoes, cut-side up, on the baking sheet. Broil until the insides are brown and crisp, about 2 minutes, watching closely so that they don't burn.

Fill each potato with a dollop of cold sour cream and sprinkle with chives. Serve!

CINCINNATI
SPAGHETTI

8 ounces spaghetti

1 tablespoon olive oil

1 medium yellow onion, diced small

¾ teaspoon salt, plus a pinch

2 garlic cloves, minced

1 (15-ounce) can lentils, rinsed and drained, or 1½ cups cooked brown or green lentils

1 tablespoon mild chili powder

2 teaspoons smoked sweet paprika

1 teaspoon ground cumin

½ teaspoon ground cinnamon

½ teaspoon dried oregano

Ground cloves

Cayenne pepper (optional)

1 (15-ounce) can crushed tomatoes (preferably fire roasted)

1 cup vegetable broth, purchased or homemade (page 203)

2 teaspoons unsweetened cocoa powder

1 (25-ounce) can kidney beans, rinsed and drained, or 2¼ cups cooked kidney beans

1 avocado, pitted, peeled, and diced small, for garnish

Thinly sliced scallions, for garnish

There's something about Ohio cuisine…well, specifically, there's Cincinnati chili. It's a confusing chili to outsiders, typically made with ground meat (lentil meat spoken here), a thin (for chili) sauce laced with surprising (for chili) spices like cinnamon and cloves. The kicker is the touch of cocoa powder, which adds a rich and alluring depth. Oh. One last thing: Perhaps you gleaned this from the recipe title but it's served over…spaghetti. The first time my brother-in-law, a native Ohioan, presented this curious mix to me, I was offended. But I became an instant addict. Typically the chili is topped with heaps of shredded cheddar and raw onions. I prefer avocado and sliced scallion!

Bring a pot of salted water to a boil over high heat. Cook the spaghetti according to the package directions. Drain and set aside.

In the meantime, preheat a 4-quart pot over medium heat. Heat the oil, then sauté the onion with a big pinch of salt until translucent, 3 to 5 minutes. Add the garlic and sauté until fragrant, about 30 seconds.

Add the lentils and a few splashes of water. Use a spatula to mash them a bit as they cook, until they hold together. If your spatula isn't strong enough to accomplish this, just use a fork. You don't want to turn them to mush—a few whole lentils are okay.

Stir in the chili powder, paprika, cumin, cinnamon, oregano, a big pinch of cloves, and the remaining ¾ teaspoon salt. If you like things a little spicy, add a pinch of cayenne.

Add the crushed tomatoes, broth, and cocoa powder. Stir to combine. Cover the pot, leaving the lid ajar so that steam can escape, and turn up the heat till it boils. Lower the heat and simmer for 10 minutes. Add the kidney beans and heat through.

Add the cooked spaghetti to the chili and toss to coat (a pasta spoon works well for this). Serve topped with avocado and scallions.

Tip

The smoked paprika is a nice little addition, but if all you've got is regular, then go ahead and use it. Maybe add a little liquid smoke if you've got it?

CHIPOTLE MAC *And* CHEESE

with Roasted Brussels Sprouts

1 pound brussels sprouts, quartered

1 tablespoon olive oil

Salt

1 cup raw cashews, soaked in water for at least 2 hours and drained

1 cup vegetable broth, purchased or homemade (page 203)

4 chipotle peppers in adobo sauce, seeded (see Tip)

2 garlic cloves, peeled

2 tablespoons nutritional yeast flakes

2 tablespoons chickpea miso or mellow white miso

8 ounces macaroni

Chipotle mac and cheese! I probably don't need to say anything else—you're already rummaging through your pantry for a can of chipotles and some cashews to soak. Mac and cheese is, after all, the ultimate comfort food. A box of macaroni might as well come with sweatpants, a cozy blanket, and an entire season of *Mad Men* DVDs.

Preheat the oven to 425°F. Line a large rimmed baking sheet with parchment paper for the brussels. Bring a pot of salted water to a boil over high heat for the pasta.

Toss the quartered brussels sprouts with the olive oil and a big pinch of salt. Transfer to the lined baking sheet and bake until lightly browned, about 18 minutes. No need to flip 'em.

Meanwhile, make the cheese sauce. In a blender, combine the cashews, vegetable broth, chipotles, garlic, yeast, miso, and a pinch of salt. Puree until completely smooth; this can take up to 5 minutes depending on the strength of your machine. Periodically stop the machine to keep it from overheating, and scrape down the sides of the blender jar with a rubber spatula to make sure you get everything.

When the pasta water comes to a boil, add the macaroni and cook according to the package directions. Drain the macaroni in a colander and immediately return it to the pot and stir in the sauce. Place the pot over low heat and stir until the sauce is thickened a bit and everything is deliciously creamy, 3 minutes or so. Taste and adjust for salt, toss in the brussels sprouts, and serve!

 Tip

Sometimes people forget that chipotles are still hot and can give you jalapeño hands if you touch the seeds. Use squares of plastic wrap to protect your fingers when handling them. Seed them by placing one flat on the cutting board, splitting it down the center with a paring knife, and using that knife to scrape out the seeds. Immediately scrape the seeds into the sink and wash them away, to prevent any further contact, then place the seeded chipotle directly in the blender. The reason we're removing the seeds, in case you're wondering, is that the seeds are really spicy. With the seeds removed, you can use more chipotles, thus getting more smoky flavor without all the heat. If you prefer a completely nonspicy version, use 1 roasted red pepper (homemade or from a jar) in place of the 4 chipotles.

HALFTIME
MEATBALL SLIDERS

2 (8-ounce) packages tempeh

1 cup water

1 tablespoon tamari or soy sauce

1 tablespoon olive oil

3 tablespoons ketchup

1 tablespoon Dijon mustard

½ teaspoon dried oregano

½ teaspoon dried thyme

½ teaspoon salt

Freshly ground black pepper

½ cup very finely chopped yellow onion

1 cup panko bread crumbs

Olive oil, for pan-frying

FOR SERVING:

12 slider buns

½ recipe Bestest Pesto (page 64)

½ recipe Marinara Sauce (page 65)

Tips

You can make the meatballs a few days ahead and store them in a zip-top bag in the refrigerator. To reheat, preheat the oven to 350°F, place the meatballs on a rimmed baking sheet, and drizzle them with a little olive oil so they don't dry out. Heat them for about 15 minutes.

For this recipe, take care to chop the onion very finely. Pea-size pieces work best to get some onion in every bite. If they're too large, they'll pop out of the meatball mixture, making it difficult to hold together.

Pesto or marinara? It's so difficult to decide which craving to answer. Well, stop wasting time choosing—you're missing the kitten bowl! Go for half and half this halftime. A big juicy tempeh meatball sits in a slider between two end zones of chunky marinara and bright garlicky pesto. Smoosh that baby down and get it in your face. Find pretzel slider buns if you can, because those really add to the magic.

Crumble the tempeh into a 2-quart pot. Add the water, tamari, and olive oil. Cover and bring to a boil over high heat. Once boiling, lower the heat and simmer, with the lid slightly ajar so that steam can escape, for 15 minutes. Most of the water should be absorbed. If there is excess water, drain it. Transfer the tempeh to a mixing bowl and place it in the freezer to cool. It should take 10 minutes or so; give it a stir after 5 minutes to make it cool evenly.

Once the tempeh is cool, add the ketchup, mustard, oregano, thyme, salt, and a few grinds of black pepper and mix well. Mix in the onion. Now add the bread crumbs and use your hands to mix until everything holds together very well. If it seems loose, add extra bread crumbs by the tablespoon until you can form very tight, compact balls. Scoop up golf ball–size portions and roll them between your hands to form the balls.

Preheat a large nonstick pan (preferably cast iron) over medium heat. Coat the pan with a thin layer of olive oil. Add the meatballs one by one, rolling them in the pan to coat in oil. If your pan is not big enough to fit all the balls comfortably, do them in two batches. Pan-fry for about 10 minutes, rolling them frequently, to cook evenly.

Toast the slider buns. Scoop a generous amount of pesto on one half of each bun and marinara on the other. Place a meatball inside, close it up, and eat.

PHILLY CHEESESTEAK
CASSEROLE

SERVES
8–12

TOTAL
1 HOUR 15 MINUTES
ACTIVE
30 MINUTES

FOR THE CHEESE:

1½ cups raw cashews, soaked in water for at least 2 hours and drained

½ cup water

½ cup refined coconut oil, melted

2 tablespoons mellow white miso

1 tablespoon fresh lemon juice

2 tablespoons nutritional yeast flakes

1 teaspoon salt

FOR THE CASSEROLE:

Soft white bread, cut into ½-inch slices (see Tip)

3 tablespoons plus 1 teaspoon olive oil

2 large yellow onions, cut into ¼-inch-thick half-moons

2 green bell peppers, seeded and cut into ¼-inch strips

Salt

1 recipe Chickee-Style Seitan (page 18) or 2 pounds store-bought equivalent, cut into ¼-inch strips

Freshly ground black pepper

1 cup bread crumbs

──────── *Tip* ────────

Toasty bread lines the bottom of the casserole, forming the base. Ideally, use a soft, hoagie-type roll, but any soft white bread will work. You'll need 6 or 8 slices. Avoid a super chewy baguette or anything with lots of nuts or seeds or whole wheat, because you don't want to accidentally serve anything vaguely healthy on this special day.

It is so difficult to bring a tray of individual cheesesteaks over to a friend's house on game day—and believe me, I've tried. This handy casserole gets all that cheesesteaky wonderfulness in a convenient casserole form that you can strut around town with. Seitan, green bell pepper, and big strips of onion are sautéed and tossed around in a cheesy sauce, then coated in bread crumbs and baked until golden. It's not a bad way to cheesesteak!

MAKE THE CHEESE: In a blender, combine the cashews, water, coconut oil, miso, lemon juice, nutritional yeast, and salt. Puree until completely smooth; this can take up to 5 minutes depending on the strength of your machine. Periodically stop the machine to prevent it from overheating, and scrape down the sides of the blender jar with a rubber spatula to make sure you get everything. Keep refrigerated in a tightly sealed container until ready to use.

MAKE THE CASSEROLE: Preheat the oven to 350°F. Coat a 9-by-13-inch casserole dish with nonstick cooking spray. Line the bottom of the dish with a single layer of bread slices.

Preheat a large skillet over medium-high heat. Add 1 tablespoon of the oil. When the oil is hot, sauté the onions and bell peppers with a pinch of salt until seared and softened, about 7 minutes. Transfer to a large bowl that will be able to fit the seitan as well.

In the same skillet, still on medium-high heat, heat 2 tablespoons of the oil. When it is hot, sauté the seitan until seared, about 5 minutes. Add the seitan to the bowl of peppers and onions, add a few grinds of black pepper, and toss to combine. Scoop in the cheese and toss to combine. The cheese doesn't have to be perfectly distributed—it's okay if some spots are cheesier than others.

In a small bowl, toss the bread crumbs with the remaining 1 teaspoon olive oil to coat. Sprinkle the bread crumbs over the top of the casserole and bake until the bread crumbs are golden brown, about 30 minutes.

Remove from the oven and grind on some more black pepper. Let the casserole cool for about 15 minutes, then serve!

BESTEST
PESTO

¼ cup walnut halves

¼ cup pine nuts

2 garlic cloves, peeled

2½ cups fresh basil leaves

½ cup fresh cilantro leaves

2 tablespoons fresh thyme leaves

2 tablespoons nutritional
   yeast flakes

¼ cup water

1 teaspoon salt

¼ cup olive oil

1 tablespoon fresh lemon juice

Freshly ground black pepper

When I want to feel my Brooklyn roots, I go classic: basil, pine nuts, olive oil. Still, even those simple flavors aren't safe from my whims. This is the recipe for exactly the pesto that I crave—classic ingredients with a few minor adjustments. If you aren't crazy about cilantro like I am, though, feel free to add more basil.

Half of the pine nuts are replaced with walnuts, a combo that started out as a cost-saving measure, but now I just prefer the flavor and texture. Of course I always toast 'em first to bring out the flavor. I keep it mostly basil, but a little bit of cilantro brightens things up, and some thyme because I'm Isa and I love thyme.

A splash of lemon heightens the flavors and provides some tang, and just a little nooch gives some creaminess and cheeziness. I replace half of the oil in a traditional pesto with some water, and it's none the worse for it. I actually prefer it this way because it's not greasy.

Preheat a large, heavy-bottomed skillet (preferably cast iron) over medium-low heat. Add the walnuts and toast them, tossing often, for 5 minutes. Then add the pine nuts and cook, still tossing, for an additional 5 minutes. The nuts should turn a few shades darker and smell warm and toasty.

Transfer the toasted nuts to a food processor. Add the garlic and pulse everything into fine crumbs. Add the basil, cilantro, thyme, nutritional yeast, water, and salt and puree until relatively smooth, scraping down the sides at least once to make sure you get everything. Stream in the olive oil and blend until well combined. Blend in the lemon juice and a few grinds of black pepper. Taste and adjust for salt and pepper. Keep covered and refrigerated until ready to use.

MARINARA
SAUCE

1 tablespoon olive oil

1 small yellow onion, finely chopped

3 garlic cloves, minced

1 tablespoon brown sugar

1 teaspoon dried thyme

1 teaspoon dried oregano

½ teaspoon crushed red pepper flakes

Freshly ground black pepper

1 (28-ounce) can crushed tomatoes with basil

1 teaspoon salt

Marinara is the simplest sauce to make, yet home cooks have a knack for overcomplicating it. I've seen usually law-abiding citizens add everything from vinegar to cumin to their beautiful sauce. Cumin! Well, here's how I like it. Super basic, super delicious. Tomatoes, garlic, basil, oregano, and a little thyme. Keep the rest of the spice rack far, far away.

Preheat a 2-quart pot over medium-low heat. Add the oil. When the oil is hot, sauté the onion until slightly browned, about 5 minutes. Add the garlic and sauté until fragrant, about 30 seconds. Add the brown sugar and cook until the sugar is dissolved and coating all the onions, about 1 minute. Mix in the thyme, oregano, red pepper flakes, and a few grinds of black pepper. Add the tomatoes and salt and stir everything together. Cover the pot, leaving a little gap for steam to escape, and cook for 15 minutes. Taste and adjust for salt and seasoning and serve!

VEGAN
MAYO

½ cup cold unsweetened almond milk or soy milk (see Tip)

1½ tablespoons ground flaxseed

2 teaspoons sugar

1 teaspoon ground mustard

1 teaspoon onion powder

¼ teaspoon salt

1 tablespoon white wine vinegar

1 tablespoon fresh lemon juice

1 cup canola oil

———— *Tips* ————

The kind of milk you use here is way important. Choose the most neutral-tasting milk you can find. Do not go for hemp or oat milk here. Choose unsweetened, unflavored almond or soy milk for the best results.

Depending on the strength of your blender, your times may differ. The important thing is to pay attention to the consistency of the mayo through each step. No matter what, you have to get the flaxseed good and blended, so that the flecks are barely noticeable. That activates its gloopy properties and will also make your mayo prettier. The other important thing to remember is that the oil needs to be added little by little.

Most people figure it out as children: Are you a mayo person or not? I definitely am. I need few excuses to slather, dip, and otherwise deface any morsel with some mayonnaise. There are plenty of decadent and delicious vegan varieties on the market these days (and, yes, plenty of not so great ones, too). But there's just something so homey about making your own! A connection, I guess—to the land, to your kitchen, to life, and probably mostly to your blender. This homemade version is so fresh and delicious, it just levels up everything it touches. And in this book, and entertaining in general, so many things depend on mayo, this is a great time to experiment with making your own.

Combine the milk and ground flaxseed in a blender. Blend on high speed until the flax is barely detectable and the mixture is frothy, about a minute.

Add the sugar, ground mustard, onion powder, salt, vinegar, and lemon juice, blending for a few seconds to combine.

Now begin to add the oil. With the blender running, use the hole at the top to stream in a tablespoon or two at a time, blending for about 30 seconds after each addition (if you're using a high-speed blender like a Vitamix, 5 to 10 seconds should do it). Give your blender a break every now and again so that it doesn't heat up the mayo. You should notice it thickening by the halfway point. By the time you've used three-quarters of the oil, it should be spreadable. And with the last addition, you should have a nice, thick mayo. If it seems watery, just keep blending.

The taste of this mayo is very strong at first, but the vinegar and salt mellow out over time, so don't adjust it straight from the blender. Transfer to a glass Tupperware, seal tightly, and refrigerate for a few hours, and it will thicken even further as the flavor mellows and becomes perfect. Use within a week.

Mini RASPBERRY CHEESECAKES

FOR THE CRUSTS:

1 (10-ounce) package chocolate wafer cookies

½ cup all-purpose flour

¼ cup sugar

¼ cup plus 2 tablespoons refined coconut oil, melted

2 tablespoons unsweetened almond milk (or your favorite nondairy milk)

FOR THE CHEESECAKE:

½ cup raw cashews, soaked in water for at least 2 hours and drained

1 cup fresh raspberries

⅓ cup mashed banana

1 (12-ounce) package extra-firm silken tofu

¼ cup fresh lemon juice

3 tablespoons refined coconut oil, melted

1 tablespoon pure vanilla extract

¾ cup sugar

2 tablespoons cornstarch

½ teaspoon salt

FOR THE DRIZZLE:

½ cup semisweet chocolate chips

1 teaspoon refined coconut oil

Cheesecake. Need I go on? Little tiny cheesecakes that you can have all to yourself, that are tart and sweet and drizzled with spoonful after spoonful of chocolate. Now your day is complete.

MAKE THE CRUSTS: Preheat the oven to 350°F. Line a standard-size 12-cup muffin tin with paper liners.

Combine the chocolate wafer cookies, flour, sugar, melted coconut oil, and almond milk in a food processor and process until fine and crumbly. Divide the mixture evenly among the muffin cups, then press it firmly down to form crusts.

Bake for 10 minutes. Set the crusts aside to cool, but leave the oven on.

MAKE THE CHEESECAKE: While the crusts are cooling, in a blender, combine the cashews, raspberries, banana, tofu, lemon juice, coconut oil, vanilla, sugar, cornstarch, and salt. Puree until completely smooth; this can take up to 5 minutes depending on the strength of your machine. Periodically stop the machine to keep it from overheating, and scrape down the sides of the blender jar with a rubber spatula to make sure you get everything. Pour the cheesecake mixture into the muffin cups, leaving ½ inch space at the top.

Bake until the cheesecakes are set and no longer jiggly, 22 to 25 minutes. Set aside to cool.

MAKE THE DRIZZLE: Once the cheesecakes are relatively cool, microwave the chocolate chips and the coconut oil at 50 percent power, stirring every 30 seconds, until melted and smooth. You can use a spoon to drizzle it over the cheesecakes, or you can put it into a plastic bag and snip off the corner for a prettier drizzle.

Refrigerate for 3 hours to set completely before serving.

MAKES

12

BROWNIES

TOTAL
30 MINUTES
ACTIVE
20 MINUTES

PEANUT BUTTER
BROWNIES

FOR THE PEANUT BUTTER SWIRL:

½ cup creamy natural peanut butter

⅓ cup powdered sugar, sifted

1 tablespoon refined coconut oil, melted

½ teaspoon pure vanilla extract

Pinch salt

FOR THE BROWNIES:

3 ounces semisweet chocolate chips

¼ cup refined coconut oil

⅓ cup unsweetened almond milk (or your favorite nondairy milk), at room temperature

1 teaspoon pure vanilla extract

1 tablespoon cornstarch

⅔ cup granulated sugar

¾ cup plus 2 tablespoons all-purpose flour

3 tablespoons Dutch-process cocoa powder

½ teaspoon baking powder

⅛ teaspoon salt

When you're, like, four years old, your first favorite dessert flavor is bound to be chocolate and peanut butter. And when you're forty...not much changes. In between you might want to toy around with other favorites (matcha? chai?), but come now, you will always return to your first. These brownies are deep and rich and have a satisfying, addictive peanut butter swirl that looks as neato as it tastes.

MAKE THE PEANUT BUTTER SWIRL: In a mixing bowl, stir together all the swirl ingredients until smooth. Set aside.

MAKE THE BROWNIES: Preheat the oven to 350°F. Line an 8-inch square metal pan with aluminum foil, then coat the foil with nonstick cooking spray.

In a large metal bowl set over a saucepan of simmering water, melt the chocolate with the coconut oil, stirring with a rubber spatula, until smooth. Remove from the heat.

In a mixing bowl, whisk together the milk, vanilla, and cornstarch. Add the warm chocolate mixture to the mixing bowl and whisk until well combined. Add the sugar and mix well.

Sift in the flour, cocoa, baking powder, and salt and fold until combined (a few lumps are okay). Pour the batter into the prepared pan and spread it to the edges.

Drop spoonfuls of the peanut butter mixture onto the brownie batter in the pan, then use a butter knife to swirl it in. Bake until a toothpick inserted in the center comes out mostly clean, 18 to 20 minutes.

When cool enough to handle, lift the foil out of the pan, slice the brownies, and serve!

3

Chinese

NEW
YEAR

ALL NEW YORKERS KNOW

that every year there are

TWO PLACES TO BE OR,

depending on how you look at it,

TWO PLACES TO AVOID:

TIMES SQUARE ON New Year's Eve and Chinatown during Chinese New Year. For me, Chinese New Year is not to be missed. A fifty-foot dragon sweeping down Canal Street. People hanging off the fire escapes throwing confetti. Paper everywhere. Red lanterns swinging. Red balloons in bunches, some flying up through the buildings and into the sky. The windiest streets in NYC form their own kind of dragon, made up of lights and confetti and people. Oh yeah, and all the food!

This is my disclaimer: What follows is the Chinese New Year menu of a Jewish girl from Brooklyn who has never been anywhere near China. Chinese New Year is a two-week-long journey involving traditions, deities, and customs that I'm not familiar with. But it is nonetheless a celebration that is close to my heart because the day of the parade was always an exciting time for me. I want my homegrown celebration to include my favorite flavors from the Chinese foods I grew up with, as well as a few playful takes on some classic dishes.

From these dishes you can set up your celebration as a coursed dinner if you like, choosing a soup, an app, and an entree, or go ahead and serve things up dim sum style, with five or six dishes, giving everyone a taste of everything. Drink oolong tea, lychee juice, and pomelo mimosas.

HOT *And* SOUR SOUP

1 ounce dried wood ear mushrooms

2 cups boiling water

2 teaspoons toasted sesame oil

2 garlic cloves, minced

2 teaspoons minced fresh ginger

1 (8-ounce) can bamboo shoots, rinsed and drained

4 cups vegetable broth, purchased or homemade (page 203)

¼ cup rice vinegar

3 tablespoons tamari or soy sauce

2 teaspoons sugar

1 teaspoon ground white pepper

1 tablespoon cornstarch

½ cup cold water

8 ounces fresh shiitake mushrooms, tough stems trimmed, sliced

4 cups sliced bok choy (see Tip), stems and leaves kept separate

1 cup chopped scallions, for garnish

Hot chile oil, for garnish (optional)

Tip

Bok choy is one of my favorite veggies, because it's like two ingredients in one: The stems are crunchy and fresh, while the leaves wilt to silk. To prep for this recipe, thinly slice the white stems right up to where the leaves begin. Then tear the leaves into smaller pieces (about the size of a Post-it note).

This soup is a mainstay of any Chinese-American menu, and it brings back a million memories to almost everyone. For me, there was nothing like walking into a Chinese restaurant in January in my beat-up Converse, soaked through from the snow, carrying my journal and a couple of magazines to flip through. I almost want to call it Wet Shoes Soup. But I made this soup with the idea that it wasn't just for you to hoard alone but to share with everyone. Share those thoughts and feelings and soup, ladle by ladle, with friends and family instead of just your journal. It's not an entree soup (read: there's no tofu in it). Rather, meaty shiitakes and traditional wood ear mushrooms give it bulk, while delicate bites of bok choy add some crunch and green. The "hot" comes from a generous pinch of white pepper, but I also like to drizzle each bowl with hot chile oil if I've got some around.

Place the wood ears in a cereal bowl and submerge them in the boiling water. Cover the bowl (a little plate works well) and let them sit for 30 minutes to soften. Remove the wood ears and chop them into bite-size pieces. Reserve the water from the soaking.

Preheat a 4-quart soup pot over low heat. Add the sesame oil. When the oil is hot, sauté the garlic and ginger for 30 seconds or so, being careful not to burn them. Add the wood ears and reserved soaking water, along with the bamboo shoots, vegetable broth, vinegar, tamari, sugar, and white pepper. Cover the pot and bring the liquid to a full boil.

In the meantime, in a measuring cup, whisk the cornstarch into the cold water until dissolved. Mix this slurry into the soup, then add the shiitakes and bok choy stems. Cook to thicken, about 5 minutes. Add the bok choy leaves and stir to wilt them.

Taste for spiciness/saltiness/sourness and adjust as necessary. Serve hot, garnished with scallions and dotted with hot chile oil, if desired.

Steamed
CHICKY DUMPLINGS

MAKES
16
DUMPLINGS

TOTAL
1 HOUR 30 MINUTES
ACTIVE
45 MINUTES

FOR THE DOUGH:

2 cups all-purpose flour

¾ cup just-boiled water

FOR THE FILLING:

1 (15-ounce) can chickpeas, rinsed and drained, or 1½ cups cooked chickpeas

1 cup shredded green cabbage

¼ cup shredded peeled carrot

1 tablespoon minced garlic

1 tablespoon toasted sesame oil

¼ teaspoon salt

¼ teaspoon freshly ground black pepper

¼ teaspoon crushed red pepper flakes

Tip

Grate the veggies on the medium holes of a box grater for the best texture.

Dumplings can be complicated, but these are not. Lightly mashed chickpeas are an unexpected filling that makes total sense: With a little sesame oil and garlic, no one would ever guess that it isn't chicken. And the best part is that you don't even have to cook the filling beforehand. It all comes together quickly in a mixing bowl. So, go ahead and make dumplings from scratch! The dough is really easy if you use a standing mixer fitted with a paddle, but you can simply knead with your hands instead. These look really pretty if you serve them on cabbage leaves.

MAKE THE DOUGH: Put the flour in the bowl of your standing mixer and turn it on low. Add the boiled water in a slow, continuous stream until a ball forms. Let the dough knead until soft and elastic, about 3 minutes.

Turn out the dough onto a lightly floured surface and knead it a bit just to form into a smooth ball. Place the ball in a plastic bag, and let it rest for at least 30 minutes. You can also refrigerate the dough overnight, but be sure to bring it back to room temperature before using.

MAKE THE FILLING: Lightly mash the chickpeas until no whole ones are left, but they aren't completely mushy. Add the cabbage, carrot, garlic, sesame oil, salt, black pepper, and crushed red pepper and mix well.

MAKE THE DUMPLINGS: Have ready a parchment-lined tray to hold the dumplings.

Turn out the rested dough onto a lightly floured surface and divide it into 16 equal pieces. The dough should be very soft and pliable and easy to work with.

Roll a piece of dough into a 4½-inch circle that's ⅛ inch thick. Place a heaping tablespoon of the filling on half of the circle, fold over the other half, and pinch the edges together to seal everything into a half-moon-shaped dumpling. Place the dumpling on the tray until ready to steam. Continue until all the dough and filling are used.

Heat up your steamer. Rub each dumpling with a little oil to prevent sticking. Steam until translucent and shiny, 15 to 20 minutes. Serve immediately.

MAKES
16
BUNDLES

TOTAL
30 MINUTES
ACTIVE
30 MINUTES

Cold SESAME NOODLE BUNDLES

12 ounces dry udon noodles

1 garlic clove, peeled

1 tablespoon chopped fresh ginger

⅓ cup toasted sesame oil

⅓ cup rice vinegar

⅓ cup tamari or soy sauce

¼ cup warm water

2 teaspoons sriracha

1 cup creamy natural peanut butter

¼ cup brown sugar

16 large romaine leaves

Black sesame seeds

16 whole scallions

Tip

Udon noodles are increasingly easy to find in any old supermarket, but if you can't find them or just plain don't feel like using them, you can substitute linguine in this recipe.

All the greatness of cold sesame noodles without the inconvenience of needing a plate and utensils! These flavorful little bundles come tied up in a scallion. It can't get any cuter or more delicious. Perfect for picking up and shoving into your face or, if you prefer, you can serve it on a plate like a princess. Long noodles mean long life, so don't go breaking your noodles before boiling them. Use the longest noodles you can find in the biggest pot of boiling water. You can make these a few hours ahead and keep them on a serving tray covered in plastic wrap until ready to serve.

First, bring a large pot of salted water to a boil. Cook the udon noodles according to the package directions.

While that's going on, prepare the dressing. Put the garlic and ginger in a blender and pulse to chop them up a bit. Add the sesame oil, rice vinegar, tamari, warm water, sriracha, peanut butter, and brown sugar and puree until it's completely smooth. Add a little extra warm water if needed to thin.

When the noodles are ready, drain them and run them under cold water to cool them completely. When the noodles are cool, transfer them to a large mixing bowl and toss them with the dressing to coat.

To assemble each bundle, place a bunch of noodles down the center of a romaine leaf, leaving a little bit of space at the top and bottom. Sprinkle with black sesame seeds. Tie each leaf crosswise with a whole scallion to form a bundle. Serve!

RICE PAPER ROLLS
with Red Curry Peanut Sauce

MAKES 16 ROLLS

TOTAL 45 MINUTES
ACTIVE 45 MINUTES

FOR THE RED CURRY PEANUT SAUCE:

¼ cup water

3 tablespoons creamy natural peanut butter

1 tablespoon red curry paste

1 tablespoon fresh lime juice

1 teaspoon agave

1 teaspoon sriracha (or more to taste)

FOR THE RICE PAPER ROLLS:

1 head napa cabbage, a few leaves reserved for the platter, the rest thinly sliced

1 large carrot, peeled and cut into matchsticks

1 ripe avocado, pitted, peeled, and thinly sliced, drizzled with lemon or lime juice to prevent browning

A lot of fresh cilantro sprigs (about ½ bunch)

1 cup fresh mint leaves

16 (8½-inch) rice paper wrappers

Tip

To keep these rolls really fresh, even if you make them a day in advance, you have to store them properly. Line a tray with damp paper towels, then arrange the rolls in a single layer. Cover with another layer of damp paper towels and cover the tray tightly in plastic wrap.

The most important characteristic of a rice paper roll is freshness: fresh ingredients and fresh wrappers. The rice paper should be supple, and the temperature should be chilly. Inside, there should be clean flavors and crunch. I like to save the assertive spicy notes for the sauce. These rolls contain my favorite raw cabbage, napa, with its gardeny flavor and snap; carrots, cut into matchsticks, for their color and crunchiness; and avocado, to add a creamy fattiness that is the perfect foil for all the veggies. And you can't have rice paper rolls without fresh herbs! Mint and cilantro make the flavors pop.

The peanut dipping sauce employs a little cheating ingredient: red curry paste. This way, we don't have to do any more chopping or cooking—everything goes into a little blender and 30 seconds later a spicy, peanutty, gingery, tangy sauce appears. Magic!

MAKE THE RED CURRY PEANUT SAUCE: Put all the sauce ingredients into a small blender and blend until smooth. Add a few more tablespoons water if needed to thin it out. Taste for seasoning and keep sealed until ready to use.

GET ROLLING: Have a large dinner plate ready to roll on. Also, have a baking dish lined with moist paper towels for the finished rolls. This will keep them fresh and prevent sticking.

Lay out the cabbage, carrot, avocado, cilantro, and mint on a cutting board.

Get out a large bowl, wide enough to accommodate the rice paper wrappers. Fill the bowl with really, really warm water—but not too hot to handle. You'll have to refresh the water a few times while rolling, to keep it warm.

Slide three or four rice paper wrappers into the warm water, one at a time, and let them steep for a minute or so, until nice and soft.

Remove one wrapper from the water. Handle it gently and patiently, and spread it out on the plate. It won't be perfect, but that's okay, just get it as flat as you can without being too fussy.

Place a bit of cabbage, a few carrot sticks, a slice or two of avocado, and a generous amount of cilantro in the lower third of the wrapper. Add a few mint leaves.

Now fold the sides over the filling, and roll up the bottom of the roll, tucking it over the filling and continuing to roll until it's, well, a roll!

Place the roll in the baking dish and cover with more damp paper towels to keep fresh. Continue making rolls until you've used up all your filling ingredients.

If you like to be fancy, you can cut each roll in half and stand them, cut-side up, on a cabbage leaf. Serve with the sauce.

ROLL, DON'T RIP

Here are some tips for how to become an expert roller,
and how to never ever rip a wrapper. But the truth is that if one rips,
it really doesn't matter. Eat it anyway (as a test subject!) or empty
out the ingredients and start again. NBD.

Add the wrappers to the warm water one at a time. If you put them all in at once in a pile, they'll stick together.

Have a clean towel nearby, to dry your hands. This keeps the slipperiness to a minimum. Also, wipe down your rolling plate every now and again to keep it from becoming too slippery.

Don't overfill the rolls. You can see in the pic on page 78 how much filling to add, but don't worry: If you're using too much filling, you'll figure it out quickly.

Avoid having sharp, pointy ingredients right at the surface of the wrapper. Carrot sticks and cilantro stems like to poke through the wrapper, so try to prevent that.

Reserve extra napa cabbage leaves for lining your serving plate. The wrappers like to stick to the surface of plates, but they lift away easily from cabbage leaves.

GENERAL
Tso's
SEITAN

FOR THE SAUCE:

½ cup vegetable broth, purchased or homemade (page 203)

3 tablespoons agave

2 tablespoons tamari or soy sauce

2 tablespoons mirin

1 tablespoon minced garlic

1 tablespoon sriracha

1 tablespoon cornstarch

1 teaspoon ground ginger

1 teaspoon crushed red pepper flakes

FOR THE CRISPY SEITAN:

¼ cup white rice flour

2 tablespoons cornstarch

¼ teaspoon ground white pepper

½ recipe Chickee-Style Seitan (page 18) or 1 pound store-bought equivalent, cut into bite-size pieces

Vegetable oil, for frying

Steamed white rice, for serving

Did you watch that General Tso documentary on Netflix? Probably. If not, let me give you the rundown: Everyone loves General Tso and no one knows who he was! But this is the yummiest thing you will ever eat. Our entire country agrees. Sweet, tangy, salty, spicy, sticky sauce smothering crispy fried meaty stuff. It is everything you want in life.

TO MAKE THE SAUCE: Whisk together all the sauce ingredients in a 4-quart saucepan. Heat the sauce over medium-high heat, stirring constantly, until glossy and thick, about 5 minutes. Remove the pan from the heat and set aside until the seitan is ready.

TO MAKE THE CRISPY SEITAN: Put the rice flour, cornstarch, and white pepper in a large zip-top plastic bag and shake to combine. Add the seitan pieces to the bag and shake to coat.

Have ready a few brown paper bags or a baking sheet lined with paper towels to absorb the oil. Pour 3 inches of oil into a deep, heavy pot. Cast iron works great. Bring the oil to frying temperature, about 350°F. It's ready when a little pinch of seitan thrown in sizzles and fries with lots of bubbles but doesn't smoke.

Fry the seitan pieces until golden brown and extra crispy, 3 to 4 minutes. Transfer to the paper bags or paper towels to absorb excess oil.

Add the crispy seitan pieces to the saucepan and toss to coat with the sauce. Serve with white rice.

MU SHU PANCAKES

MAKES
8
PANCAKES

TOTAL
2 HOURS
ACTIVE
1 HOUR

FOR THE PANCAKES:

2 cups all-purpose flour

½ teaspoon salt

¾ cup boiling water

1 tablespoon olive oil

Toasted sesame oil, for brushing and cooking

FOR THE FILLING:

1 tablespoon toasted sesame oil

1 yellow onion, cut into thin half-moons

1 red bell pepper, seeded and cut into thin strips

3 garlic cloves, minced

1 tablespoon minced ginger

8 ounces cremini mushrooms, thinly sliced

8 ounces green cabbage, thinly sliced

FOR THE SAUCE:

1 teaspoon cornstarch

⅓ cup cold water

⅓ cup hoisin sauce

2 tablespoons mirin

2 tablespoons tamari or soy sauce

1 tablespoon sriracha (use less if you are a spice wimp)

⅛ teaspoon salt

Freshly ground black pepper

Sliced scallions, for garnish

One of my fondest memories of eating out in NYC is going out for mu shu pancakes with my best friend shortly after we went vegetarian as teenagers. We would stuff each pancake with lots of saucy shredded veggies and proceed to stuff our faces. It seemed very fancy and ceremonious to me, and always led to great conversation and adventure. Now you can re-create that fun at home! They're a great appetizer if you serve one to each person, but they also make for a fabulous entree if you serve two each.

If you'd like to serve these as an entree, and desire additional meatiness, sauté up to 8 ounces thinly sliced Chickee-Style Seitan (page 18) in a little toasted sesame oil. Remove the seitan from the pan, proceed with the rest of the recipe, then return the seitan to the mixture at the end. You can also try thinly sliced tofu, if you like!

MAKE THE PANCAKES: Sift the flour and salt together into a medium mixing bowl, then make a well in the center. Pour the boiling water into the well, along with the olive oil, and use a fork to mix. When the dough comes together, transfer it to a floured surface and knead until it is smooth and pliable, about 5 minutes. Put the dough back in the bowl, cover with plastic wrap, and let rest for about 30 minutes.

On a lightly floured surface, roll out the dough into a long snake, about 1 inch wide. Cut the snake into 16 even pieces and roll each piece into a ball, then flatten them slightly into disks.

Now we will form the pancakes. Brush the top of one disk with a little sesame oil, then place another disk on top. On a lightly floured surface, flatten the double disk a bit with the palm of your hand. Now roll it out into an 8-inch circle. Transfer the pancake to a plate and cover with plastic wrap. Proceed to form the other 7 pancakes.

Now it's time to cook them! Preheat a large pan (preferably cast iron) over medium-low heat. Brush the pan with a very thin layer of sesame oil. Cook each pancake individually for about 2 minutes on each side. The pancake should puff up, with the occasional bubble here and there and toasty brown speckles. Stack the pancakes on a plate and tent with aluminum foil until ready to serve.

MAKE THE FILLING: Preheat a large, heavy-bottomed pan (preferably cast iron) over medium-high heat. Heat the oil, then sauté the onion and bell pepper until slightly softened, about 2 minutes. Add the garlic and ginger and cook until fragrant, about 30 seconds. Add the mushrooms and sauté until they release their moisture, about 3 minutes.

Tip

You'll notice that you are rolling together two pancakes to create one flaky layered one. I have a dark secret: This was a happy accident. I misread a recipe that said to roll them together and separate them after cooking. What? That's impossible! But, luckily, the texture is awesome when they are rolled together, and there is no need to pull them apart. They come out wonderfully puffy and flaky and way better than store-bought.

Add the cabbage and stir to incorporate with the other ingredients. The pan will look too full, but don't worry—the cabbage will cook down. Cover the pan and cook, tossing occasionally, until the cabbage is wilted and lightly browned, about 5 minutes.

MAKE THE SAUCE: Meanwhile, in a small bowl, vigorously whisk the cornstarch into the cold water with a fork. Once it is smooth, mix in the hoisin, mirin, tamari, sriracha, and salt.

Lower the heat under the filling to medium and add the sauce to the pan, stirring to combine. Add a few grinds of black pepper. Cook until the sauce thickens and bubbles, about 3 minutes.

SERVE: Let the filling mixture cool slightly, and then spoon it into the pancakes. Roll 'em up, sprinkle with chopped scallions, and serve.

SEARED
DRAGON
GREEN BEANS
with Almonds

½ cup sliced almonds

2 tablespoons refined coconut oil

1 pound green beans, trimmed

4 garlic cloves, minced

1 tablespoon sriracha

1 tablespoon tamari or soy sauce

¼ teaspoon salt

If you're serving a buffet, it's nice to have a few simple things amid all that's going on, with ingredients that really pop. These green beans do just that. With toasted almonds, sriracha, and lots and lots of garlic that's added at the end to ensure maximum garlic strength, this humble little recipe might just steal the whole show.

Preheat a large nonstick pan (preferably cast iron) over medium-low heat. Add the almonds to the dry pan and let them toast until fragrant and lightly browned, 3 to 5 minutes. Transfer the almonds to a plate, wipe the pan with a towel (carefully, don't burn yourself!), and return it to the stove.

Turn the heat up to medium-high and add 1 tablespoon of the coconut oil. When the coconut oil is melted, toss in the green beans and cook them, stirring occasionally, until they are seared in a few spots. They should still have a lot of snap to them and be fairly firm.

Push the beans over to one side of the pan. Add the remaining 1 tablespoon coconut oil and immediately dump the minced garlic into the oil, letting it cook for 15 seconds or so but being careful not to let it burn. Now mix the garlic in with the beans to coat them.

Add the sriracha, tamari, and salt. Turn off the heat and toss the beans to coat. Immediately transfer the beans to a serving plate and sprinkle with the sliced almonds to serve.

CURRY
PORK FRIED RICE

SERVES

6

TOTAL
45 MINUTES
ACTIVE
45 MINUTES

1 small beet, scrubbed and chopped

1 cup water

1 teaspoon liquid smoke

2 cups diced Chickee-Style Seitan (page 18), or store-bought equivalent

3 tablespoons refined coconut oil

3 cups small broccoli florets

1 large carrot, peeled and cut into thin half-moons

1 small red onion, diced

Salt

2 garlic cloves, minced

½ cup chopped fresh cilantro

4 cups cooked and cooled jasmine rice (see Tip)

2 teaspoons oriental curry powder (like S&B brand)

¼ teaspoon crushed red pepper flakes

2 tablespoons tamari or soy sauce

1 tablespoon fresh lime juice

1 teaspoon agave

Sriracha, for serving

No Chinese buffet spread is complete without fried rice! I love this curried version, rich with coconut oil, and it's my favorite method for cooking fried rice magnificently. First you cook the veggies, to get them the perfect texture—not too tender, with some crunch, and nicely seared. Then you do a quick sauté to brown the seitan. (You can also use cubed tofu if you don't feel like having fun with seitan.) Then come the aromatics, followed by cold rice, which keeps the grains from getting mushy.

Oriental curry powder is completely different from, say, an Indian madras curry powder. It's more floral and herbal, with anise and coriander. And it takes fried rice to new heights.

MAKE THE PORKY SEITAN: Boil the chopped beet in the water in a tiny pan. Simmer until the water is thick and red, about 10 minutes. Transfer to a mixing bowl to cool. Add the liquid smoke and toss with the seitan. Let sit for about 20 minutes, until the outside of the seitan is dyed red. Remove the seitan from the water and place on paper towels to drain. Set aside until ready to use.

MAKE THE FRIED RICE: Preheat a large, heavy-bottomed pan (preferably cast iron) over medium-high heat. Heat 1 tablespoon of the coconut oil. When it melts, sauté the broccoli florets and carrot until the broccoli is lightly charred, about 5 minutes. Transfer the broccoli and carrot to a large plate.

Add another 1 tablespoon coconut oil and let it melt. Sauté the seitan, tossing frequently, until lightly browned, about 3 minutes. Transfer the seitan to the plate with the broccoli and carrot.

Add the last tablespoon of oil. Sauté the onion with a pinch of salt for 3 minutes. Add the garlic and cilantro and sauté for about a minute. The cilantro will wilt and everything will smell aromatic and wonderful.

Now add the cold rice, curry powder, and red pepper flakes and cook, tossing often, for 5 minutes.

Return the broccoli, carrot, and seitan to the pan, then drizzle in the tamari, lime juice, and agave. Cook until the rice is lightly browned, 3 minutes or so. Taste and adjust for salt. Serve with plenty of sriracha!

Tip

You can often buy frozen jasmine rice in the freezer section (duh) of fancy supermarkets. Otherwise, cook 2 cups of rice a day ahead. Spread out the rice on a baking sheet to cool so it won't clump together. Once cooled, transfer to a zip-top bag and refrigerate until ready to use.

PEKING
PORTOBELLOS

FOR THE MUSHROOMS:

4 medium-size portobello
mushroom caps

Sliced scallions, for garnish

FOR THE SAUCE:

½ cup hoisin sauce

2 tablespoons rice wine vinegar

2 tablespoons sriracha

1 tablespoon toasted sesame oil

1 tablespoon grated fresh ginger

1 tablespoon grated orange zest

2 tablespoons brown sugar

¼ teaspoon Chinese five-spice
powder

It's time to see portobellos in a whole new way: crispy, caramelized skin with a meaty, juicy center. The portobellos are roasted first to release some of the juices, then broiled in a sweet and tangy sauce with a hint of orange zest.

Preheat the oven to 425°F. Place an oven-safe cooling rack or roasting rack over a rimmed baking sheet to catch the drippings.

Place the portobellos, gill-side down, on the rack and roast for 12 minutes.

In the meantime, grab a medium mixing bowl and whisk together all the ingredients for the sauce.

When the portobellos are done roasting, lay them on paper towels and gently press to release any excess moisture.

Turn the oven to broil and set your oven rack about 8 inches from the flame. Lightly grease a rimmed baking sheet and place the portobellos, gill-side up, on the baking sheet. Spoon about half of the sauce over the mushrooms and spread it with the back of the spoon to coat.

Broil the portobellos for about 5 minutes, checking frequently that the sauce is not burning. The skin should get somewhat crisp and caramelized.

Flip the portobellos and spoon most of the remaining sauce over each cap. Reserve about ¼ cup sauce for serving. Broil until the skin is browned and crisp, about 5 minutes more.

Slice the portobellos on a bias and drizzle with a little of the reserved sauce. Garnish with sliced scallions and serve.

Tips

Remove the portobello gills for this recipe to prevent any sogginess. Simply remove the stem with a gentle turn, then use a tablespoon to carefully scrape out the gills. Use care not to break the portobello!

This recipe calls for 4 medium-size mushrooms, but as you've probably noticed at some point, portobellos can vary dramatically in size. Use common sense for cooking times if your specimens seem very large or very small, although don't go too small or you will lose the juicy interior.

If you don't have a metal roasting rack or oven-safe cooling rack, don't despair! Instead, roast the mushrooms on parchment paper. Then, halfway through roasting, drain the pan, change the parchment, and continue roasting.

TOFU SHORT RIBS

with Gingery Mashed Root Vegetables

SERVES 8

TOTAL
1 HOUR 15 MINUTES
ACTIVE
1 HOUR 15 MINUTES

FOR THE TOFU:

2 (14-ounce) packages super-firm tofu, drained

2 tablespoons vegetable oil

1 tablespoon tamari or soy sauce

FOR THE RIB SAUCE:

2 tablespoons cornstarch

1 cup cold vegetable broth, purchased or homemade (page 203)

1 cup hoisin sauce

⅓ cup pure maple syrup

⅓ cup tamari or soy sauce

⅓ cup rice vinegar

¼ cup tomato paste

1 tablespoon sriracha

2 teaspoons liquid smoke

1½ tablespoons garlic powder

1 tablespoon onion powder

¾ teaspoon Chinese five-spice powder

FOR THE ROOT MASH:

8 ounces parsnips, peeled and cut into 1-inch chunks

8 ounces rutabaga or turnip, peeled and cut into 1-inch chunks

1 pound sweet potatoes, peeled and cut into 1-inch chunks

2 tablespoons refined coconut oil

1 tablespoon minced fresh ginger

2 garlic cloves, minced

1 teaspoon salt

All the licky, succulent flavor of a rib but without the...rib! Smother the sauce all over the gingery root veg mash and it's like a winter parade for your taste buds. These ribs make a dazzling presentation as a centerpiece for your spread, so serve them family style on your coolest serving platter. To get this recipe together in about an hour, preheat the oven for the tofu first. In the meantime, start putting the sauce together. While the sauce heats, get the tofu in the oven. And while those things are working away, throw together your root mash.

MAKE THE TOFU: Preheat the oven to 350°F. Put the tofu on a large rimmed baking sheet and coat it on both sides with the oil and tamari. Bake for 15 minutes, then flip the slices and bake for 15 minutes more.

MAKE THE RIB SAUCE: While the tofu is in the oven, in a 2-cup measuring cup, use a fork to vigorously whisk the cornstarch into the vegetable broth until it's mostly dissolved. Add the remaining sauce ingredients and mix well.

Transfer the sauce to a small saucepot and heat over medium heat, stirring occasionally, until it comes to a boil. Once boiling, lower the heat to a low simmer and let the sauce thicken for about 5 minutes. Remove from the heat.

Smother the cooked tofu with the rib sauce, return it to the oven, and bake for 15 minutes more. Remove the pan from the oven and tent it with aluminum foil to keep warm until ready to serve.

MAKE THE ROOT MASH: Put the parsnips and rutabaga in a 4-quart pot and submerge them in water by 2 inches. Cover the pot and bring the water to a boil over high heat. Uncover and boil the parsnips and rutabaga for 10 minutes, then add the sweet potatoes. Continue to boil until everything is fork-tender, about 10 minutes more.

Drain the veggies and transfer them to a medium mixing bowl.

Heat a small pan over low heat and add the coconut oil. When it is melted, sauté the ginger and garlic just until golden, about a minute. Add the ginger and garlic to the bowl of boiled root veg, along with the salt.

Mash everything very well, then taste and adjust for salt.

SERVE: Spread out the hot root veg mash on a serving platter. Arrange the ribs over the mash, then spoon on the remaining sauce. Serve immediately, with large serving spoons.

4
Valentine's
DAY

IF YOU DON'T COOK
for someone you love
ON VALENTINE'S DAY,
you are awful.

THERE'S NO TWO ways about it. Forget about how many hours you volunteer at the doggy shelter. Forget about how many old ladies you've helped cross the street. None of that matters anymore. You are just a cold-hearted person who doesn't love anyone.

Now that that's established, let's talk Valentine's Day food! This chapter has recipes ranging from beginner (like Strawberry Mâche Salad) to more advanced (Porcini-Crusted Tofu, madame?), but, truly, they will all mean a lot to whomever you're feeding. I've also organized a few menus if you'd like to go all out!

It's a good time to experiment with flavor. A hint of orange in the French toast, like a secret message. An unexpected whiff of vanilla in the sweet potato soup, like a promise that nothing will ever be ordinary. Aromatic seeds and spices, a leafy green they've never heard of with an accent over the A so you know it's fancy. Oh, and hearts. And strawberries. Lots and lots and lots of those.

MENUS

I have a few menu ideas, depending on what you're feeling like.
I know that the recipes say "serves 4" or whatever but, for one thing, I have no
idea how many people you're dating and, for another, who doesn't love Valentine's
leftovers? Or maybe you're gonna have seconds and then work
all those calories off in the sack. Some of these menus would also work for a
"Galentine's" dinner, or some other sort of V-Day get-together, where
you're feeding somewhat of a crowd.

Fancy-Shmancy Menu

Sweet Potato Soup with Ginger & Vanilla

Beeting Heart Salad with Champagne Vinaigrette

Porcini-Crusted Tofu with Shallot Pan Gravy
(serve with cilantro-scallion mashed potatoes, page 319)

Mini Almond Pound Cakes

Italian Edition
(aka Garlic Breath Is for Lovers)

Strawberry Mâche Salad

Arancini with Almond Cheese

Green Lasagna Rolls

Chocolate Yogurt Bundt Cake

Show Them You Curry

Potato Samosas in Phyllo

Pistachio Lentil Biryani

Cauliflower Tikka Masala

ALMOND-CRUSTED
FRENCH TOAST
with Strawberries

MAKES
6
TOASTS

TOTAL
25 MINUTES
ACTIVE
25 MINUTES

¼ cup all-purpose flour

1 tablespoon cornstarch

⅛ teaspoon salt

½ cup unsweetened almond milk (or your favorite nondairy milk)

½ cup coconut milk from a well-stirred can

1 teaspoon finely grated orange zest

1 teaspoon pure vanilla extract

1 cup sliced almonds

6 (¾-inch-thick) slices sourdough bread

Refined coconut oil, for the pan

Sliced strawberries, for serving

Pure maple syrup, for serving

——— *Tip* ———

It's essential that you use a spatula thin enough to get under the toast and keep the almond coating intact. You don't want to lose all that deliciousness!

This is "I love you" fare. So, if you're just beginning a relationship and you don't feel like spending the rest of your life with that person, and you don't want them to fall madly and passionately in love with you, then maybe opt for some frozen waffles instead.

Crunchy aromatic almonds coat the outside of thick sourdough French toast in a rich coconut milk batter with just a hint of orange. You bite through the crunchy exterior to the soft doughy insides and ahhhh. Get the perfect bite with some strawberries and maple syrup, then wait for the magic to happen. Don't forget to bring this to your loved one on a vintage breakfast tray with coffee and creamer and maybe a long-stemmed rose, and don't forget the diamond-studded fork. Also, ride in on a white horse.

Preheat the oven to 250°F to keep the toasts warm. Preheat a large nonstick pan over medium heat.

In a wide mixing bowl, whisk together the flour, cornstarch, and salt. Whisk in the almond milk and coconut milk until relatively few lumps are left. Mix in the orange zest and vanilla.

Have ready a large sheet of wax paper or parchment. Spread out the sliced almonds on a dinner plate. Dip each bread slice into the wet batter and let the excess drip off. Then, press each side of the bread into the almonds to coat. Set aside on the wax paper.

When the pan is hot enough, pour in a thin layer of coconut oil (about a tablespoon) and use a spatula to coat the bottom of the pan. Cook three slices of the coated bread until the almonds are browned and toasty, about 4 minutes per side. Add extra oil when you flip the toasts. Place the cooked toasts on a baking sheet in the oven to keep warm until ready to serve.

To serve, place three slices of toast overlapping on each plate, and fan some strawberries out over the toasts. Serve with maple syrup on the side.

BROCCOLI STRATA

FOR THE BREAD AND VEGGIES:

3 tablespoons olive oil

1 medium yellow onion, thinly sliced

1 red bell pepper, seeded and diced small

6 cups broccoli florets

3 garlic cloves, minced

1 teaspoon dried thyme

1 teaspoon dried rosemary

1 teaspoon salt

Freshly ground black pepper

8 cups French bread cubes (1½-inch cubes)

Chopped fresh chives, for garnish

FOR THE CUSTARD:

1 (14-ounce) package soft tofu

½ cup vegetable broth, purchased or homemade (page 203)

2 tablespoons fresh lemon juice

2 teaspoons Dijon mustard

1 tablespoon cornstarch

1 teaspoon ground turmeric

¼ teaspoon salt

Strata is kind of what it sounds like...a breakfast stratosphere. It's a casserole of layered bread and veggies, all baked in a lush custard. If you're planning on a Galentine's Day potluck brunch, this is your ticket! It's a beautiful, homey casserole, dotted with pretty flecks of red pepper. Serve with breakfast potatoes, a side salad, and avocado toast and everyone is all set.

If you're serving this as a more romantic endeavor, you can use a large heart-shaped cookie cutter (say, 5 inches or so) to make heart-shaped individual stratas. Save the leftover pieces of the casserole for lunch the next day, when nothing has to be fancy.

MAKE THE BREAD AND VEGGIES: Preheat the oven to 350°F. Lightly grease a 9-by-13-inch casserole or baking pan.

Preheat a large, heavy-bottomed pan (preferably cast iron) over medium heat. Add 2 tablespoons of the oil. When the oil is hot, sauté the onion and bell pepper until the onion is softened, about 3 minutes. Add the broccoli, garlic, thyme, rosemary, salt, and a few grinds of black pepper and sauté until the broccoli is softened but still has some snap, about 10 minutes.

Transfer the mixture to the prepared casserole and scatter the bread cubes on top. Drizzle the remaining 1 tablespoon oil over the bread and toss everything together.

MAKE THE CUSTARD: Combine all the custard ingredients in a blender, crumbling the tofu as you add it. Puree until completely smooth, scraping down the sides of the blender jar to make sure you get everything.

Pour the custard over the bread and veggies and use a spatula to press the custard into the bread. You want to get as much custard as you can into the vegetable mixture without actually stirring things up.

Bake the strata until it is browned on top and fairly firm to the touch, 50 to 60 minutes. Allow the strata to cool for about 10 minutes, then garnish with chives, slice, and serve.

Strawberry MÂCHE SALAD

FOR THE DRESSING:

3 tablespoons whole-grain mustard

3 tablespoons balsamic vinegar

2 tablespoons grapeseed oil

1 garlic clove, Microplaned or minced to a paste

Pinch salt

Freshly ground black pepper

FOR THE SALAD:

½ cup slivered almonds

4 ounces mâche

12 ounces strawberries, hulled and quartered

¼ cup thinly sliced red onion

10 fresh basil leaves, thinly sliced

What better day than Valentine's to branch out to something special? Mâche is a velvety salad green with a complex flavor; it's earthy, nutty, grassy, and peppery all at once. It's pronounced like "mosh" for all you punks, and it's also called lamb's lettuce. If you can't find it, a spinach-arugula blend would be really nice, too. The result is dizzyingly delicious with the addition of fresh basil and toasted almonds. If you've never strawberried a salad, tonight's the night.

MAKE THE DRESSING: Just mix all the dressing ingredients together in a little bowl. Ta-dah!

MAKE THE SALAD: Preheat a small pan over medium-low heat. Toast the almonds in the dry pan, tossing frequently, until honey brown, about 5 minutes. Remove from the heat and set aside.

To assemble the salad, in a large mixing bowl, toss together the mâche, strawberries, and red onion. Add the dressing, and toss to coat. Top with the almonds and basil, and serve!

BEETING HEART
SALAD
with Champagne Vinaigrette

SERVES
6

TOTAL
1 HOUR
ACTIVE
20 MINUTES

FOR THE BEETS:

4 softball-size beets (about 2½ pounds), cut into ½-inch slices
2 tablespoons olive oil
Salt

FOR THE DRESSING:

2 teaspoons olive oil
1 cup sliced shallots
¼ cup grapeseed oil
3 tablespoons champagne vinegar
1 tablespoon Dijon mustard
1½ teaspoons sugar
½ teaspoon salt

FOR THE SALAD:

1 pound mixed greens

This salad is fun, easy, and beautiful—just like you! It's the perfect accompaniment to a decadent Valentine's Day dinner. Champagne vinegar is intriguingly delicious and makes the salad sound super fancy, but you can get away with white wine vinegar, too, and no one will be the wiser. Serve with Porcini-Crusted Tofu with Shallot Pan Gravy (page 108) for maximum effectiveness.

MAKE THE BEETS: Preheat the oven to 375°F. Line a rimmed baking sheet with parchment paper.

Put the beet slices on the baking sheet, toss with the olive oil, and season with salt. Bake, tossing once, until the beets are nice and tender, about 40 minutes.

Remove the beets from the oven and wait until they are cool enough to handle. Use a metal heart-shaped cookie cutter to punch out heart shapes. If you'd rather not do shapes, you can cut the slices into half-moons for the salad.

MAKE THE DRESSING: Preheat a large pan over medium heat. Heat the olive oil, then sauté the shallots until translucent, about 5 minutes.

Transfer the shallots to a blender, along with the remaining dressing ingredients, and blend until smooth. Taste and adjust for salt. Refrigerate until ready to use.

ASSEMBLE THE SALAD: In a large mixing bowl, toss together the greens and the dressing. Portion the salad onto individual plates and top each with roasted beets to serve.

Tips

It's important that you use big beets here, so that you have plenty of surface space for creating the heart shapes. (This works best if the heart-shaped cookie cutter is about an inch in diameter. You can also throw in other fun shapes, like a sun or a flower.) No need to peel the beets, just wash them well. You'll have scraps of leftover beets after cutting out the hearts, but that's life. You can use them in a juicer if you've got one, or make some borscht. You're smart. You'll figure it out.

Use a pretty mix of spring greens, with varying colors, for maximum prettiness! Maybe some radicchio or red cabbage to add to the beauty.

SWEET POTATO SOUP

with Ginger & Vanilla

SERVES
6–8

TOTAL
30 MINUTES
ACTIVE
15 MINUTES

1 tablespoon olive oil

1 medium yellow onion, diced medium

½ teaspoon salt, plus a pinch

2 tablespoons chopped fresh ginger

½ teaspoon crushed red pepper flakes

3 pounds garnet yams, peeled and cut into 1-inch chunks

4 cups vegetable broth, purchased or homemade (page 203)

1 vanilla bean, split and scraped (see Tip)

2 tablespoons fresh lime juice

1 tablespoon pure maple syrup

Lime wedges, for serving (optional)

Tip

My favorite method of scraping the seeds out of a vanilla bean is to cut the bean in half across the waist, using a steak knife. Then split open each half lengthwise, and use the steak knife to scrape out all the delicious vanilla beaniness.

Here's the vision: vanilla bean and ginger holding hands in a field of sweet potato, with pretty bursts of lime lighting their way, and just a touch of heat. This soup is pure aromatherapy, with ginger and vanilla wafting through the winter air, like a lover's caress. Only much better-smelling.

Preheat a 4-quart soup pot over medium heat. Heat the oil, then sauté the onion with a pinch of salt until translucent, about 3 minutes. Add the ginger and red pepper flakes and sauté for another minute or so.

Add the yams, veggie broth, and remaining ½ teaspoon salt. Cover and bring to a boil. Once boiling, lower the heat to a slow simmer and cook until the potatoes are tender, 5 more minutes or so.

Once tender, add the vanilla seeds. Use an immersion blender to puree the soup until smooth. Or transfer the soup in batches to a blender or food processor to puree. Be sure to let the steam escape in between pulses so that the steam doesn't build up and explode all over you. Then transfer the soup back to the pot.

Stir in the lime juice and maple syrup. Taste and adjust for salt, and thin the soup with a little water, if necessary.

You can serve the soup immediately, but the flavor develops a lot as it sits. The lime mellows out and the vanilla becomes more pronounced, especially the next day. Serve garnished with lime wedges, if you like. You may also want to do a coconut swirl, or something like that, if you're feeling fancy.

POTATO SAMOSAS

in Phyllo

MAKES
24
SAMOSAS

TOTAL
1 HOUR 30 MINUTES
ACTIVE
45 MINUTES

FOR THE FILLING:

1½ pounds Yukon Gold potatoes, scrubbed and cut into ½-inch dice

3 teaspoons refined coconut oil

2 teaspoons yellow mustard seeds

1 medium yellow onion, diced small

1 cup peeled, diced carrots (see Tip)

1 teaspoon salt, plus a pinch

2 garlic cloves, minced

1 tablespoon minced fresh ginger

1 teaspoon ground cumin

¼ teaspoon ground turmeric

¼ teaspoon garam masala

¼ teaspoon crushed red pepper flakes

1 tablespoon fresh lime juice

½ cup water

½ cup frozen peas

FOR THE ASSEMBLY:

Olive oil, for brushing

24 sheets frozen phyllo dough, thawed

Presenting everybody's favorite Indian stuffed pastry, now made a wee bit flakier. Phyllo makes a wonderful wrapper for samosas, and I think it makes samosas a breeze if you're feeling lazy about making dough. This is a classic filling: potatoes, carrots, peas...you know the drill. It's a combination that pleases everyone and an absolutely ideal start for a fancy Indian-inspired feast. Serve with Pear Chutney (page 373).

PREPARE THE FILLING: Put the potatoes in a 4-quart pot and fill with water until submerged. Cover the pot and bring the water to a boil over high heat. Once boiling, immediately lower the heat to a simmer and cook for about 10 minutes. The potatoes should be fork-tender. Drain the potatoes and return them to the pot. Lightly mash them, so that they are still chunky but with some mushiness mixed in. Ten or so mashes should get you there.

Preheat a large, heavy-bottomed pan (preferably cast iron) over medium-high heat. Add 1 teaspoon of the coconut oil, let it melt, then add the mustard seeds. Cover the pan and let the seeds pop for 30 seconds or so. They should be fragrant and popping rapidly—if they are not, turn up the heat.

Remove the lid. (The seeds may still be popping a bit, but adding the next few ingredients will make them stop popping.) Add the onion and carrots, plus another 1 teaspoon coconut oil and a pinch of salt, and sauté until the carrots are soft, about 10 minutes.

Add the garlic and ginger and cook until fragrant, about 1 minute. Mix in the cumin, turmeric, garam masala, and red pepper flakes. Lower the heat and add the last 1 teaspoon coconut oil. Let it melt, then add the potatoes, lime juice, and remaining 1 teaspoon salt. Pour in the water and stir to incorporate. Cook until the spices are well incorporated and the water is evaporated. You may need to add a few more splashes if the mixture seems dry.

Fold in the frozen peas. They will cool the mixture down and make it easier to handle. Taste for salt and spices. Set aside until cool to the touch.

Recipe Continues

For me, a samosa isn't complete without a few popped mustard seeds. Just remember: When they pop, they pop. *Like popcorn. So have a lid at the ready to make sure they don't pop all over you! I think the seeds make these a lot of fun to cook. And if you haven't ever popped a mustard seed, the expletives will make it even more fun.*

Baby carrots work like a charm here. They're already peeled and already small, so you're halfway there. When you dice them, make sure they aren't any bigger than the peas.

ASSEMBLE THE SAMOSAS: Preheat the oven to 350°F. Line two large rimmed baking sheets with parchment.

Prepare a clean, dry surface with plenty of elbow room. Pour some olive oil into a small bowl and have a pastry brush handy.

Unwrap the thawed phyllo dough. Carefully place one sheet in front of you vertically and brush it with oil. Layer and repeat with two more sheets. Cover the other sheets with a damp towel to prevent them from drying out.

Use a paring knife to slice the triple stack lengthwise into thirds.

Place a heaping tablespoon of filling at the bottom of one of the strips. Fold the phyllo and filling diagonally and keep folding upward, diagonally, until you have a triangle. Brush the triangle with oil and continue with the remaining samosas. Place the finished samosas on the lined baking sheets. Repeat with the remaining phyllo and filling.

Bake, flipping the samosas and rotating the pans once, until nicely browned on both sides, about 18 minutes total.

GREEN
LASAGNA ROLLS

MAKES

10

ROLLS

TOTAL
1 HOUR 15 MINUTES
ACTIVE
45 MINUTES

FOR THE NOODLES:

1 pound lasagna noodles

FOR THE WHITE SAUCE:

1 cup raw cashews, soaked in water for at least 2 hours and drained

½ cup water

2 teaspoons cornstarch

½ teaspoon salt

FOR THE PESTO:

2 garlic cloves, peeled

3 cups fresh basil leaves, loosely packed

½ cup pepitas (shelled pumpkin seeds), plus extra for garnish

⅓ cup olive oil

¼ cup vegetable broth, purchased or homemade (page 203)

1 tablespoon fresh lemon juice

2 tablespoons nutritional yeast flakes

½ teaspoon salt

Several pinches freshly ground black pepper

FOR THE RICOTTA:

1 (14-ounce) package extra-firm tofu, crumbled

2 tablespoons nutritional yeast flakes

1 tablespoon olive oil

1 tablespoon fresh lemon juice

½ teaspoon salt

FOR THE SPINACH:

2 tablespoons olive oil

6 garlic cloves, minced

10 ounces baby spinach

Here, tofu ricotta is elevated with the addition of some pumpkin seed pesto. The mellow flavor of pumpkin seeds really lets the basil shine. The sautéed spinach is really, really garlicky, as is the pesto, so this makes the perfect date night meal.

What I really love about these rolls, besides how flavorful they are, is the texture. Baking the rolls makes the noodles soft but still toothsome, with little crunchy bits on the edges. Smothered in cashew cream and pesto and finished off with a scattering of additional pumpkin seeds, these lasagna rolls will fulfill even the wildest fantasies: creamy, crunchy, velvety, chewy, and hearty all at once.

MAKE THE NOODLES: Bring a big pot of salted water to a boil and cook the noodles according to the package instructions until al dente, stirring occasionally to make sure they don't stick together. If they seem to be, use metal tongs to gently peel them apart. Once cooked, drain them in a colander and run them under plenty of cold water to make sure they stop cooking and don't stick together. Set aside.

MAKE THE WHITE SAUCE: Meanwhile, combine the cashews, water, cornstarch, and salt in a blender. Puree until completely smooth; this can take up to 5 minutes depending on the strength of your machine. Periodically stop the machine to keep it from overheating, and scrape down the sides of the blender jar with a rubber spatula to make sure you get everything. Set aside.

MAKE THE PESTO: Put the garlic cloves in a blender and pulse a bit to chop. Add the remaining pesto ingredients and blend. The pesto should still have some texture and not be completely smooth. If necessary, thin with a few tablespoons of water to get it into a spreadable consistency.

MAKE THE RICOTTA: In a medium mixing bowl, mash the tofu with your hands until it resembles ricotta cheese. Mix in ¼ cup of the pesto you just made (reserve the rest for serving), along with the nutritional yeast, olive oil, lemon juice, and salt, and stir until well combined. Set aside.

MAKE THE SPINACH: Preheat a large, heavy-bottomed skillet (preferably cast iron) over medium-low heat. Add the olive oil. When the olive oil is hot, sauté the garlic until fragrant, about 30 seconds. Add the spinach and cook, stirring often, until wilted, about 3 minutes. Immediately transfer the spinach to a plate to stop it from cooking further.

Recipe Continues

You won't need all the lasagna noodles called for, but go ahead and boil the whole package to allow for some breakage. Sauté the leftovers and broken ones for dinner the next night.

The amount of ricotta made is just enough to fill the rolls, so go easy with the taste testing and don't overfill the rolls, or you might not get ten out of the deal.

Put the pesto in a little plastic bag with a hole cut out of the corner to pipe it nicely over the rolls. Then just spread it a bit with a spoon and it's real pretty-like.

Make the white sauce before the pesto to cut down on cleaning a little bit. You can pour the white sauce out and then just rinse the blender without having to do a major cleaning, since who cares if a little bit of cashew cream ends up in your pesto.

ASSEMBLE AND BAKE: Preheat the oven to 350°F. Lightly grease a 9-by-13-inch casserole dish.

Spread 3 tablespoons of the ricotta evenly over one lasagna noodle, leaving a little room around the side edges and ½ inch at each end.

Scatter about 3 tablespoons of the spinach over the ricotta. Starting at the bottom end, roll up the noodle and place it, seam-side down, in the prepared casserole dish. Continue with the remaining noodles. When all the rolls are in the pan, pour the white sauce over them in thick ribbons.

Bake until the edges of the rolls are lightly browned and the white sauce is thickened, 20 to 25 minutes. If after 25 minutes the rolls are not browning but the edges are crispy, place the pan under a broiler on low heat for a minute or two, keeping a very close eye on them so that they don't burn.

Slather the rolls with the reserved pesto, garnish with additional pumpkin seeds, and serve!

PISTACHIO LENTIL
BIRYANI

2 tablespoons refined coconut oil

1½ teaspoons cumin seeds

1½ teaspoons mustard seeds

¼ cup thinly sliced garlic

1½ cups white basmati rice

1 teaspoon salt

1 teaspoon garam masala

½ teaspoon crushed red pepper flakes

¼ teaspoon ground turmeric

3½ cups water

1 teaspoon finely grated lemon zest

½ cup beluga lentils (see Tip)

½ cup shelled pistachios

½ cup raisins

— *Tip* —

The lentils for this recipe need to be cooked al dente, lest they get lost in the rice. Beluga lentils work perfectly here, because they cook up nice and firm. If you don't have any, then green or brown will do. Definitely do not use red, because they are way too tender and will fall apart.

I've always been of the opinion that basmati rice in and of itself is flavorful enough with a little salt and coconut oil, so the addition of cumin, mustard seed, and garlic is really just the icing on the cake...er, rice. Biryani is delicate enough to work as a backdrop for the main event—I intend for this dish to go with the Cauliflower Tikka Masala (page 112)—but it's also hearty enough on its own, with the lentils and pretty green pistachios.

Preheat a 2-quart pot over medium heat. Melt 1 tablespoon of the coconut oil in the pot and then mix in the cumin and mustard seeds. Cover the pot and let the seeds pop for about a minute or until the popping slows down, stirring occasionally.

Lower the heat a bit, add the garlic and the other tablespoon of coconut oil, and sauté until the garlic is golden, about 2 minutes. Add the rice, salt, garam masala, red pepper flakes, and turmeric and stir to coat. Add the water and lemon zest. Cover and bring to a boil. Once boiling, lower the heat as low as possible, cover the pan, and cook until the water is mostly absorbed, about 20 minutes.

While the rice is cooking, bring a small pot of water to a boil over medium-high heat. Add the lentils, reduce the heat to a simmer, and cook until al dente, about 20 minutes. Drain the lentils well.

Stir the lentils, pistachios, and raisins into the rice. Cover the pot and let the raisins soften for 15 minutes or so. Fluff with a fork and serve.

PORCINI-CRUSTED TOFU
with Shallot Pan Gravy

FOR THE TOFU:

1 (14-ounce) package extra-firm tofu, pressed

1¼ cups vegetable broth, purchased or homemade (page 203)

¼ cup red wine vinegar

3 tablespoons tamari or soy sauce

FOR THE CRUST:

1 ounce dried porcini mushrooms

¼ cup fine bread crumbs

1 garlic clove, minced

Pinch each dried tarragon, rosemary, and thyme, crushed with your fingers

⅛ teaspoon salt

Freshly ground black pepper

FOR THE SHALLOT GRAVY:

2 tablespoons olive oil

2 cups thinly sliced shallot

2 garlic cloves, minced

1¾ cups vegetable broth, purchased or homemade (page 203)

Salt

Freshly ground black pepper

YOU'LL ALSO NEED:

Olive oil, for cooking

Cilantro-scallion mashed potatoes (page 319), for serving

This recipe came to me when I was trying to drift off to sleep one night and was suddenly seized by a terrifying thought: "I have never porcini-crusted *anything*." Maybe porcini crusting went out of style with the Rachel haircut, but it's still my idea of a fancy meal.

Porcinis remind me of wet leaves, red wine, and cozy, cloudy evenings. Their sensuous, woodsy flavor just oozes romance. They're a little pricey, but dried ones aren't too bad for a special occasion. You grind them up in the blender, mix with bread crumbs and seasonings, and voilà! Delicious crust. Even though you might not make this recipe any old day of the week (but you might), it isn't difficult to do. My favorite part is that the accompanying gravy is made with both the leftover marinade and the leftover crusting mixture.

MARINATE THE TOFU: Cut the tofu crosswise into 8 even slices. Cut each of these diagonally (corner to corner) so that you have 16 long triangles.

In a large bowl, mix the broth, vinegar, and tamari, add the tofu, and let it marinate in the refrigerator for at least 1 hour and up to 8 hours, turning when you can. Drain the tofu, reserving ¼ cup of the marinade to use in the gravy.

MAKE THE CRUSTING MIXTURE: In a blender, pulse the porcinis until they're powdery. Now toss them in a wide bowl, along with the bread crumbs, garlic, dried herbs, salt, and a few grinds of black pepper. Reserve ¼ cup of this crusting mixture to use in the gravy.

MAKE THE SHALLOT GRAVY: Preheat a medium saucepan over medium heat. Heat the oil, then cook the shallot until browned, about 8 minutes. Add the garlic and cook until fragrant, about 30 seconds. Add the reserved ¼ cup crusting mixture and toss to coat. Now add the vegetable broth and reserved ¼ cup marinade. Let cook until nicely thickened, 10 minutes or so. Taste and adjust for salt and pepper. Keep covered and warm until ready to serve.

COOK THE TOFU: Preheat a large, heavy-bottomed pan (preferably cast iron) over medium-high heat. While it's heating, dredge half of the tofu slices in the crusting mixture and place on a plate. Pour a very thin layer of oil in the pan and cook the dredged tofu slices until golden brown, about 4 minutes per side. Use a thin metal spatula (as thin as possible) so that you can easily get under the tofu to flip it. A thick spatula might cause the breading to fall off. While the first batch of tofu is cooking, dredge the second batch. Transfer the cooked tofu to a plate and tent with aluminum foil to keep warm while you cook the second batch.

SERVE: Scoop some mashed potatoes onto each plate and smother them in gravy. Scatter a few roasted beets around. Place a few slices of tofu on top and garnish with extra scallions (from the mashed potatoes) or whatever fresh herbs you have on hand. Serve!

ARANCINI

with Almond Cheese

MAKES
16
ARANCINI

TOTAL
2 HOURS
ACTIVE
30 MINUTES

FOR THE RISOTTO:

2 cups Arborio rice

2 tablespoons olive oil

5 cups vegetable broth, purchased or homemade (page 203)

1 cup dry white wine

2 teaspoons finely grated lemon zest

½ teaspoon salt

FOR THE BREADING:

¾ cup plain bread crumbs

½ teaspoon dried thyme

Salt

Freshly ground black pepper

FOR THE ARANCINI:

1 recipe Almond Ricotta (page 299)

Olive oil, for frying and drizzling

1 recipe Marinara Sauce (page 65)

Freshly ground black pepper, for garnish

Fresh basil chiffonade, for garnish

Tip

Because this is simply going to be formed into a ball and fried, you can skip the usual step in making risotto where you add broth bit by bit and instead just cook the rice all at once, stirring occasionally.

Gaze upon these rice balls and ask yourself, "Can this really be happening?" Risotto and almond cheese...sold. But wait, they're also formed into a ball and breaded and fried. These were a staple for me growing up in Brooklyn. I'd get a big fat one, wrapped in parchment, and walk the city streets just stuffing it into my face. For today, let's make it a more elegant experience. Serve with marinara and garnish with a little parsley. You can still stuff it into your face—just be a little more civilized about it.

MAKE THE RISOTTO: Line a rimmed baking sheet with parchment paper.

Preheat a medium saucepot over medium heat. Pour in the rice and oil and stir with a slanted wooden spoon until coated. Add the broth, wine, lemon zest, and salt. Cover and bring to a boil. Reduce the heat to medium-low, cover, and simmer, stirring occasionally, until all the liquid is absorbed, about 30 minutes. The rice will be sticky and look a little mushy, but it should still have texture.

Spread out the rice on the lined baking sheet and set aside until cool enough to handle.

MAKE THE BREADING: Combine the bread crumbs, thyme, a pinch of salt, and a few grinds of black pepper in a shallow dish. Set aside.

MAKE THE ARANCINI: Line another rimmed baking sheet with parchment paper.

Wash your hands frequently as you form the balls, and keep them damp, so that the rice doesn't stick to your hands.

Roll and gently flatten a scant ¼ cup rice in the palm of your hand. Make an indentation in the center and add about 1½ teaspoons almond ricotta. Fold the rice around the filling to enclose it and gently roll it into a ball. You should have eight balls total.

Roll each rice ball in the bread crumb mixture and place them on the clean lined baking sheet. Refrigerate for about 30 minutes to make sure that they're good and firm.

Heat ½ inch olive oil in a cast iron pan over medium heat. It's ready when you sprinkle a pinch of bread crumbs in and it sizzles rapidly. Cook the balls until golden brown, flipping with a slotted spoon to make sure they fry evenly.

To serve, ladle some marinara sauce into each bowl and add a few arancini—whole or sliced in half. Drizzle them with a little olive oil, grind some black pepper on top, and garnish with sliced basil.

CAULIFLOWER
TIKKA MASALA

FOR THE CAULIFLOWER:

2 medium heads cauliflower

4 tablespoons olive oil

½ teaspoon salt

FOR THE SAUCE:

3 tablespoons refined coconut oil

2 medium yellow onions, thinly sliced

2 teaspoons salt, plus a pinch

6 garlic cloves, minced

2 tablespoons minced fresh ginger

¼ cup chopped fresh cilantro

1 teaspoon fennel seeds, crushed

1 teaspoon ground cumin

1 teaspoon sweet paprika

½ teaspoon ground cardamom

½ teaspoon cayenne pepper

1 (24-ounce) can crushed fire-roasted tomatoes

2 (14-ounce) cans coconut milk

2 tablespoons tomato paste

2 tablespoons fresh lime juice

FOR THE GARNISH:

¼ cup sliced almonds, toasted

Chopped fresh cilantro

Tikka masala is a Bangladeshi/British dish of tart and creamy tomato curry, usually served with chicken, but come on, people don't still eat chicken, do they? Here, cauliflower is given the tikka treatment in an amazingly flavorful and slurpiful dish! The cauliflower is cut into big meaty pieces and roasted to perfection, then smothered in sauce and topped with toasted almonds for a little crunch. Tikka masala isn't typically baked in a casserole, but I found that it really helps bring together the cauliflower and the sauce. The most time-efficient way to prepare it is to first put the cauli in to roast, and then start the sauce.

ROAST THE CAULIFLOWER: Preheat the oven to 425°F. Line two large rimmed baking sheets with parchment.

Remove the leaves from one head of cauliflower and trim the stem. Cut the cauliflower in half lengthwise and lay both sides flat on the cutting board. Now cut the halves into ½-inch-thick slices. Put the pieces on one lined baking sheet and toss with 2 tablespoons of the oil and ¼ teaspoon of the salt to coat. Arrange the slices in a single layer on the baking sheet. Repeat with the other cauliflower and the remaining oil and salt.

Roast, rotating and swapping the pans halfway through, until the cauliflower is browned, about 25 minutes. Remove from the oven and set aside.

MAKE THE SAUCE: Preheat a 4-quart pot over medium heat. Heat the oil, then sauté the onions with a pinch of salt until lightly brown, 5 to 7 minutes. Add the garlic and ginger and sauté for a minute more. Add the cilantro and stir until wilted.

Add the fennel seed, cumin, paprika, cardamom, and cayenne; stir to toast for 30 seconds or so. Stir in the tomatoes, coconut milk, tomato paste, lime juice, and remaining 2 teaspoons salt. Cover and bring the mixture to a simmer. Once simmering, lower the heat and simmer for 10 minutes.

ASSEMBLE: Pour some sauce into a 9-by-13-inch casserole. Layer in half of the cauliflower and cover with half of the remaining sauce. Layer in the remaining cauliflower and pour on the remaining sauce. Bake for 20 minutes.

Remove from the oven, scatter the almonds and cilantro over the top, and serve.

CHOCOLATE YOGURT
BUNDT CAKE

1½ cups granulated sugar

1¼ cups plain or vanilla coconut yogurt

¾ cup unsweetened almond milk (or your favorite nondairy milk)

½ cup canola oil

1 tablespoon pure vanilla extract

2½ cups all-purpose flour

1 cup unsweetened cocoa powder

1 tablespoon baking powder

1 teaspoon salt

⅓ cup boiling water (see Tip)

1 cup semisweet chocolate chips

2 tablespoons powdered sugar, for dusting

Fresh strawberries, for serving

Tip

Measure the boiling water after it boils, not before. That way you can be sure that some of it didn't evaporate in the boiling process.

This is the cake to fulfill all your chocolate cake cravings. It's the kind of cake that's super moist and melts in your mouth and melts your heart and makes you forget about the snow outside that might never melt! A little (or big) slice served up with some whipped cream is wonderful for date night. Or fill it with strawberries for a crowd-pleasing centerpiece. I love it simply sprinkled with powdered sugar, but if you absolutely cannot accept cake without icing, then try some ganache (page 206) drizzled over.

Preheat the oven to 350°F. Lightly grease a 12-cup Bundt pan.

In a large mixing bowl, whisk together the granulated sugar, yogurt, milk, and canola oil until smooth, about a minute. Mix in the vanilla.

Sift in about half of the flour and the cocoa powder, baking powder, and salt. Mix until almost smooth, then add the remaining flour and the boiling water. Mix again until smooth. The batter will be relatively thick.

Fold in the chocolate chips. Transfer the batter to the prepared pan and bake for 55 to 60 minutes. A knife inserted into the center should come out clean, but because of the chocolate chips it might be hard to tell. Just make sure there's not a bunch of batter on it.

Let the cake cool for 20 minutes or so, then invert it onto a cooling rack to cool completely. Because the cake is so moist, it may take a little tapping to get the cake to release.

Once the cake is completely cool, dust it with powdered sugar and serve with strawberries!

MINI ALMOND POUND CAKES

MAKES
8
MINI POUND CAKES

TOTAL
1 HOUR 30 MINUTES
ACTIVE
20 MINUTES

1 (7-ounce) tube almond paste

6 ounces extra-firm silken tofu (half of a 12-ounce package of Mori-Nu)

1 cup unsweetened almond milk (or your favorite nondairy milk)

1 cup sugar

1 teaspoon pure vanilla extract

½ cup refined coconut oil, melted

2 cups all-purpose flour

1½ teaspoons baking powder

½ teaspoon salt

Tip

You can make a cute little bite-size dessert outta these, which might be perfect for spring holiday snacking. Slice a few of the loaves ¼ inch thick and top with a dollop of cream and a sliced strawberry. Now you've got a great little treat that's easy to grab. You can also make these into individual cakes (or, fine, call them cupcakes) by using a muffin tin. Baking time will be around 24 minutes. Top with cream and a sliced strawberry.

These cakes are just lovely and darling. The crumb is somehow both dense and fluffy. The edges are crispy and sweet. And the almond flavor is simply bangin'. And you know how I came up with the recipe? From my box of almond paste! Yes, I shamelessly ripped open the package and veganized one of the recipes that came inside. It's such a wonderful recipe, I can see why it's on a box!

Preheat the oven to 350°F. Lightly grease an 8-compartment mini loaf pan.

Break up the almond paste into small pieces and drop them into a blender. Add the tofu, almond milk, and sugar. Blend until smooth, scraping down the sides with a rubber spatula to make sure you get everything. Add the vanilla and stream in the melted coconut oil and blend again.

Transfer the mixture to a large mixing bowl. Sift in the flour, baking powder, and salt and whisk until smooth. An electric hand mixer will work best because the batter is quite thick, but a strong metal whisk will get the job done, too.

Fill each mini loaf compartment about three-quarters full—about ½ cup of batter each. Bake for 30 minutes, then lower the heat to 325°F and continue baking until the loaves are lightly browned and firm to the touch, about 10 more minutes.

Remove from the oven and let cool for a few minutes. When the pan is cool enough to touch, invert it to release the cakes, then transfer them to a cooling rack to cool completely.

5

MARDI GRAS

Confession:

I'VE NEVER BEEN TO NEW ORLEANS

and I'm no expert on

MARDI GRAS.

BUT I HAVE ogled food magazines with Mardi Gras menus...and I'm an expert on ogling. Combine that with hours and hours of Southern cooking shows plus all the seasons of *True Blood,* and I think I've got the cuisine down!

But, seriously, somewhere along the line, way after I went vegetarian, I became obsessed with these flavors. Peppery, herby, creamy, zesty, spicy...how can you not? And so I love to celebrate the festival every year with a feast, some beads, and a big old sign saying "SHOW US YOUR MITTS!"

Whether you want to have a little Fat Tuesday brunch or a four-course dinner, these recipes have you covered.

BLACKENED SCRAMBLED TOFU

& Garlicky Polenta Grits

SERVES
4

TOTAL
40 MINUTES
ACTIVE
40 MINUTES

FOR THE SPICE BLEND:

1 teaspoon dried thyme, crushed with your fingers

½ teaspoon sweet paprika

½ teaspoon smoked paprika

¼ teaspoon ground coriander

⅛ teaspoon cayenne pepper (optional, if you want it spicy)

FOR THE TOFU:

1 tablespoon olive oil

1 small onion, thinly sliced

3 garlic cloves, minced

1 (14-ounce) package extra-firm tofu

2 tablespoons fresh lemon juice

1 teaspoon salt

Freshly ground black pepper

½ cup halved cherry or grape tomatoes

Here, tofu is scrambled in big chunks with lots of onion and garlic and then coated in dried herbs and spices, including two different kinds of paprika because you only live once. Some cherry tomatoes make it juicy and tangy. The grits are actually polenta, because I'm kind of a yuppie, with lots of garlic tossed in at the end. But feel free to use grits instead. Serve with sautéed greens. Lots of 'em. To get this done quickly, start the broth for the polenta and then get started on the tofu.

MAKE THE SPICE BLEND: Mix 'em all up in a small cup.

MAKE THE TOFU: Preheat a large, heavy-bottomed pan (preferably cast iron) over medium-high heat. Heat the oil, then sauté the onion until softened, about 5 minutes. Add the garlic and sauté for 30 seconds.

Break the tofu into bite-size pieces and add them to the pan. Sauté for about 10 minutes, using a thin metal spatula to stir often (a wooden or plastic one won't really cut it). You want to really get under the tofu when you are stirring, scrape the bottom, and don't let it stick to the pan—that is where the good, crispy stuff is. The tofu should get browned on at least one side, but you don't need to be too precise about it. The water should cook out of it and not collect too much at the bottom of the pan. If that is happening, turn up the heat and let the water evaporate.

Add the lemon juice, salt, and a few grinds of black pepper and sauté for another minute. Add the spice blend and mix to incorporate. Add the tomatoes and cook until they are warmed through and slightly broken down, about 5 minutes. Taste for salt and seasoning and keep warm until ready to serve.

Recipe Continues

FOR THE GRITS:

4 cups vegetable broth, purchased or homemade (page 203)

¼ teaspoon salt (or to taste, depending on how salty your broth is)

1 cup polenta corn grits (such as Bob's Red Mill brand)

1 tablespoon olive oil

4 garlic cloves, minced

FOR SERVING:

Sautéed greens

Chopped scallions, for garnish

—————— *Tip* ——————

The polenta definitely makes more than you need for the tofu, so pour the excess into a square Tupperware while it's still hot. Let it cool and then refrigerate for up to 3 days. When ready to eat, slice into squares and pan-fry.

MAKE THE GRITS: Bring the vegetable broth and salt to a boil in a 2-quart pot. Lower the heat to a simmer. Add the polenta in a slow steady stream, whisking constantly. Whisk until the polenta is thickened, about 5 minutes. Keep the heat low, cover the pot, and let the polenta cook for 20 more minutes or so, stirring occasionally.

When the polenta is thick and almost done, preheat a small pan over medium-low heat. Add the olive oil. When the oil is hot, sauté the garlic just until it begins to sizzle, being careful not to burn. Stir for 30 seconds, then transfer to the cooked polenta and mix well.

SERVE: Spoon some polenta onto each plate and scoop on some tofu, overlapping it a bit. Complete the plate with sautéed greens, then garnish with chopped scallions. Serve!

CHICKPEA
Crab MORNAY

1 cup raw cashews, soaked in water for at least 2 hours and drained

1½ cups vegetable broth, purchased or homemade (page 203)

2 tablespoons chickpea miso or mellow white miso

3 tablespoons olive oil

1½ cups thinly sliced scallions, plus extra for garnish (roughly 1 bunch total)

3 tablespoons all-purpose flour

2 tablespoons dry sherry

2 tablespoons finely chopped nori

¼ teaspoon salt

¼ teaspoon crushed red pepper flakes

Freshly ground black pepper

1 (15-ounce) can chickpeas, rinsed and drained, or 1½ cups cooked chickpeas

¼ cup chopped fresh parsley

1 tablespoon fresh lemon juice

Crusty bread or toast points, for serving (optional)

Prepared phyllo or puff pastry shells, for serving (optional)

--- *Tip* ---

A chickpea roux is perfect for making this gluten-free. Just replace the all-purpose flour with chickpea flour. It has a more pronounced toasty chickpea flavor, but that's actually a bonus here.

Crab Mornay always shows up in food mags, looking creamy and chunky and delicious in a fondue pot or poured into tart shells. It's typically made with lump crabmeat, but lightly mashed chickpeas do the trick here. Chickpea miso works its wonders for the nuanced cheesy flavor, and a little crumbled nori lends the taste of the sea. The result is a rich seafood dip, perfect for, well, dipping, with some crusty bread or toast points. Or, as more of a formal hors d'oeuvre, poured into prepared shells.

Combine the cashews, vegetable broth, and miso in a blender. Puree until smooth; this can take up to 5 minutes depending on the strength of your machine. Periodically stop the machine to keep it from overheating, and scrape down the sides of the blender jar with a rubber spatula to make sure you get everything.

Preheat a 4-quart saucepan over medium heat. Heat the oil, then sauté the scallions just until a little wilted, about 2 minutes. Now we'll make a roux: Use a slanted wooden spatula and stir constantly while sprinkling the flour into the scallions. Once all the flour is in, keep stirring until the flour is toasted and golden, about 5 minutes more.

Slowly stir in the cashew mixture, mixing constantly to make sure that clumps don't form. Stir in the sherry, nori, salt, red pepper flakes, and a few grinds of black pepper. Let the mixture heat through and bubble, stirring only occasionally, until it's nicely thickened, about 7 minutes.

Lightly mash the chickpeas in a bowl. Fold the chickpeas, parsley, and lemon juice into the pan to heat through. Garnish with extra scallions and serve warm, with crusty bread or toast points or in prepared tart shells.

BISCUITS *and* WHITE PEPPER GRAVY

MAKES
16
BISCUITS

TOTAL
1 HOUR
ACTIVE
45 MINUTES

FOR THE BISCUITS:

2 teaspoons apple cider vinegar

1 cup unsweetened almond milk (or your favorite nondairy milk)

2¼ cups all-purpose flour

4 teaspoons baking powder

1 tablespoon sugar

¾ teaspoon salt

⅛ teaspoon baking soda

⅓ cup refined coconut oil, at room temperature

FOR THE GRAVY:

½ cup raw cashews, soaked in water for at least 2 hours and drained

2 cups vegetable broth, purchased or homemade (page 203)

3 tablespoons olive oil

3 tablespoons all-purpose flour

½ teaspoon salt

½ teaspoon ground white pepper

Chopped fresh parsley, for garnish

The minute these biscuits touch your lips you'll feel it: fluffy, buttery bliss! They're the ideal biscuit. The gravy is kept really simple, but don't be skeptical of the short ingredients list. The roux creates plenty of toasty goodness, with a bit of heat from the white pepper. Use a vegetable broth that you really love (try homemade, page 203), because the flavor will shine through. Serve these family style, with the biscuits in a basket and the gravy in a boat, letting guests pour on what they like. Or plate them with some gravy poured over a biscuit or two, and fresh parsley sprinkled on top.

MAKE THE BISCUITS: Preheat the oven to 425°F.

In a small bowl, stir the apple cider vinegar into the almond milk and set aside.

Sift the flour, baking powder, sugar, salt, and baking soda together into a large mixing bowl and make a well in the center. Cut the coconut oil into the dough with a pastry cutter or two knives held together, until it resembles coarse crumbs. Pour in the milk mixture and gently combine with a fork, being careful to not overmix.

Turn out the dough onto a floured surface and form into a 1-inch-thick disk. Use a 2-inch cookie cutter or a drinking glass to cut out biscuits. Lightly flour the cutter to prevent sticking.

Place the biscuits on a rimmed baking sheet 2 inches apart, then gently press the remaining dough back together and cut out more biscuits, adding them to the baking sheet.

Bake until puffy and golden brown, about 15 minutes, then transfer to a rack to cool.

MAKE THE GRAVY: Combine the cashews and vegetable broth in a blender. Puree until completely smooth; this can take up to 5 minutes depending on the strength of your machine. Periodically stop the machine to keep it from overheating, and scrape down the sides of the blender jar with a rubber spatula to make sure you get everything.

Preheat a saucepot over medium heat. Heat the oil, then sprinkle in the flour, using a slanted wooden spoon to stir until the flour is completely smooth and browned, about 5 minutes.

Lower the heat. Slowly add the cashew cream mixture, stirring constantly with a big fork. The roux should absorb into the cream as you pour, thickening it. Keep stirring until thick and smooth, about 3 minutes. Add the salt and white pepper and continue to heat for another 2 minutes or so.

Serve the biscuits with the hot gravy, garnished with chopped parsley.

CORN FRITTERS
with Tomato Jam

FOR THE TOMATO JAM:

1 tablespoon olive oil

1 small white onion, diced medium

2 teaspoons minced fresh ginger

1 (28-ounce) can diced fire-roasted tomatoes, drained

2 tablespoons balsamic vinegar

2 tablespoons brown sugar

FOR THE FRITTERS:

½ cup unsweetened almond milk (or your favorite nondairy milk)

2 tablespoons ground flaxseed (preferably golden)

1½ cups fresh or frozen (thawed) corn kernels

¼ cup all-purpose flour

1 tablespoon granulated sugar

¼ teaspoon salt

Freshly ground black pepper

½ red bell pepper, very finely chopped

Refined coconut oil, for the pan

Baby arugula leaves, for serving

Tip

You only need the tomatoes from the can, not the juice. But you don't have to toss the juice—save it for making salsa or pour it into a veggie soup.

A taste of the summer, any time of the year! These simple flavors pop like crazy. Little pan-fried cakes of corn with specks of red pepper are made buttery and decadent with coconut oil. The tomato jam is the perfect tangy accompaniment, with just a hint of fresh ginger to make it sing. You can use fresh or frozen corn here—if using frozen, let it thaw first.

MAKE THE TOMATO JAM: Preheat a 2-quart saucepan over medium heat. Heat the oil, then sauté the onion until lightly browned, 5 to 7 minutes. Add the ginger and cook until fragrant, about 1 minute. Add the tomatoes, vinegar, and brown sugar. Bring to a boil, then lower the heat and simmer until reduced, about 15 minutes. Set aside until ready to use. (The jam tastes great at room temperature, so there's no need to keep it warm.)

MAKE THE FRITTERS: In a blender, puree the milk and flaxseed. Add half of the corn and pulse to blend a bit—don't puree it smooth. About 10 pulses should get the job done. Pour the mixture into a medium mixing bowl. Vigorously whisk in the flour, granulated sugar, salt, and a few grinds of black pepper. Fold in the remaining corn and the bell pepper.

Line a plate with paper towels. Heat a large nonstick pan over medium heat. Cast iron works perfectly here. Add enough coconut oil to coat the bottom of the pan. When it melts, drop the batter into the pan by the rounded tablespoon and fry until set and golden, about 3 minutes each side. Add more coconut oil as needed. Transfer the fritters to the paper towels and tent with aluminum foil to keep warm as you prepare the next batch.

Serve the fritters warm with tomato jam and arugula leaves.

EGGPLANT
PO' BOY

FOR THE EGGPLANT:

2 pounds eggplant (2 small ones), cut crosswise into ½-inch slices

Salt

Canola oil, for frying

FOR THE SLAW:

1 cup vegan mayo, purchased or homemade (page 203)

2 teaspoons red wine vinegar

2 teaspoons sugar

½ teaspoon salt

3 cups thinly sliced red cabbage

½ cup shredded peeled carrot

¼ cup shredded radish

FOR THE SLURRY:

¾ cup unsweetened almond milk (or your favorite nondairy milk)

1 teaspoon fresh lemon juice

¼ cup cornstarch

FOR THE BREADING:

1 cup all-purpose flour

¼ cup cornmeal

2 teaspoons sweet paprika

1 teaspoon dried thyme

½ teaspoon garlic powder

½ teaspoon cayenne pepper

Several pinches freshly ground black pepper

FOR THE SANDWICHES:

4 (8-inch) French breads

Vegan mayo, purchased or homemade (page 67)

Sliced tomatoes

Big fat golden slices of breaded fried eggplant seasoned just right. Creamy crunchy tangy drippy slaw. This is the sub to end all subs!

PREP THE EGGPLANT: Place the eggplant slices on a rimmed baking sheet and sprinkle with a light layer of salt. This will draw out the moisture. Let the eggplant sit for 20 minutes, then use a paper towel to absorb the moisture that has come out.

MAKE THE SLAW: Meanwhile, in a large mixing bowl, stir together the mayo, vinegar, sugar, and salt. Add the cabbage, carrot, and radish and mix well. Cover with plastic wrap and refrigerate until ready to use.

BACK TO THE EGGPLANT: First, make the slurry: Whisk together the almond milk, lemon juice, and cornstarch with a fork until the cornstarch is dissolved. Next, combine the breading ingredients on a large dinner plate.

Dip an eggplant slice in the slurry, shaking off the excess. Coat the eggplant in the breading and set on another plate. Repeat until all the eggplant is coated.

Preheat a large cast iron pan over medium-high heat. Have ready a plate lined with paper towels to absorb the oil. Add about an inch of oil to the pan. When it's about 350°F, and a bit of breading thrown into the oil creates bubbles quickly, add a single layer of eggplant.

Fry the eggplant in batches until golden brown, about 3 minutes per side, then transfer to the paper towels to drain the oil.

ASSEMBLE THE PO' BOYS: Split the French breads in half and coat each side with mayo. Place tomatoes on the bottom half. Layer on the eggplant slices. Top the eggplant with some slaw, replace the top half of the bread, and serve.

 Tip *Because the eggplant has been salted, I don't put salt in the breading. So taste one after it's been breaded and cooked. If it needs salt, just sprinkle some on while the eggplant is still warm.*

CAULIFLOWER & SHIITAKE
ÉTOUFFÉE

2 cups vegetable broth, purchased or homemade (page 203)

1 ounce dried shiitake mushrooms

3 to 4 tablespoons olive oil

1 medium yellow onion, finely diced

2 celery ribs, thinly sliced

1 green bell pepper, seeded and diced

1 teaspoon salt, plus a pinch

4 garlic cloves, minced

2 teaspoons Cajun spice mix

½ teaspoon crushed red pepper flakes

¼ cup all-purpose flour

2 bay leaves

2 tablespoons finely chopped nori

1 medium head cauliflower, cut into small florets

1 (15-ounce) can kidney beans, rinsed and drained, or 1½ cups cooked kidney beans

¼ cup chopped fresh parsley

¼ cup chopped fresh chives, plus extra for garnish

Étouffée is fun to say, fun to eat, and not too hard to make, either. Being a Louisiana dish, it's typically a seafood stew made with crawfish, which sounds a little like cauliflower, so why not? I also use some dried mushrooms for chewiness and kidney beans for a protein punch. Besides those little vegan adjustments that absolutely nobody will notice, I try to stick to traditional ingredients—or what I think are traditional ingredients, if years of watching Emeril are to be believed: the holy trinity of onion, celery, and bell pepper, some roux action, and Cajun spice mix. BAM! Vegan étouffée. I use a little nori (as usual) for some sea flavor, but I think it's optional here, especially if you're already making the Chickpea Crab Mornay (page 123) or somethin' else kinda fishy.

In a small saucepan, bring the vegetable broth to a boil. Put the shiitakes in a small bowl and pour in the veggie broth. Cover the bowl with a little plate to keep it warm and let the shiitakes steep while you're cooking everything else, at least 30 minutes.

Preheat a 4-quart pot over medium heat. Heat 2 tablespoons of the oil, then sauté the onion, celery, and bell pepper with a pinch of salt until softened, about 5 minutes. Add the garlic, Cajun spice mix, red pepper flakes, and remaining 1 teaspoon salt and sauté until fragrant, 30 seconds or so.

Now we'll make the roux. Add another tablespoon of oil and, using a slanted wooden spatula, stir constantly as you sprinkle in the flour. Keep stirring to toast the flour, adding another tablespoon of oil if necessary. Cook until the roux is thick and pasty and browned, about 10 minutes.

Remove the shiitakes from the veg broth and set aside. Now stream the vegetable broth into the pot, stirring constantly so that the roux does not clump. As soon as the mixture is smooth, add the shiitakes, bay leaves, nori, and cauliflower and simmer with the lid slightly ajar, until the cauliflower is just tender, about 10 minutes. Stir in the kidney beans, parsley, and chives. Taste and adjust for salt and seasoning, and add a little extra vegetable broth if necessary to thin.

Turn off the heat and let the étouffée sit for 10 minutes for the flavors to meld, then serve, garnished with more chives.

GUMBO Z'HERBES

TOTAL 1 HOUR
ACTIVE 30 MINUTES

⅓ cup olive oil

½ cup all-purpose flour

1 teaspoon salt

2 medium yellow onions, thinly sliced

4 celery ribs, thinly sliced

2 green bell peppers, seeded and diced

6 garlic cloves, minced

2 jalapeños, seeded and thinly sliced

3 pounds greens (see headnote), tough stems removed and leaves torn into bite-size pieces

8 cups vegetable broth, purchased or homemade (page 203)

2 bay leaves

2 teaspoons filé powder

Freshly ground black pepper

Stewed greens in a thick spicy stew...it's *all* about the greens with this gumbo. I think it's the prettiest and the most delicious if you use a blend of leafies, so grab a bunch of kale, a bunch of mustard greens, some chard...whatever looks the freshest. Some of the veggies are blended up as the base and some are left lush and whole, for a big old dose of green in every bite.

Start with the roux. Preheat a large soup pot over medium heat. Heat the oil, then sprinkle in the flour, using a slanted wooden spoon to stir until completely smooth and browned, about 5 minutes.

Add the onions, celery, bell peppers, garlic, and jalapeños to the pot, stirring to coat. Cook until the veggies are fragrant and soft, 5 to 7 minutes, stirring often.

Add the greens and 2 cups of the vegetable broth and cook until the greens have wilted. Use an immersion blender to blend for 10 seconds or so, just until some of the greens are pureed but there are still lots of leaves left whole.

Add the remaining 6 cups vegetable broth, the bay leaves, the filé powder, and a few grinds of black pepper. Cook for 30 more minutes. Remove the bay leaves; taste and adjust for salt before serving.

CREOLE
LENTIL LOAF

2 tablespoons olive oil

1 medium yellow onion, diced small

2 celery ribs, thinly sliced

1 green bell pepper, seeded and diced small

2 garlic cloves, minced

½ cup chopped fresh parsley

1 (15-ounce) can lentils, rinsed and drained, or 1½ cups cooked brown or green lentils

¾ cup vegetable broth, purchased or homemade (page 203)

¾ cup chopped pecans

2 teaspoons smoked paprika

1 teaspoon dried thyme

¾ teaspoon salt

¼ teaspoon ground allspice

Freshly ground black pepper

2 cups bread crumbs

⅓ cup ketchup

1 teaspoon Dijon mustard

2 tablespoons brown sugar

½ cup roughly chopped celery leaves, for garnish

A good old-fashioned lentil loaf never hurt no one. Smother this one in ketchup glaze and serve it up with mashed potatoes and peas or on French bread as a sandwich. This loaf has a little Creole love going on—and chopped pecans for extra-special texture.

Preheat the oven to 350°F. Line an 8-by-4-inch loaf pan with parchment paper, leaving about an inch of overhang on all sides. This is how you will lift the loaf out of the pan later.

Preheat a large, heavy-bottomed pan (preferably cast iron) over medium-high heat. Heat the oil, then sauté the onion, celery, bell pepper, and garlic until the vegetables are softened and lightly browned, about 10 minutes. Stir in the parsley just until it wilts, and remove the pan from the heat.

In a large mixing bowl, lightly mash the lentils so that they are semi-mashed. There should still be some texture, and some whole ones left are totally okay. Stir in the cooked vegetables, broth, pecans, paprika, thyme, salt, allspice, and a few grinds of black pepper. Lastly, add the bread crumbs and mix until somewhat firm. Transfer the lentil mixture to the prepared loaf pan, smoothing out the top.

In a small bowl, stir together the ketchup, mustard, and brown sugar to make the glaze. Spread the glaze on the surface of the loaf. Bake for 45 minutes. Remove the loaf from the oven and let set for about 15 minutes. Carefully pull up on the parchment to lift the loaf out of the pan. Place on a serving tray, slice, and serve, garnished with the celery leaves.

ANDOUILLE & CANNELLINI
JAMBALAYA

6 tablespoons olive oil

3 andouille sausages, either store-bought or homemade (page 316), cut crosswise into ½-inch slices

1 large yellow onion, diced small

1 green bell pepper, seeded and diced small

2 celery ribs, diced small

¼ cup thinly sliced garlic

1 teaspoon salt, plus a pinch

½ cup sherry vinegar

2 bay leaves

2 tablespoons chopped fresh thyme

2 teaspoons onion powder

1 teaspoon dried oregano

1 teaspoon sweet paprika

Freshly ground black pepper

2 cups red rice

1 cup diced tomato

4 cups vegetable broth, purchased or homemade (page 203)

1 (15-ounce) can cannellini beans, rinsed and drained, or 1½ cups cooked cannellini beans

Chopped fresh parsley, for garnish

Jambalaya is the exact dish you want to warm you right up. It's so homey and comforting; fluffy rice, meaty sausages, and flavor through and through. This one is pretty classic, with smoky sausages, holy trinity aromatics, and Creole seasoning, because some classics just don't need a twist. The only out-of-the-ordinary thing I like to do is use red rice, because I love its pretty color and aromatic flavor. But you can use any long-grain rice you like (keep in mind that brown will take about 20 minutes longer in the oven).

Preheat a Dutch oven over medium-high heat. Heat 2 tablespoons of the oil, then sauté the sausage until nicely browned, about 5 minutes. Transfer the sausage to a plate.

Add the remaining 4 tablespoons oil and sauté the onion, bell pepper, celery, and garlic, along with a pinch of salt, until lightly browned, about 7 minutes.

Add the sherry vinegar to the pan to deglaze, scraping the bottom with a slanted wooden spoon to get any of the good bits that are sticking. Stir in the bay leaves, thyme, onion powder, oregano, paprika, remaining 1 teaspoon salt, and a few grinds of black pepper.

Add the rice and toss to coat with the veggies. Stir in the tomato. Stream in the vegetable broth, stirring well. Return the sausages to the pot, along with the beans, and stir gently to distribute.

If using an oven-safe pot, cover and bake until the rice is tender, about 45 minutes. If not, transfer the jambalaya to a deep casserole dish, cover tightly with aluminum foil, and bake for 45 minutes.

Remove from the oven, give the jambalaya a stir, remove the bay leaves, and let cool for about 10 minutes. Garnish with fresh parsley and serve.

Tip

This recipe works best in a stove-to-oven pot, like a Dutch oven. If you don't have one, make it in a 4-quart pot and then transfer it to a deep casserole dish to bake.

SERVES
8–12

KITTEE'S
KING CAKE

**TOTAL
3 HOURS
ACTIVE
1 HOUR**

FOR THE DOUGH:

1¼ teaspoons active dry yeast

¼ cup warm water

½ cup warm unsweetened almond milk (or your favorite nondairy milk)

¼ cup refined coconut oil, melted

2 tablespoons ground flaxseed

1 tablespoon cornstarch

2½ cups all-purpose flour

¼ cup granulated sugar

½ teaspoon salt

FOR THE FILLING:

2 apples

1 tablespoon fresh lemon juice

2 tablespoons refined coconut oil

¼ cup granulated sugar

1 teaspoon ground cinnamon

½ teaspoon cornstarch

¼ teaspoon salt

½ cup raisins

FOR THE ICING:

3 tablespoons unsweetened almond milk (or your favorite nondairy milk)

1½ cups powdered sugar

1 teaspoon pure vanilla extract

Colored sugar, if desired (green, gold, purple)

When it comes to stuff I know nothing about, I defer to the experts! Thus, my friend Kittee and her perfect little king cake. It's filled with apples and cinnamon and, as is tradition, you can stick a little baby figurine in there before icing. I don't know why, I'm from Brooklyn. But I do know that this Danish-like pastry is totally delightful.

MAKE THE DOUGH: In a small bowl, whisk together the yeast and warm water and set aside.

In a blender on high speed, blend the milk, melted coconut oil, flaxseed, and cornstarch until it gets to a goopy consistency and the flax is in tiny specks.

In a large bowl or the bowl of a stand mixer, combine 2 cups of the flour, the sugar, and the salt. Mix in the flax mixture and the yeast mixture, stirring until all the flour is incorporated. Turn out onto a floured counter and knead the dough, adding the remaining flour a few tablespoons at a time until the dough is no longer sticky, just a little tacky, and springs back when you touch it. Use up to ½ cup extra flour if needed.

Clean out the mixing bowl and spray it with oil, place the dough ball in the bowl and oil the top, then cover with plastic wrap and set in a warm place. Let it rise to double in size, about an hour.

MAKE THE FILLING: While the dough rises, peel, core, and dice the apples, keeping them in cold water with the lemon juice to prevent oxidizing. In a medium saucepan, melt the coconut oil over medium heat and mix in the sugar, cinnamon, cornstarch, and salt. Drain the apples and add them, along with the raisins, and stir to combine. Once the liquid starts to boil, turn down the heat a little and continue to cook until the apples are tender but not mushy, then transfer to a bowl to cool.

ASSEMBLE: Preheat the oven to 350°F and line a rimmed baking sheet with parchment. Turn out the dough onto your counter. Roll it out into a rectangle about 14 by 20 inches. Spread the filling over the dough, leaving an inch of free border all around, then start rolling up the dough starting from one long side. Work slowly and carefully to keep the roll tight, then pinch the seam really well. Form the tube into a ring, pinching the seams really well to keep the filling from spilling out, then transfer to the lined baking sheet. Bake until the cake is golden and crispy on top, 40 to 45 minutes, then let cool completely.

MAKE THE ICING: When the cake has cooled, mix the milk into the powdered sugar a teaspoon at a time until it's icing consistency, then stir in the vanilla extract. Pour the icing over the cake and sprinkle the colored sugar on top, if you wish. Voilà!

6

OSCARS PARTY

THIS CHAPTER
is all about
FINGER FOODS.

O R, MORE ACCURATELY, it's about the ability to stuff your face with one hand and hold a cocktail in the other, while keeping your eyes on the TV and watching beautiful people win awards for movies you keep meaning to see. And if you can do it all in fancy clothing, so much the better.

Hosting an Oscars party doesn't take very much prep. Make sure that your TV is in working condition and pull all your chairs out of their corners to face it. Throw some comfy pillows and blankets on the floor and doggone it, you've got yourself a home theater.

As far as serving, have a bunch of tiny plates and cocktail napkins all over. Break out the fancy serving trays and the cute toothpicks you ordered off the internet. If you'd like to circle the crowd wearing white gloves and holding glorious trays of hors d'oeuvres, that can be fun. Who doesn't want to float around the room saying things like "Asparagus Cigar, m'lord?" and "Snuggy Bunny for you, madame?"

My suggestion is to pick two warm hors d'oeuvres, two cold ones, and a dip or two. Make the cold ones a day or two in advance and then the day of will be easy and breezy, and you'll be the showstopper.

OTHER HORS D'OEUVRES FROM THIS BOOK
That You Can Totally Serve at Your Oscars Party

SNUGGY
BUNNIES
(Carrots in a Blanket)

36 baby carrots (about 1 pound)

2 tablespoons olive oil

½ teaspoon salt

1½ teaspoons smoked paprika

1 sheet frozen puff pastry, thawed

1 tablespoon toasted sesame seeds

Dijon mustard, for serving

— *Tip* —

Purchase the thicker variety of baby carrot if you can. The thin ones kind of reduce into nothingness. Make sure they are just a little under ½ inch in diameter.

I don't have to tell you that these are the cutest things in the world! Darling little roasted carrots in puff pastry, because bunnies love carrots, and real pigs deserve real blankets. They're sprinkled with a little paprika for smokiness, but the flavors are kept simple, relying more on the gentle roasting of the carrot, which sweetens a bit as it cooks. There are sesame seeds for fanciness, and I serve these with a hit of mustard just to drive the point home. I love this recipe because there isn't much prep to do at all—most of the time spent is wrapping the baby carrots in their blankets.

Preheat the oven to 450°F. Line a rimmed baking sheet with parchment.

Toss the carrots with the olive oil and ¼ teaspoon of the salt to coat. Arrange them in a single layer on the baking sheet, cover the baking sheet tightly with aluminum foil, and roast until tender, about 20 minutes.

Remove the foil, sprinkle the paprika and the remaining ¼ teaspoon salt over the carrots, and toss to coat again. Transfer the carrots to a plate. Keep the oven on because you'll be using it again. Discard the old parchment and place a new sheet of parchment on the baking sheet.

Place the pastry sheet on a lightly floured surface and roll it out into a rectangle approximately 11 by 15 inches. With a paring knife, cut the pastry into long thin strips that are about 3 inches long and 1 inch wide, depending on the size of your carrots. A little bit of carrot should be able to stick out of each side once wrapped.

Wrap each carrot in a piece of puff pastry, seal the edge with a little water, and place it, seam-side down, on the parchment. Brush the tops of the snuggies with water and sprinkle with sesame seeds, gently pressing the seeds into the pastry. Pop them back into the oven until golden and puffy, 10 to 15 minutes. Serve with mustard.

GRILLED POLENTA

with Tapenade

MAKES
32
PIECES

TOTAL
2 HOURS
ACTIVE
30 MINUTES

FOR THE POLENTA:

3 cups vegetable broth, purchased or homemade (page 203)

1 teaspoon salt

1 tablespoon olive oil, plus more for brushing

2 cups quick-cooking polenta

FOR THE TAPENADE:

3 garlic cloves, peeled

3 cups pitted kalamata olives

2 tablespoons olive oil

1 teaspoon mellow white miso

FOR THE GARNISH:

1 tablespoon grated lemon zest

Fresh chives, cut into 1-inch pieces

Grill marks always seem to impress, and polenta, with its bright yellow hue, is a prime candidate for the grill. The salty tapenade is divine with the mild polenta and lets the char shine through.

MAKE THE POLENTA: Lightly grease a 9-by-13-inch metal baking pan.

In a medium saucepan, bring the broth and salt to a boil over medium-high heat. Drizzle in the olive oil. Lower the heat and slowly stream in the polenta, whisking constantly for about 3 minutes, then letting it cook the rest of the way on low heat until it's soft and mushy, about 10 more minutes.

Spread the polenta into the prepared pan. Use a rubber spatula to smooth out the top. Refrigerate until it is fully set, about 1 hour. If you won't be serving it right away, cover it with plastic wrap until it's ready to use.

MAKE THE TAPENADE: Pulse the garlic in a food processor fitted with a metal blade. Once finely chopped, add the remaining tapenade ingredients and pulse into a chunky paste. Refrigerate in a tightly sealed container until ready to use.

GRILL THE POLENTA: Brush the top of the polenta with a little olive oil and invert the pan onto a cutting board to release it. Now brush the other side with more oil. Use a long chef's knife to cut the polenta into squares, four across and eight down.

Preheat a lightly greased cast iron grill pan over medium-high heat. Grill the polenta squares until grill marks appear, 3 to 4 minutes per side. Use a thin metal spatula to get under the polenta to flip it, to make sure the polenta doesn't stick. This will have to be done in two batches.

Spoon a little tapenade over each square, right in the center. Garnish with lemon zest and a chive and serve.

ASPARAGUS CIGARS

with Horseradish Mayo

2 tablespoons olive oil, plus extra for brushing

24 asparagus spears, trimmed to about 5 inches

4 garlic cloves, minced

2 teaspoons grated lemon zest

1 teaspoon salt

Freshly ground black pepper

12 sheets frozen phyllo dough, thawed

2 tablespoons prepared horseradish

1 tablespoon fresh lemon juice

¾ cup vegan mayo, purchased or homemade (page 67)

Crisp, lemony asparagus is wrapped in a flaky pastry and served with zesty horseradish mayo. Sounds kinda fancy, but it is really easy to make. Choose thick asparagus for this recipe, so that it holds its shape and gives a substantial bite. Just be careful not to ruin your Oscars dress with all that flaky pastry or a fallen spoonful of mayo.

Preheat the oven to 350°F. Line a large rimmed baking sheet with parchment.

Preheat a large, heavy-bottomed pan (preferably cast iron) over medium-high heat. Heat the oil, then sauté the asparagus until bright green and slightly tender, about 5 minutes. Add the garlic, lemon zest, salt, and pepper and sauté for a minute more. Remove the asparagus from the heat and transfer to a plate to cool.

Prepare a clean, dry surface with plenty of elbow room. Pour some olive oil into a small bowl and have a pastry brush handy.

Unwrap the thawed phyllo dough. Carefully place one sheet in front of you vertically and brush it with oil. Layer and repeat with two more sheets. Cover the other sheets with a damp towel to prevent them from drying out.

Use a paring knife to slice the triple stack crosswise into sixths.

Wrap one asparagus stalk in a strip of phyllo so that the tip is sticking out a bit. Brush with oil once more and place it, seam-side down, on the baking sheet. Repeat with the remaining asparagus and phyllo.

Bake until nicely browned, about 12 minutes.

While the asparagus is baking, in a small bowl, stir the horseradish and lemon juice into the mayo.

Transfer the asparagus to a serving tray and serve with the bowl of horseradish mayo and a spoon for dipping.

SHIITAKE
BLT
BITES

MAKES

24

PIECES

TOTAL
45 MINUTES
ACTIVE
20 MINUTES

1 pound shiitake mushrooms, tough stems trimmed, sliced a little over ¼ inch thick

¼ cup tamari or soy sauce

1 tablespoon olive oil

2 teaspoons liquid smoke

⅓ cup vegan mayo, purchased or homemade (page 67)

24 (¾-inch) French bread cubes

24 (1-inch) iceberg lettuce chunks

12 cherry tomatoes, halved

Tips

A dark-colored baking sheet works best here, to help crisp up the shiitake bacon.

Maybe this is obvious, but this recipe will make fabulous BLT sammies as well! You can get four average-size BLTs per recipe. I recommend adding avocado as well.

These are so ready to be popped right into your mouth! Smoky, bready, creamy, crunchy, and fresh...all in one tiny little bite. Shiitakes are baked in a smoked tamari sauce until wonderfully crisp. Then little French bread cubes are smeared with some mayo and skewered with a chunk of lettuce and a juicy little cherry tomato. And then...where did they all go?! You'll need 4-inch-long toothpicks to skewer these.

Preheat the oven to 425°F. Lightly grease a rimmed baking sheet.

Toss the sliced shiitakes in a bowl with the tamari, olive oil, and liquid smoke. Use your hands to coat.

Arrange the mushroom slices on the baking sheet in a single layer. Bake until very crisp on the edges, 12 to 15 minutes. Remove from the oven and let them cool right on the baking sheet. They'll cook a little more from the heat of the baking sheet and become even crispier.

Spread a little mayo on each bread cube. Skewer onto a toothpick, mayo-side up, and then skewer on the lettuce, shiitake bacon, and cherry tomato. Place in a circle on a serving tray.

Pistachio-Crusted
CASHEW CHEESE
& STRAWBERRY
SKEWERS

MAKES
ABOUT
24
SKEWERS

TOTAL
4 HOURS
(for setting)
ACTIVE
30 MINUTES

1½ cups raw cashews, soaked in water for at least 2 hours and drained

½ cup refined coconut oil, melted

2 tablespoons mellow white miso

1 tablespoon fresh lemon juice

2 tablespoons nutritional yeast flakes

1 teaspoon salt

¾ cup shelled pistachios

24 strawberries, hulled and cut in half

Tip

Work quickly with the cheese, because if you handle it for too long, the heat from your hands can make it too soft to work with. If that happens, simply refrigerate it for a few minutes. Once all the balls are made, get them into the fridge as soon as possible, until as close to serving time as possible.

Cheese balls coated in pistachios and topped with a little strawberry: Can it get any fancier? Maybe if you were using gold-plated skewers. These are pretty little things with beautifully mingling flavors; the mild miso in the cheese offsets the sweet, tangy strawberries. The cheese taste is probably most comparable to a chèvre. They aren't difficult to make, either. The only reason the time is so long is that the cheese needs time to set. If you make the cheese a day or two ahead, it sets best.

Combine the cashews, coconut oil, miso, lemon juice, nutritional yeast, and salt in a blender. Puree until completely smooth; this can take up to 5 minutes depending on the strength of your machine. Periodically stop the machine to keep it from overheating, and scrape down the sides of the blender jar with a rubber spatula to make sure you get everything.

Transfer the mixture to a tightly sealed container and refrigerate for at least 3 hours or overnight.

When you're ready to make the cheese balls, line a tray with waxed paper or parchment.

Pulse the pistachios in a food processor until they become fine crumbs. You can also achieve this by finely chopping them. Transfer to a plate.

Scoop up about 1½ tablespoons of the cheese and roll it into a ball. It's okay if the ball isn't perfectly smooth at this point—just handle it as lightly as possible. Place the cheese ball in the pistachios and coat it all over. Now roll it again, and this time it should be easier to form into a ball because it's coated in pistachios. Place the pistachio-coated balls on the lined tray. Refrigerate immediately for about 30 minutes to firm up.

Skewer a cheese ball onto a toothpick, then a strawberry. Place on a serving tray and serve!

Smoky
EGGPLANT-WRAPPED
FIGS

¼ cup tamari or soy sauce

1 tablespoon olive oil, plus extra for drizzling

2 teaspoons liquid smoke

1 teaspoon red wine vinegar

1 large eggplant (about 1 pound), cut into ⅛-inch-thick half-moons

12 dried Mission figs, halved

Guests really think you put in the extra effort when something is wrapped. I mean, it takes 2 seconds, but it really shows you care and makes them think you are better than them. Smoky, crispy, juicy eggplant bacon wrapped around a warm, sweet, sticky fig. So precious and delectable!

Mix the tamari, olive oil, liquid smoke, and vinegar in a wide bowl. Add the eggplant slices and toss to coat. Let marinate for about 30 minutes, tossing occasionally.

Preheat the oven to 425°F. Line two large rimmed baking sheets with parchment paper. Coat the parchment lightly with nonstick cooking spray.

Arrange the eggplant slices in a single layer on the baking sheets. Bake for 8 minutes, then rotate the pans and flip the eggplant slices and bake until lightly crispy in some places, about 5 more minutes. Remove from the oven and turn the heat down to 350°F.

Transfer the eggplant slices to a cooling rack to cool. They should cool down fairly quickly.

Wrap each fig half in an eggplant slice and secure with a toothpick. Put them back on the baking sheet and bake for about 5 minutes, just to warm the figs. Serve!

CREAM CHEE
TOASTS
with Sundried Tomato and Basil

MAKES
24
TOASTS

TOTAL
20 MINUTES
ACTIVE
30 MINUTES

24 (½-inch-thick) baguette slices

3 tablespoons olive oil

2 cups white bean cream chee (page 28) or purchased cream cheese

1 (8-ounce) jar oil-packed sundried tomatoes, drained

Large-flake salt (like Maldon)

Freshly ground black pepper

⅓ cup basil chiffonade

This is a really lazy bite full of classic flavors. Creamy white bean cream cheese spread on a slice of toast is a nice contrast to pungent sundried tomatoes. A little basil freshens everything up. Make the cream cheese the night before and these take no time at all.

Preheat the oven to 350°F.

Brush both sides of the bread slices with olive oil, then arrange in a single layer on a rimmed baking sheet. Bake, turning once, until golden and toasty, 10 to 12 minutes.

Dollop a big tablespoon of cream chee onto each toast. Top with a sundried tomato. (Sundried tomato sizes vary, so if yours are large, cut them into 1-inch pieces.) Sprinkle with salt and black pepper and finish with a healthy sprinkle of basil. Serve!

Pesto

CHICKPEA SALAD
BRUSCHETTA

MAKES
24
PIECES

TOTAL
30 MINUTES
ACTIVE
20 MINUTES

FOR THE BREAD:
3 tablespoons olive oil
2 garlic cloves, minced
Salt
24 (½-inch-thick) baguette slices

FOR THE PESTO:
⅓ cup walnuts
1 garlic clove, peeled
1 cup loosely packed fresh basil
   leaves
½ cup loosely packed fresh cilantro
   leaves
¼ teaspoon salt
¼ cup olive oil
¼ cup vegan mayo, purchased or
   homemade (page 67)
1 tablespoon fresh lemon juice
1 tablespoon mellow white miso

FOR THE SALAD:
1 (15-ounce) can chickpeas, rinsed
   and drained, or 1½ cups cooked
   chickpeas
Freshly ground black pepper
1 celery rib, finely chopped
Salt

FOR THE GARNISH:
Chopped tomato
Chopped fresh basil
Freshly ground black pepper

It's not quite springtime, but this garlic bread thinks it is. This is a fun play on chicken salad, with lightly mashed chickpeas in a pesto mayo dressing, topped with juicy tomatoes. It packs a ton of flavor into an easy finger food. If you are already serving a lot of bread, you can easily turn this into a lettuce cup with an endive or radicchio leaf. So fresh!

MAKE THE BREAD: Preheat the oven to 350°F.

In a small bowl, stir together the olive oil, garlic, and a pinch of salt. Brush both sides of the bread slices with the garlic oil and transfer to a rimmed baking sheet. Bake, turning once, until golden and toasty, 10 to 12 minutes.

MAKE THE PESTO: While the bread is in the oven, preheat a large, heavy-bottomed skillet (preferably cast iron) over medium-low heat. Toast the walnuts in the dry skillet for 5 to 10 minutes, tossing often.

Transfer the toasted nuts to a food processor. Add the garlic and pulse everything into fine crumbs. Add the basil, cilantro, and salt and pulse to combine. Add the olive oil, mayo, lemon juice, and miso and blend until relatively smooth.

MAKE THE SALAD: Mash the chickpeas in a large mixing bowl until they are broken down but not pureed. Mix in the pesto and a few grinds of black pepper until well combined. Fold in the celery; taste and adjust for salt and pepper.

ASSEMBLE: Spoon a few tablespoons of chickpea salad onto each baguette slice, garnish with tomato and basil, and sprinkle with black pepper. Serve!

 Tip   *Even though it adds a deeper flavor, if you don't feel like toasting the nuts, no biggie. Just toss 'em right into the blender and wink at the camera.*

Swanky
MUSHROOM
PÂTÉ

2 tablespoons refined coconut oil

1 medium yellow onion, diced large

¾ teaspoon salt, plus a pinch

3 garlic cloves

¼ teaspoon dried thyme

¼ teaspoon dried tarragon

¼ teaspoon crushed red pepper flakes

8 ounces cremini mushrooms, thinly sliced

Freshly ground black pepper

1 ounce dried porcini mushrooms

½ cup pumpkin seeds, plus additional for garnish

1 cup cooked or canned navy or great northern beans, rinsed and drained

2 tablespoons truffle oil, plus extra for drizzling

1 tablespoon fresh lemon juice

1 tablespoon nutritional yeast flakes (optional)

Chopped fresh parsley, for garnish

Coarse salt, for garnish

Crackers or toast points, for serving

This is a luxurious pâté, with a deep, rich, woodsy flavor that will have mushroom lovers swooning. You can use glass Tupperware, round or square, to mold the pâté; even a regular old cereal bowl will work as long as it's big enough. Serve with super fancy crackers and a beautiful vintage serving knife.

Preheat a large, heavy-bottomed pan (preferably cast iron) over medium heat. Heat the oil, then sauté the onion with a pinch of salt until lightly browned, 5 to 7 minutes.

Add the garlic, thyme, tarragon, and red pepper flakes and sauté for another minute. Add the cremini mushrooms, remaining ¾ teaspoon salt, and a few grinds of black pepper. Sauté until the mushrooms are fully cooked, about 8 minutes.

In the meantime, put the dried mushrooms in a blender and pulse until they turn into a fine powder. This could take a few minutes. When you lift the lid of the blender, some powder may come floating out, so consider yourself warned.

Add the pumpkin seeds and pulse into coarse crumbs.

At this point the cremini mushrooms should be fully cooked. Set aside about 2 tablespoons of the mushrooms for garnishing the pâté. Add the rest to the blender, along with the white beans, truffle oil, lemon juice, and nutritional yeast (if using). Puree until relatively smooth, scraping down the sides often.

Line a 3-cup container (a glass Tupperware works great) with plastic wrap. Transfer the pâté to the container and smooth out the top. Cover and refrigerate for at least 3 hours, or until firm enough to unmold.

Place your serving plate over the pâté, then gently invert so that the container is upside down on the plate. Lift the container to unmold the pâté, and peel off the plastic wrap.

To garnish, top with the reserved mushrooms and a sprinkle of pumpkin seeds. Drizzle with additional truffle oil, and finish with chopped parsley and a little coarse salt. Serve with crackers or toast points.

EDAMAME-MINT
HUMMUS

4 garlic cloves, peeled

1 (1-pound) bag frozen edamame, thawed (about 3 cups)

¾ cup tahini

6 tablespoons olive oil

3 tablespoons fresh lemon juice

1 teaspoon salt

1 teaspoon crushed red pepper flakes

½ cup water

3 tablespoons chopped fresh mint

Pita points, for serving

─── *Tip* ───

Be sure to thaw your edamame before using in this recipe. Leaving it in the fridge overnight usually does the trick!

Hummus doesn't always have to be humble. Sometimes it can be show-offy and unexpected. Even though edamame hummus may line the hummus shelves, mint makes this one really special and impossible to stop dipping into.

Pulse the garlic in a food processor fitted with a metal blade, just until it's chopped up. Add the edamame and pulse again to get it mushed up.

Add the tahini, olive oil, lemon juice, salt, and red pepper flakes and blend until really smooth, using water as needed to thin it and scraping down the sides as necessary. You may need up to ½ cup water; the hummus will thicken up again as it sets and you want it very velvety smooth.

Add the mint and pulse to combine, until the mint is in little flecks.

Taste and adjust for salt. Transfer to a tightly sealed container and keep refrigerated until ready to serve. Serve with soft pita points.

MAKES ABOUT 16 CUPS

SALTED CARAMEL CORN

with Peanuts

TOTAL
1 HOUR 30 MINUTES
ACTIVE
20 MINUTES

---

16 cups (4 quarts) plain popped popcorn

1 cup roasted peanuts (optional)

1 cup brown sugar

½ cup refined coconut oil

¼ cup pure maple syrup

¾ teaspoon salt

¼ teaspoon baking soda

1 teaspoon pure vanilla extract

1 teaspoon large flake salt (like Maldon)

Oscar night is incomplete without popcorn! This sweet and salty caramel concoction will steal the show. The method (which I stole from the internet) is an absolutely brilliant one. The caramel corn is baked in a low oven, guaranteeing perfect little morsels that won't burn. Serve in martini glasses for extra-special fanciness.

Preheat the oven to 250°F. Lightly grease two large rimmed baking sheets, jelly roll pans, shallow roasting pans, or disposable aluminum pans.

Divide the popped popcorn between the two greased pans. Add the peanuts to the popped corn, if using. Set aside.

In a saucepan, combine the brown sugar, coconut oil, maple syrup, and salt and bring to a boil over medium heat, stirring occasionally. Once boiling, stir constantly for about 5 minutes, lowering the heat if needed to keep it from burning.

Remove the pan from the heat and stir in the baking soda and vanilla. The mixture will be light and foamy. Immediately pour it over the popcorn in the pans, and stir to coat.

Bake for 1 hour, removing the pans from the oven and giving them a stir every 15 minutes. Line a flat surface (like your countertop) with waxed paper. Dump the popcorn mixture onto the waxed paper and separate the pieces. Sprinkle with the flaky salt. Cool completely, then transfer to airtight containers until ready to serve.

MAKES
12
CUPCAKES

TOTAL
1 HOUR 30 MINUTES
ACTIVE
45 MINUTES

PINK GRAPEFRUIT
CUPCAKES

FOR THE CANDIED PEEL:
1 large pink grapefruit
1 cup granulated sugar
½ cup water

FOR THE CUPCAKES:
¾ cup unsweetened almond milk
   (or your favorite nondairy milk)
½ cup fresh grapefruit juice
⅓ cup canola oil
¾ cup granulated sugar
1 tablespoon grated grapefruit zest
1 teaspoon pure vanilla extract
1⅓ cups all-purpose flour
1 teaspoon baking powder
½ teaspoon baking soda
¼ teaspoon salt

FOR THE ICING:
3 cups powdered sugar, sifted
½ cup refined coconut oil, melted
¼ cup fresh grapefruit juice
½ teaspoon pure vanilla extract
Salt

Grapefruit reminds me of the '60s, and that's when Hollywood was full of glamour! Thus these glamorous cupcakes. Candied grapefruit peel sits atop these citrusy cakes like a sparkling jewel. They are dainty and sweet and just perfect for eating three of.

MAKE THE CANDIED PEEL: With a paring knife, cut off the top and bottom ends of the grapefruit. Following the curve of the fruit, cut away the outermost peel, leaving some of the white pith intact on the peel. Cut the peel lengthwise into just-under-½-inch-wide strips.

Put the strips in a 4-quart pot and cover with cold water. Bring to a boil over medium-high heat, then drain. Repeat this step two more times.

Put the peel back in the pot, add the sugar and ½ cup fresh water, and bring to a boil over medium-high heat. Reduce the heat and simmer until the peel is translucent, 15 to 20 minutes. Drain the sugar water and transfer the peels to a wire rack to dry, 2 to 4 hours. When dry, place in airtight containers and store in a cool, dry place.

MAKE THE CUPCAKES: Preheat the oven to 350°F. Line a standard-size muffin tin with paper or foil cupcake liners. Coat them lightly with nonstick cooking spray.

In a large mixing bowl, beat together the milk, grapefruit juice, oil, sugar, grapefruit zest, and vanilla.

Sift in the flour, baking powder, baking soda, and salt. Mix until relatively smooth.

Fill the lined muffin cups two-thirds of the way and bake for 18 to 22 minutes. Remove from the oven, and when the pan is cool enough to touch, transfer the cupcakes to a cooling rack to cool completely.

MAKE THE ICING: In a mixing bowl, whisk together the powdered sugar, melted coconut oil, juice, vanilla, and a pinch of salt until smooth. Refrigerate for 30 minutes.

In a standing mixer, whip the chilled icing on medium-high speed until light and fluffy. Frost the cupcakes using a butter knife, or pipe on the icing using a pastry bag fitted with the tip of your choice. Garnish with candied grapefruit peel and serve.

7

St. Patrick's
DAY

IT'S ST. PATRICK'S DAY!

So, guess what?

EVERYTHING HAS TO be green! Luckily, this is a vegan cookbook so we have no shortage of green ingredients to go around. And let's not forget the potatoes and beer. These homey comfort foods are full of carby goodness.

Brooklyn has always had a huge Irish population, and the little fishing village I grew up in called Sheepshead Bay had its own St. Patrick's parade. I loved to watch all the bakeries suddenly pop up with green pastries and the streets line with Irish flags.

I like to have a beer or two occasionally, but instead of getting wasted, let's stuff our faces and drink Shamrockin' Shakes. That's how I party.

AVOCADO CABBAGE ROLLS

FOR THE CILANTRO VINAIGRETTE:

1 garlic clove, peeled

½ cup lightly packed fresh cilantro (stems and leaves)

3 tablespoons fresh lime juice

3 tablespoons water

2 tablespoons olive oil

1 tablespoon Dijon mustard

1 teaspoon agave

½ teaspoon salt

Several pinches freshly ground black pepper

FOR THE CABBAGE ROLLS:

1 large head green cabbage

2 cups steamed white rice, cooled

1 cucumber, seeded and diced small

½ cup thinly sliced scallion

½ cup chopped fresh cilantro

1 tablespoon minced garlic

2 tablespoons olive oil

2 tablespoons fresh lime juice

½ teaspoon grated lime zest

½ teaspoon salt

¼ teaspoon ground cumin

¼ teaspoon freshly ground black pepper

¼ teaspoon crushed red pepper flakes

2 firm but ripe avocados, pitted, peeled, and cubed

Here's a little Latin twist on cabbage rolls, with a zesty avocado rice salad wrapped up in lightly cooked cabbage leaves and dipped in vinaigrette. Those frozen bags of cooked rice come in really handy for these rolls.

MAKE THE CILANTRO VINAIGRETTE: Combine all the vinaigrette ingredients in a small blender or food processor and blend until very smooth. Keep tightly sealed and refrigerated until ready to use. (You can make the vinaigrette up to 5 days ahead of time.)

MAKE THE CABBAGE ROLLS: Bring a large pot of water to a boil. Remove the core and any damaged outer leaves from the cabbage. Add the cabbage to the boiling water and boil until soft and tender, and the leaves separate easily, about 3 minutes. Remove from the water and allow to cool enough to handle.

In a large mixing bowl, combine the rice, cucumber, scallion, cilantro, garlic, olive oil, lime juice and zest, salt, cumin, black pepper, and red pepper flakes. Mix until well combined. Carefully fold in the avocado cubes.

Place ¼ cup of the avocado-rice mixture in the center of 1 large cabbage leaf. Fold it up like a tiny burrito, making sure to tuck in the ends.

Place on a serving tray, then repeat with the remaining cabbage leaves and filling. Cover the tray with plastic wrap and chill until ready to serve. Serve with the cilantro vinaigrette.

COLCANNON

3 pounds Yukon Gold potatoes, scrubbed and cut into 1½-inch chunks

1¾ teaspoons salt

4 tablespoons olive oil

4 cups chopped kale (from about 1 bunch)

½ cup unsweetened almond milk (or your favorite nondairy milk), at room temperature

Freshly ground black pepper

Here's my version of the classic Irish dish of potatoes and greens. I've kept the recipe really short to let the simple flavors speak for themselves. Serve with Corned Beet & Cabbage (page 164) and your feast is complete. Or, you know, just call a friend and eat these right out of the pot.

Put the potatoes in a medium pot and cover with cold water. Sprinkle 1 teaspoon of the salt into the water. Cover and bring the water to a boil over high heat. Lower the heat to a simmer and cook the potatoes until fork-tender, about 12 minutes.

In the meantime, preheat a large pan over medium heat. Heat 1 tablespoon of the olive oil, then sauté the kale until completely wilted, about 3 minutes.

Drain the potatoes, then return them to the pot. Do a preliminary mash with a potato masher, just to get them broken up. Add the milk, remaining 3 tablespoons oil, remaining ¾ teaspoon salt, and a few grinds of black pepper and mash until fluffy. Add the kale and mix to combine. You may want to add a bit more milk or oil, if needed. Taste and adjust for salt and pepper, and serve!

HERBED COUSCOUS *and* KALE SALAD

with Green Apple

SERVES
8

TOTAL
20 MINUTES
ACTIVE
20 MINUTES

FOR THE DRESSING:

2 garlic cloves, peeled

½ cup chopped fresh parsley

¼ cup chopped fresh chives

¼ cup fresh basil leaves

2 tablespoons fresh thyme leaves

⅓ cup fresh lemon juice

¼ cup olive oil

¼ cup water, plus more to thin

2 tablespoons Dijon mustard

2 teaspoons sugar

1 teaspoon salt

Several pinches freshly ground
   black pepper

FOR THE SALAD:

½ cup pine nuts

4 cups cooked couscous

8 cups baby kale

2 thinly sliced green apples

Fluffy couscous readily soaks up flavors, especially in this salad. The dressing of parsley, chives, basil, and thyme makes it completely addictive. Some pine nuts provide toasty crunch, and there's just a hint of sweetness from the green apples. Baby kale works like a dream here: just tender enough to add raw, but still holding on to some of its rugged chewiness. If you can't find any, I'd recommend spinach instead of adult kale, for its tenderness.

MAKE THE DRESSING: Put the garlic in a blender and pulse to chop it up a bit. Add all the remaining dressing ingredients and puree until very smooth. Add a little more water to thin it if needed. Taste and adjust for salt. Keep tightly sealed and refrigerated until ready to use.

MAKE THE SALAD: Preheat a small, heavy-bottomed pan over medium heat. Toss in the pine nuts and toast, stirring often, for about 5 minutes. They should be varying shades of toasty brown, and smell toasty and yummy. Transfer them to a plate to cool.

In a large mixing bowl, toss together the couscous, kale, and apples. Add the dressing and toss to coat. Transfer to a serving bowl, top with the toasted pine nuts, and serve.

 Tips   *Slice the apples right before tossing the salad together so they don't discolor.*

This salad calls for the couscous to be cooked already, so take that into account before starting the recipe. It's just a matter of pouring hot water over the grains and covering. So, cook the couscous according to the package directions, then spread it out on a baking sheet to cool completely. Do this the night before and this salad will be ready in hardly any time at all.

SAUSAGE-STUFFED LEEKS

1 (8-ounce) package tempeh, cut into quarters

6 large leeks

2 tablespoons olive oil, plus more for drizzling

1 small onion, finely diced

3 garlic cloves, minced

1 tablespoon tamari or soy sauce

2 tablespoons tequila (optional)

2 chipotle peppers in adobo sauce, seeded and finely chopped (see Tip on page 61)

1 tablespoon adobo sauce from the can of chipotles

2 tablespoons fresh lime juice

2 tablespoons brown sugar

1 teaspoon ground cumin

1 teaspoon smoked paprika

1 teaspoon dried oregano

½ teaspoon salt

Freshly ground black pepper

½ cup panko bread crumbs

Crushed red pepper flakes, for garnish

Smoked salt, for garnish

Tip

Smoked sea salt is a great addition to these little guys if you've got it. You can use it in place of the salt in the recipe, to add that extra touch of smokiness. And you can also sprinkle a bit on at the end to finish them.

Sausage casings made out of leeks! Spicy, seasoned tempeh is stuffed into steamed leeks and baked, making the cutest little cruelty-free sausages ever. These take a little work, but they're super impressive and worth it. Choose leeks that are really large, since you won't be using the dark green parts. Make sure that the white and light green parts are about 6 inches long. And give your guests steak knives so they can easily slice into the leeks.

Prepare a steamer. Steam the tempeh for 20 minutes. It will get plump and be ready to absorb all of the fabulous flavors.

In the meantime, prepare the leeks. You need only the white and light green parts, so trim off the root end and the tough green leaves. You will be left with the tender bottoms that should measure between 5 and 6 inches long. Remove any tough outer layers. Now cut each piece in half (across the waist) so that you have a total of 12 pieces, each 2 to 3 inches long. Rinse the leeks under cold running water if there is still any dirt remaining.

When the tempeh is done steaming, crumble it into tiny pieces into a medium mixing bowl.

Now, steam the leeks until soft, about 10 minutes. Transfer the leeks to a cutting board and let cool until you can handle them. Once cooled, carefully press out the centers, leaving 2 to 3 outer layers, forming a tube.

Preheat the oven to 375°F. Lightly grease an 8-inch square baking dish.

Okay, now let's make the sausage mixture. Preheat a large, heavy-bottomed pan (preferably cast iron) over medium heat. Heat the oil, then sauté the onion and garlic until softened and fragrant, about 3 minutes. Add the crumbled tempeh and the tamari and cook until the tempeh is lightly browned, about 5 minutes. Splash in the tequila, if using, and cook for a minute more.

Return the tempeh to the mixing bowl and let it get cool enough to handle. Add the chipotles and sauce, lime juice, brown sugar, cumin, paprika, oregano, salt, and a few grinds of black pepper. Mix until well combined. Add the panko and mix just until everything holds together.

Stuff some sausage mixture into each leek tube. Pack it in tightly, then place the stuffed leeks in a single layer in the prepared baking dish. Drizzle the leeks lightly with olive oil. Cover with aluminum foil and bake for 25 minutes. Remove the foil and bake until the leeks begin to brown, about 20 minutes more.

Serve hot, garnished with red pepper flakes and smoked salt.

PEPPERONI
POTATO SOUP
with Kale

SERVES
8

TOTAL
30 MINUTES
ACTIVE
30 MINUTES

FOR THE SOUP:

1 tablespoon olive oil

1 small yellow onion, diced medium

½ teaspoon salt, plus a pinch

3 garlic cloves, minced

1 teaspoon dried thyme

1 pound Yukon Gold potatoes, scrubbed and cut into ¾-inch chunks

1 cup chopped peeled carrot

3 cups vegetable broth, purchased or homemade (page 203)

½ teaspoon ground turmeric

Freshly ground black pepper

1 pound kale, cut into bite-size pieces

2 pepperonis, homemade (page 314) or store-bought, chopped into ½-inch chunks

2 tablespoons fresh lemon juice

FOR THE CASHEW CREAM:

¾ cup raw cashews, soaked in water for at least 2 hours and drained

1½ cups vegetable broth, purchased or homemade (page 203)

2 tablespoons mellow white miso

2 tablespoons tomato paste

2 tablespoons nutritional yeast flakes

Potatoes and kale and pepperoni in a cheddary cashew base…it's everything you need for a chilly March evening. This recipe would be a wonderful start if you're serving Irish Stout Stew (page 167) as an entree, but it's also a fabulous casual dinner all on its own if you're just slinging back a couple of beers or Shamrockin' Shakes (page 170) and not doing a whole whoop-di-do for the occasion.

FIRST, GET THE SOUP STARTED: Preheat a 4-quart pot over medium heat. Heat the oil, then sauté the onion with a pinch of salt just until softened, about 3 minutes. Add the garlic and thyme and sauté just until fragrant, 30 seconds or so.

Add the potatoes, carrot, broth, turmeric, remaining ½ teaspoon salt, and a few grinds of black pepper. Cover and bring to a boil, then reduce the heat to a simmer. Cook, covered, until the potatoes and carrot are very tender, about 10 minutes.

IN THE MEANTIME, MAKE THE CASHEW CREAM: Combine the cashews, vegetable broth, miso, tomato paste, and nutritional yeast in a blender. Puree until completely smooth; this can take up to 5 minutes depending on the strength of your machine. Periodically stop the machine to keep it from overheating, and scrape down the sides of the blender jar with a rubber spatula to make sure you get everything.

FINISH THE SOUP: When the potatoes and carrots are tender, add the cashew cream to the soup. Use an immersion blender to puree about half of the soup. You still want it to be chunky, with some whole bits of potato and carrot. Add the kale and cook, partially covered, for 5 minutes.

Add the pepperoni and lemon juice. Taste and adjust for salt and seasoning and turn off the heat. The soup tastes best if you let it sit for 10 minutes or so before serving. Also, it thickens even more as it cools, so you'll need to thin out leftovers…if there are any!

Tip *Make the pepperonis a day in advance and serve the leftovers on pizza. You can also use store-bought vegan pepperoni for this recipe, but homemade is yummier, of course.*

CORNED BEET
And CABBAGE

SERVES
6

TOTAL
3 HOURS
ACTIVE
30 MINUTES

FOR THE BRINE:

4 whole cardamom pods
1 tablespoon whole allspice berries
1 tablespoon whole cloves
1 tablespoon whole black peppercorns
1 gallon water
4 bay leaves
1 cinnamon stick
1 cup coarse sea salt
½ cup tightly packed brown sugar
1 tablespoon ground mustard
1 tablespoon ground coriander
1 tablespoon crushed red pepper flakes
2 teaspoons ground ginger
1 teaspoon caraway seeds

FOR THE BEET SEITAN:

8 ounces beets, trimmed and chopped into 1-inch pieces
3 garlic cloves, peeled and halved
1 tablespoon olive oil
½ teaspoon salt
1¼ cups vital wheat gluten
½ cup chickpea flour
⅓ cup all-purpose flour
1 tablespoon dried parsley
1 teaspoon freshly ground black pepper
½ cup finely diced yellow onion
1 tablespoon minced garlic
Super Simple Sautéed Cabbage (facing page), for serving

You can't have St. Patrick's Day without some twist on a briny braise and cabbage! A beety seitan loaf is simmered in fragrant brine for a lovely earthy meaty loaf that lights up the kitchen while cooking. It's definitely a project, but actual hands-on cooking time is minimal, and when you're done you can add "brined corned beet" to your list of life accomplishments.

PREPARE THE BRINE: Toast the cardamom, allspice, cloves, and peppercorns in a dry pan over medium heat until fragrant. Toss often, and take care not to burn them. This should take only about 1 minute.

Pour the water into a large stockpot and add the toasted spices, along with the remaining brine ingredients. Stir to combine and set aside.

MAKE THE SEITAN: First, we will roast the beets and garlic to bring out the flavor.

Preheat the oven to 425°F. Coat the beets and garlic in the olive oil and salt and wrap them in foil. Place the foil package on a rimmed baking sheet and roast for 45 minutes, turning once. Remove the baking sheet from the oven, carefully open the foil, and allow the roasted beets and garlic to cool enough to handle. Transfer the beets and garlic to a food processor fitted with a metal blade and puree until smooth.

In a large mixing bowl, mix the vital wheat gluten, chickpea flour, all-purpose flour, parsley, and pepper. Make a well in the center and add the beet puree, diced onion, and garlic. Knead the mixture into an elastic dough; this should take about 5 minutes.

Form the dough into a log about 8 inches long, cover with a dishtowel, and allow to rest for 20 minutes. (You can do this right in the bowl.)

Wrap the seitan log tightly in cheesecloth and tie the ends closed. Place the wrapped log in the pot of cold brine and bring to a boil over high heat. Reduce the heat to medium-low and simmer for 4 hours, turning the seitan every so often.

Remove the pot from the heat and allow to cool enough to handle. Remove the cheesecloth and store the seitan in the brine until ready to use. Serve with the cabbage.

 Tip *For this recipe you'll need cheesecloth, which is available online or at kitchen stores and well-stocked supermarkets.*

SAUTÉED CABBAGE

SERVES
8

TOTAL
30 MINUTES
ACTIVE
30 MINUTES

2 tablespoons olive oil

1 medium yellow onion, thinly sliced

¾ teaspoon salt, plus a pinch

2 tablespoons minced garlic

1 average-size head green cabbage, shredded

Freshly ground black pepper

Chopped fresh dill, for garnish

This is just as the title suggests: sautéed cabbage with a little onion and garlic. Super simple but super tasty.

Preheat a large, heavy-bottomed pan (preferably cast iron) over medium heat. Heat the oil, then sauté the onion with a pinch of salt until lightly browned, 5 to 7 minutes. Add the garlic and sauté until fragrant, about 30 seconds.

Add the cabbage, the remaining ¾ teaspoon salt, and a few grinds of black pepper and cook, tossing often, until the cabbage is soft and wilted and reduced in size by about half, about 7 more minutes.

Serve garnished with fresh dill.

IRISH STOUT STEW

with Potato Biscuits

FOR THE STEW:

1 ounce dried porcini mushrooms

3 cups vegetable broth, purchased or homemade (page 203)

2 tablespoons olive oil

1 large onion, diced medium

1¼ teaspoons salt, plus a pinch

4 garlic cloves, minced

8 ounces cremini mushrooms, thinly sliced

2 celery ribs, thinly sliced

2 teaspoons dried thyme

1 teaspoon dried rosemary

8 ounces carrots, peeled and cut into thin half-moons

1¼ cups stout beer

2 tablespoons tomato paste

Freshly ground black pepper

⅓ cup all-purpose flour

1 cup cold water

2 (15-ounce) cans kidney beans, rinsed and drained, or 3 cups cooked kidney beans

FOR THE BISCUITS:

1½ cups all-purpose flour

2 tablespoons sugar

1 tablespoon baking powder

1 teaspoon salt

1 cup leftover mashed potatoes (see Tip)

½ cup cold water

3 tablespoons olive oil

Chopped fresh parsley, for garnish

Oh my lucky stars, this is good—a fluffy potato biscuit soaking up a deeply savory gravy that is at once mysterious and familiar. The stout really gives this dish an allure, and two kinds of mushrooms make it meaty and earthy and just umami like nobody's business. Kidney beans and lots of veggies make it really homey and filling. And ya know, for a special occasion, it's not tooooo fussy.

MAKE THE STEW: Put the porcinis in a large bowl. If the porcinis are large, tear them into bite-size pieces. Bring the vegetable broth to a boil in a saucepan on the stovetop or in the microwave and pour it over the porcinis. Cover the bowl with a plate to keep it hot while you prep everything you need for the recipe. This will soften them and make the recipe go a bit faster.

Preheat a Dutch oven over medium heat. Heat the oil, then sauté the onion and a pinch of salt until translucent, 4 to 7 minutes. Add the garlic and cook until fragrant, about a minute.

Add the sliced cremini mushrooms (not the porcinis yet), celery, thyme, and rosemary and sauté until the mushrooms release their moisture and brown slightly, about 5 minutes.

Add the carrots, stout, tomato paste, remaining 1¼ teaspoons salt, and a lot of freshly ground black pepper and bring to a boil. The liquid should reduce in about 3 minutes. Add the porcinis and vegetable broth, cover, and bring to a full boil for 5 minutes or so, to finish cooking and softening the porcinis.

In a measuring cup, whisk the flour into the cold water with a fork until no lumps are left. Slowly add the slurry to the pot, mixing well as you go. Let the soup thicken for 5 minutes or so. Add the kidney beans, turn off the heat, and cover the pot to keep the soup warm.

MAKE THE BISCUITS: Preheat the oven to 425°F.

In a large mixing bowl, sift together the flour, sugar, baking powder, and salt. In a separate bowl, use a fork to mix the mashed potatoes, water, and olive oil. The mixture should be very loose and mushy.

Recipe Continues

This recipe calls for "leftover mashed potatoes," but you may not have any lying around! To make about 1 cup as called for here, pierce a russet potato all over with a fork and microwave for 4 to 6 minutes, then scoop it out of the peel and mash with ¼ cup unsweetened nondairy milk, 2 tablespoons olive oil, and a pinch of salt. Let cool, then measure and use!

If you don't have a stovetop-to-oven pot, then simply make the stew, transfer it to a 9-by-13-inch casserole dish, and form the biscuits into a rectangle instead of a circle. Slice and arrange them on top of the casserole and bake as directed.

Make a well in the center of the flour and add the potato mixture. Mix with a fork until a stiff dough starts to form, then turn out the dough onto a clean surface and knead a few times to smooth it out. Flatten the dough into a disk 2 inches smaller than the pot with the stew in it. Cut the disk like a tic-tac-toe board into 9 pieces and arrange the pieces on top of the cooked stew.

Bake, uncovered, until the biscuits are lightly browned on top and the stew bubbles up thickly around them, about 20 minutes. Let the stew sit for 15 minutes or so, then garnish with parsley and serve.

Super Fancy

ROASTED
CARROTS *And* CABBAGE
WEDGES

SERVES
8

TOTAL
1 HOUR 10 MINUTES
ACTIVE
20 MINUTES

1 large head green cabbage

4 large carrots, peeled and cut into ¼-inch coins

¼ cup olive oil

1 teaspoon minced garlic

1 tablespoon chopped fresh thyme

1 teaspoon chopped fresh dill, plus more for garnish

¾ teaspoon salt

½ teaspoon dried tarragon

¼ teaspoon crushed red pepper flakes

Freshly ground black pepper

Cabbage wedges and carrot coins are coated in an herbed oil and then roasted until tender and juicy. This is a fancier way to serve cabbage, but still not too much work!

Preheat the oven to 375°F. Line a rimmed baking sheet with parchment paper.

Remove any damaged outer leaves from the cabbage. Cut the head in half and remove the core, then cut into eight equal wedges.

Place the cabbage wedges and carrot coins on the lined baking sheet.

In a mixing cup, stir together the oil, garlic, thyme, dill, salt, tarragon, red pepper flakes, and a few grinds of black pepper. Drizzle the herbed oil over the cabbage and carrots and toss to coat. Rearrange them in a single layer on the baking sheet.

Bake until the carrots are tender and the outer edges of the cabbage are browned, about 45 minutes.

Place one wedge on each plate and sprinkle on the carrot coins. Garnish with dill and serve.

MAKES

4

CUPS

TOTAL
1 HOUR
ACTIVE
15 MINUTES

SHAMROCKIN' SHAKES

1 ripe avocado

1 (14-ounce) can coconut milk

2 cups unsweetened almond milk
(or your favorite nondairy milk)

½ cup agave

2 tablespoons fresh lemon juice

½ teaspoon pure vanilla extract

½ cup fresh mint leaves

A mint ice cream shake is definitely the funnest drink of all time! This version of the classic fast food shake is *au naturel* and dare I say even more delish. Avocado and coconut create the frostiest base for all the fresh mint. The recipe doubles and triples perfectly, so make enough for the whole block.

Cut the avocado in half, remove the pit, and scoop the flesh into a medium container. Pour in the coconut milk. Put the container in the freezer for 45 minutes. The mixture should be really, really cold but not frozen, although a little iciness is okay.

Transfer the avocado-coconut mixture to a blender. Add all the other ingredients and blend until smooth. Serve cold and frosty.

IRISH CREAM WHOOPIE PIES

MAKES
8
PIES

TOTAL
1 HOUR 30 MINUTES
ACTIVE
45 MINUTES

FOR THE CAKES:

2 cups all-purpose flour

½ cup unsweetened cocoa powder

1¼ teaspoons baking soda

1 teaspoon salt

1 cup unsweetened almond milk (or your favorite nondairy milk)

2 teaspoons apple cider vinegar

⅓ cup refined coconut oil, at room temperature

1 cup packed brown sugar

⅓ cup unsweetened applesauce, at room temperature

1 teaspoon pure vanilla extract

FOR THE FILLING:

2 tablespoons whiskey

2 tablespoons hot water

2 tablespoons unsweetened cocoa powder

2 teaspoons instant coffee granules

½ cup refined coconut oil, melted

2½ cups powdered sugar, sifted

½ teaspoon pure vanilla extract

¼ teaspoon pure almond extract

Pinch salt

Tip

An ice cream scoop works perfectly for getting pretty rounded cookies onto the baking sheet. If you don't have one, filling up a ¼-cup measuring cup three-quarters of the way ought to do it.

The scrumptious Irish cream filling in these fluffy chocolaty cakes is smoky and mysterious from the whiskey, with hints of chocolate, coffee, and almond. If you'd like to leave the alcohol out for the children and straight edgers, simply use a little almond milk instead.

MAKE THE CAKES: Preheat the oven to 350°F. Lightly grease two large rimmed baking sheets.

In a mixing bowl, sift together the flour, cocoa powder, baking soda, and salt.

In a measuring cup, whisk together the milk and apple cider vinegar and set aside to curdle.

In a separate mixing bowl, use an electric mixer to beat together the coconut oil and brown sugar until very well combined, about 5 minutes. Add the applesauce and vanilla and beat for another minute.

Now at low speed, alternately add the flour mixture and milk mixture in batches, starting and ending with the flour, until all the ingredients are well combined.

Spoon the batter in 3-tablespoon mounds onto the greased baking sheets, leaving about 2 inches of room between them to allow for spreading. You should have eight mounds on each sheet. Bake, rotating and swapping the pans about halfway through, until the cakes are puffy and the tops are firm but with some spring in them, 12 to 15 minutes.

Transfer the cakes to cooling racks to cool completely before filling.

MAKE THE FILLING: In a mixing bowl, use a fork to mix the whiskey, hot water, cocoa powder, and instant coffee until dissolved. Add the melted coconut oil and powdered sugar alternately, in batches, and mix with an electric beater. Add the vanilla and almond extracts and the salt, mixing until everything is well incorporated. Refrigerate for 30 minutes.

In a standing mixer, whip the chilled filling on medium-high speed until light and fluffy.

ASSEMBLE THE PIES: Transfer the filling to a pastry bag fitted with a large metal tip. Pipe about 2 tablespoons of filling on one cake, and sandwich it with another cake. If you don't have a pastry bag, just neatly spread 2 tablespoons of filling onto the cake with a butter knife. Keep the whoopie pies chilled until ready to serve.

8
EASTER

SPRING IS IN THE AIR!
The bunnies are hopping, the
TULIPS AND DAFFODILS ARE
blooming, and it's time for
THE EGG HUNT.

OKAY, IF YOU'RE VEGAN, you can just stuff some biodegradable plastic eggs with vegan candy and hide them. Then go find them all by yourself.

This section is an homage to early spring, but also to gatherings where you linger throughout the day, grabbing a snack here or there. Oh, and eggs. A lot of these recipes tip a hat to those little orbs. We don't have to give up all the things we love about eggy foods. There are little potatoes that look like deviled eggs, cucumber cups stuffed with a tofu egg salad, and even a quiche made with white beans!

And don't worry, the classics are represented, too. Instead of rack of lamb (sad face), there are skewers of mushrooms with mint sauce. Glazed tofu isn't going to fool anyone into thinking it's a ham, but it's still juicy, smoky, and superfun. And if you're Greek, you're no stranger to a big casserole of pastitsio as the Easter centerpiece. Dig in!

Cream of CARROT SOUP

1 tablespoon refined coconut oil

1 medium yellow onion, diced medium

½ teaspoon salt, plus a pinch

3 garlic cloves, minced

1 tablespoon minced fresh ginger

3½ cups vegetable broth, purchased or homemade (page 203)

3 pounds carrots, peeled and cut into ½-inch pieces, greens chopped for garnish

1 cup coconut milk from a well-stirred can, plus extra for garnish

2 tablespoons pure maple syrup

2 tablespoons fresh lime juice

Freshly ground black pepper

What a vibrant way to kick off the holiday! This fresh, gingery carrot soup is rich and creamy thanks to the coconut milk. Make it really pretty by drizzling some extra coconut milk into each bowl and garnishing with carrot greens.

Preheat a 4-quart pot over medium heat. Heat the oil, then sauté the onion with a pinch of salt until lightly caramelized, about 7 minutes. Add the garlic and ginger and sauté until fragrant, about 30 seconds.

Add the broth and remaining ½ teaspoon salt and scrape the bottom of the pan to deglaze. Add the carrots, cover the pot, and bring to a low boil. Boil until the carrots are completely softened, about 15 minutes. Add the coconut milk, maple syrup, and lime juice and heat everything through.

Use an immersion blender to blend the soup smooth and creamy. If you don't have an immersion blender and need to use a food processor or blender, remember that steam can build up in there and hurt you, so lift the lid every few seconds to let steam escape.

Thin the soup with a little water if necessary, then taste and adjust for sweetness, salt, and pepper. If you like, swirl a little coconut milk on the top of each serving for extra prettiness and sprinkle on some chopped carrot greens.

EGGPLANT CAPONATA
BRUSCHETTA

FOR THE CAPONATA:

1 large eggplant (about 1¼ pounds), cut into ¾-inch dice

3 tablespoons olive oil, plus a spray bottle of olive oil

¼ teaspoon salt

1 medium yellow onion, thinly sliced

1 celery rib, very thinly sliced

3 garlic cloves, minced

3 tablespoons brown sugar

1 (15-ounce) can crushed tomatoes

¼ cup roughly chopped kalamata olives

Freshly ground black pepper

2 tablespoons red wine vinegar

FOR THE BRUSCHETTA:

24 (½-inch-thick) baguette slices

3 tablespoons olive oil

Fresh basil chiffonade, for garnish

Caponata is a classic Sicilian sweet and sour eggplant salad, laced with olives and finished off with fresh basil. I find that it brightens up any appetizer spread. I like to roast the eggplant, which makes it lush and smoky and perfect to spoon over toasted bread as a bruschetta.

MAKE THE CAPONATA: First, roast the eggplant. Preheat the oven to 350°F and line a large rimmed baking sheet with parchment paper.

Put the eggplant on the baking sheet and drizzle with 2 tablespoons of the olive oil and the salt, tossing to coat. Eggplant likes to absorb oil, so try to drizzle as thinly as possible to cover as much of the eggplant as possible. Arrange the eggplant in a single layer and spray with olive oil for good measure.

Bake for 40 minutes, tossing every 15 minutes or so and spraying with a little extra olive oil.

In the meantime, prepare everything else. Preheat a large, heavy-bottomed skillet (preferably cast iron) over medium heat. Heat the remaining 1 tablespoon olive oil, then sauté the onion until translucent, about 3 minutes. Add the celery and cook until the onion is lightly browned, about 5 more minutes. Add the garlic and sauté until fragrant, about 30 seconds.

Sprinkle in the brown sugar and cook for a minute or so, tossing to coat and caramelize the onions. Mix in the tomatoes, olives, and a few grinds of black pepper and cook for 10 minutes, mixing often.

Stir in the red wine vinegar and taste for salt (I add salt now instead of at the beginning, because olives release salt as they cook).

Keep the tomato mixture covered and warm until the eggplant is cooked. When the eggplant is ready, toss it into the mixture and mix well.

Transfer the caponata to a bowl and let it cool for at least 30 minutes to allow the flavors to meld. If you're not serving it immediately, refrigerate it in a sealed container. (It tastes even better the next day—just bring it to room temperature before serving.)

MAKE THE BRUSCHETTA: Preheat the oven to 350°F.

Brush both sides of the bread slices with the olive oil and lay them out in a single layer on a rimmed baking sheet. Bake, turning once, until golden and toasty, 10 to 12 minutes.

To serve, spoon a few tablespoons of caponata on each bread slice and top with a bit of the basil chiffonade.

MARINATED POTATOES

with Fresh Dill

SERVES
6

TOTAL
30 MINUTES
(plus marinating time)
ACTIVE
15 MINUTES

1¾ pounds baby potatoes
½ cup red wine vinegar
¼ cup olive oil
4 garlic cloves, minced
½ cup roughly chopped fresh dill
½ teaspoon salt

Tip

Use whole small potatoes here because the skin makes them steam just right. Make sure they are no bigger than a golf ball. They pop a little as you take a bite, releasing all the yummy flavor they've absorbed. Red or yellow potatoes will both work just fine.

This is a really nice make-ahead side, and so much more than plain old potato salad. Baby potatoes are steamed to the exact right tenderness and then bathed in a garlicky vinaigrette—the longer the potatoes marinate, the more flavor they pick up. I like to let them sit overnight.

Get your steamer ready.

Scrub the potatoes and poke a few fork holes in the skins to allow the marinade to be absorbed. Steam the potatoes until just fork-tender, about 15 minutes.

In the meantime, combine the vinegar, oil, garlic, dill, and salt in a zip-top bag.

Remove the potatoes from the steamer and immediately transfer them to the marinade to cool. Once they stop steaming, seal the bag and marinate in the refrigerator overnight. Serve cold or at room temperature.

SAUTÉED
RADISHES
with Garlic & Chives

2 tablespoons olive oil

8 ounces radishes, halved

6 garlic cloves, thinly sliced

2 tablespoons thinly sliced fresh chives

1 tablespoon fresh lemon juice

2 teaspoons grated lemon zest

½ teaspoon salt

Freshly ground black pepper

Radishes have been relegated to a cold salad topping for far too long! They have a spicy, peppery, earthy flavor that really comes out when they're sautéed. Serve with lots of sliced garlic and chives and say hello to your new favorite vegetable.

Preheat a large, heavy-bottomed skillet (preferably cast iron) over medium heat. Heat 1 tablespoon of the oil, then sauté the radishes until lightly browned and tender but still with some snap, about 5 minutes.

Push the radishes aside, add the remaining 1 tablespoon oil, and sauté the garlic until golden. Transfer the radishes to a serving bowl and toss with the chives, lemon juice and zest, salt, and a few grinds of black pepper. Serve!

CUCUMBER CUPS

with *Picnic Tofu Salad*

MAKES
16

TOTAL
30 MINUTES
ACTIVE
30 MINUTES

2 English cucumbers, at least 12 inches long

1 (14-ounce) package extra-firm tofu

¾ teaspoon ground turmeric

1 tablespoon hot water

¼ cup vegan mayo, purchased or homemade (page 203)

2 tablespoons fresh lemon juice

½ teaspoon salt

Freshly ground black pepper

¼ cup chopped fresh dill, plus extra for garnish

¼ cup finely chopped dill pickles

1 small carrot, peeled

There's something so Midwestern about these, it just warms my little-house-on-the-prairie heart. Cucumbers are filled with a dilly, pickly tofu salad, and the result is completely darling. I like to use seedless English cucumbers to fill because they are uniform in shape and really easy to work with.

Cut the cucumbers into approximately 2-inch sections. Using a melon baller or a small spoon, scoop out one end of each section, leaving a ¼-inch-thick rim around the edges and a ½-inch-thick base at the bottom; set aside.

In a medium mixing bowl, mash the tofu well, using your hands or an avocado masher. In a tiny bowl, whisk the turmeric into the hot water to get the color to activate. Add it to the tofu, along with the mayo, lemon juice, salt, and a few grinds of black pepper. Fold in the dill and pickles. Grate the carrot directly into the bowl and stir to combine. Taste and adjust for salt and pepper.

Using a melon baller or small spoon, scoop the tofu mixture into the cucumber cups. Garnish with more black pepper and extra dill and serve.

DEVILISH
POTATOES

1½ pounds small, thin-skinned potatoes, like Yukon Gold (about 10)

1 tablespoon olive oil

Salt

½ cup raw cashews, soaked in water for at least 2 hours and drained

¾ cup vegetable broth, purchased or homemade (page 203), or water

½ teaspoon ground turmeric

2 teaspoons fresh lemon juice

1 teaspoon kala namak black salt or ¾ teaspoon regular salt

Freshly ground black pepper

Sweet paprika, for garnish

Fresh dill sprigs, for garnish

Who doesn't love a tender roasted potato with a creamy, eggy filling? Sprinkled with a little paprika and a sprig of dill, these taste as irresistible as they look. Pop them into one of those vintage egg trays and impress everyone.

Preheat the oven to 350°F. Line a rimmed baking sheet with parchment paper.

Cut the potatoes in half and put them on the baking sheet. Drizzle the potatoes with the olive oil and sprinkle with a pinch of salt. Rub the potatoes to coat, then arrange them cut-side down. Bake until the potatoes are tender, about 30 minutes.

In the meantime, combine the cashews, vegetable broth, and turmeric in a blender. Puree until completely smooth; this can take up to 5 minutes depending on the strength of your machine. Periodically stop the machine to keep it from overheating, and scrape down the sides of the blender jar with a rubber spatula to make sure you get everything.

When the potatoes are tender, remove them from the oven. When cool enough to handle but still warm, scoop out the centers with a melon baller or small teaspoon, leaving about a ¼-inch lining of potato inside.

In a medium mixing bowl, mash the scooped-out potato until smooth. (It's important that they're still warm so that they mash well.) Add the cashew cream mixture, lemon juice, black salt, and a big pinch of black pepper and continue to mash until well incorporated. Chill in the fridge for about 30 minutes so that the mixture stiffens up.

Once cool, scoop the mixture into a pastry bag fitted with a medium serrated tip and fill the potatoes. Sprinkle with paprika and top with a little sprig of dill. Keep chilled until ready to serve, although they are great at room temp, too.

Tips

If you don't actually have a vintage egg tray, cut off just a tiny sliver of potato at the bottom before you stuff them, to prevent wobbling. But a little wobble isn't going to hurt anyone.

Try to find egg-shaped Yukon Gold potatoes that are all as close in size as possible. As you can see from the pic, they aren't going to be totally perfect, but that adds to the cuteness.

If you don't have a pastry bag, you can snip off a ½-inch corner of a plastic bag and pipe the filling that way. Alternatively, just use a rounded tablespoon to scoop it in. But try a pastry bag and pastry tip (I used Wilton #4B)—it's fun!

SHROOM
KABOBS
with Mint Yogurt Sauce

MAKES
10–12
KABOBS

TOTAL
1 HOUR
ACTIVE
30 MINUTES

FOR THE KABOBS:

10 ounces shiitake mushrooms (try to find ones with large, flat caps)

½ cup olive oil

1 tablespoon agave

¼ cup chopped fresh mint

2 tablespoons chopped fresh rosemary

1 teaspoon salt

Freshly ground black pepper

FOR THE MINT YOGURT SAUCE:

1 garlic clove, peeled

¾ cup plain unsweetened coconut yogurt

1 tablespoon fresh lime juice

½ cup finely chopped fresh mint

¼ cup chopped scallion

Tips

If you're using an outdoor gas grill, remember to soak your wooden skewers in water for an hour or so before skewering to prevent them from burning.

If you can't find plain unsweetened coconut milk yogurt, coconut milk makes a nice alternative. It's not as tangy, but it's still wonderful. Add some extra lime juice to up the tang.

These glazed mushroom skewers with their creamy, tangy, minty sauce make for a succulent and meaty entree—obviously far superior to the traditional (sob) rack of lamb. Choose shiitakes with large caps for maximum meatiness.

MAKE THE KABOBS: Have ready a rimmed baking sheet lined with parchment, plus 10 or 12 bamboo skewers.

Remove the stems from the mushrooms. Cut each cap in half so you have two half-moon shapes. Carefully thread three or four half-moons (depending on the size of your mushrooms) onto each skewer at an angle, so that as much mushroom surface as possible can lie on the grill. Place the kabobs on the lined baking sheet.

To make the glaze, in a small bowl, whisk together the olive oil, agave, mint, rosemary, salt, and a few grinds of black pepper. Brush the glaze liberally all over both sides of each kabob. Reserve any leftover glaze. Lightly cover the baking sheet with plastic wrap and allow the kabobs to rest for 15 to 20 minutes. You can make the yogurt sauce while you're waiting.

MAKE THE YOGURT SAUCE: Pulse the garlic in a blender. Add the yogurt and lime juice and puree. Now add the mint and scallion and pulse until well combined, but not totally pureed. The herbs should look like tiny flecks throughout the sauce.

GRILL THE KABOBS: Preheat a stovetop grill pan to medium-high heat. Grill the kabobs until grill marks are present and the mushrooms are soft and have released moisture, 2 to 3 minutes per side. Brush the mushrooms with any leftover glaze while grilling.

Serve the kabobs with the yogurt sauce for spooning on.

WHITE BEAN
And BROCCOLI
QUICHE

2 tablespoons olive oil

3 cups small broccoli florets

¾ teaspoon salt, plus a pinch

1 medium yellow onion, diced medium

2 garlic cloves, minced

1 tablespoon fresh thyme leaves

¼ teaspoon dried tarragon

1 cup raw cashews, soaked in water for at least 2 hours and drained

1 (15-ounce) can navy beans, rinsed and drained, or 1½ cups cooked navy beans

2 tablespoons cornstarch

¼ teaspoon ground nutmeg

Freshly ground black pepper

1 recipe (single) Pastry Crust (page 358)

½ cup halved cherry tomatoes

I don't like to play favorites, but this quiche kills it at potlucks. It's the first thing people reach for at any lunch spread, with its buttery crust, pretty green speckles, and little cherry tomato rim. And it doesn't disappoint! Broccoli is the real star of each bite, set in a soufflé-like base.

Preheat a large skillet over medium-high heat. Heat 1 tablespoon of the olive oil, then sauté the broccoli with a pinch of salt until softened, about 7 minutes.

Transfer the broccoli to a plate to cool a bit. Add the remaining 1 tablespoon olive oil and sauté the onion, garlic, thyme, and tarragon just until the onion is softened, about 3 minutes. Transfer them to the broccoli plate to cool.

Meanwhile, dump the cashews into a food processor fitted with a metal blade. Pulse until they are chopped up. Add the beans, cornstarch, remaining ¾ teaspoon salt, nutmeg, and a few grinds of black pepper and puree until relatively smooth. It will still be a bit grainy, but that's okay—just make sure no big chunks of nuts or beans are left.

When the vegetables have cooled to the touch, add them to the food processor. Pulse a few times, scraping down the sides in between, so that the broccoli is chopped into pea-size pieces or thereabouts, and well distributed. You don't want it pureed completely. Keep the filling mixture refrigerated until ready to use.

Preheat the oven to 350°F. Parbake the pie crust for 10 minutes.

Remove the crust from the oven. Spoon the quiche filling evenly into the crust and smooth out the top. Place the halved cherry tomatoes facedown around the rim of the crust to form a ring.

Bake the quiche until lightly browned and bouncy to the touch, 40 to 45 minutes. Let it cool for about 20 minutes before serving. Serve warm or at room temperature.

Sweet & Smoky
GLAZED
TOFU HAM

FOR THE MARINADE:

¼ cup olive oil

¼ cup tamari or soy sauce

¼ cup pure maple syrup

2 tablespoons liquid smoke

¼ cup packed brown sugar

2 teaspoons garlic powder

2 teaspoons onion powder

1 teaspoon smoked paprika

FOR THE TOFU:

1 (14-ounce) package extra-firm tofu, pressed

8 thin orange slices

20 to 25 whole cloves

FOR THE GLAZE:

½ cup fresh orange juice

2 tablespoons smooth apricot jam

1 tablespoon whiskey

2 tablespoons packed brown sugar

¼ teaspoon ground ginger

¼ teaspoon smoked salt

¼ teaspoon freshly ground black pepper

Are you crazy? Don't put an adorable pig at the center of your table! Put an adorable block of tofu instead! This is a sassy take on ham that will definitely bring smiles (or at least curious side glances) to your guests' faces. It's also, as the title suggests, sweet and smoky and elegant in a '70s kind of way, with notes of orange and maple. It's easy to double, or even triple, the recipe if this will be your main course. (Thank you to my friend Joni Newman for developing this recipe.)

MAKE THE TOFU: In a shallow dish, whisk together all the marinade ingredients. Place the block of tofu in the marinade, turn to coat, and marinate in the refrigerator for at least 4 hours, and up to overnight.

Preheat the oven to 375°F. Line a 9-by-13-inch baking pan with parchment paper.

Arrange the orange slices in an even layer in the center of the parchment. Place the marinated tofu block on the bed of oranges.

Carefully score the top of the tofu block with a sharp knife in a diamond pattern, about ¼ inch deep. Press the whole cloves into the intersections of the cuts (at the corners of the diamonds). Bake for 1 hour.

IN THE MEANTIME, MAKE THE GLAZE: Combine all the glaze ingredients in a small saucepot and bring to a boil over medium-high heat. Reduce the heat to low and simmer until reduced by half and thickened, about 20 minutes. Remove from the heat and set aside.

After the tofu has baked for 1 hour, remove it from the oven and pour the glaze evenly all over the top. Bake for an additional 30 minutes.

Allow the tofu to cool for about 5 minutes before slicing to serve.

SO VEGGIE
PASTITSIO

FOR THE PASTA AND SAUCE:

1 pound bucatini or ziti pasta

2 tablespoons olive oil

1 small onion, finely chopped

1 teaspoon salt, plus a pinch

3 garlic cloves, minced

8 ounces cremini mushrooms, chopped

2 medium zucchini, diced small

1 teaspoon dried thyme

1 teaspoon dried oregano

½ teaspoon ground cinnamon

Freshly ground black pepper

½ cup dry red wine

½ cup nutritional yeast flakes

1 (15-ounce) can lentils, rinsed and drained, or 1½ cups cooked brown or green lentils

1 (28-ounce) can crushed tomatoes with basil

FOR THE PINE NUT CREAM:

1 garlic clove, peeled

½ cup pine nuts

1 (14-ounce) package soft tofu

3 tablespoons fresh lemon juice

1 teaspoon cornstarch

1¼ teaspoons salt

Oh, layery baked casserole goddess of pasta, meaty lentils, veggies, and cream! Pastitsio is sometimes called Greek lasagna, and you'll soon see why. The little hints of cinnamon and red wine, though, make it uniquely pastitsio. The traditional tube-shaped pasta looks so cool and artsy when you cut into it, so have your Instagram at the ready.

MAKE THE PASTA AND SAUCE: Bring a large pot of salted water to a boil over high heat. Cook the pasta according to the package directions, then drain and set aside until ready to use. In the meantime, prepare the sauce.

Preheat a large, heavy-bottomed saucepan over medium heat. Heat 1 tablespoon of the olive oil, then sauté the onion with a pinch of salt until translucent, about 3 minutes. Add the minced garlic and sauté for 30 seconds or so.

Add the mushrooms and zucchini, along with the remaining 1 tablespoon olive oil, thyme, oregano, cinnamon, remaining 1 teaspoon salt, and a few grinds of black pepper. Cook, stirring often, until the veggies are very tender and cooked down, about 10 minutes.

Pour in the red wine and turn the heat up to reduce the wine. This should take about 5 minutes. Once reduced, lower the heat and mix in the nutritional yeast and lentils. Give the mixture a few good mashes with a small avocado masher or fork, just to get some of the lentils mashed to help thicken the sauce. Add the crushed tomatoes and simmer for 10 more minutes.

MAKE THE PINE NUT CREAM: Meanwhile, in a food processor fitted with the metal blade, pulse the garlic to get it chopped up. Add the pine nuts and get those nice and chopped as well. Add the tofu, lemon juice, cornstarch, and salt and puree until thick, creamy, and relatively smooth. Use a rubber spatula to scrape down the sides and make sure you get everything.

ASSEMBLE: Preheat the oven to 400°F and lightly grease a 9-by-13-inch casserole dish.

Add the cooked pasta to the tomato sauce and toss to coat completely. Transfer the pasta and sauce to the prepared casserole, distributing it all evenly. Top with the pine nut cream and smooth it out with a rubber spatula. Bake until the top is lightly browned and a few cracks have formed in the topping, 35 to 40 minutes. Allow to cool for at least 10 minutes before slicing and serving.

CLASSIC
CARROT CAKE

MAKES
1
CAKE

TOTAL
3 HOURS
ACTIVE
30 MINUTES

FOR THE CAKE:

2 cups all-purpose flour

1 tablespoon ground cinnamon

1 teaspoon ground ginger

½ teaspoon ground nutmeg

1 teaspoon baking soda

1 teaspoon baking powder

½ teaspoon salt

¾ cup unsweetened almond milk (or your favorite nondairy milk)

2 tablespoons ground flaxseed

1½ cups granulated sugar

½ cup olive oil

½ cup unsweetened applesauce

2 teaspoons pure vanilla extract

3 cups shredded carrots

1 cup coarsely chopped walnuts

1 cup raisins

FOR THE FROSTING:

3 cups powdered sugar

½ cup refined coconut oil, melted

2 tablespoons fresh lemon juice

2 tablespoons unsweetened almond milk (or your favorite nondairy milk)

½ teaspoon pure vanilla extract

Salt

3 tablespoons shredded coconut or chopped walnuts, for garnish

This is a classic recipe for this beloved dessert, with walnuts, raisins, plenty of spice, and, of course, a generous amount of shredded carrot. Olive oil gives the cake a surprisingly buttery flavor that isn't too heavy. The frosting is thick and lemony and lets all the flavors really shine. This makes a great layer cake, but it's pretty awesome as a sheet cake, too. Just pick your poison!

MAKE THE CAKE: Preheat the oven to 350°F. Lightly grease a 9-by-13-inch baking pan or two 9-inch round baking pans.

Sift the flour, cinnamon, ginger, nutmeg, baking soda, baking powder, and salt into a mixing bowl.

In another large mixing bowl, beat together the milk and flaxseed until smooth. Beat in the sugar, olive oil, applesauce, and vanilla until well combined.

Add the dry ingredients to the wet ingredients and mix until no large lumps remain. Fold in the carrots, walnuts, and raisins.

Pour the batter into the prepared pan(s) and bake until a knife inserted in the middle comes out clean, 40 to 45 minutes for a sheet pan or 32 to 35 minutes for cake pans. Transfer to a cooling rack to cool completely before frosting.

MAKE THE FROSTING: In a medium mixing bowl, blend the powdered sugar, melted oil, juice, milk, vanilla, and a pinch of salt with a hand mixer on low speed until incorporated. Turn the mixer to medium-high speed and continue to blend until smooth. Refrigerate for 30 minutes.

Whip the chilled frosting on medium-high speed until light and fluffy.

FROST THE CAKE: For a sheet cake: Using a spatula or spoon, spread the frosting over the cake. Sprinkle with the coconut or walnuts. Cut into squares and serve.

For a layer cake: Using a spatula or spoon, frost the top of one cake with half of the icing. Place the second cake on top and frost the top with the rest of the icing. Sprinkle with the coconut or walnuts. Cut into wedges and serve.

Glazed
BLUEBERRY *And*
MEYER LEMON
SCONES

TOTAL
1 HOUR 30 MINUTES
ACTIVE
30 MINUTES

FOR THE SCONES:

1¼ cups unsweetened almond milk (or your favorite nondairy milk)

1 tablespoon Meyer lemon juice

3 cups all-purpose flour

½ cup granulated sugar

2 tablespoons baking powder

½ teaspoon salt

½ cup refined coconut oil

1½ teaspoons pure vanilla extract

1 heaping tablespoon grated Meyer lemon zest

2 cups fresh blueberries

FOR THE GLAZE:

2 cups powdered sugar

2 tablespoons Meyer lemon juice

1 tablespoon refined coconut oil, melted

½ teaspoon pure vanilla extract

— *Tip* —

It's fun to do that traditional rounded triangle scone shape. It makes you feel kinda refined, like you've got it all together. Late with your taxes or have a run in your stockings? No problem, not when you've got triangular scones. But if you want to drop 'em instead, use a ¼-cup measure and plop 12 scones onto the baking sheet.

Trust me, I've had many scones, and these are perfect—all bursty with blueberries and glazy with Meyer lemons. They are exactly what you want with tea or at brunch. You can use regular old lemons if you like; the flavor will be a little tarter.

MAKE THE SCONES: Preheat the oven to 375°F. Lightly grease a large rimmed baking sheet.

In a measuring cup, whisk together the milk and lemon juice and set aside to curdle.

Combine the flour, sugar, baking powder, and salt in a large mixing bowl. Add the coconut oil in small clumps, then use your fingers or a pastry cutter to cut it into the flour until the flour texture becomes pebble-like.

Create a well in the center and add the milk mixture, vanilla, and zest. Mix with a wooden spoon until about half of the flour is incorporated. Fold in the blueberries and mix until all the ingredients are just moistened, taking care not to overmix.

Place a piece of parchment on the counter. Divide the dough into two blobs. Shape each blob into a disk, roughly 8 inches in diameter. Using a sharp knife, cut one disk in half. Then cut each of those halves into thirds, so that you have 6 cute triangles. Transfer the triangles to a baking sheet, then repeat with the other blob of dough.

Bake until the tops are lightly browned and firm to the touch, 22 to 26 minutes.

MAKE THE GLAZE: While the scones are baking, sift the powdered sugar into a large bowl. Add the lemon juice, coconut oil, and vanilla and stir vigorously until a thick and smooth but pourable icing forms. If it seems way too thick, add warm water by the teaspoon until the desired texture is achieved.

When the scones are done, transfer them to a cooling rack, allow to cool slightly, and then drizzle with glaze while still warm. Serve immediately, or allow the glaze to set for a few minutes first. If you'd like a thicker, opaque glaze, wait until the scones are cool to drizzle.

9
PASSOVER

I've always relished

THE PASSOVER TABLE.

YOU SIT AROUND asking questions, playing games, and eating matzoh ball soup! What's not to love?

But Passover and veganism can be, well, tricky. Even with a few years of Hebrew school under my belt, I'm still not sure what foods are okay to eat at Passover. It all depends if you're Ashkenazi or Sephardic and a few million other things. So, let's just say that I avoided the big one in this chapter: leavened bread. For all other dishes that may or may not be allowed, check with your rabbi or the internet. Now, on to the fun part!

TEMPEH
SHEPHERD'S PIE
with Whipped Sweet Potatoes

SERVES
8–12

TOTAL
2 HOURS
ACTIVE
45 MINUTES

FOR THE SWEET POTATO LAYER:
3 pounds sweet potatoes, scrubbed

3 tablespoons refined coconut oil

¾ teaspoon salt

¼ teaspoon ground nutmeg

FOR THE FILLING:
2 (8-ounce) packages tempeh

2 cups water

⅓ cup tamari or soy sauce

3 tablespoons plus 1 teaspoon
   refined coconut oil

1 large onion, cut into ½-inch dice

4 garlic cloves, minced

3 tablespoons chopped fresh thyme

½ teaspoon anise seeds

Freshly ground black pepper

1 pound cremini mushrooms,
   roughly chopped

2 cups sliced green beans (1-inch
   pieces)

2 tablespoons cornstarch

2 cups vegetable broth, purchased
   or homemade (page 203)

2 tablespoons tomato paste

¼ cup thinly sliced fresh chives, for
   garnish

Piped sweet potatoes make a stunning presentation that does not disappoint. Underneath that forkful of sweet, creamy heaven is a savory, meaty gravy with just a hint of anise. Baking the potatoes whole in their jackets locks in the sweetness and makes the recipe come together quickly and efficiently. You'll never boil a sweet potato again!

START THE SWEET POTATO LAYER: Preheat the oven to 375°F. Line a rimmed baking sheet with parchment paper. Put the sweet potatoes on the baking sheet and bake until very soft and mushy. This could take up to an hour depending on the size of your sweet potatoes, but check them after 45 minutes.

Let the sweet potatoes cool until they're at a temperature you can handle. They should still be warm but not burning hot.

Cut the sweet potatoes in half lengthwise and peel away the skin (or scoop out the flesh if the skin won't peel easily). Discard the skin and put the potatoes in a large mixing bowl along with the coconut oil, salt, and nutmeg. The mixture should be warm enough to easily melt the coconut oil. Use a hand mixer or immersion blender to whip the mixture until creamy.

PREPARE THE FILLING: In a large saucepan, crumble the tempeh into bite-size pieces. Add the water, tamari, and 1 teaspoon of the oil. Cover the pan and bring the water to a boil over medium-high heat. Let it boil for 10 minutes.

Remove the lid and continue to boil until most of the liquid has evaporated, about 5 more minutes. Drain the tempeh in a colander, give the pan a quick rinse, and return it to the stovetop over medium heat.

Heat the remaining 3 tablespoons oil, then sauté the onion until translucent, about 3 minutes. Add the garlic, thyme, anise seeds, and a few grinds of black pepper and sauté for another minute, just until fragrant. Add the mushrooms and green beans and cook to soften, 3 minutes or so. Stir in the tempeh, raise the heat a bit, and cook until the tempeh is lightly browned, about 10 minutes.

Meanwhile, in a large measuring cup, whisk the cornstarch into the broth until mostly dissolved. Whisk in the tomato paste. When the tempeh is browned, add the cornstarch mixture to the pan and mix well. Let the mixture cook until it is gravy-like and thickened, about 3 minutes. Taste and adjust for salt and seasoning.

ASSEMBLE: Preheat the oven to 375°F. Lightly grease a 9-by-13-inch casserole dish.

Transfer the tempeh mixture to the casserole.

If you're using a pastry bag, fill it with some of the sweet potato mixture. Pipe the sweet potato over the top of the casserole in zigzag layers. You can go widthwise, lengthwise, or diagonal, whichever you prefer. If you aren't using a pastry bag, spoon the filling over the top with a serving spoon, using the back of the spoon to press it into the filling, gently creating hills.

Bake until lightly browned, about 30 minutes. Let cool for 10 or 15 minutes, then garnish with chives and serve.

Roasted RED PEPPER and HAZELNUT DIP

MAKES
2
CUPS

TOTAL
1 HOUR
ACTIVE
15 MINUTES

4 red bell peppers

1 cup hazelnuts

1 tablespoon olive oil, plus more for garnish

½ cup thinly sliced shallot

½ teaspoon salt, plus a pinch

2 garlic cloves, minced

Freshly ground black pepper

1 tablespoon red wine vinegar

1 teaspoon agave

— Tip —

To simplify this recipe, you can forgo roasting the red peppers and just use drained roasted red peppers from a jar.

This is a Passover staple for my family. I like to take credit for everything, but I think my sister Michelle first started the tradition, with a red pepper dip that she makes for everything. This is Passover-friendly, peppery, and nutty. You need a little color on that matzoh!

Preheat the oven to 350°F. Line two rimmed baking sheets with parchment paper.

Place the red peppers on one baking sheet. On the other, spread out the hazelnuts in a single layer. Put both in the oven.

Toast the hazelnuts, shaking the pan once to rotate the nuts, until the skins look crisp and the hazelnuts are golden, 12 to 15 minutes. Leave the peppers in the oven, but remove the hazelnuts and wrap them in a towel for about 5 minutes. This will loosen their skins. Rub the nuts in the towel to remove the skins. If they aren't perfectly peeled, don't worry, just do your best. Set aside.

Turn the oven up to 425°F. Turn the peppers over with tongs and roast for another 20 minutes or so. They're ready when they're blackened and collapsed. Remove them from the oven and immediately transfer them to a paper bag to steam the skin off as they cool. Put the bag in the fridge. Once cool, peel off the skin and remove all the seeds.

Preheat a large skillet over medium-high heat. Heat the oil, then sauté the shallot with a pinch of salt until lightly browned, 5 to 7 minutes. Add the garlic, remaining ½ teaspoon salt, and several grinds of black pepper and sauté for 30 seconds more. Turn off the heat.

Set aside 5 or so hazelnuts for garnish. Pulse the remaining hazelnuts in a food processor until they're ground into a fine powder. Add the roasted red peppers, shallot mixture, red wine vinegar, and agave. Puree until fairly smooth. Taste and adjust for salt, then refrigerate in a tightly sealed container until ready to use.

Transfer the dip to a serving dish and garnish with the reserved hazelnuts, a little olive oil, if desired, and some freshly ground black pepper. Serve!

GINGER-ORANGE
TZIMMES

2½ pounds sweet potatoes, peeled and cut into cubes

1 cup pitted prunes

¼ cup fresh orange juice

2 tablespoons olive oil

2 tablespoons pure maple syrup

2 tablespoons grated fresh ginger

1 tablespoon grated orange zest

½ teaspoon ground cinnamon

½ teaspoon salt

Tzimmes—syrupy sweet potatoes with plump prunes, laced with ginger and orange—always brightens up the Passover plate! And, like most Passover food, it's fun to say, too.

Preheat the oven to 425°F. Lightly grease a large rimmed baking sheet.

Toss all the ingredients together in a large mixing bowl. Transfer to the baking sheet. Cover with aluminum foil and bake for 30 minutes.

Remove the foil, mix everything up, and bake until everything is tender and juicy, another 10 minutes or so. Serve!

ROASTED BEET BORSCHT

3 pounds red beets, trimmed and scrubbed

4 tablespoons olive oil

1 cup thinly sliced shallot

¾ teaspoon salt, plus a pinch

3½ to 4 cups vegetable broth, purchased or homemade (page 203)

3 tablespoons sherry vinegar

So Very Sour Cream (page 368), for garnish

Chopped fresh dill, for garnish

Borscht is beautifully simple and also just plain beautiful. Roasting the beets gives this borscht a naturally sweet, caramelly flavor that needs very little futzing over. A little sour cream, some dill, and you've got yourself an unforgettable bowl of soup. Use beets that are uniform in size so that they cook evenly.

Preheat the oven to 350°F.

Wrap the beets individually in aluminum foil and place them on a rimmed baking sheet. Bake, turning once about halfway through, until they are very easily pierced with a steak knife, about 1 hour. Transfer the beets to a cooling rack until cool enough to handle.

In the meantime, preheat a large pan over medium heat. Heat 2 tablespoons of the olive oil, then sauté the shallot with a pinch of salt until it becomes honey brown, about 10 minutes.

Once the beets are cooled, unwrap the foil, slide off the peels, and put the beets in a blender or food processor. Add the sautéed shallot, remaining 2 tablespoons olive oil, 3½ cups vegetable broth, vinegar, and remaining ¾ teaspoon salt and puree until completely smooth. Use up to ½ cup more vegetable broth if needed to achieve the desired consistency.

Transfer the soup to a 4-quart pot and heat over medium-low heat. When hot, ladle into soup bowls and serve garnished with a dollop of sour cream and a sprinkle of dill.

MAKES
ABOUT
3
CUPS

TOTAL
2 HOURS
ACTIVE
20 MINUTES

CHAROSET

1½ cups shelled walnuts

1½ cups pitted dates

2 Granny Smith apples, peeled

3 tablespoons sweet wine, such as Manischewitz

2 tablespoons pure maple syrup

¾ teaspoon ground cinnamon

Freshly ground black pepper

Ground allspice

Ground ginger

Your first Passover bite will undoubtedly be charoset, so let's make it the best. But first, some real talk: Charoset is not pretty. You can dress it up if you like, but it's ground-up nuts. And apples. And dates. And it's a million shades of brown. And then you spread it on a piece of beige matzoh. And that, my friends, is life. Your charoset is not going on Pinterest. It's going in your mouth. And it represents mortar and sand and the desert and slavery, so appreciate it for its good qualities. I grew up making it by hand, not in the food processor (did the Israelites have food processors?), and so shall you.

In a medium pan, toast the walnuts over medium-low heat until a few shades darker and aromatic, about 5 minutes. Transfer the walnuts to a large cutting board and coarsely chop them until they resemble gravel. Transfer to a mixing bowl.

Chop the dates as finely as possible, wetting your knife occasionally so that the dates don't stick. Transfer to the mixing bowl.

Use a box grater to grate the apples into the mixing bowl. Toss everything together.

Add the wine, maple syrup, cinnamon, a few grinds of black pepper, and a pinch each of allspice and ginger and mix well. Cover tightly with plastic wrap and chill for at least 2 hours and up to overnight before serving.

VEGETABLE BROTH

MAKES

3

QUARTS

TOTAL
2 HOURS
ACTIVE
15 MINUTES

1 tablespoon olive oil

3 medium yellow onions, unpeeled, roughly chopped

1 teaspoon salt

2 large carrots, roughly chopped

2 parsnips, roughly chopped

4 garlic cloves, peeled and smashed with the flat side of a knife

12 celery ribs, roughly chopped

1 loosely packed cup fresh dill

1 loosely packed cup fresh parsley

3 quarts water

There's a time and a place for packaged veggie broth, and there are some really delicious ones out there, but when you really want the love to shine, making your own is so easy, so aromatic, and so fulfilling.

Preheat a very large pot (at least 6 quarts) over medium heat. Add the oil. When the oil is hot, sauté the onions with the salt for 5 minutes. Add the carrots, parsnips, garlic, celery, dill, parsley, and water. Cover and bring to a boil. Reduce the heat and let simmer for 1½ hours, uncovered. It should reduce by about one-quarter.

Remove the pot from the heat and let the broth come to a temperature that isn't too hot to handle. Strain the broth through a cheesecloth-lined colander or strainer into a large bowl. Press the vegetables with a gentle but firm pressure to get all the moisture out.

Transfer the broth to airtight containers and refrigerate until ready to use.

Flaxen
MATZOH BALL
SOUP

**SERVES
6–8**

**TOTAL
3 HOURS
ACTIVE
30 MINUTES**

FOR THE MATZOH BALLS:

1¼ cups matzoh meal (or about 4 sheets matzoh, crumbled)

½ teaspoon salt

½ teaspoon freshly ground black pepper

½ cup vegetable broth, purchased or homemade (page 203)

3 tablespoons olive oil

2 tablespoons ground flaxseed

2 teaspoons potato starch

¼ cup grated peeled carrot

FOR THE SOUP:

6 cups vegetable broth, purchased or homemade (page 203)

⅓ cup thinly sliced peeled carrot

Handful chopped fresh dill, plus more for garnish

Freshly ground black pepper, for garnish

This is the shining star of every Jewish holiday. It doesn't matter what's on the rest of the table—there could be bowls of gold doubloons, but everyone will reach right over them for those matzoh balls! The flavor is very delicate, so definitely make your own broth for this even if you normally use store-bought.

MAKE THE MATZOH BALLS: In a mixing bowl, combine the matzoh meal, salt, and pepper and set aside.

In a blender, whiz together the broth, olive oil, and flaxseed until the mixture is frothy and a little goopy, about 30 seconds. Pulse in the potato starch.

Pour the blender mixture into the matzoh meal mixture and combine until everything is moist. Add the grated carrot and mix until it's well distributed.

Cover the bowl tightly with plastic wrap and refrigerate for at least an hour and up to overnight. You can't skip this step; it's important in making sure that the matzoh balls do not fall apart when boiled.

When you are ready to form the balls, fill a large stockpot with enough water to fit all the matzoh balls with minimal touching. Salt the water generously, cover, and bring to a boil. Once boiling, lower to a simmer.

Have ready a parchment-lined surface to prevent sticking. Also have handy a wet rag to wipe your hands on while you're forming the matzoh balls.

Remove the matzoh mixture from the fridge. Form it into tightly packed, walnut-size balls. When all the balls are prepared, drop them carefully into the slow-rolling boiling water with a spatula or slotted spoon. Cover the pot and simmer for about 20 minutes, checking occasionally to see if the water is still at a slow-rolling boil. If it's too high, they might break; too low, and they will get mushy. They usually rise to the top and then sink when they are ready. Transfer them to the parchment.

MAKE THE SOUP: Pour the broth into a separate pot. Add the sliced carrot and dill. Bring the broth to a low boil over medium heat.

When the broth is hot, use a slotted spoon to carefully remove the matzoh balls from the parchment and place two or three in each bowl. Ladle the broth over the matzoh balls so that they're covered only about halfway. Garnish with some more fresh dill and black pepper and serve.

COCONUT
CREAM PIE
with Bittersweet Ganache

FOR THE CRUST:
1 recipe Matzoh Graham Cracker Crust (facing page)

FOR THE FILLING:
½ cup raw cashews, soaked in water for at least 2 hours and drained

1 (14-ounce) can coconut milk, at room temperature

¾ cup unsweetened almond milk (or your favorite nondairy milk)

⅔ cup sugar

½ teaspoon agar powder

3 tablespoons refined coconut oil

1 teaspoon pure vanilla extract

1 teaspoon coconut extract (optional—another teaspoon of vanilla will work, too)

1½ cups shredded unsweetened coconut

FOR THE BITTERSWEET GANACHE:
¼ cup coconut milk from a well-stirred can

6 ounces bittersweet chocolate

Rich, sweet coconut filling contrasts beautifully with bittersweet ganache. It's like a candy bar in pie form!

BAKE THE CRUST: Preheat the oven to 350°F. Press the crust into a 9-inch pie plate. Bake for 15 minutes, then remove from the oven and set aside.

MAKE THE FILLING: Combine the cashews and coconut milk in a blender. Puree until completely smooth; this can take up to 5 minutes depending on the strength of your machine. Periodically stop the machine to keep it from overheating, and scrape down the sides of the blender jar with a rubber spatula to make sure you get everything.

In the meantime, stir together the almond milk, sugar, and agar powder in a 2-quart saucepot. Bring the mixture to a boil, stirring pretty consistently. Once boiling, lower the heat so that you're just getting small bubbles. Let the mixture cook for about 5 minutes, then add the coconut oil and stir until melted.

With the blender running, stream the hot mixture into the cashew cream until thoroughly blended, then add the extracts and pulse a few times to combine. Stir in the shredded coconut, but don't blend it again, just mix it with a spatula—you want the coconut to remain intact. (It's important that the mixture goes in hot, and is poured into the crust immediately, to prevent it from setting up before it's in the pie.)

Transfer the mixture to the prepared pie crust and refrigerate until set, at least 5 hours. The filling is very thin at first, but that is how it's supposed to be—don't worry, because it will thicken as it sets.

MAKE THE BITTERSWEET GANACHE: Once the pie filling has set, bring the coconut milk to a boil in a small saucepan. Lower the heat, add the chocolate, and let it melt, stirring constantly with a rubber spatula. Remove the pan from the heat and let it sit for 10 minutes or so, then pour the ganache over the pie. Let the pie set in a cool place for about an hour and then serve. If you're not serving it immediately, cover it with plastic wrap and refrigerate.

MATZOH
GRAHAM CRACKER
CRUST

1½ cups matzoh meal (or about
   4 sheets matzoh, crumbled)

⅓ cup brown sugar

¼ teaspoon ground cinnamon

⅛ teaspoon ground nutmeg

⅛ teaspoon salt

¼ cup refined coconut oil, melted

2 to 3 tablespoons water

A little coconut oil, cinnamon, nutmeg, and magic turn matzoh into graham crackers! This is a great Passover-friendly crust for any filled pie that calls for a graham cracker crust, but it's especially lovely with Coconut Cream Pie with Bittersweet Ganache (facing page).

In a large mixing bowl, combine the matzoh meal, brown sugar, cinnamon, nutmeg, and salt. Drizzle in the coconut oil and mix well with your fingertips. Add water by the tablespoon just until the crust holds together.

10
CINCO *de* MAYO

I have a sneaking suspicion that

THIS WILL BE THE MOST

bookmarked section in

THIS COOKBOOK.

EVEN IF YOU don't know what the holiday actually commemorates (a battle that Mexico won over the French, duh, Google it), most people, Mexican or not, use it as a day to celebrate everything we love about Mexico: the fashion, the music, and, most important, the food.

The recipes herein are boldly flavored, colorful, and just plain fun. A trip to the Mexican grocery isn't required for most of them, but there are a few specialty ingredients you might want to grab.

BURRITO
POTATO SALAD

2 pounds baby red potatoes, cut in half (or into 1-inch pieces)

2 ripe avocados

2 tablespoons fresh lime juice

½ teaspoon salt

1 jalapeño, seeded and roughly chopped

1 small red onion, roughly chopped

1 medium tomato, roughly chopped

¼ cup loosely packed fresh cilantro leaves, plus additional for garnish

1 (25-ounce) can black beans, rinsed and drained, or 2 cups cooked black beans

½ cup crushed, lightly salted yellow tortilla chips, for serving

———— *Tips* ————

Because avocado browns so quickly, wait until the last minute to throw together the dressing. If you need to make it ahead, keep it refrigerated until ready to serve—but don't refrigerate it for more than an hour or so.

Once made, to keep the salad as fresh as possible, squeeze additional lime juice over the top and press a piece of plastic wrap directly on top of the salad, then cover the bowl with additional plastic wrap.

Since I'm always putting potatoes in my burritos, I had a dangerous thought: What would happen if I put a burrito in my potato salad? The result is a tangy, hearty, and irresistible mix of black beans and potatoes in a creamy guacamole dressing, with a handful of crushed tortillas over the top.

Put the potatoes in a 4-quart pot and cover them with salted cold water. Cover the pot and bring the water to a boil over medium-high heat. Lower the heat to a simmer and cook until the potatoes are easily pierced with a fork, about 10 more minutes. Drain in a colander and let cool.

Once the potatoes have cooled, prepare the dressing. Cut each avocado in half, remove the pit, and scoop the flesh into a food processor. Add the lime juice and salt and puree until smooth, scraping down the sides with a spatula as needed. Once smooth and creamy, add the jalapeño, onion, tomato, and cilantro. Pulse until they are incorporated but not completely blended. You should still be able to see small chunks of tomato and onion.

Transfer the potatoes to a large mixing bowl and use a spatula to mix in the avocado dressing, tossing to coat the potatoes. Fold in the black beans. When ready to serve, scatter the crushed tortilla chips over the top and add some extra cilantro.

MEXICAN
CAESAR SALAD

FOR THE DRESSING:

½ cup tahini

½ cup water, plus more for thinning

2 tablespoons fresh lime juice

1 tablespoon whole-grain Dijon mustard

1 tablespoon minced garlic

¼ cup nutritional yeast flakes

1 teaspoon ground cumin

1 teaspoon chipotle powder, plus extra for garnish

½ teaspoon salt

FOR THE SALAD:

1 pound romaine lettuce, chopped

1 (25-ounce) can black beans, rinsed and drained, or 2 cups cooked black beans

2 avocados, pitted, peeled, and diced

2 cups blue tortilla chips

½ cup pepitas (shelled pumpkin seeds)

½ cup fresh cilantro leaves, for garnish

Even though Caesar salad was invented in Mexico, making all Caesar salads technically Mexican, this one is even more so. Traditional Caesar, with its tang and creaminess, meets Mexican flavors like cumin and chipotle. At its crunchy romaine heart, this is a simple throw-together salad, but all the flavors and textures make it something really special. If you'd like a warm element in this salad, try some seared or roasted broccoli.

MAKE THE DRESSING: In a small bowl, stir together the dressing ingredients until completely smooth, adding tablespoons of water as needed (see Tip). Taste and adjust for salt and seasoning. It should be slightly salty, because the saltiness will subside when you dress the salad.

MAKE THE SALAD: In a very large mixing bowl, toss the lettuce with the dressing. Once well combined, fold in the beans, avocados, and chips. Some chips may break, but that's okay. Transfer to a large serving bowl and top with the pepitas. Sprinkle with a little extra chipotle powder, if you like spice (but be gentle, because it can quickly get too spicy). Garnish with cilantro and serve.

Tips   *If you use the kind of tahini that is very smooth and liquidy, then the dressing will come together with nothing but a fork to stir it. But if your tahini is thick and more solid, use a blender and additional water as needed.*

Some chipotle powder sprinkled on the top adds great color, but if you aren't already serving lots of tomatoey, salsa-y stuff, some chopped tomatoes would be pretty, too.

SPICY
TOMATO RICE

2 teaspoons cumin seeds

2 tablespoons olive oil

1 small yellow onion, finely chopped

2 jalapeños, seeded and thinly sliced

4 garlic cloves, minced

¾ teaspoon salt, plus a pinch

2 teaspoons coriander seeds, crushed

1½ cups chopped tomato

2 tablespoons tomato paste

1 cup white jasmine rice

½ teaspoon cayenne pepper

1¼ cups water

Without rice, your Cinco de Mayo spread would look empty! This one is bright red and very festive. This is a basic recipe that you can make more or less spicy by adjusting the amount of cayenne or swapping out the jalapeños for something hotter.

Preheat a 2-quart pot over medium heat. Lightly toast the cumin seeds for about 1 minute, just until fragrant. Add the oil, then sauté the onion, jalapeños, and garlic with a pinch of salt until the onion and jalapeños soften, about 5 minutes.

Stir in the crushed coriander seeds. Add the chopped tomato and remaining ¾ teaspoon salt and cook them down until they become saucy, about 5 minutes.

Add the tomato paste and stir to incorporate it and heat through. Add the rice and stir to cover it with all the goodness in the pot, then add the cayenne and water and bring it to a boil. Give it a stir and lower the heat as low as it can go. Cover and cook until the water is completely absorbed, about 20 minutes. Serve.

TOMATILLO POSOLE

with Pintos & Avocado

2 tablespoons olive oil

1 large yellow onion, diced small

2 jalapeños, seeded and thinly sliced

2 poblano peppers, seeded and diced medium

1 teaspoon salt, plus a pinch

4 garlic cloves, minced

2 teaspoons ground cumin

1 teaspoon dried oregano

1½ cups dry white wine

1½ pounds tomatillos, husked, rinsed, and roughly chopped

3 cups vegetable broth, purchased or homemade (page 203)

½ cup loosely packed fresh cilantro

¼ cup chopped scallions

1 to 2 teaspoons sugar (optional)

1 (25-ounce) can pinto beans, rinsed and drained, or 2 cups cooked pinto beans

1 (30-ounce) can hominy, drained

1 tablespoon fresh lime juice

FOR THE GARNISH:

So Very Sour Cream (page 368) (optional)

2 avocados, pitted, peeled, and sliced

½ cup thinly sliced radish

¼ cup pepitas (shelled pumpkin seeds)

I like to think of posole as Mexican matzoh ball soup. With fluffy hominy and brothy slurpiness, it's comfort food at its best. And just as with matzoh ball soup, every family has a recipe they swear by. This version is tart from the tomatillos, with just the right amount of peppery spice from the jalapeños and poblanos. And the pinto beans make it a filling dish that can stand on its own for a weeknight dinner if you feel so inclined. Garnish with avocados for creaminess and pepitas for a little crunch, and you've got Cinco de Mayo all in one pot.

Preheat a 4-quart pot over medium-high heat. Heat the oil, then sauté the onion, jalapeños, and poblanos with a pinch of salt until everything is softened and the onion is browned, about 10 minutes.

Add the garlic, cumin, and oregano. Sauté until the garlic is fragrant, about 1 minute. Add the white wine, tomatillos, and remaining 1 teaspoon salt and raise the heat a bit to let the wine reduce and the tomatillos release their juices, about 5 minutes.

Add the vegetable broth, cilantro, and scallions. Lower the heat to a simmer, cover, and cook for 20 more minutes.

Use an immersion blender to partially puree everything (or transfer the soup to a food processor in batches and puree, then return to the pot).

Taste for tartness: If it's bitter, add a teaspoon or two of sugar to level things out. Add the beans and hominy and simmer for a few more minutes until everything is heated through. Stir in the lime juice.

Ladle the posole into bowls, garnish with the sour cream (if using), avocados, radish, and pepitas, and serve.

BROILED
CORN
with Coconut & Lime

¼ cup refined coconut oil, melted

1 tablespoon grated lime zest

1 teaspoon salt

½ teaspoon crushed red pepper flakes

8 ears corn, husked and cut in half

Charred corn is a great treat on its own. Now imagine making it extra special with buttery coconut oil, lots of fresh lime zest, and a little heat from red pepper flakes. Okay, are you drooling? It's just as wonderful as you think it would be. I like to chop the ears of corn in half because they look really cute and are a bit easier to eat, but you can leave them whole if you prefer.

Place an oven rack about 6 inches from the broiler element and turn on the broiler. Lightly grease a rimmed baking sheet.

In a small bowl, mix the melted coconut oil, lime zest, salt, and red pepper flakes.

Place the corn on the baking sheet. Drizzle with the coconut oil mixture and use your hands to rub the corn all over, making sure to coat it completely.

Broil the corn, keeping a close eye on it and turning it with tongs as it chars. This could take 6 to 10 minutes total, depending on the heat of your broiler.

Transfer to a serving tray and serve hot!

Spicy PINTO-SEITAN CUTLETS

MAKES
4
CUTLETS

TOTAL
50 MINUTES
ACTIVE
10 MINUTES

1 cup cooked or canned pinto beans, rinsed and drained

1 cup vegetable broth, purchased or homemade (page 203)

3 tablespoons tamari or soy sauce

1 tablespoon olive oil

1 tablespoon tomato paste

⅓ cup nutritional yeast flakes

1 tablespoon mild chili powder

1 teaspoon dried oregano

1 teaspoon ground cumin

¼ teaspoon salt

1½ cups vital wheat gluten

These cutlets are a breeze to put together. Because they're so assertively flavored, there's no need to add any other seasonings when you use them in a recipe. They're perfect for slicing up for a taco filling (as in the Seitan de Mayo Carnitas, page 221), dicing up in a chili, or even just sautéing for a taco salad.

Before mixing the ingredients, get your steamer ready, bringing the water to a full boil. The rest of the recipe comes together very quickly.

Have ready four large square sheets of aluminum foil. In a large bowl, mash the pinto beans well, until no whole ones are left. Add the broth, tamari, olive oil, tomato paste, nutritional yeast, chili powder, oregano, cumin, and salt. Mix well with a fork, then add the vital wheat gluten. Mix for a bit until it becomes too stiff to mix with a fork, and then lightly knead it with your hands.

Divide the dough in half and then in half again to make four equal pieces. Form each piece into a patty that is about 6 inches wide. Place each patty in the center of a foil square and fold the foil into a parcel. Don't wrap it too tightly— leave a little bit of room inside because the seitan will expand as it cooks.

Place the wrapped patties in the steamer and steam for 40 minutes. That's it! You can unwrap and enjoy immediately or refrigerate until ready to use.

SUPER-CLASSIC GUACAMOLE

MAKES ABOUT **4** CUPS

TOTAL 15 MINUTES
ACTIVE 15 MINUTES

4 ripe avocados

½ teaspoon salt

2 tablespoons fresh lime juice

¼ cup minced white onion

¼ cup diced tomato

1 tablespoon seeded minced jalapeño

2 tablespoons chopped fresh cilantro

Guac is all about the avocados. So long as you use perfectly ripe ones—not toooo green and not at all brown—then you really can't go wrong. Well, actually, you can: Finding the right balance is key! Just enough lime, onion, salt, and spice to bring out the creamy rich flavor, but not so much to cover it up. I love to add a little bit of tomato for body, too. This recipe is a good place to start, but it's definitely a season, taste, adjust thing, so find your perfect guac balance!

Cut the avocados in half lengthwise and remove the pits. Scoop the avocado stuff into a mixing bowl. Sprinkle in the salt and lime juice. Use an avocado masher or strong fork to give it a good mash. Add the remaining ingredients and mash like crazy, until the guacamole is creamy and the tomato has broken up. Taste and adjust the flavors if needed. Serve immediately (see Tip).

Tip *If you can, make the guacamole as close to serving time as possible. If that's not doable, toss in the avocado pits, sprinkle some additional lime juice over the top, and place plastic wrap directly on the surface of the guac before refrigerating. This will help prevent browning.*

SALSA FRESCA

MAKES ABOUT **4** CUPS

TOTAL 60 MINUTES
ACTIVE 10 MINUTES

4 cups small-diced tomatoes

1 cup small-diced red onion

¼ cup fresh lime juice

½ cup finely chopped fresh cilantro

3 tablespoons minced seeded jalapeño

½ teaspoon salt

Several pinches freshly ground black pepper

Choose the ripest, reddest, most beautifulest tomatoes that you can find, and your salsa fresca will be a hit every time.

Simply toss everything in a bowl and let marinate for an hour or so. Keep refrigerated in a sealed container until ready to use.

MUSHROOM-SPINACH
QUESADILLAS

FOR THE CHEESE:

1½ cups raw cashews, soaked in water for at least 2 hours and drained

½ cup water

¼ cup refined coconut oil, melted

¼ cup canned chipotles in adobo sauce, seeded (see Tip, page 61)

2 tablespoons mellow white miso

1 tablespoon fresh lemon juice

2 tablespoons nutritional yeast flakes

2 teaspoons onion powder

1 teaspoon ground turmeric

1 teaspoon salt

FOR THE MUSHROOMS AND SPINACH:

2 tablespoons olive oil

3 garlic cloves, minced

8 ounces cremini mushrooms, thinly sliced

¼ teaspoon salt

¼ cup chopped fresh cilantro

4 cups baby spinach

FOR THE ASSEMBLY:

8 (8-inch) flour tortillas

1 recipe Salsa Fresca (page 217)

1 recipe Super-Classic Guacamole (page 217) or diced avocado (optional)

A melty, smoky, spicy cheese spread mingles with garlicky mushrooms and spinach in these quesadillas. Not to be cheesy, but these are a fiesta in your mouth. I think they taste best (and also look super cool) when grilled, but if you don't have a grill pan, just cook them in a large skillet.

MAKE THE CHEESE: Combine all the cashew cheese ingredients in a blender. Puree until completely smooth; this can take up to 5 minutes depending on the strength of your machine. Periodically stop the machine to keep it from overheating, and scrape down the sides of the blender jar with a rubber spatula to make sure you get everything.

Transfer to a tightly sealed container and let set for at least 3 hours or overnight.

MAKE THE MUSHROOMS AND SPINACH: Preheat a large skillet over medium heat. Heat the oil, then sauté the garlic for about 1 minute, being careful not to let it burn. Add the mushrooms and sprinkle in the salt, then toss to coat the mushrooms in the oil and garlic. Cook, stirring occasionally, until the mushrooms have released their moisture and are lightly browned, 5 to 7 minutes.

Stir in the cilantro. Add the spinach and toss it with all the ingredients. Turn off the heat and allow the spinach to wilt, giving it a stir every few minutes. Once the spinach is wilted, transfer the mixture to a bowl. If there is any extra liquid in the pan, just leave it there or it will make your quesadillas soggy.

ASSEMBLE: Lightly oil a grill pan and preheat it over medium heat.

Lay out two tortillas and spread a few tablespoons of the cheese on each, keeping it about ¼ inch away from the edges.

Spoon about ⅓ cup of the mushroom and spinach stuff on top of one of the quesadillas, then place the other one on it, cheese-side down.

Cook until grill marks appear and the cheese spread is melty, about 3 minutes per side. Repeat to make the other three quesadillas.

Use a pizza cutter to cut each quesadilla into halves or quarters. Top with salsa and guac, if using, and serve.

 Tip

Even if you have a high-speed blender, like a Vitamix, it's still necessary to soak the cashews so that they're soft enough to blend without much added liquid.

Seitan
DE MAYO
CARNITAS

2 tablespoons olive oil

1 medium red onion, cut into thin half-moons

2 jalapeños, seeded and cut into long strips

Salt

2 Spicy Pinto-Seitan Cutlets (page 216), shredded or cut into thin strips (see Tip)

2 garlic cloves, minced

2 medium tomatoes, cut into ¼-inch-thick half-moons

¼ cup roughly chopped fresh cilantro

8 (8-inch) flour or corn tortillas, warmed

These are flavors no one ever tires of: spicy, garlicky, meaty deliciousness. Carnitas are, essentially, shredded meat tacos. Here, spicy pinto-seitan cutlets are thinly sliced and tossed with simple, fresh flavors. Serve this alongside the Burrito Potato Salad (page 210) or just with some rice and lots of guacamole.

Preheat a large pan over medium-high heat. Heat 1 tablespoon of the oil, then sauté the onion and jalapeños with a pinch of salt just until slightly softened, about 3 minutes.

Add the sliced seitan, plus 2 more teaspoons oil, and sauté until lightly browned, about 5 minutes. Now push everything aside to clear a little space in the pan and add the garlic, drizzling it with the remaining 1 teaspoon olive oil. Sauté just until fragrant, 15 seconds or so, and mix it in with everything else.

Now add the tomatoes and cilantro and cook for about 5 more minutes. The tomatoes should break down a bit and everything should appear juicy.

Taste and adjust for salt and serve with the warmed tortillas.

Tip   *Here's a great way to get the sliced seitan to appear shredded: Cut the cutlets in half, so that you have two wide, flat pieces. Place the flat side on the cutting board and, with a chef's knife, "carve" the seitan on a bias. Make the slices about ⅛ inch thick, and it's okay (even preferable) if the slices aren't completely uniform. Sloppy slices will give the seitan a more organic feel. Don't worry if you don't get this method totally right the first time—practice makes perfect! No one becomes a vegan butcher overnight.*

ALMOND CHURRO BISCOTTI

MAKES
18
BISCOTTI

TOTAL
3 HOURS
ACTIVE
20 MINUTES

FOR THE BISCOTTI:

⅓ cup unsweetened almond milk (or your favorite nondairy milk)

2 tablespoons ground flaxseed

¾ cup granulated sugar

½ cup canola oil

1 teaspoon pure vanilla extract

¼ teaspoon pure almond extract

1⅔ cups all-purpose flour

2 tablespoons cornstarch

2 teaspoons baking powder

½ teaspoon salt

½ teaspoon ground cinnamon

⅛ teaspoon ground allspice

¾ cup slivered almonds

All the fun of a churro, now in biscotti form! They've got great snap and crunch and the spicy fun flavor of cinnamon sugar—just right for café con leche or a few shots of espresso. These are a bit easier to serve than a churro because they keep well and you don't have to break out the deep fryer. One especially nice variation is to use only ½ cup almonds and add ½ cup white chocolate chips.

MAKE THE BISCOTTI: Preheat the oven to 350°F. Line a rimmed baking sheet with parchment paper.

In a large mixing bowl, vigorously whisk together the almond milk and flaxseed until a bit frothy, about 1 minute. Mix in the sugar, oil, and extracts. Sift in the flour, cornstarch, baking powder, salt, cinnamon, and allspice. Stir to combine, and just before the dough comes together, knead in the slivered almonds. Knead to form a stiff dough.

On the parchment, form the dough into a log and press it into a rectangle about 12 inches long and 4 inches wide. Bake until lightly puffed and browned, 26 to 28 minutes. Let the log cool on the baking sheet for about 30 minutes.

Once cool, preheat the oven to 325°F. Carefully transfer the baked log to a cutting board. With a heavy, very sharp knife, cut the log crosswise into ½-inch slices. The best way to do this is in one motion, pushing down—don't "saw" the slices off or they could crumble. Place the slices, curved-sides up, ½ inch apart on the baking sheet, and bake until the biscotti appear dry and toasted, 20 to 25 minutes. Transfer to a cooling rack to cool completely.

FOR THE GLAZE:

2 cups powdered sugar

2 tablespoons unsweetened almond milk (or your favorite nondairy milk)

1 tablespoon refined coconut oil, melted

½ teaspoon pure vanilla extract

FOR SPRINKLING:

¼ cup granulated sugar

1 tablespoon ground cinnamon

MAKE THE GLAZE: Sift the powdered sugar into a large bowl. Add the milk, coconut oil, and vanilla and stir vigorously until a thick and smooth but pourable icing forms. If it seems way too thick, add warm water by the teaspoon until the desired texture is achieved.

In a separate little bowl, mix the sugar and cinnamon for sprinkling.

Place the cooling rack in or over a sink, or somewhere that can get really messy. Push all the biscotti side by side so that they're touching. Take a large spoon and drizzle the glaze over the biscotti, covering as much of the tops as possible. Let the excess glaze drip into the sink. While the glaze is still wet, sprinkle the cinnamon sugar over the top.

Remove the rack from the sink and put it in a cool place to let the frosting set. Store the biscotti in a single layer in a sealed container in the refrigerator if not serving immediately.

SPICY CHOCOLATE CUPCAKES

with Hot Candied Pecans

MAKES
12
CUPCAKES

TOTAL
2 HOURS
ACTIVE
30 MINUTES

FOR THE CUPCAKES:

1 cup unsweetened almond milk (or your favorite nondairy milk)

1 teaspoon apple cider vinegar

¾ cup sugar

⅓ cup canola oil

1½ teaspoons pure vanilla extract

1 teaspoon grated orange zest

1 cup all-purpose flour

⅓ cup unsweetened cocoa powder

¾ teaspoon baking soda

½ teaspoon baking powder

¼ teaspoon salt

¼ teaspoon cayenne

FOR THE PECANS:

½ cup pecan pieces

1 teaspoon refined coconut oil

2 tablespoons pure maple syrup or agave

1 tablespoon sugar

¼ teaspoon salt

⅛ teaspoon cayenne pepper

FOR THE CHOCOLATE GLAZE:

⅔ cup unsweetened almond milk (or your favorite nondairy milk)

4 ounces bittersweet chocolate, finely chopped

1 tablespoon pure maple syrup or agave

A little cayenne kicks these moist, rich chocolate cupcakes up into the unforgettable category. Then they're glazed with more chocolate and topped with sweet, salty pecans that have more cayenne. I made these just a little spicy so as not to scare off anyone who absolutely can't handle heat, but if you're looking to really do some damage, you can double the cayenne in both the cake and the pecans.

MAKE THE CUPCAKES: Preheat the oven to 350°F. Line a standard-size muffin tin with paper or foil cupcake liners.

In a large bowl, whisk together the milk and vinegar and set aside for a few minutes to curdle.

Add the sugar, oil, and vanilla extract to the milk mixture and mix vigorously until foamy. Mix in the orange zest. Sift in the flour, cocoa powder, baking soda, baking powder, salt, and cayenne. Mix until no large clumps of flour are left.

Fill the lined muffin cups three-quarters of the way. Bake until a toothpick inserted into the center comes out clean, 18 to 20 minutes. Transfer to a cooling rack and let cool completely.

MAKE THE PECANS: Have ready a plate lined with parchment. Preheat a small pan over medium heat. Toast the pecans for 2 minutes. Add the coconut oil and toss to coat. Stir in the maple syrup, sugar, salt, and cayenne and cook until bubbly, about 2 minutes. Spread the coated pecans out on the parchment and let cool.

MAKE THE CHOCOLATE GLAZE: In a small pan, bring the milk to a boil over medium heat. Turn off the heat and use a rubber spatula to stir in the chocolate and maple syrup, until smooth. Let cool for about 15 minutes.

ASSEMBLE: Break the pecans apart into smaller pieces. Spoon the glaze onto the cupcakes. Top with the pecans. Set aside in a cool place to let the chocolate set before serving.

11

MOTHER'S *and* FATHER'S DAYS

At first, this section had been
TWO SEPARATE CHAPTERS
for Mother's Day and
FATHER'S DAY.

BUT THEN I decided, why be so gender normative? Who knows, maybe your mom loves Japanese food and your dad loves quiche? Maybe you have two dads who both love French toast? Maybe you were raised by an Italian grandma whom you simply must introduce to vegan Alfredo?

The point of these holidays is to show appreciation for whoever is responsible for how awesome you turned out. Brunch is well represented, or you can go all out with a full dinner menu. But definitely make the effort to put a smile on someone's face on these special days!

MAKES
6
PANCAKES

TOTAL
30 MINUTES
ACTIVE
30 MINUTES

Blueberry
BUCKWHEAT PANCAKES

¾ cup all-purpose flour

½ cup buckwheat flour

2 tablespoons sugar

2 teaspoons baking powder

¾ teaspoon salt

1 cup unsweetened almond milk (or your favorite nondairy milk)

1 teaspoon apple cider vinegar

1 tablespoon ground flaxseed

½ cup water

1 tablespoon canola oil, plus more for the pan

1 teaspoon pure vanilla extract

1 cup blueberries

Tip

After years of just dealing with it, I've stopped making pancakes with frozen blueberries. It makes them cook unevenly! And of course it does: They're frozen, completely changing the temperature of the pancakes. So, if frozen is all I've got, I let them thaw first and then drain them.

I love the sultry flavor of buckwheat flour. Here, it's mixed with regular flour to produce a fluffy pancake, with its wholesome flavor providing the perfect backdrop for juicy berries.

In a large mixing bowl, sift together the flours, sugar, baking powder, and salt. Make a well in the center.

Measure the milk into a 2-cup or larger measuring cup. Add the vinegar and ground flaxseed and use a fork to vigorously mix the ingredients until foamy. This will take a minute or so.

Pour the milk mixture into the center of the dry ingredients. Add the water, canola oil, and vanilla and use a fork to mix just until all the dry ingredients are moist. It doesn't need to be smooth, as long as you make sure to get all the ingredients incorporated.

Preheat a large nonstick pan (I use cast iron) over medium-low heat as you let the batter rest for 10 minutes.

After the batter has rested, fold the blueberries into the batter. Lightly coat the pan in oil. Add ⅓ cup of batter for each pancake, and cook for about 4 minutes, until bubbly in the middle and dry around the edges. Flip the pancakes, adding a new coat of oil to the pan, and cook for another 3 minutes or so.

Rest the pancakes on a cooling rack tented with aluminum foil until ready to serve. To reheat leftovers, put the pancakes on a rimmed baking sheet, cover with foil, and bake in a 300°F oven for 5 minutes or so.

QUICHE
LORRAIN'T

2 tablespoons olive oil

3 medium sweet onions, like Vidalia or Walla Walla, thinly sliced

1 teaspoon salt, plus a pinch

1 recipe (single) Pastry Crust (page 358)

¾ cup raw cashews (no need to soak!)

¼ teaspoon ground nutmeg

1 (14-ounce) package extra-firm tofu

1 tablespoon mellow white miso

1 to 2 tablespoons water (optional)

1 recipe shiitake bacon (page 145)

Thinly sliced fresh chives, for garnish

The basics of quiche Lorraine are bacon, Swiss cheese, and caramelized onion. This one ain't! (I mean, besides the onion, smarty-pants.) For the bacon, we turn to another quiche favorite: mushrooms, this time in the form of smoky shiitake bacon. For the pungent Swiss cheese flavor, a little mellow white miso does the trick. A flaky pie crust never hurt, either. The result will be smoky, salty, creamy, and just downright eggy enough to satisfy any brunch craving.

Preheat a heavy-bottomed skillet (preferably cast iron) over low heat. Heat the oil, then add the onions, along with a pinch of salt, and toss to coat. Cover the skillet, leaving a little gap for steam to escape. Cook, stirring every 5 minutes or so, until the onions turn a nice, mellow amber color, about 20 minutes. Don't let the onions burn, but a couple of darker spots are fine.

Remove the lid and turn up the heat to medium. Keep cooking, stirring often, for another 10 minutes. The onions should become darker, and some of the moisture should evaporate.

Preheat the oven to 350°F. Press the pastry crust into a 9-inch pie plate and set aside.

In a food processor fitted with the metal blade, pulse the cashews into fine crumbs. Add the remaining 1 teaspoon salt and the nutmeg. Crumble the tofu into the food processor, along with the miso, and blend until relatively smooth. If it seems too thick and is not pureeing, add a tablespoon or two of water. Add ½ cup of the caramelized onions to the food processor and pulse a few times to combine.

Transfer the cashew mixture to a large mixing bowl and stir in the rest of the caramelized onions, as well as the shiitake bacon. Taste and adjust for salt. Use a rubber spatula to get everything into the pie crust and smooth out the top. Bake until the edges of the quiche are lightly browned, about 40 minutes.

I suggest letting the quiche sit for 20 minutes before you dig in. It tastes best when it is moderately warm, not piping hot. It's also great at room temperature. Garnish with chives to serve.

TAHINI MOM SALAD

FOR THE DRESSING:

½ cup tahini

½ cup water

⅓ cup fresh lemon juice

2 tablespoons olive oil

2 teaspoons grated garlic (see Tip)

½ teaspoon salt

FOR THE SALAD:

1 pound crisp greens (red romaine and butter lettuce are good choices)

1 cup halved cherry tomatoes

1 cup thinly sliced cucumbers

2 cups sunflower sprouts

Freshly ground black pepper

Lemon wedges, for garnish

Tip

If you don't have a Microplane grater for the garlic, then mince it as finely as possible, until it's almost a paste. If you're worried you don't have the skills for that, then drop all the dressing ingredients in a blender and whiz away!

In the '90s, I waitressed at about 87 percent of the vegan restaurants that existed in New York City. And in that time, I believe I served about 87 percent of the mothers in this country. Each and every one of them ordered a salad just like this: baby greens, sprouts, tomato, cucumber, and tahini dressing. Those are the facts. Here's another one: This is a great, all-purpose, easy-as-tahini side-type salad when you want a lot of punch but don't want to spend a lot of time because you have a million other things to do. The dressing goes well on sautéed greens or broccoli, too. It's perfect next to the Quiche Lorrain't (facing page).

MAKE THE DRESSING: Stir together the dressing ingredients in a small bowl or a coffee mug. Use a fork to blend it smooth. Mix in additional tablespoons of water to thin the dressing, if needed. Taste and adjust for salt and seasoning. It should be slightly salty, because the saltiness will subside when you dress the salad.

MAKE THE SALAD: In a gigantic mixing bowl, toss together the greens, tomatoes, and cucumbers. Add the dressing and use tongs to coat. Transfer to a serving bowl or individual plates, top with the sprouts, and grind on plenty of black pepper. Serve with lemon wedges.

SEITAN NEGIMAKI

MAKES
16
ROLLS

TOTAL
3 HOURS
ACTIVE
40 MINUTES

⅓ cup hoisin sauce

¼ cup mirin

3 tablespoons water

2 teaspoons sriracha, plus extra for optional garnish

1 teaspoon toasted sesame oil

1 teaspoon grated fresh ginger

1 recipe Chickee-Style Seitan (page 18) or 2 pounds store-bought equivalent

2 bunches scallions, green parts only, cut into 3- to 4-inch pieces

A few tablespoons toasted sesame seeds

--------- *Tip* ---------

If you're cooking these on an outdoor grill, soak the toothpicks in water for at least 15 minutes beforehand so that they don't burn too badly.

Beautifully grilled teriyaki rolls stuffed with vibrant scallions—swoon! The characteristics that I wanted to really shine were the charred grilled flavor and, of course, the scallions. The simple marinade of hoisin and mirin really does its job, keeping things juicy with the perfect marriage of sweet and savory. This recipe makes more seitan than you'll need, but that's okay—any leftover seitan will be great in a stir-fry. It may take a couple of tries before you get the strips perfectly thin for wrapping.

In a large mixing bowl, whisk together the hoisin, mirin, water, sriracha, sesame oil, and ginger.

Cut the seitan into long strips about ⅛ inch thick. Don't worry about making them perfectly even. Just make sure that each slice can wrap around your pinky nicely, without breaking or being unruly. Once you have 16 slices, put them in the bowl with the marinade for an hour, flipping occasionally.

After an hour, move all the seitan to one side of the marinade bowl and add the scallion pieces, coating them in the marinade. Your bowl should now be one side seitan and one side scallion, more or less.

Form the rolls on a large dinner plate, to avoid messiness. Place one slice of marinated seitan on the plate. Lay 4 or 5 scallions across, so that the scallions will poke out of the ends by an inch or so. Now roll the seitan around the scallions and secure it with a toothpick or two. Make sure that the toothpicks are going in the same direction, parallel to each other, so that you'll be able to grill them without toothpick interference.

Once all the rolls are formed, heat an outdoor grill or stovetop grill pan over medium heat. In an average-size grill pan, you will have to cook the rolls in two batches. Spray or brush the grill with oil and cook the rolls until grill marks appear on one side, about 4 minutes. Use a thin metal spatula to get under the rolls and flip them, spraying with more oil as necessary. Cook on the other side until grill marks appear, another 4 minutes.

Transfer the rolls to a serving plate. When ready to serve, drizzle with any leftover marinade and some more sriracha if you like it spicy (it's okay to leave it off) and sprinkle with toasted sesame seeds. Serve!

PAN BAGNAT

2 (15-ounce) cans chickpeas, rinsed and drained, or 3 cups cooked chickpeas

½ cup vegan mayo, purchased or homemade (page 67), plus more for serving

1 tablespoon whole-grain Dijon mustard

1 tablespoon red wine vinegar, plus more for serving

½ cup halved kalamata olives

⅓ cup very finely chopped yellow onion

3 tablespoons capers with brine

Salt

Freshly ground pepper

8 kaiser rolls, cut in half, for serving

Baby greens, for serving

Sliced tomatoes, for serving

This is a Provençal recipe meaning "bathed bread." Yeah, I'm in. Traditionally, it's made with tuna, so I turned on the old vegan magic and used mashed chickpeas instead. In this case, the bread is bathed in homemade mayo and a drizzle of red wine vinegar and studded with olives and capers, making for a briny, creamy, tangy sandwich. Make sure you have plenty of towels around as you eat it, because it might give your hands a bath, too. This is the perfect picnic sandwich, so if you're spending the day at a botanical garden or strolling through the park, wrap a few in parchment and snuggle them in some Tupperware.

In a large mixing bowl, use an avocado masher or a strong fork to mash the chickpeas well. They should retain some of their texture and not appear pureed. A few whole ones left are okay.

Mix in the mayo, mustard, and vinegar and give it a few more mashes. Mix in the olives, onion, and capers. Add salt and pepper to taste.

To assemble the sandwiches, drizzle both sides of each roll with a teaspoon or so of red wine vinegar. Slather on the mayo. Top with a heaping scoop of chickpea salad, and then the greens and tomatoes. Close the sandwich and enjoy.

TRUFFLED
ALMOND ALFREDO
with *Really Garlicky Broccoli*

FOR THE ALFREDO:

1 cup slivered almonds

1¼ cups vegetable broth, purchased or homemade (page 203)

2 tablespoons black truffle oil

1 tablespoon fresh lemon juice

¼ cup nutritional yeast flakes

½ teaspoon salt

Freshly ground black pepper

8 ounces linguine

FOR THE BROCCOLI:

1 tablespoon plus 1 teaspoon olive oil

6 cups broccoli florets and thinly sliced stems

Salt

6 garlic cloves, minced

2 tablespoons chopped fresh parsley

Tips

Slivered almonds are great here because their skins are already removed, which makes the sauce smoother and keeps it looking creamy and pristine.

Truffle oil gives this pasta an allure that screams "Fancy day!" even if it's just you on the couch binge-watching Orange Is the New Black. *It's a fun ingredient to have around, and, although it's a little pricey, it ain't nothing compared to the cost of an actual truffle.*

This Alfredo is deceptively simple but totally creamy, with a hint of nuttiness. The almonds act a little bit differently than cashews do in similar creamy applications, because they retain some of their texture. I love that quality for this recipe because it reminds me of hard cheese, which is a must for Alfredo. Combined with a li'l lemon and nooch, this gets the job done!

For an all-out Italian feast, I love to start with Arancini with Almond Cheese (page 111) and serve the Alfredo with really *really* REALLY garlicky broccoli. The secret to getting it good and garlicky is adding the garlic at the end. That way the garlic doesn't burn, but you can take your time getting the broccoli cooked just right.

MAKE THE ALFREDO: In a blender, combine the almonds, broth, truffle oil, lemon juice, nutritional yeast, salt, and a few grinds of black pepper. Puree until relatively smooth; this can take up to 5 minutes depending on the strength of your machine. Periodically stop the machine to keep it from overheating, and scrape down the sides of the blender jar with a rubber spatula to make sure you get everything. Keep refrigerated in a tightly sealed container until ready to use.

Bring a large pot of salted water to a boil over high heat. Cook the linguine according to the package directions.

MAKE THE BROCCOLI: In the meantime, preheat a large, heavy-bottomed pan (preferably cast iron) over medium heat. Heat 1 tablespoon of the oil, then sauté the broccoli with a big pinch of salt, tossing often, until it is bright green, 5 to 7 minutes. Add a few splashes of water if it seems dry.

Now push the broccoli to one side of the pan and add the garlic. Immediately drizzle the remaining 1 teaspoon olive oil over the garlic and toss to coat, then integrate the garlic with the broccoli and cook for another minute.

ASSEMBLE: Drain the pasta and immediately return it to the pot you boiled it in. Add the sauce and parsley and toss to coat. Taste and adjust for salt and seasoning. Serve with the broccoli!

BOUILLABAISSE

with Roasted Yellow Squash & Chickpeas

SERVES
6–8

TOTAL
30 MINUTES
ACTIVE
30 MINUTES

FOR THE SQUASH:

2 average-size yellow squash, cut into ¼-inch-thick half-moons

Olive oil, for drizzling

Salt, for sprinkling

FOR THE STEW:

1 tablespoon olive oil

2 cups finely sliced fennel bulb (1 medium-ish bulb should be enough), fronds reserved for garnish

1 medium yellow onion, thinly sliced

1 teaspoon salt, plus a pinch

3 garlic cloves, minced

1 (28-ounce) can diced fire-roasted tomatoes, drained

1 pound Yukon Gold potatoes, scrubbed and cut into 1-inch chunks

½ cup red lentils

5 to 6 cups vegetable broth, purchased or homemade (page 203)

½ sheet nori, crumbled or cut into tiny pieces

2 bay leaves

6 fresh thyme sprigs

1 teaspoon grated orange zest (see Tip)

⅛ teaspoon cayenne pepper

Freshly ground black pepper

1 (25-ounce) can chickpeas, rinsed and drained, or 2 cups cooked chickpeas

I wish I had a really interesting story to tell about me and bouillabaisse and my French lineage, but the truth is, the word just got stuck in my head one day and I became intrigued. It's a Provençal fisherman's stew, a bit spicy, usually served with crusty bread and a creamy, peppery spread called *rouille*.

To mimic the pretty shapes of the clams that poke out of the stew every which way, I decided to go with yellow squash, cut into half-moons. Since boiled summer squash can get mushy, I opted to roast the squash and toss it in at the end. Forgive the fussiness, but sometimes a little extra work produces great rewards. The roastiness brings a lot to the bowl.

This isn't your run-of-the-mill chickpea tomato stew. It's got so much interesting goodness going on: fennely bites, a little orange undertone, and just a hint of the sea. It's a vegan bouillabaisse that even a French fisherman would love. Okay, fine, a French fisherman would probably laugh at me and call me terrible things in French. But it's still totally delicious.

MAKE THE SQUASH: Preheat the oven to 425°F. Line a large rimmed baking sheet with parchment paper.

Toss the yellow squash on the baking sheet with a drizzle of olive oil and a sprinkle of salt. Spread the squash out, then roast for 10 minutes. Flip the squash and roast for another 5 minutes. Remove from the oven and set aside.

MAKE THE STEW: Meanwhile, preheat a 4-quart pot over medium heat. Heat the oil, then sauté the fennel and onion with a pinch of salt until translucent, 5 to 7 minutes. Add the garlic and sauté until fragrant, about 30 seconds.

Add the tomatoes, potatoes, lentils, 5 cups broth, nori, bay leaves, thyme sprigs, zest, remaining 1 teaspoon salt, cayenne, and a few grinds of black pepper. Cover the pot and bring the liquid to a boil. Once boiling, lower the heat to a simmer and leave the lid ajar so that steam can escape.

Simmer until the potatoes are tender and the red lentils are cooked, about 15 minutes, then add the chickpeas and turn the heat to its lowest setting. Cook, uncovered, for 15 more minutes. This gives the lentils more time to turn mushy and lets the flavors develop without overcooking the potatoes. Add up to 1 cup more vegetable broth if needed to keep the stew brothy. Cook for 10 minutes, then turn off the heat and let the stew sit for at least 10 minutes to allow the flavors to marry. Taste and adjust for salt and seasoning. Remove the bay leaves and thyme sprigs.

FOR THE *ROUILLE*:

½ cup slivered almonds

2 garlic cloves, peeled

4 roasted Fresno peppers or 1
   roasted red bell pepper, seeded

¼ cup water

2 teaspoons Dijon mustard

¼ teaspoon salt

½ cup olive oil

FOR SERVING:

Chopped fresh parsley

Capers

Toasted bread

MAKE THE *ROUILLE*: While the stew is cooking, preheat a large pan over medium heat. Toast the almonds in the dry pan, tossing them frequently, until they're honey brown in spots. Transfer to a blender and let cool for 2 minutes or so.

Add the garlic to the blender and pulse the mixture into coarse crumbs. Add the peppers, water, mustard, and salt and blend into a thick paste. Stream in the olive oil and blend until thick and smooth, giving the motor on your blender a rest every minute or so. If the *rouille* is too thick, use a little water to thin—not too much, though, just enough to get it smooth and spreadable.

Taste and adjust for salt and refrigerate until ready to use. It does thicken a bit as it chills.

SERVE: Ladle the stew into bowls and top with the roasted squash. Garnish with fresh parsley, fennel fronds, and capers. Serve with toasted bread spread thickly with *rouille*.

Tips

I love the flavor that fire-roasted canned tomatoes bring to the party, but use only the tomatoes, not the juice. You can reserve that for another soup on another day! It freezes well in a small zip-top bag.

One average-size navel orange should get you enough zest for this recipe. Use a Microplane grater and eyeball the amount. It's too frustrating to actually measure a teaspoon of zest, in my opinion.

Roast the peppers for the rouille *while the squash is roasting. That makes it super easy to pull together.*

GRILLED RAMEN

½ cup hoisin sauce

3 tablespoons rice wine vinegar

1 tablespoon tamari or soy sauce

1 tablespoon fresh lime juice

1 tablespoon brown sugar

1 (14-ounce) package extra-firm tofu, pressed and cut crosswise into 8 slabs

8 ounces plain ramen noodles (see headnote)

1 recipe hot Miso Dashi Broth (page 243)

4 baby bok choy, cut in half lengthwise

2 tablespoons toasted sesame oil, plus more for the grill

Salt

4 ounces shiitake mushrooms, tough stems trimmed

1 ripe avocado, pitted, peeled, and diced small, for garnish

1 cup thinly sliced scallions, for garnish

--- *Tip* ---

To make this recipe not such a pain in the tuchus, make the broth a day ahead and marinate the tofu overnight. The next day, you're essentially just boiling the noodles and grilling some stuff. And it is so worth it!

Curly noodles in a homemade dashi broth, topped with grilled hoisin tofu, shiitake mushrooms, bok choy, and some diced avocado—OMG, it's grilled ramen! And it is beyond sublime, the kind of food that brings the room to a hush as everyone takes their first slurpy bites.

You definitely want the right noodles for this! A trip to an Asian grocery should provide you with a wall of ramen to choose from. We're not talking about the kind that come with a flavor packet, just a plain old block of curly-looking noodles.

In a wide, shallow bowl, whisk together the hoisin, vinegar, tamari, lime juice, and brown sugar. Add the tofu slabs to the marinade and set aside for at least 2 hours and up to overnight, flipping occasionally.

When the tofu has marinated, cook the noodles according to the package directions, then immediately cool them under cold running water and set aside. Also, make sure your broth is piping hot and ready to go, since everything else will happen rather quickly.

Preheat your outdoor grill or stovetop grill pan to medium.

Brush the bok choy halves with sesame oil and sprinkle with a little salt. Grill them cut-side down until grill marks appear, about 5 minutes. If you're using an outdoor grill, keep the leaves away from the direct flame, if possible, since they will burn if they get too close to the fire.

Remove the tofu from the marinade, but reserve the marinade. Brush the grill with a little sesame oil and place the tofu on the grill as well, cooking along with the bok choy for about 5 minutes. Once the tofu is on the grill, dunk the mushrooms in the marinade.

Transfer the bok choy to a plate. Flip the tofu and grill for 5 minutes on the other side. Use a thin metal spatula to flip, so that you can really get under the tofu and it doesn't stick. In the meantime, place the marinated mushrooms on the grill and let them grill for 5 minutes as well.

Now remove the tofu and mushrooms from the grill. It's time to assemble your ramen!

Transfer the cooked noodles to the hot broth to heat them through, just for about 30 seconds. Divide the noodles and broth among big bowls. Slice the tofu slabs on a bias and divide them among the bowls. Add the bok choy, mushrooms, and avocado in little piles. Scatter scallions across the top and serve immediately!

ZUCCHINI NOODLES

with Peanut Sauce

FOR THE DRESSING:

1 cup creamy natural peanut butter

1 cup water

½ cup rice wine vinegar

2 tablespoons sriracha

2 tablespoons agave

2 tablespoons tamari or soy sauce

2 tablespoons chopped fresh ginger

½ teaspoon salt

FOR THE SALAD:

3 pounds zucchini

2 pounds cherry or grape tomatoes, cut in half

1 pound cucumbers, cut into half-moons (about 1½ cups)

1 cup finely diced red onion

1 cup roasted salted peanuts

2 cups chopped fresh herbs, such as Thai basil, mint, or cilantro (or a mix of all three)

If you're like me, you have genetically perfect jet-black goth hair, you watch too much HGTV, and you crave peanut sauces. *Seriously* crave them. Like, a would-it-be-weird-to-have-this-for-breakfast-type craving.

These zucchini noodles are just as satisfying as a big bowl of stir-fried noodles. They're totally slurpy, flavorful, filling, and just, you know, peanutty. They're a fresh start to any meal, but they go especially nicely with Seitan Negimaki (page 232) and Grilled Ramen (page 241).

MAKE THE DRESSING: Combine all the dressing ingredients in a small blender and blend until smooth. That's it! Keep sealed and refrigerated until ready to use.

MAKE THE SALAD: Cut the zucchini lengthwise, on a mandoline or by hand, into ⅛-inch slices. Stack those slices and cut them lengthwise into long noodly strips. (Or see the Tip about making noodles.)

Toss the zucchini noodles with the dressing, reserving some of the dressing for drizzling. Taste and adjust for salt.

Top each serving with tomatoes, cucumbers, red onion, and peanuts. Drizzle with extra dressing as desired. Finish with fresh herbs and serve!

Tip *You can make zucchini noodles on a mandoline or the rustic way, with a peeler. If you're using a mandoline, slice the zucchini the long way on the mandoline, then use a knife to cut it into strips. If you're using a peeler, simply peel the zucchini into rustic shapes of various sizes. Or maybe you even have a spiralizer! How very twenty-first century.*

MISO DASHI BROTH

1 tablespoon oil (peanut, toasted sesame, and canola are all good choices)

1 large yellow onion, diced large

3 garlic cloves, peeled and smashed with the flat side of a knife

2 teaspoons salt, plus a pinch

2 large carrots, peeled and cut into chunks

1 (1-inch) piece ginger, peeled and sliced

12 cups cold water

2 sheets kombu, cut into 3-inch strips

3 tablespoons mellow white miso

2 tablespoons mirin

Dashi, if you're not familiar, is the deeply umami Japanese broth used to make ramen. Traditionally, it includes some fishy ingredients. Literally. Here, we're simply making a veggie broth with a healthy dose of kombu, for a slight taste of the sea, and miso, for that fermented deliciousness.

Preheat a large pot over medium-high heat. Heat the oil, then sauté the onion and garlic with a pinch of salt for about 5 minutes, just to get a little caramelization going.

Add the carrots, ginger, and water. Cover and bring to a boil. Once boiling, lower the heat a bit and leave the lid slightly ajar so that steam can escape. Simmer to reduce by a third; this will take about 30 minutes. Add the kombu and cook for an additional 30 minutes. All told, it should simmer for a little over an hour, and reduce to 8 cups. Remove the kombu at this point so that it doesn't get slimy.

Add the miso, mirin, and remaining 2 teaspoons salt and stir. Let simmer for an additional 2 minutes, then turn off the heat.

Put a separate large pot in the sink. Place a handled strainer so that it sits securely on top of the pot. Line the strainer with a few layers of cheesecloth, leaving plenty of overhang. Pour in the vegetables and broth and let strain for about 20 minutes.

Bunch up the cheesecloth and squeeze so that the vegetables release as much moisture and flavor as possible.

Taste and adjust for salt, and now your broth is ready to use!

ELVIS CUPCAKES

MAKES

12

CUPCAKES

TOTAL
2 HOURS 30 MINUTES
ACTIVE
45 MINUTES

FOR THE CUPCAKES:

2 very ripe medium bananas

⅔ cup unsweetened almond milk (or your favorite nondairy milk)

⅓ cup canola oil

1½ teaspoons pure vanilla extract

1 teaspoon apple cider vinegar

¾ cup granulated sugar

1¼ cups all-purpose flour

1½ teaspoons baking powder

½ teaspoon salt

FOR THE PEANUT BUTTER FROSTING:

½ cup creamy natural peanut butter, at room temperature

1 teaspoon pure vanilla extract

2½ cups powdered sugar

¼ cup unsweetened almond milk (or your favorite nondairy milk), warmed

2 tablespoons refined coconut oil, melted

Salt

FOR THE COCONUT BACON:

1 tablespoon liquid smoke

2 teaspoons tamari or soy sauce

2 teaspoons pure maple syrup

1 teaspoon water

1½ cups large flaked coconut

FOR THE CARAMELIZED BANANAS:

3 tablespoons brown sugar

1 ripe banana, sliced into 12 coins

This cupcake will have you shaking your hips! A fluffy banana cupcake with peanut butter frosting and caramelized banana and, to top it all off, smoky, salty coconut bacon, all in honor of the King of Rock's favorite sammich. Serve them in animal print cupcake liners and you'll be able to feel the shag carpet beneath your feet in the Jungle Room.

MAKE THE CUPCAKES: Preheat the oven to 350°F. Line a standard-size muffin tin with paper or foil liners.

Break the bananas into chunks and place them in a blender, along with the almond milk, oil, vanilla, and apple cider vinegar. Blend until smooth.

Transfer the mixture to a large mixing bowl. Use an electric mixer to mix in the sugar. Then sift in the flour, baking powder, and salt and mix just until the batter is smooth and falls in ribbons.

Fill the lined muffin cups two-thirds of the way full and bake until a knife stuck in the center comes out clean, 20 to 22 minutes. Cool completely before frosting.

MAKE THE PB FROSTING: Scoop the peanut butter and vanilla into a large mixing bowl. Sift in the powdered sugar and pour the warm almond milk over the ingredients. Use a hand mixer to beat everything together until relatively smooth. Add the coconut oil and beat again. This time it should get really smooth and fall from the blades of the mixer in ribbons. If it seems stiff, add a splash of milk to loosen it up. Add a big pinch of salt and mix to incorporate. Cover with plastic wrap and refrigerate for at least an hour to firm up.

MEANWHILE, MAKE THE COCONUT BACON: Preheat the oven to 325°F. Line a rimmed baking sheet with parchment paper.

Combine the liquid smoke, tamari, maple syrup, and water in a large mixing bowl. Pour in the flaked coconut and gently toss to coat.

Spread out the coated coconut on the lined baking sheet. Bake for 20 to 25 minutes, flipping every 10 minutes. Keep a close eye so that it browns but does not burn. Remove from the oven and spread out on a plate to cool.

Recipe Continues

MEANWHILE, MAKE THE CARAMELIZED BANANAS: Have ready a large sheet of parchment paper. Sprinkle the brown sugar onto a dinner plate. Press each banana slice into the sugar on both sides to lightly coat.

Preheat a large pan over medium heat. Spray with a little cooking spray. Cook the banana slices until the sugar melts, about a minute, being careful not to let them burn. Spray the banana slices with cooking spray and flip, then cook on the other side for another minute or so.

Transfer the bananas to the parchment paper to cool.

ASSEMBLE: Crumble the coconut bacon into small pieces on a large dinner plate.

Use a strong fork to mix the chilled peanut butter frosting, which will appear somewhat crusty. That's just the powdered sugar firming up. A brisk stir will get it creamy again. Use a spoon to frost each cupcake with a few tablespoons of frosting. Use the back of the spoon to smooth the frosting in a spiral motion, making sure the frosting goes all the way to the edges.

Roll the edges of the cupcakes in the coconut bacon.

Top each cupcake with a caramelized banana and serve! If you're not serving immediately, store them in a covered container in the refrigerator so that the bananas stay fresh.

CINNAMON-RAISIN
SWIRL BREAD

MAKES
1
LOAF

TOTAL
4 HOURS
ACTIVE
45 MINUTES

FOR THE BREAD:
¾ cup raisins

½ cup warm water

2¼ teaspoons active dry yeast (one 0.75-ounce packet)

2½ to 3 cups all-purpose flour

2 tablespoons sugar

1 teaspoon salt

½ cup unsweetened almond milk (or your favorite nondairy milk), warm

2 tablespoons refined coconut oil, melted

FOR THE CINNAMON SWIRL:
¼ cup sugar

1 tablespoon ground cinnamon

2 tablespoons refined coconut oil, melted

FOR THE GLAZE:
2 tablespoons agave

2 tablespoons water

I have a serious cinnamon-raisin-bread problem: I can't stop eating it. Something takes over, and by the end of the day, the whole loaf gets gone, even the butts. So, I never buy it and I only bake it for special occasions. Like Mother's or Father's Day! Let the cinnamony goodness waft through your home and see if you can resist eating the whole thing.

MAKE THE BREAD: Put the raisins in a bowl and cover them with warm water, letting them plump for at least 10 minutes. Drain and set aside.

Meanwhile, in a small bowl, whisk together the ½ cup warm water and the yeast and set aside for 5 minutes to bloom.

In a large bowl, combine 2½ cups of the flour, the sugar, and the salt and form a well in the middle. Into the well, pour the yeast mixture, the milk, and the melted coconut oil. Start mixing from the center, pulling in the flour little by little until fully incorporated. Turn out the dough onto a floured countertop and knead, adding flour a tablespoon at a time until the dough isn't sticky anymore and springs back when you poke it.

Toss the raisins with a little flour to absorb the excess moisture, then fold them into the dough in two batches, adding a little more flour if the dough gets sticky. When the raisins are evenly distributed, wipe out the mixing bowl and coat it with nonstick cooking spray. Put the dough ball in and spray the top, then cover the bowl with plastic wrap. Set the bowl somewhere warm until the dough has doubled in size, 1 to 2 hours.

MAKE THE CINNAMON SWIRL: Once the dough has risen, lightly grease a 9-by-5-inch loaf pan.

In a small bowl, combine the sugar and cinnamon and set aside.

On a floured countertop, roll the dough into a rectangle, about 5 inches wide and 18 inches long, with the small side facing you.

Brush the dough with the melted coconut oil and sprinkle on the cinnamon sugar. Roll it up tightly, starting from the small side nearest you, and pinch the seam closed at the end. Place the roll in the prepared loaf pan, seam-side down. Cover with plastic wrap and set in a warm place until puffy, 30 to 40 minutes.

Preheat the oven to 350°F.

MAKE THE GLAZE: In a small bowl, mix the agave and water, then brush it on top of the loaf. Bake until the bread is golden brown on top, 30 to 45 minutes. Turn out onto a cooling rack immediately and let cool completely before slicing and serving.

RHUBARB CRUMB CAKE

FOR THE CRUMB TOPPING:

2 cups all-purpose flour

½ cup granulated sugar

⅓ cup brown sugar

4 teaspoons ground cinnamon

½ teaspoon baking powder

½ cup refined coconut oil, at room temperature (see Tip)

FOR THE CAKE:

1½ cups unsweetened almond milk (or your favorite nondairy milk)

½ cup canola oil

⅓ cup unsweetened applesauce

1 tablespoon pure vanilla extract

2 teaspoons apple cider vinegar

2½ cups all-purpose flour

⅔ cup granulated sugar

4 teaspoons baking powder

1 teaspoon salt

1½ cups sliced rhubarb, in ¼-inch slices

Powdered sugar, for serving (optional)

Rhubarb is the cranberry of springtime. It's so fresh and tart, and bakes up beautifully, giving this coffee cake little brushstrokes of pink throughout. There is no shortage of crumbs on this cake, so serve this to your mom for Mother's Day and watch her get crumbs all over her mom blouse.

Preheat the oven to 350°F. Lightly grease a 9-by-13-inch pan.

MAKE THE CRUMB TOPPING: In a small mixing bowl, mix the flour, sugars, cinnamon, and baking powder. Cut in the coconut oil with your fingers or a pastry cutter to form a nice large crumb. Some of the topping is still going to be sandy and that's fine, just so long as you have mostly nice, big crumbs.

MAKE THE CAKE: In a large mixing bowl, mix the milk, oil, applesauce, vanilla, and vinegar. Sift in the flour, sugar, baking powder, and salt and mix until smooth. Fold in the rhubarb.

Pour the batter into the prepared pan. Evenly sprinkle on the crumb topping and pat it down just a bit. Bake until a knife inserted in the center comes out clean, 40 to 45 minutes. Let cool for at least an hour before slicing and serving. If desired, sift powdered sugar over the top.

 Tip *The coconut oil should be soft and slightly melty for the crumb topping. Make sure it's at the right temperature before preparing everything else. If it's too cold and hard, run the jar under warm water for a minute. If it's too warm and liquidy, place it in the fridge until it's stiffened up a bit.*

12

FOURTH
of JULY

THIS SECTION IS MORE

than just what to serve

BEFORE YOU WATCH THE

fireworks.

YOU CAN LOOK at it as a summertime cookout manifesto! From chilled soups to grilled pizzas, all your hot weather cravings are covered. Of course you'll find recipes for the best burgers and hot dogs for the grill here, too.

When I was growing up in the big city, our cookouts were usually in Prospect Park, where you could rent a little picnic space, complete with grill and table. You'd have to book months in advance, though, because you were competing for a slot with a few million other New Yorkers who didn't have backyards, either. Everyone would bring blankets and lounge out in the grass, play some Wiffle ball, and try to blast their boom box louder than then their neighbor's boom box.

Even though I have a backyard now, that's still pretty much my setup. No one really eats at the picnic table—instead, that's where the spread is. Everyone sits on blankets or in lawn chairs, while I (wo)man the grill, working really hard and trying to make people feel guilty for not helping. And the boom box is gone, but everyone is still fighting over whose Spotify to blast.

To make things as easy as possible, have the chilled soups ready to go a day or two in advance. Your pizza dough can be frozen a week in advance and thawed the day before.

Chilled
FRESH CORN
SOUP

6 cups fresh corn kernels (from about 8 ears)

½ cup chopped scallion, white and light green parts only, plus more for garnish

1½ cups unsweetened almond milk (or your favorite nondairy milk)

1½ cups vegetable broth, purchased or homemade (page 203)

3 tablespoons olive oil, plus more for garnish

2 tablespoons fresh lime juice

1 teaspoon salt

½ teaspoon ground white pepper

Thinly sliced radishes, for garnish

Fresh basil chiffonade, for garnish

This fresh corn soup is light and lovely, and tastes as pure as a Nebraskan field. If you're already heating up the grill, baking a cobbler, and who knows what else, it's nice to have a no-cook recipe in your back pocket. (But please don't keep soup in your back pocket!) Make this and your guests will think you did way more than whiz up a few ingredients and run them through a sieve. Depending on the size of your blender, you may have to do this in two batches.

In a blender, combine the corn, scallion, almond milk, broth, olive oil, lime juice, salt, and white pepper. Puree until as smooth as possible.

Strain the soup through a sieve into a large sealable pitcher or Tupperware. Press down on the mixture if the sieve gets clogged, to get as much liquid out as possible. Taste and adjust for salt and seasoning. Chill for at least 1 hour before serving.

To serve, ladle the soup into bowls and garnish with a drizzle of olive oil and some sliced radishes, basil, and scallion.

CHILLED
PEA SOUP
with Mint

SERVES
8

**TOTAL
2 HOURS**
(includes chilling)
**ACTIVE
1 HOUR**

2 tablespoons refined coconut oil

1 cup chopped scallion, white and
light green parts only, plus more
for garnish

6 cups fresh peas (from 6 pounds
of pea pods)

5 cups vegetable broth, purchased
or homemade (page 203)

1 cup coconut milk from a well-
stirred can

2 tablespoons fresh lemon juice

½ cup fresh mint leaves, plus more
for garnish

1 teaspoon salt

Olive oil, for garnish

Nothing makes you feel like you're one with the universe on a hot summer day quite the way a chilled pea soup does. It's so green in taste and hue, so citrusy and refreshing, and so very minty. If you were never a fan of cold soups, this will make you a believer. Yes, shelling 6 pounds of peas might be a pain in the tuchus, but often you can find already shelled peas at your local overpriced organic grocery store. Or you can get a couple of friends to help! Otherwise, that is what the 1-hour active time is all about.

Preheat a 4-quart pot over medium heat. Melt the coconut oil, then sauté the scallion just until softened, about 2 minutes.

Add the peas and broth and bring to a boil. Reduce the heat and simmer until the peas are tender, about 5 minutes. Turn off the heat and add the coconut milk, lemon juice, mint, and salt. Let the soup cool a bit, then transfer it to a blender and puree until completely smooth. Taste and adjust for salt.

Refrigerate the soup for at least 1 hour before serving. To serve, ladle into bowls and garnish with a drizzle of olive oil and a scattering of scallion and mint leaves.

Chilled
GOLDEN BEET *and* GINGER SOUP

SERVES
8

TOTAL
2 HOURS
(includes chilling)
ACTIVE
20 MINUTES

2 pounds yellow beets, trimmed and scrubbed

1 (14-ounce) can coconut milk

3 tablespoons fresh lime juice

½ teaspoon salt

2 teaspoons olive oil

3 garlic cloves, minced

1 tablespoon minced fresh ginger

1½ to 2 cups vegetable broth, purchased or homemade (page 203)

1 teaspoon agave or pure maple syrup (optional)

Thinly sliced scallions, for garnish

Sriracha, for garnish

This soup is smooth and velvety and just as invigorating as a run through your neighbor's sprinkler on a hot summer day. Golden beets taste like the old reliable red beet went out dancing with a butternut squash way past curfew. It's got that great earthy backdrop, but a tangy sweetness is the first taste. Look for beets that are somewhere between the size of a golf ball and a tennis ball, so that they roast quickly and evenly.

Preheat the oven to 350°F. Wrap the beets individually in aluminum foil. Place them on a rimmed baking sheet and bake, turning once about halfway through, until they are very easily pierced with a steak knife, about 1 hour.

Remove the beets from the oven and let them become cool to the touch. They'll keep softening as they cool, and that is good! Put them in the fridge to cool completely.

Once cool, unwrap the beets, slide off the peels, and put them in a blender or food processor. Add the coconut milk, lime juice, and salt and puree until relatively smooth.

Preheat a small pan over medium-low heat. Heat the oil, then sauté the garlic and ginger for no more than a minute, being careful not to let them burn. Add 1½ cups vegetable broth to deglaze the pan, then turn off the heat.

Transfer the broth mixture to the blender or food processor and puree with the beet mixture until very smooth and velvety. Taste and adjust for salt and seasonings.

Transfer the blender jar to the fridge and chill for at least an hour. It should be cold all the way through. If it's too thick, add up to ½ cup more vegetable broth and blend again.

Serve topped with scallions and dotted with sriracha.

GREEN GAZPACHO

SERVES
8

TOTAL
1 HOUR 15 MINUTES
(includes chilling)
ACTIVE
15 MINUTES

4 medium-size green or yellow heirloom tomatoes, chopped (about 4 cups)

1 cup chopped seedless cucumber

2 jalapeños, seeded

½ cup chopped scallion

½ cup fresh cilantro leaves

¼ cup olive oil

2 tablespoons fresh lime juice

1 teaspoon salt

1 to 2 cups vegetable broth, purchased or homemade (page 203)

FOR GARNISH:

Olive oil

Freshly ground black pepper

Pea tendrils or chopped fresh herb of choice

This gazpacho requires zero cooking, making it a go-to for any summertime party. It's a nice change of pace from red gazpacho (which will put everyone at the party instantly to sleep). It's fresh, zesty, fruity, and spicy with tomato, cucumber, jalapeño, and cilantro. As you blend it, the olive oil makes it wonderfully creamy. I especially love it as a shooter, so if you want to begin the meal with a palate cleanser, serve this soup in ice-cold shot glasses.

The directions here are very easy. Combine all the ingredients (start with 1 cup broth) in a blender or food processor. Blend until as smooth as possible, adding extra broth as necessary. Taste and adjust for salt and seasoning. Transfer to the fridge to cool for at least an hour. Serve topped with a drizzle of olive oil, a few grinds of black pepper, and a few pea tendrils or chopped herbs.

BOW TIE *And* BUTTER BEAN SALAD

with *Fresh Dill*

SERVES
8–10

TOTAL
2 HOURS
(includes chilling)
ACTIVE
30 MINUTES

12 ounces farfalle (bow tie) pasta

½ cup vegan mayo, purchased or homemade (page 67)

3 tablespoons distilled white vinegar

1 teaspoon sugar

1 teaspoon onion powder

½ teaspoon salt

Freshly ground black pepper

1 cup sliced cucumbers, in thin half-moons

1 cup sliced radishes, in thin half-moons

½ cup shredded peeled carrot

¼ cup chopped fresh dill

1 (15-ounce) can butter beans, rinsed and drained, or 1½ cups cooked butter beans

This is the pasta salad to end all pasta salads. Bow ties are the perfect little gentlemen, and they collect plenty of dressing in their creases. And the seriously underappreciated butter bean is a big, creamy bean that holds its shape nicely in a salad. Dill brightens everything up with its fresh, summery flavor, making it perfect for any warm-weather spread. One pasta salad to conquer all!

Bring a large pot of salted water to a boil over high heat. Cook the pasta according to the package instructions, then drain in a colander and run under cold water to cool. Refrigerate to cool even further.

In a large mixing bowl, whisk together the mayo, vinegar, sugar, onion powder, salt, and a few grinds of black pepper. Then add the chilled pasta to the dressing, along with the cucumbers and radishes, and mix well. Add the carrot and dill and toss to mix. Stir in the butter beans. Taste and adjust for salt and pepper.

Cover the bowl with plastic wrap and chill for at least 2 hours to let the flavors meld. Serve cold.

Spicy
TEMPEH-STUFFED
AVOCADO

2 (8-ounce) packages tempeh

2 tablespoons tamari or soy sauce

½ cup vegan mayo, purchased or homemade (page 67)

3 tablespoons rice vinegar

1 tablespoon sriracha

2 teaspoons toasted sesame oil

½ teaspoon salt

½ cup finely sliced scallion, green and white parts only

8 avocados

Fresh lemon juice, for brushing

Shredded radish, for garnish

Black sesame seeds, for garnish

This is my take on a spicy tuna roll filling, stuffed into an avocado. It's an idea taken from sushi restaurants that serve much, much fancier stuffed avocados. But you don't have to be fancy to be delicious! This is succulent and spicy and will be hoarded by guests, so make sure everyone gets one.

Tear the tempeh into bite-size pieces and put them in a small saucepan. Cover them with water and add the tamari. Cover the pot and bring the water to a boil over medium-high heat, then turn down the heat and simmer for 15 minutes. Drain and transfer the tempeh to a mixing bowl to cool.

Once cool, add the mayo, vinegar, sriracha, sesame oil, and salt and stir with a fork, mashing the tempeh as you go. Fold in the scallion. Taste and adjust for salt and seasoning. Cover with plastic wrap and refrigerate until ready to serve.

Prepare the avocados as close to serving time as possible. Cut each avocado in half and remove the pit. Peel the skin off the avocado (see the Tip). Use your fingertips to brush the avocado with lemon juice, which will prevent it from browning. Overstuff the avocado halves with the tempeh salad. Top with shredded radish and sesame seeds and serve!

Tip   *I prefer to stuff avocados that have no peel, because they're more fun to eat and easier to smother with all that stuffed deliciousness. The easiest way to skin an avocado is to chill it in advance, and make sure it's the perfect ripeness: not over, and not under. However, sometimes avocados aren't willing to cooperate. They're overripe, or the skin is sticking, or they're otherwise just being jerks. In that case, serving stuffed avocado in the skin is perfectly acceptable and much easier to keep fresh.*

MELON SALAD

with Mint & Lime

SERVES
8

TOTAL
20 MINUTES
ACTIVE
20 MINUTES

½ cup fresh lime juice

1 tablespoon agave

5 cups diced peeled cantaloupe, in ¾-inch pieces (from 2 average-size cantaloupes; see Tip)

Salt

2 avocados, pitted, peeled, and cut into ¾-inch dice

½ cup lightly packed fresh mint leaves (chopped if leaves are very large)

Crushed red pepper flakes (optional, if you'd like some spice)

Even though it's perfectly legit to enjoy a melon with nothing but a spoon and some candlelight, it takes only a few extra steps for something even more special. Pairing melons with acid and herbs is a versatile formula, so if you've got, say, watermelon and basil, then try that, switching the lime to balsamic vinegar. Make it work with what you've got. The whole point is that simple flavors can be heavenly for your taste buds and make your dish duties disappear.

In a large bowl, stir together the lime juice and agave. Add the cantaloupe and a pinch of salt and toss to coat. Let sit for about 5 minutes so that the cantaloupe releases some of its juice and the flavors meld.

Toss in the avocados and mint leaves and a big pinch of red pepper flakes, if desired. Taste and adjust for salt. You may want to adjust the sweetness and limey-ness as well. Serve immediately!

Tip *Prepping the cantaloupe is easy for this salad. Cut it in half and scoop out the seeds. Then turn the melon flat-side down on a cutting board and use your chef's knife to peel away the skin. A little green is okay, but try to get it so that you mostly have orange. Then simply dice away.*

Crunchy
POTATO
SALAD

SERVES
10–12

TOTAL
2 HOURS
(includes chilling)
ACTIVE
20 MINUTES

2 pounds baby red potatoes, cut in half or into 1-inch pieces

½ cup vegan mayo, purchased or homemade (page 67)

¼ cup Dijon mustard

2 tablespoons white wine vinegar

2 teaspoons agave

½ teaspoon salt

1 cup thinly sliced peeled carrots

3 celery ribs, thinly sliced

1 cup thinly sliced sugar snap peas

Freshly ground black pepper

This is a verrrry traditional potato salad with carrots, celery, and my top-secret ingredient for extra crunchiness: sugar snap peas! In addition to the crispiness they bring to the party, once you taste their fresh flavor you'll wonder where they've been all your potato salad's life.

Put the potatoes in a 4-quart pot and cover with salted cold water. Cover the pot and bring the water to a boil over high heat. Lower the heat and simmer until the potatoes are easily pierced with a fork, about 10 minutes. Drain in a colander and let cool.

In a very large mixing bowl, whisk together the mayo, mustard, vinegar, agave, and salt. Transfer the cooled potatoes to the mixing bowl and toss to coat them in the dressing. Fold in the carrots, celery, and sugar snap peas, along with several grinds of black pepper. Transfer to a pretty serving bowl, cover tightly with plastic wrap, and refrigerate until ready to serve.

SERVES
10–12

TOTAL
2 HOURS
(includes chilling)
ACTIVE
20 MINUTES

2½ pounds russet potatoes, peeled and cut into 1-inch chunks

¾ cup vegan mayo, purchased or homemade (page 67)

¼ cup Dijon mustard

3 tablespoons distilled white vinegar

2 teaspoons agave

2 teaspoons kala namak black salt or 1½ teaspoons regular salt

1 teaspoon ground turmeric

½ cup grated peeled carrot

2 celery ribs, thinly sliced

1 cup chopped scallion, light green and white parts only

1 (14-ounce) package extra-firm tofu, diced small

Freshly ground black pepper

Sweet paprika, for garnish

Chopped fresh dill, for garnish

If you love (or loved) hard-boiled eggs in your potato salad, then prepare to be delighted. Tofu, turmeric, and pungent kala namak black salt team up to form a trifecta of egginess. If you feel like tricking your uncle Herbie into eating tofu, this might be the ticket. (But tricks aside, it's also just a really great potato salad.) It's important to get the potatoes into the dressing while they are still warm, because the heat activates the color in the turmeric to get you that bright eggy yellow you're looking for. I love this on top of a burger or as a side. See the photo on page 280.

Put the potatoes in a 4-quart pot and cover them with salted cold water. Cover the pot and bring the water to a boil over high heat. Lower the heat and simmer until the potatoes are easily pierced with a fork, about 10 minutes. Drain in a colander.

Meanwhile, in a very large mixing bowl, whisk together the mayo, mustard, vinegar, agave, kala namak, and turmeric. Transfer the warm potatoes to the mixing bowl and toss to coat them in the dressing. Fold in the carrot, celery, scallion, and tofu, along with several grinds of black pepper. Taste and adjust for salt and seasoning. Cover the bowl tightly with plastic wrap and refrigerate until ready to serve.

Serve topped with a light dusting of paprika and fresh dill.

STUFFED
CHERRY
TOMATOES
with Basil

24 large cherry tomatoes

Coarse salt

1½ cups white bean cream chee (page 28) or purchased cream cheese

Freshly ground black pepper

½ cup fresh basil chiffonade

Olive oil, for drizzling

These will be gobbled up in an instant! The classic flavors never fail to please, and it's a really great and easy way to showcase the fresh cherry tomatoes that usually pop up in July. Make sure your cherry tomatoes are on the larger side, to get the most bang for your buck. If you don't have a pastry bag, a plastic zip-top bag with a corner cut out will work just dandily.

Cut a thin slice off the top of each tomato. Scoop out and discard pulp. Sprinkle with a little salt and turn the tomatoes upside down on a paper towel to drain.

Use a pastry bag fitted with a medium-size circle tip to fill the tomatoes with the cream chee. Grind on some black pepper and top with basil chiffonade. Finish with a drizzle of olive oil and a sprinkling of coarse salt. Serve!

Seattle Pizza, page 271

GRILLED PIZZA
GRILLS JUST WANNA HAVE FUN

If you don't have a wood-burning pizza oven right in
your kitchen, the grill is the next best heat source for the kind of pizza that
might get written up in the *New York Times* as, like, the best-ever
"I can't believe you never heard of this" pizza. A crisp exterior with a chewy and
airy bite that's just this side of burnt—to me that is pizza perfection.
It's easy to achieve, especially if you learn from my mistakes. After many misfires
resulting in folded, ripped, and otherwise no-fun pizza crusts,
I picked up a few tips:

1. *Forget about circles.* In fact, forget about any shape you know. Instead of thinking your crust looks deformed, go for "rustic" and your grilled pizzas will be a different kind of perfect every time. I find that an ovalish-rectanglish shape works really well, and is easy enough to flip. It's also easy to cut into triangles by slicing zigzags crosswise.

2. *Use cold dough.* If you're grilling, it's a safe bet that it's warm outside, so your dough is going to be floppy. It helps to keep the dough refrigerated until you're ready; that way it doesn't flap in the breeze like so much laundry on the line when it's time to grill it. Your dough will come out thicker, but that's okay because it will be sturdy.

3. *Grill both sides.* Obviously, on a traditional pizza, you add the toppings before baking. With grilled pizza, it's way easier to grill one side, flip the pizza, and then add the toppings. You get two sets of grill marks *and* your dough cooks evenly. Win-win!

CHEESY PIZZA

with Olives & Basil

Cornmeal

1 recipe Rustic Pizza Dough
(page 43)

Olive oil, for brushing and drizzling

1 recipe Pizza Awesomesauce
(page 268)

1 recipe Swirly Pizza Cheese
(facing page)

½ cup sliced oil-cured black olives

20 fresh basil leaves

Brooklyn has the best pizza in the world. I'm just stating the facts! These are the flavors that are closest to my pizza-shaped heart, the classics: tomato, basil, olive. And this is one of the easiest grilled pizzas to pull together.

Preheat the grill to medium-high heat.

Sprinkle some cornmeal onto a clean countertop with lots of elbow room, then press and roll one of the dough balls into an ovalish-rectanglish shape or as much of a circle as you can.

Brush some olive oil on the top, then carefully, but not too carefully, flip the crust onto the grill, oiled-side down.

Cook for about 5 minutes, rotating with a spatula once in a while for even heating. It should be nice and dark with a few grill marks on the bottom.

Brush the top with olive oil and flip the crust. Ladle on half of the sauce and spread it out, leaving about an inch of space around the edges.

Drizzle on half of the cheese sauce and scatter half of the olives all over. Close the lid of the grill and let cook for about 3 minutes. The bottom should be firm and cooked through, with some grill marks. Transfer from the grill to a large cutting board. Drizzle on some olive oil and scatter half of the fresh basil leaves all over. Slice and serve as soon as possible. Repeat with the next pizza.

Swirly PIZZA CHEESE

1 cup raw cashews, soaked in water for at least 2 hours and drained

¾ cup water

2 tablespoons fresh lemon juice

1 tablespoon mellow white miso

2 tablespoons nutritional yeast flakes

½ teaspoon salt

Whether you're drizzling, splotching, zigzagging, or swirling, this cheesy sauce will meet all your pizza needs. And best of all, it's really simple to make. Cashews provide the creamy base, while miso and lemon make it tangy with just a little salty, aged edge.

Combine all the ingredients in a blender. Puree until completely smooth; this can take up to 5 minutes depending on the strength of your machine. Periodically stop the machine to keep it from overheating, and scrape down the sides of the blender jar with a rubber spatula to make sure you get everything. Keep refrigerated in a tightly sealed container until ready to use.

PIZZA AWESOMESAUCE

MAKES
ENOUGH SAUCE
FOR 2 PIZZAS,
PLUS DIPPING

TOTAL
1 HOUR
ACTIVE
15 MINUTES

10 medium-size garlic cloves, peeled

2 tablespoons olive oil, plus more for drizzling

1 teaspoon salt, plus more for sprinkling

2 (28-ounce) cans fire-roasted whole tomatoes

1 medium onion, diced medium

3 garlic cloves, minced

1 teaspoon dried oregano

1 teaspoon dried thyme

¼ teaspoon ground fennel seeds

Freshly ground black pepper

1 tablespoon sugar

2 tablespoons tomato paste

This is the pizza sauce I make when I want to go all out with flavor: rich and garlicky, with what I think is the perfect amount of herby flavor. You don't have to make the roasted garlic, but it adds a wonderful dimension of sweet, mellow flavor. If you don't make it, increase the minced garlic to 5 cloves, because garlic!

First, roast the garlic. Preheat a toaster oven (or regular oven) to 375°F. On a square of aluminum foil, drizzle the garlic cloves with olive oil and sprinkle with salt. Toss to coat. Fold securely in the foil and bake for about 45 minutes, until absolutely every corner of your apartment smells like Little Italy (and the cloves are nice and soft).

Meanwhile, drain the tomatoes and reserve the liquid for thinning if needed. Preheat a 4-quart pot over medium heat. Heat the remaining 2 tablespoons oil, then sauté the onion with a pinch of salt until translucent, about 5 minutes. Add the minced garlic, oregano, thyme, fennel, and a few grinds of black pepper and sauté until fragrant, 30 seconds or so.

Crush the tomatoes with your hands as you add them to the pot and stir to deglaze. Mix in the sugar and remaining 1 teaspoon salt. Cook the tomatoes down for about 10 minutes, stirring occasionally. It should appear saucy and bubbly.

Add the tomato paste and roasted garlic cloves. Use an immersion blender to blend into a relatively smooth sauce. Cook for another 5 minutes. If it seems too thick, add the reserved tomato juice by the tablespoon.

Use immediately, or refrigerate in a tightly sealed container until ready to use.

Miami Pizza, page 271

Portland Pizza

PIZZA PARTY

Here are some of my favorite pizza variations, inspired by a few different cities. Pick your poison. These ingredients are for one pizza each, but scale up or down as needed!

The Portland

Bestest Pesto (page 64), Swirly Pizza Cheese (page 267), 4 ounces thinly sliced trumpet mushrooms, olive oil, salt and freshly ground black pepper, ¼ cup toasted hazelnuts, scant ¼ cup raspberries, ½ cup baby arugula

If you'd like this to be even more Portlandy, use hazelnuts instead of the other nuts in the pesto recipe and arugula instead of all the herbs.

Follow the directions for Cheesy Pizza (page 266) up until you flip the crust. Spread pesto all over the pizza, leaving about ½ inch around the edge. Swirl, plop, or zigzag on the cheese. Scatter the mushrooms on top and drizzle with olive oil. Season with salt and pepper. Place the pizza back on the grill, close the lid, and let it cook for about 3 minutes. Transfer to a cutting board and top with the hazelnuts, raspberries, and arugula.

The Miami

Pizza Awesomesauce (page 268), Swirly Pizza Cheese (page 267), 2 tablespoons sliced jalapeño rings, ½ cup eggplant bacon (page 148), olive oil, salt and freshly ground black pepper, ⅓ cup diced nectarine, fresh cilantro sprigs

Follow the directions for Cheesy Pizza (page 266) up until you flip the crust. Spread sauce all over the pizza, leaving about ½ inch around the edge. Swirl, plop, or zigzag on the cheese. Scatter the eggplant bacon and jalapeño rings on top and drizzle with olive oil. Season with salt and pepper. Place the pizza back on the grill, close the lid, and let it cook for about 3 minutes. Transfer to a cutting board and top with the nectarines and cilantro sprigs.

The Seattle

1 small bulb fennel (fronds reserved), olive oil, salt, 1 teaspoon minced garlic, ¼ cup cooked lentils, thinly sliced red apples (like Fuji or Braeburn), Almond Ricotta (page 299)

Brush the fennel with olive oil and season with a little salt. Grill on both sides until tender, about 5 minutes total. Transfer to a cutting board and slice thinly. Follow the directions for Cheesy Pizza (page 266) up until you flip the crust. Brush the grilled dough very liberally with olive oil, sprinkle with the garlic and about ½ teaspoon salt, then add dollops of ricotta. Place the pizza back on the grill, close the lid, and let it cook for about 3 minutes. Transfer to a cutting board. Scatter the grilled fennel, lentils, and apples all over the top, and garnish with the reserved fennel fronds.

Grilled
CAULIFLOWER
STEAKS

2 very large cauliflower heads
¼ cup olive oil, or more as needed
1 teaspoon salt
Freshly ground black pepper

Tip

Steaming the cauliflower first is really the key to the juiciest steaks. It ensures that the cauli is cooked through, so really all you're doing is adding the grill marks without burning or overcooking or undercooking. Perfect steaks, every time!

Cauli steaks are all the rage these days! It's for one simple reason: They are freaking delicious, like a succulent cloud from heaven, plus grill marks. I am giving you a very basic recipe, in part because they are just wonderful without any bells and whistles, but also so that you can use them in various ways to integrate with other flavors. You can go ahead and serve them on top of potato salad (or any salad), drizzle them with Bestest Pesto (page 64), or dip them in tahini dressing (page 231). Pick out the biggest heads of cauliflower you can find, and reserve any cauli scraps for soup or a puree.

First, prepare a large steamer. While that's heating up, prepare the steaks. Trim the cauliflower, removing the leaves and most of the stem. Place one head on a cutting board, stem-side down, and slice down the center. Now slice, from the cut side, into 1-inch-thick steaks. Repeat with the second head of cauliflower.

Steam the cauliflower in batches until tender with just a little snap left, about 3 minutes. Let cool completely before proceeding with the recipe.

Place the steaks on a rimmed baking sheet in as much of a single layer as possible. Drizzle with the olive oil and sprinkle with the salt and a few grinds of black pepper. Use your hands to rub each steak all over, making sure it's well coated in oil. The oil makes sure that the cauliflower doesn't stick to the grill and tastes as awesome as possible, so don't be shy.

Preheat the grill to medium-high. Cook the cauliflower steaks until dark grill marks appear, about 3 minutes per side. Serve!

Grilled
PORTOBELLO
SANDWICHES

8 portobello mushroom caps

1 cup dry white wine

¼ cup tamari or soy sauce

¼ cup balsamic vinegar

2 tablespoons olive oil, plus more for brushing

8 garlic cloves, minced

8 focaccia squares, sliced sandwich-style

Vegan mayo, purchased or homemade (page 67), for serving

A few handfuls baby arugula, for serving

Sweet onion slices, like Walla Walla or Vidalia, for serving

Tomato slices, for serving

Grilling brings out the juicy best in these portobellos, so I use the bare minimum of ingredients to let them really flaunt their flavor. A little (cheap!) chardonnay for depth of flavor, tamari for a bit of saltiness, balsamic for a touch of zest, and garlic because, well, it's garlic! Choose firm, light-colored mushrooms with fresh, healthy-looking gills that spring back when you gently rub your finger across them. Don't remove the gills—they are loaded with flavor and texture, not to mention they soak up garlic and marinade like no one's business. Gently rinse the caps before marinating and you will be A-OK. Skip the bun here and go for a bready focaccia that can stand up to the portobello juices that are bound to make you lick your fingers.

Place the portobellos, gill-side up, on a rimmed baking sheet.

In a small bowl, whisk together the wine, tamari, vinegar, olive oil, and garlic. Spoon the marinade mixture over the portobellos. Let marinate for at least 30 minutes, spooning the marinade back onto the mushrooms every 10 minutes or so.

Lightly grease the grill and preheat it to medium-high heat. It's important to keep some oil nearby for brushing the grill throughout the cooking process. You can use a grill brush or a paper towel wadded up and grasped in your tongs.

Place the mushrooms, gill-side up, on the grill. Close the lid and let the shrooms cook for about 5 minutes, lifting the lid to baste them with the marinade every few minutes. Use tongs to turn the mushrooms 90 degrees to make crosshatched grill marks; cook for about 3 more minutes. Flip the mushrooms over and cook for about 3 more minutes. Your cooking time may vary depending on the size of your portobellos and the temperature of your grill. You know the mushrooms are done when you press on the center (where the stem used to be) with tongs and it's very soft and juicy.

Transfer the mushrooms to a plate and let rest for about 5 minutes. This lets the flavors develop, and the juices taste even yummier when they are a little bit cooled down. You can use this time to slice your bread and prep the veggies.

Slather the focaccia with mayo, assemble the sandwiches with the mushrooms, arugula, onion, and tomato, and sink your teeth in.

GRILLED TOFU
with Peanut Sauce

MAKES
12
SKEWERS

TOTAL
30 MINUTES
ACTIVE
20 MINUTES

FOR THE SAUCE:

2 garlic cloves, peeled

1 tablespoon minced fresh ginger

¾ cup creamy natural peanut butter

½ cup water, plus more as needed

¼ cup rice vinegar

3 tablespoons tamari or soy sauce

4 teaspoons agave

2 teaspoons sriracha

1½ teaspoons toasted sesame oil

¾ teaspoon salt

FOR THE TOFU:

2 (14-ounce) packages extra-firm tofu, pressed

¼ cup tamari or soy sauce

2 tablespoons olive oil

1 tablespoon toasted sesame oil

Toasted sesame seeds, for garnish

Chopped scallions, for garnish

Tofu on the grill is a beautiful thing! It takes to grill marks like a dream, charring up to be Instagram-perfect in minutes. This version doesn't require a marinade, just a quick dip in some soy and sesame oil. Then it's smothered in a very simple peanut sauce that packs a punch but is very easy to whip up. Serve over greens, or over additional grilled veggies like red peppers and summer squash—you'll definitely want more stuff to sop up sauce with. You will need twelve 8-inch wooden skewers for this recipe; remember to soak them in water for 30 minutes before putting them on the grill, to prevent them from burning.

MAKE THE SAUCE: Combine all the sauce ingredients in a blender and puree until completely smooth. Thin with water as necessary to get a thick but pourable sauce. Taste and adjust for salt and seasoning. The sauce can be made up to 3 days in advance and stored in a tightly sealed container in the refrigerator.

MAKE THE TOFU: Cut one block of tofu crosswise into 8 slabs. Then cut the slabs in half lengthwise so that you have 16 rectangles. Repeat with the second block of tofu.

In a wide, shallow dish, mix the tamari and both oils. In batches, dip the tofu rectangles in the mixture to lightly coat, then set aside on a separate plate.

Lightly grease your grill, and preheat it to medium-high heat. Thread three or four tofu rectangles on each skewer, leaving space at the bottom for handling.

Place the skewers on the grill so that the tofu lies flat. Let cook until grill marks appear, about 3 minutes, then use a very thin metal spatula to flip and cook the other side for 3 minutes. Remove from the grill.

You can serve the skewers family style on a platter, with the sauce and garnishes on the side. Or serve on individual plates, drizzled with sauce and sprinkled with the sesame seeds and scallions.

Eggplant
CHIMICHURRI
KABOBS

FOR THE EGGPLANT:

2 pounds eggplant, cut into 1½-inch chunks

½ teaspoon salt

FOR THE CHIMICHURRI:

6 garlic cloves, peeled

1½ cups loosely packed fresh cilantro leaves

1½ cups loosely packed fresh parsley leaves

⅓ cup red wine vinegar

⅓ cup olive oil

⅓ cup vegetable broth, purchased or homemade (page 67)

1½ teaspoons dried oregano

¾ teaspoon salt

¾ teaspoon crushed red pepper flakes

When meat eaters want something vegetarian, they naturally gravitate toward eggplant. And nowhere does it shine so brightly as on the grill, so meaty and juicy! It makes perfect sense to pair it with chimichurri, the herby Argentine steak sauce. You will need twelve 8-inch wooden skewers for this recipe; remember to soak them in water for 30 minutes before grilling to prevent them from burning.

PREP THE EGGPLANT: In a large mixing bowl, sprinkle the eggplant with the salt. Toss to coat and transfer to a colander. Place the colander in the sink to let the eggplant drain for about 30 minutes (the salt will coax out some moisture). Wipe out the bowl to be used again later.

MAKE THE CHIMICHURRI: Meanwhile, pulse the garlic in a blender to get it chopped up. Add the remaining chimichurri ingredients and blend until relatively smooth, with a little texture left.

FINISH THE EGGPLANT: Return the eggplant to the large mixing bowl and add half of the chimichurri. Let the eggplant marinate at room temperature for about an hour.

Lightly grease your grill and set it to medium-high heat. Thread 4 or 5 chunks of eggplant on each skewer.

Place the skewers on the grill and cook, brushing with extra chimichurri and turning the skewers every few minutes to get all sides charred, about 8 minutes total. You may need to use a thin metal spatula to turn the skewers, to prevent sticking.

Transfer the skewers to a serving plate and spoon the remaining chimichurri over them to serve.

Crackly
POTATO
KABOBS

2 pounds baby potatoes (about 36)

¼ cup olive oil

2 teaspoons grated lemon zest

1 teaspoon coarse salt

Freshly ground black pepper

Sauce suggestions: tahini dressing (page 231), Bestest Pesto (page 64), queso (page 45), maple-mustard dressing (page 49)

This is how baby potatoes were meant to be! Blanching the potatoes ahead of time makes them tender and creamy inside, and leaving the skin on creates a charred volcanic exterior. You can serve these with any number of sauces you like, or just alongside your veggie burger as is. Honestly, perfectly grilled potatoes need little more than salt, pepper, and a little lemon to turn them into flavor explosions.

Choose potatoes that are around 1½ inches in diameter, and pick ones that are mostly the same size so that they cook evenly. You will need sixteen 8-inch wooden skewers for this recipe; remember to soak them in water for 30 minutes before grilling to prevent them from burning.

In a 4-quart pot, submerge the potatoes in lightly salted cold water. Cover the pot and bring the water to a boil over high heat. Reduce the heat and simmer until the potatoes are tender, about 10 minutes. Drain them in a large colander and set aside to cool a bit.

In a large mixing bowl, toss the potatoes with the olive oil, lemon zest, salt, and plenty of black pepper.

Lightly grease your grill and heat it to medium-high heat. Thread four or five potatoes onto each skewer, leaving about an inch of space at the bottom.

Place the skewers on the grill and cook, turning the skewers as the potatoes char, until the skins are charred and crackly, about 5 minutes total. You may need to use a thin metal spatula to help turn the skewers if they start to stick to the grill.

Transfer the skewers to a serving plate and spoon on whatever sauce you are using, or you can pull them off the skewer to serve in a bowl, as a little potato side dish with burgers or what have you.

MAKES

6

BURGERS

TOTAL
45 MINUTES
ACTIVE
20 MINUTES

Classic VEGGIE BURGERS

2 tablespoons olive oil, plus more for brushing

1 small yellow onion, diced medium

Salt

8 ounces cremini mushrooms, thinly sliced

3 garlic cloves, minced

½ teaspoon dried thyme

½ teaspoon fennel seeds, crushed

Freshly ground black pepper

1 (15-ounce) can lentils, rinsed and drained, or 1½ cups cooked lentils

1 tablespoon ground flaxseed

2 tablespoons tamari or soy sauce

2 tablespoons water

2 teaspoons fresh lemon juice

¼ teaspoon liquid smoke (optional)

1 cup bread crumbs

½ cup finely chopped walnuts

Lentils and walnuts and mushrooms...this veggie burger has everything! And it holds up on the grill just great. I love a huge scoop of Eggy Potato Salad (page 262) on top to complete life.

Preheat a large, heavy-bottomed nonstick pan (preferably cast iron) over medium-high heat. Heat the oil, then sauté the onion with a pinch of salt for 3 minutes. Add the mushrooms, garlic, thyme, fennel, and a few grinds of black pepper and sauté until the mushrooms are cooked, 7 to 10 minutes.

In a food processor fitted with the metal blade, puree the lentils with the flaxseed, tamari, water, lemon juice, and liquid smoke (if using) until smooth.

Add the mushroom mixture to the food processor, along with ½ cup of the bread crumbs, and pulse to combine. Do not puree it smooth; leave a little bit of texture.

Transfer the mixture to a large mixing bowl. Add the remaining ½ cup bread crumbs and the chopped walnuts and combine thoroughly. The mixture should hold its shape very well.

Let the mixture chill and firm up for about 30 minutes before proceeding.

Divide the burger mix into six equal portions. Form the six portions into patties.

Lightly grease the grill and preheat it to medium-high. Brush each burger with a little olive oil and cook on each side for about 5 minutes. The grill marks should be dark and the burgers should feel very firm.

These burgers taste great right off the grill, but they can also sit at room temperature and be lightly reheated on the grill if needed.

BURGERTIME FOREVER

The Classic Veggie Burger (page 279) is very versatile. You can swap out a few ingredients, or add a few toppings, to come up with a different burger for every day of the week—or year! Here are a few of my favorites.

White Bean Burgers with Coleslaw Swap the lentils for white beans. Swap the walnuts for slivered almonds. Leave out the tamari and fennel. Add an extra ½ teaspoon salt and 2 extra tablespoons water. When you pulse in the mushrooms, also pulse in ¼ cup fresh dill. Serve with Vegan Mayo (page 67) and coleslaw (page 128) and plenty of pickles.

Black Bean Burgers with Guacamole Swap the lentils for black beans. Swap the fennel for 1 teaspoon ground cumin. When you pulse in the mushrooms, also pulse in ¼ cup fresh cilantro. Serve with Super-Classic Guacamole (page 217), lettuce, tomato, red onion, and hot sauce.

Pizza Burgers Make the burgers as directed. After grilling the first side, flip and top with Marinara Sauce (page 65) or Pizza Awesomesauce (page 268) and use a squirt bottle to drizzle with Swirly Pizza Cheese (page 267). Cook for another 5 minutes.

BBQ Veggie Burgers with Grilled Pineapple Make the burgers as directed. Grill pineapple slices just until grill marks appear. Have ready a mixing bowl with your favorite BBQ sauce, warmed a bit. Coat each burger in the sauce and serve with the grilled pineapple and sliced avocado.

SMOKY
DOGS

6 ounces extra-firm silken tofu (half of a 12-ounce package)

1 cup vegetable broth, purchased or homemade (page 203)

¼ cup ketchup

2 tablespoons tamari or soy sauce

1 tablespoon olive oil

1 teaspoon liquid smoke

1½ cups plus 2 tablespoons vital wheat gluten

¼ cup nutritional yeast flakes

1 tablespoon onion powder

2 teaspoons sweet paprika

½ teaspoon salt

¼ teaspoon ground white pepper

——— *Tip* ———

This sounds mean, but don't use "environmentally friendly" parchment paper or you run the risk of the hot dogs sticking to it. Regular old parchment gets you that smooth hot doggy skin you desire.

It isn't summer without a big, sloppy hot dog in your hand and mustard all over your face. (Or if you're a weirdo like my sister, ketchup. Weird.) These smoky dogs are so much yummier than store-bought vegan dogs and, although impressive, they aren't hard to make. They grill up so lovely, with a skin that goes "pop" as you bite into it.

In a food processor fitted with the metal blade, puree the tofu, broth, ketchup, tamari, olive oil, and liquid smoke until completely smooth, scraping down the sides with a rubber spatula to make sure you get everything.

In a large mixing bowl, mix together the vital wheat gluten, nutritional yeast, onion powder, paprika, salt, and white pepper.

Make a well in the center and add the tofu mixture. Use the rubber spatula to mix until well combined, and then use your hands to further knead the mixture until it's a well-formed dough with a little spring to it.

Prepare your steamer. Have ready eight large squares of parchment and eight sheets of aluminum foil.

Divide the dough into eight equal pieces. Roll each piece into a hot dog shape. Now place one hot dog at the bottom of a square of parchment and roll it up. Then do the same in a piece of foil, this time tightly sealing the ends like a Tootsie Roll. Repeat with the remaining dogs.

Steam the hot dogs for about 40 minutes, until very firm.

Let the dogs cool completely before unwrapping. Then preheat a grill to medium-high heat. Unwrap the cooled dogs and grill, turning them once, until grill marks appear, about 3 minutes.

Serve with your favorite accompaniments.

Little
BLUEBERRY
GALETTES

2 cups fresh blueberries (about a pint)

3 tablespoons sugar

1 tablespoon cornstarch

1 teaspoon grated lemon zest

Salt

2 recipes (double) Pastry Crust (page 358)

1 tablespoon unsweetened almond milk (or your favorite nondairy milk)

1 tablespoon pure maple syrup

A galette is a rustically beautiful way to enjoy summer berries without having to "perfect" a pie crust. It's a free-form pie, so anything goes, and it looks pretty no matter what. These little ones can be eaten with a fork or handheld, if you like your pie in grab-and-go form. Serve with your favorite ice cream!

Preheat the oven to 375°F. Line a large rimmed baking sheet with parchment paper and coat it lightly with nonstick cooking spray.

In a large bowl, combine the blueberries, sugar, cornstarch, lemon zest, and a pinch of salt. Toss to coat well, then set aside.

On a lightly floured surface, roll out the pastry crust dough to ¼-inch thickness. Use a small bowl or cookie cutter to cut out 4-inch disks. You will need to gather your scraps and cut out disks twice to get a total of eight. Place the pastry disks on the prepared baking sheet and mound some blueberry filling in the center of each.

Fold ½ inch of pastry over the edge of the filling all the way around, pinching and crimping to seal. In a small bowl, whisk together the milk and syrup. Brush the edges of the pastry with the mixture.

Bake the galettes until the pastry is golden and the filling is bubbly, 20 to 25 minutes. Serve warm (let cool a bit first) or chilled.

13

ROSH HASHANAH and YOM KIPPUR

THESE HOLIDAYS HAVE
always indicated that
BITTERSWEET TRANSITION
from summer to fall.

REMEMBER BEING A child, walking to temple, summer memories fresh in my mind but autumn leaves swirling around my brand-new Mary Janes.

Little did I realize then that this was absolutely the best season for produce!

Okay, so these are the high holy days of Judaism. Come Rosh Hashanah, the feast begins. This is the Jewish new year, and our plates get full. Go for a roast with braised veggies and plenty of beautiful golden challah. Make sure that you try the Bagel & Nox (page 28), too—because no New Year should be without a full bagel spread. It's the circle of life!

Then comes Yom Kippur, the Day of Atonement, when you fast. The matters at hand are so much more important than food. (Although, honestly, even after so many years of Jewish sleepaway camp, I'm still not sure I know what the matters at hand are.) But what to eat when you break the fast? Casseroles, sweet potatoes, and full-on-flavor salads!

CHALLAH
FRENCH TOAST

1½ cups unsweetened almond milk
(or your favorite nondairy milk)

3 tablespoons cornstarch

⅓ cup chickpea flour

Refined coconut oil, for pan-frying

1 loaf day-old Challah (page 305),
cut into ¾-inch-thick slices

Tip

*To keep the French toast warm,
have ready a large plate. Place the
cooked slices on the plate and tent
with aluminum foil while cooking
the rest.*

This recipe captures love, adoration, and appreciation all in a fluffy tower of battered bread. Bake the bread at least 2 days in advance, so it can dry out a little, becoming easier to coat in batter and fry. Serve this French toast with fresh berries, powdered sugar, and pure maple syrup. Dabs of coconut oil are nice, too!

Pour the milk into a wide, shallow bowl. Mix in the cornstarch and stir with a fork until dissolved. Add the chickpea flour and mix until it is mostly absorbed; some lumps are okay.

Heat a large, heavy-bottomed nonstick pan (preferably cast iron) over medium-high heat. Add enough oil to create a thin layer on the bottom (a tablespoon or two).

Soak four slices of challah in the batter at a time. Transfer them to the hot pan, adding extra oil if necessary before the addition of each slice.

Cook until golden brown with flecks of dark brown, about 2 minutes per side. Repeat with the rest of the challah. Serve immediately.

SWEET POTATO
APPLES
with Candied Pecans

FOR THE SWEET POTATOES AND APPLES:

1½ pounds sweet potatoes, scrubbed

8 red apples (see Tip)

2 tablespoons refined coconut oil

2 tablespoons vegan honey or pure maple syrup

2 teaspoons grated fresh ginger

½ teaspoon ground cinnamon

¼ teaspoon salt

FOR THE CANDIED PECANS:

½ cup pecan halves

2 teaspoons refined coconut oil

⅛ teaspoon salt

¼ cup vegan honey or pure maple syrup

These baked apples are filled with a creamy, gingery sweet potato filling. They're the perfect sweet accompaniment to a savory September dinner when apples are just coming into season, and they're especially welcome in a Jewish holiday spread. (But I wouldn't kick 'em off a Thanksgiving table, either.)

You can use any sweet potato you like here; jewel and garnet both work well. It doesn't matter what size they are, as long as you bake them until they are very tender. There should be no resistance if you stick a steak knife through the center. This makes it much easier to get them smooth and creamy and ready to pipe into the apples.

BAKE THE SWEET POTATOES AND APPLES: Preheat the oven to 350°F. Coat a 9-by-13-inch casserole dish with a little nonstick cooking spray.

Place the whole sweet potatoes on a baking sheet. No need to cut them or poke them with a fork.

Cut the apples in half across the waist and place them, cut-side down, in the casserole. Cover tightly with aluminum foil.

Put the sweet potatoes on the lower rack of the oven and the apples on the upper rack. Bake until the apples are just softened and beginning to brown around the edges. Check after about 30 minutes—they should still be a little firm so that they hold their shape.

Remove the apples from the oven and continue to bake the sweet potatoes until completely fork-tender, 30 more minutes or so, depending on their size.

WHILE THE SWEET POTATOES CONTINUE BAKING, CANDY THE PECANS: Have ready a large plate covered with a sheet of parchment paper.

Preheat a heavy-bottomed pan (preferably cast iron) over medium-low heat. Toast the pecans in the dry pan, tossing frequently, for about 5 minutes.

Add the coconut oil and sprinkle in the salt, then toss to coat as the coconut oil melts. Add the honey and let it bubble for about 30 seconds, tossing the entire time.

Transfer to the lined plate and let cool. Once cool, break apart the pieces and roughly chop them.

Recipe Continues

I love red apples for these. They bake really nicely and look prettier than green or yellow might. Some varieties I recommend are Gala, Braeburn, or Pink Lady. They all bake differently, though, so pay attention to the time so that they don't over- or underbake.

Vegan honey is available in a few different varieties. Since things are in and out of the market so quickly these days, I don't want to recommend one over another, but they all taste luxurious. If you can't find any and don't want to order it online, you can totally use maple syrup!

If you don't have a pastry bag and a large metal tip, you can use a plastic zip-top bag with a ½-inch slit cut out of one corner. It won't be quite as pretty, but it will get the job done!

FILL THE APPLES AND SERVE: When the sweet potatoes are ready, cut them in half and scoop the yummy insides into a mixing bowl. Add the coconut oil and use a masher to make them very smooth. Mix in the honey, ginger, cinnamon, and salt. Cover and keep warm until ready to pipe.

Use a spoon to scoop out the apple cores, leaving a ½-inch rim of apple around the edges. Place them, cut-side up, in a serving dish. Transfer the sweet potato mixture to a pastry bag fitted with an extra-large metal tip and pipe it into each apple. Scatter the candied pecans on top and serve.

MACADAMIA CHEESE BLINTZES

with Cherries

MAKES
6
BLINTZES

TOTAL
1 HOUR 15 MINUTES
ACTIVE
1 HOUR 15 MINUTES

FOR THE MACADAMIA CHEESE:

2 cups macadamia nuts, soaked in water overnight and drained

¼ cup unsweetened almond milk (or your favorite nondairy milk)

2 tablespoons agave

2 tablespoons refined coconut oil, melted

1 teaspoon pure vanilla extract

⅛ teaspoon salt

1 teaspoon grated lemon zest

2 tablespoons fresh lemon juice

FOR THE CHERRY SAUCE:

6 cups pitted cherries, fresh or frozen

½ cup granulated sugar

2 tablespoons cornstarch

¼ cup cold water

FOR THE BLINTZES:

1 recipe Lacy Crêpes (page 22)

Refined coconut oil, for pan-frying

¼ cup powdered sugar, for serving

Any brunch spread with a platter of these beauties will become instantly unforgettable. If you're not familiar with blintzes, they are a stuffed Russian crêpe that is taken one step further: After they're stuffed with cheese, they're briefly pan-fried. Then they're topped with fruit—cherries look especially festive. That's some next-level stuff right there!

MAKE THE MACADAMIA CHEESE: Pulse the macadamias in a food processor a few times to break them up. Add the almond milk, agave, coconut oil, vanilla, and salt. Blend until relatively smooth, but don't overdo it so that it turns into cashew butter. It should have a thick, creamy consistency with just a bit of graininess.

Transfer the cheese to a mixing bowl. Add the lemon zest and juice and mix well. Taste and add more juice if you like. Cover and refrigerate until ready to use.

MAKE THE CHERRY SAUCE: Combine all the sauce ingredients in a saucepan. Stir to dissolve the cornstarch. Turn the heat to medium. Cook, using a wooden spoon to stir often, until the sauce is sticky and thick and the cherries have burst and released their juices, about 15 minutes. Keep warm until ready to use.

MAKE THE BLINTZES: Place ⅓ cup cheese in the lower third of a crêpe. Fold the bottom up and over the filling. Now fold in the left and right sides so that the cheese is tucked in snugly. Finally, roll up the blintz like a burrito. Repeat with all the crêpes.

Preheat a cast iron (or nonstick) pan over medium-high heat. Add some coconut oil to coat the bottom and place the blintzes, flap-side down, in the pan. Cook until golden brown, about 2 minutes per side.

Serve warm, sprinkled with powdered sugar and topped with cherry sauce.

STONE FRUIT and LENTIL SALAD

with Creamy Mustard Dressing

SERVES
6–8

TOTAL
20 MINUTES
ACTIVE
20 MINUTES

FOR THE PICKLED RED ONIONS:
¼ cup white wine vinegar
2 tablespoons sugar
Salt
1 small red onion, cut into thin half-
  moons

**FOR THE CREAMY MUSTARD
VINAIGRETTE:**
¼ cup Dijon mustard
¼ cup vegan mayo, purchased or
  homemade (page 67)
2 tablespoons chopped shallot or
  onion
1 garlic clove, minced
1 tablespoon white wine vinegar
Big pinch salt

FOR THE SALAD:
4 ounces mixed greens
1 romaine heart, chopped
1 pound stone fruit, diced
2 cups cooked French, beluga,
  brown, or green lentils (see Tip)

This salad, studded with lentils, makes the most of late summer flavors. It's hearty and light at the same time. Sweet and savory. Whimsical, yet down to earth. Full of contradiction. It's the Zooey Deschanel of salad! The pickled red onions bring a bright tang to the dish that pulls everything together. I use French or beluga lentils here because they hold their shape wonderfully. Brown or green would work, too, but don't mess with red lentils or you'll have mush salad. You can use whichever stone fruit you'd like. Mix it up, even, with plums and apricots. Add some pitted cherries. Live a little.

MAKE THE PICKLED RED ONIONS: In a small bowl, whisk together the vinegar, sugar, and a pinch of salt. Add the onions and splash them around. Let them soak while you prepare everything else, giving them a stir every now and again. You can also prepare these a few hours or even a few days ahead, for a more pickly pickled onion.

MAKE THE CREAMY MUSTARD VINAIGRETTE: Whiz all the vinaigrette ingredients together in a small blender. Taste and adjust for salt and seasoning.

MAKE THE SALAD: In a large mixing bowl, toss together the greens, romaine, fruit, and lentils. Top with the pickled onions and drizzle with the vinaigrette. Serve!

Tip

To cook 1 cup of lentils, submerge them in slightly salted water by 3 inches. Throw in a bay leaf, if you like. Cover and bring it all to a boil. Once boiling, lower the heat and simmer for about 20 minutes with the lid slightly ajar to allow steam to escape. Check for tenderness after 20 minutes, but it could take 30 or even 40 minutes for them to be Goldilocks perfect: not too soft, not too hard.

Once the lentils are tender enough, drain and spread them out in the colander to cool. (Obviously, make sure the colander has holes small enough that the lentils won't fall through.) If you need to speed-chill them, place in the freezer and give them a stir every few minutes. They'll cool in 15 minutes or so that way. Otherwise, put them in the fridge once they've stopped steaming. You can do this a few days ahead.

BROWN SUGAR
CARROTS

2 pounds large carrots, peeled and cut on a bias into 1-inch pieces

3 tablespoons olive oil

¼ cup brown sugar

1 teaspoon grated orange zest

¾ teaspoon salt

Freshly ground black pepper

1 teaspoon crushed red pepper flakes (optional)

Somehow these humble little carrots always steal the show. They are sweet and salty, with a hint of orange zest. When roasted, they become melt-in-your-mouth tender. I like to add a little spice, so a hit of red pepper flakes at the end is my favorite—but you can leave it off.

Preheat the oven to 400°F. Line a rimmed baking sheet with parchment paper.

Toss the carrots in a large mixing bowl with the olive oil, brown sugar, orange zest, salt, and a few grinds of black pepper. Arrange them on the baking sheet in a single layer and roast until caramelized and tender, 20 to 25 minutes.

Transfer to a serving tray and sprinkle with red pepper flakes, if desired. Serve!

GEFILTE
CHICKPEAS

½ sheet nori

2 (15-ounce) cans chickpeas, rinsed and drained, or 3 cups cooked chickpeas

½ cup vegan mayo, purchased or homemade (page 67)

2 tablespoons prepared horseradish

4 medium carrots, peeled, 2 grated and 2 sliced into thin coins

2 celery ribs, finely diced

3 tablespoons onion flakes

½ teaspoon salt

Freshly ground black pepper

Chopped fresh parsley, for garnish

When I first went vegan, I was in no hurry to veganize gefilte fish. However, over the years, I've come to crave fishy flavors. Now it's been so long since I've had gefilte fish, I figure, what the hey? Let's give it a vegan go! Everyone at your holiday table will appreciate this not-from-a-jar chickpea version. It's actually just a spin on my all-time favorite chickpea salad sandwich. Make this a day ahead so that it has time for the flavors to meld and to let it firm up, making it easier to form into little scoops that hold their shape.

In a small blender, pulse the nori into fine flakes. Transfer to a plate and set aside.

In a mixing bowl, use an avocado masher or a strong fork to mash the chickpeas very well. Mix in the mayo and horseradish and give them a few more mashes. Mix in the grated carrots, celery, onion flakes, and nori flakes. Add the salt and a few grinds of black pepper. Taste and adjust for seasoning.

Cover the bowl with plastic wrap and refrigerate overnight. Use an ice cream scoop to scoop little mounds onto a serving plate. Scatter the carrot coins over the mounds and sprinkle with parsley to serve.

TATER TOT
KUGEL

1 (12-ounce) package extra-firm silken tofu

⅓ cup olive oil

1 tablespoon cornstarch

2 teaspoons salt

4 pounds russet potatoes, scrubbed and cut into long pieces that will fit in your food processor's shredder

1 large onion

¾ cup matzoh meal

Freshly ground black pepper

I could have called this dish Potato Kugel, but who would care about that when the truth is that this tastes like a gigantic Tater Tot? Needless to say, it is magnificent.

Preheat the oven to 375°F. Lightly grease a 9-by-13-inch casserole dish.

In a food processor fitted with the metal blade, blend the tofu, olive oil, cornstarch, and salt until completely smooth. Transfer the mixture to a very large mixing bowl.

Rinse out the food processor and switch to the shredder attachment. Shred the potatoes and onion and transfer to the bowl with the tofu mixture. Add the matzoh meal and a healthy dose of black pepper and mix well.

Transfer the mixture to the prepared casserole and fluff the top a bit with a fork to make sure you get some crispy texture as it bakes.

Bake the kugel until browned on top and pulling away from the sides, about 1 hour 15 minutes. Let cool for 20 minutes or so, just to set it a little, before slicing and eating.

Pineapple NOODLE KUGEL

SERVES
8–12

TOTAL
1 HOUR 30 MINUTES
ACTIVE
20 MINUTES

FOR THE KUGEL:

1 pound rombi noodles or lasagna noodles, torn into 2-inch pieces

¼ cup refined coconut oil

2 (14-ounce) cans coconut milk

1 cup unsweetened almond milk (or your favorite nondairy milk)

3 tablespoons cornstarch

½ cup sugar

2 teaspoons pure vanilla extract

½ teaspoon salt

1 recipe Almond Ricotta (below)

1 (20-ounce) can crushed pineapple, drained

FOR THE TOPPING:

2 cups coarsely crushed cornflakes

2 tablespoons sugar

½ teaspoon ground cinnamon

2 tablespoons refined coconut oil, cut into bits

If you didn't go to Jewish sleepaway camp, you'll look at this recipe and say, "Pineapples and noodles and ricotta? What in the…?" But if you know what I'm talking about, you're right there with me, completely excited to get this on the table and into your belly. It's kind of a dessert, but my family always served it right alongside the brisket, so here it shall remain.

MAKE THE KUGEL: Preheat the oven to 350°F. Lightly grease a 9-by-13-inch baking dish.

Boil the noodles in salted water according to the package instructions until al dente. Drain them in a colander, then return them to the warm pot. Add the coconut oil and toss until it melts and coats the noodles.

In a blender, whiz together the coconut milk, almond milk, and cornstarch until the cornstarch is thoroughly dissolved. Add the sugar, vanilla, and salt and pulse to combine. Pour the mixture into the pasta pot, along with the almond ricotta and crushed pineapple. Stir until everything is very well combined. Transfer the mixture to the prepared baking dish.

MAKE THE TOPPING AND BAKE THE KUGEL: Stir together the cornflakes, sugar, and cinnamon and sprinkle evenly over the kugel. Dot with the coconut oil. Bake until the kugel is set and the edges are golden brown, about 1 hour. Let stand for at least 5 minutes before serving.

Almond RICOTTA

MAKES
3
CUPS

TOTAL
15 minutes
ACTIVE
15 minutes

2 cups slivered almonds

⅔ cup water

2 tablespoons refined coconut oil

2 tablespoons olive oil

¼ cup lemon juice

1½ teaspoon salt

Boil the almonds in the water for about 30 minutes. Drain and place in a blender. Add the coconut oil and puree a bit just to melt the oil.

Add the olive oil, lemon juice, and salt. Puree so that it's not completely smooth and there's some texture left. It should resemble ricotta (obviously).

Transfer to a container, cover, and refrigerate for at least 3 hours, so that it sets.

BROCCOLI
KUGEL

SERVES
8–12

TOTAL
1 HOUR 15 MINUTES
ACTIVE
30 MINUTES

3 cups rombi noodles or lasagna noodles, torn into 2-inch pieces

4 tablespoons olive oil

1 medium onion, diced small

4 cups broccoli florets

1¼ cups matzoh meal

¼ cup lightly packed chopped fresh dill

¾ teaspoon salt

½ teaspoon freshly ground black pepper

1 (12-ounce) package extra-firm silken tofu

1 cup vegetable broth, purchased or homemade (page 67)

2 tablespoons fresh lemon juice

Another kugel, this one veggiful and dilly and cozy! It's sort of like a quiche went swing dancing with a lasagna.

Preheat the oven to 350°F. Lightly grease a 9-by-13-inch baking pan.

Boil the noodles in salted water according to the package instructions until al dente. Drain and set aside.

Preheat a large pan over medium heat. Heat 2 tablespoons of the olive oil, then sauté the onion until translucent, about 3 minutes. Add the broccoli and sauté just until it's cooked through and softened, about 5 minutes. Set aside.

In a large mixing bowl, mix the matzoh meal, dill, salt, and black pepper and set aside.

In a food processor fitted with the metal blade, blend the tofu, broth, lemon juice, and remaining 2 tablespoons olive oil until totally smooth. Add the mixture to the matzoh meal in the mixing bowl, along with the pasta, onion, and broccoli, and thoroughly combine. Using your hands is the best strategy here, being careful not to break up the pasta.

Transfer the mixture to the baking dish and bake until the top is lightly browned and the edges start pulling away from the sides, 35 to 40 minutes. Wait at least 5 minutes before slicing and serving.

SUNDRIED TOMATO
SEITAN ROAST
with Braised Vegetables

SERVES
8

TOTAL
3 HOURS
ACTIVE
45 MINUTES

FOR THE SEITAN ROAST:

3 garlic cloves, peeled

¾ cup cooked or canned lentils, rinsed and drained

¼ cup oil-packed sundried tomatoes, drained

1½ cups vegetable broth, purchased or homemade (page 67)

3 tablespoons tamari or soy sauce

2 tablespoons olive oil

2 cups vital wheat gluten

⅓ cup nutritional yeast flakes

1 teaspoon sweet paprika

½ teaspoon dried thyme, crushed with your fingers

Freshly ground black pepper

FOR THE VEGGIES:

1 tablespoon olive oil

1 medium onion, cut into thin half-moons

1 teaspoon salt, plus a pinch

1 garlic clove, minced

¾ teaspoon dried rosemary

4 cups diced fresh tomatoes (½-inch dice)

1 pound Yukon Gold potatoes, scrubbed and cut into 1-inch chunks

12 ounces carrots, peeled and cut on a bias into ½-inch pieces

2 celery ribs, cut on a bias into ½-inch pieces

4 cups vegetable broth, purchased or homemade (page 67)

Freshly ground black pepper

This is the centerpiece to end all centerpieces. The kind of meal that you can imagine brings conversation to a halt and makes everyone, just for a few moments, forget all their problems and appreciate the finer things. Like braised vegetables swimming in a light tomato broth around a gorgeous roast!

MAKE THE SEITAN ROAST: Preheat the oven to 350°F. Have ready a sheet of aluminum foil that is at least 16 inches long.

In a food processor, pulse the garlic. Add the lentils, sundried tomatoes, broth, tamari, and olive oil and puree until relatively smooth.

In a large mixing bowl, mix the wheat gluten, nutritional yeast, paprika, thyme, and a few grinds of black pepper. Make a well in the center and add the lentil mixture. Stir with a wooden spoon until the mixture starts coming together to form a ball of dough. Knead until everything is well incorporated.

Shape the seitan into a log that is roughly 8 inches long. It doesn't have to be perfectly shaped; it will adjust itself as it bakes. Place the log lengthwise in the center of the foil and roll it up like a Tootsie Roll, making sure the ends are tightly wrapped. Place the log on a baking sheet and bake for 1 hour 15 minutes, turning the roll every 20 minutes for even cooking.

IN THE MEANTIME, MAKE THE VEGGIES: Preheat a 4-quart pot over medium heat. Heat the oil, then sauté the onion with a pinch of salt until lightly caramelized, about 5 minutes. Add the garlic and rosemary and sauté until fragrant, 30 seconds or so.

Mix in the tomatoes to deglaze the pan. Add the potatoes, carrots, celery, broth, remaining 1 teaspoon salt, and a few grinds of black pepper. Cover the pot and bring it to a boil. Once boiling, lower the heat and simmer, covered, until the potatoes are tender, about 15 more minutes. Then lower the heat to the lowest possible setting and cook, covered, for 20 more minutes or so, just to develop the flavors.

BACK TO THE ROAST: Once the seitan roast is cooked through, let it cool until it's not too hot to handle. Unwrap the foil and place the entire roast right in the stew. Let it soak in there for 10 minutes or so, with the heat turned off.

Remove the seitan roast from the stew, place it on a cutting board, and cut it into ¼-inch-thick slices. Now transfer the stew to a casserole dish and place the sliced roast in there. Serve!

CHALLAH

1½ cups water

½ teaspoon ground turmeric

½ cup refined coconut oil

½ cup plus 1 tablespoon sugar

⅓ cup warm water

2½ tablespoons active dry yeast

2 very overripe bananas

1 tablespoon salt

7 cups all-purpose flour, plus extra
  for kneading

2 tablespoons pure maple syrup

2 tablespoons unsweetened almond
  milk (or your favorite nondairy
  milk)

2 teaspoons poppy seeds

So fluffy and doughy. So cuddly and perfect that it even looks like a hug. Challah is such an inviting golden amber with gorgeous yolky yellow poking through. This recipe satisfies every nook and cranny of my memory growing up in Brooklyn, eating challah fresh from the bakery. The original idea to use bananas was actually from an old user-submitted recipe on my website, but it's undergone a million alterations in the past decade or so. The result is crusty and toasty on the outside and buttery and soft inside, with that beautiful yolky-yellow crumb.

Combine the water and turmeric in a small saucepot. Bring to a boil over medium heat, then immediately turn off the heat. Add the coconut oil and ½ cup of the sugar to the pot, and stir to melt the coconut oil. You want the mixture to cool so that it isn't hot to the touch but is still warm. So, just let it sit while you work on the rest of the recipe.

In a very large mixing bowl, mix the warm water and remaining 1 tablespoon sugar. Sprinkle in the yeast and set aside to get all yeasty.

In a separate bowl, mash the bananas very well, until they appear pureed. The coconut oil mixture should be cooled enough now, so proceed with the recipe.

Add the mashed banana to the yeast bowl, along with the slightly warm coconut oil mixture. Stir just to combine. Add the salt and then the flour, 1 cup at a time. Mix after each addition, and begin to knead with your hands when a dough starts to form. Once all 7 cups have been added, turn out the dough onto a lightly floured counter and begin to knead like crazy for 10 minutes or so, until the dough is nice and smooth. Add up to another ½ cup of flour as needed, until the dough is no longer tacky. Form the dough into a ball.

Wipe out the mixing bowl and lightly grease it. Add the ball of dough, spinning it into the bowl to get it lightly coated in oil. Cover the bowl with plastic wrap or a towel and set aside to rise for about 1½ hours. The dough should double in size.

Grease two rimmed baking sheets and set them aside. Also, make sure you have plenty of space for rolling out the dough ropes to create the braids.

When the dough has doubled, punch it down, knead it lightly, and divide it in half. Take one half and divide it into thirds. Roll each third into a long rope, 18 inches or so.

Now place the three ropes on one baking sheet the long way and braid 'em! Pinch the ends together to form butts. Form the second braided loaf on the other baking sheet.

Recipe Continues

Let the loaves rise for about 30 minutes. They should get nice and puffy. No need to cover them for this part.

When the loaves are almost done rising, preheat the oven to 375°F.

Mix the maple syrup and milk in a small bowl. Brush the loaves with the mixture and sprinkle on the poppy seeds. Bake the loaves on separate racks, rotating the pans and swapping racks halfway through, until golden brown, about 40 minutes. If you tap them, they should sound hollow.

Let the challahs cool for 30 minutes or so, and then they are ready to slice and serve! I love them warm and doughy like that.

If you're not serving the challahs immediately, let them cool completely, then wrap in plastic and store at room temperature for up to 2 days.

CHALLAH TOAST

Don't just stop at beautiful slices of challah! Make some challah toast. Here are two ideas, one sweet, one savory. Guests will devour these. (There's also a recipe for Challah French Toast on page 288, so go crazy and make 4 loaves!)

Challah Toast with Apple Butter & Roasted Squash

Store-bought apple butter is fine here—I mean, you made your own challah, what more do people want? Toast thick slices of challah, spread on some apple butter, and top with roasted butternut squash. Finish with some crushed red pepper flakes for a little heat.

Challah Toast with Mushroom Pâté & Caramelized Onion

Toast thick slices of challah, spread on Swanky Mushroom Pâté (page 151), and top with Caramelized Onions (page 368). Finish with something pretty and green, like sliced fresh chives or chopped parsley.

Honey
BUNDT CAKE

SERVES
12–16

TOTAL
1 HOUR 30 MINUTES
ACTIVE
20 MINUTES

3½ cups all-purpose flour

1 tablespoon baking powder

1 teaspoon baking soda

½ teaspoon salt

4 teaspoons ground cinnamon

½ teaspoon ground cloves

½ teaspoon ground allspice

1¼ cups unsweetened almond milk
(or your favorite nondairy milk)

1 cup canola oil

1 cup vegan honey or agave

¾ cup pure apple juice

½ cup unsweetened applesauce

2 teaspoons pure vanilla extract

1½ cups sugar

Oh, honey! Look forward to a sweet year ahead because that is what this cake is all about. It's moist and deep and spicy with a little tart hint of apple, and begs for a cup of coffee and a few sighs of happiness.

Preheat the oven to 350°F. Lightly grease a 10-inch Bundt pan.

In a large bowl, whisk together the flour, baking powder, baking soda, salt, and spices. Make a well in the center and add the milk, oil, honey, apple juice, applesauce, vanilla, and sugar.

Using a strong wire whisk or an electric mixer on slow speed, combine the ingredients well to make a thick batter.

Spoon the batter into the prepared pan. Bake until the cake is very firm and springs back when touched, about 1 hour, or maybe 10 minutes more.

Let the cake sit until the pan is cool enough to touch. Invert onto a cooling rack to cool completely before slicing and serving.

CHOCOLATE
BABKA

MAKES
2
LOAVES

TOTAL
3 HOURS
ACTIVE
30 MINUTES

FOR THE DOUGH:

4 cups all-purpose flour

⅓ cup plus 2 tablespoons sugar

2 teaspoons salt

1 cup unsweetened almond milk (or your favorite nondairy milk), warmed

2¼ teaspoons active dry yeast (one 0.75-ounce packet)

⅓ cup mashed very ripe banana

½ cup refined coconut oil, at room temperature

FOR THE FILLING:

12 ounces semisweet chocolate chips

¾ cup refined coconut oil

1½ cups finely ground chocolate wafer cookies

3 tablespoons agave

2 teaspoons ground cinnamon

This takes a million bowls and a million years, but listen, once a year it's worth it! A rich and buttery dough gets all twisted up with chocolate and cinnamon. You pull apart the sections, each revealing swirl after swirl of chocolaty bliss. It's babka, baby!

MAKE THE DOUGH: In a medium mixing bowl, whisk together the flour, ⅓ cup of the sugar, and the salt. In a large mixing bowl, combine the warm milk with the yeast and the remaining 2 tablespoons sugar. Let it sit and get foamy.

Mix the mashed banana into the milk mixture. Add the dry ingredients in batches, mixing well, until all ingredients are incorporated. Mix in the coconut oil. Turn out the dough onto a floured surface and knead for a good 10 minutes, until smooth and elastic.

Wipe out the mixing bowl and lightly grease it. Add the ball of dough, spinning it in the bowl to get it lightly coated in oil. Cover the bowl with plastic wrap or a towel and set aside to rise for about 1½ hours. It should double in size.

Line a large baking sheet with parchment paper and lightly coat the parchment with oil. Divide the dough in half, and form into two rough squares on the parchment. Let the dough rise again in the refrigerator for about 30 minutes.

MEANWHILE, MAKE THE FILLING: In a large metal bowl set over a saucepan of simmering water, melt the chocolate with the coconut oil, stirring with a rubber spatula, until smooth. Let cool to room temperature, then stir in the cookie crumbs, agave, and cinnamon.

MAKE THE BABKAS: Lightly coat two 9-by-4-inch loaf pans with nonstick cooking spray and line them with parchment paper, allowing 2 inches of overhang on each of the long sides.

Roll out each square of dough to a 16-inch square. Remove ½ cup of the filling mixture and set aside.

Using an offset spatula, spread half of the remaining filling in an even layer over each of the dough squares, spreading to within ½ inch of the edges. Starting at the edge nearest you, tightly roll up each dough square jelly roll–style into a tight log.

Using a sharp knife, cut the logs in half crosswise. Using your offset spatula, spread half of the reserved filling on the top and sides of one of the halves. Set one of the other halves on top in the opposite direction to form a cross. Twist the two halves together to form spirals and transfer to one of the prepared pans. Repeat with the remaining filling and log halves. Cover the loaves with a towel and let stand in a warm place until doubled in size, about 2 hours.

When the loaves are almost done rising, preheat the oven to 375°F.

Bake the loaves until puffed and well browned, about 45 minutes. Let cool slightly, then use the parchment paper to lift the babkas out of the pans and onto a cooling rack. Let cool most of the way before slicing and serving.

14
HALLOWEEN

Okay, now we really get

TO HAVE SOME FUN.

THIS CHAPTER IS all about playing with your food. But even though Halloween is kitschy, it can still be totally delish! It is, after all, autumn, and those earthy, herby flavors are in full force here, even in a casserole that looks like a monster ghost!

It's also time for candy, and plenty of it! Making candy is a fun way to spend the afternoon. Even though it's still candy, a chocolate bar you made yourself is something to feel good about. Tempering chocolate and thickening caramel—these are skills that will make you a person everyone wants to be around, because if you know how to make candy you probably know everything. And maybe, just maybe, you even have some extra candy in your back pocket.

ROASTED CARROT HUMMUS
with Beet Chips

MAKES
3
CUPS

TOTAL
45 MINUTES
ACTIVE
45 MINUTES

FOR THE HUMMUS:

1½ pounds carrots, peeled and chopped into 1-inch pieces

4 tablespoons olive oil

2 garlic cloves, peeled

1 (15-ounce) can navy or great northern beans, rinsed and drained, or 1½ cups cooked beans

¼ cup tahini

3 tablespoons fresh lemon juice

2 teaspoons ground cumin

1 teaspoon salt

Freshly ground black pepper

2 to 4 tablespoons water

Chopped fresh parsley or carrot greens, for garnish

FOR THE BEET CHIPS:

1½ pounds red beets (about 3 medium-size beets)

3 tablespoons olive oil

½ teaspoon salt

Tip

To make perfect beet chips, you really need a mandoline here. I agree, mandolines are scary! But uneven beet chips are even scarier. Use larger beets to get perfect-size chips.

Blood-red beet chips and pumpkin-hued hummus make for the most gorgeous Technicolor dip! It's Halloween in a serving bowl. I like to use white beans in the hummus instead of chickpeas because they have a mellow flavor that really lets the sweet, earthy carrot shine. If you have beautiful green carrot tops from the farmers' market, chop 'em up as a garnish instead of parsley.

MAKE THE HUMMUS: Preheat the oven to 425°F. Line a rimmed baking sheet with parchment paper.

On the baking sheet, toss the carrots with 3 tablespoons of the olive oil and spread them out in a single layer. Roast, tossing once halfway through, until tender and slightly caramelized, 20 to 25 minutes. Remove from the oven and turn the oven down to 375°F to prepare for the beet chips.

In a food processor fitted with the metal blade, pulse the garlic to get it chopped up. Add the roasted carrots, beans, tahini, lemon juice, cumin, salt, and a few grinds of black pepper and blend to get everything combined. Stream in the remaining 1 tablespoon olive oil and blend till smooth. You will need a little water to thin the hummus, so start with 2 tablespoons and blend until velvety, keeping in mind it will firm up when it chills. Transfer to a sealed container and refrigerate until ready to serve.

MAKE THE BEET CHIPS: Slice the beets as thinly as possible, preferably with a mandoline, into a very large mixing bowl. Toss and drizzle them with the olive oil to coat completely.

Divide the beets between two large rimmed baking sheets and spread out in a single layer, being careful not to crowd them.

Place the baking sheets on separate oven racks and bake. After 7 or 8 minutes, rotate and swap the baking sheets, check to see if any beets are burning, and flip them if necessary. Bake until the beets have curled up at the edges and are lightly browned, 10 to 15 minutes total.

Remove the beets from the oven, sprinkle lightly with the salt, toss, and let cool on the baking sheets (they will crisp up even more). Serve the same day for maximum crispiness, with the hummus, garnished with parsley.

MUMMY
DOGS

8 sheets frozen phyllo dough, thawed

⅓ cup olive oil

½ teaspoon salt

8 Smoky Dogs (page 282) or purchased hot dogs, cut in half crosswise

BBQ sauce and/or yellow mustard, for serving

Oh my, these hot dogs have been dead for centuries and now, to make matters worse, they're being dipped in mustard and BBQ sauce. Can life get any harder? At least guests of all ages will delight in this trashy/classy hors d'oeuvre. I definitely recommend making your own hot dogs for the occasion, but I can't stop you if you insist on your favorite store-bought brand.

Preheat the oven to 400°F. Line a rimmed baking sheet with parchment.

Place one sheet of phyllo on a clean counter in front of you. Cover the other sheets with a damp towel to prevent them from drying out.

In a small bowl, mix the olive oil and salt. Lightly brush the phyllo with the olive oil, then fold it in half lengthwise. Brush with more olive oil.

Use a paring knife to cut the phyllo lengthwise into ½-inch-wide strips. Now take a hot dog half, brush it with olive oil, and wrap a few of the phyllo strips around the hot dog sloppily, so that it looks like a mummy. Leave some of the hot dog exposed, and a little space peeking through where the face would be. This might take two or three strips. Transfer to the lined baking sheet.

Proceed with the remaining phyllo and hot dogs to make 16 mummies.

Bake until the phyllo is crispy, 20 to 25 minutes. Transfer to a serving dish and serve immediately with your favorite sauces.

Zomberoni PIZZA FACES

FOR THE PEPPERONIS:

½ cup cooked or canned pinto beans, rinsed and drained

1 cup vegetable broth, purchased or homemade (page 203)

1 tablespoon olive oil

1 tablespoon tomato paste

2 tablespoons tamari or soy sauce

1¼ cups vital wheat gluten

¼ cup nutritional yeast flakes

1 teaspoon granulated garlic

1½ teaspoons anise seeds, crushed

½ teaspoon crushed red pepper flakes

1 tablespoon smoked paprika

Lots of freshly ground black pepper

FOR THE WHITE SAUCE:

1 cup raw cashews, soaked in water for at least 2 hours and drained

¾ cup vegetable broth, purchased or homemade (page 203)

2 tablespoons nutritional yeast flakes

½ teaspoon garlic powder

½ teaspoon salt

FOR THE ACCOUTREMENT:

6 English muffins (see Tip)

3 cups Marinara Sauce (page 65)

12 fresh basil leaves

Sliced black olives

Baby bell peppers (see Tip)

Capers

A horde approaches. All googly-eyed, mouths agape, rotting teeth, and the stench! Oh, the stench! The stench is...it's just so...wait. They actually smell pretty amazing! Like a pizza shop.

But of course they do, they're zomberoni pizza faces! It's really difficult to mess this up. I mean, how can you? It's a zombie! But if you like, practice making pizza faces on a plate before going the whole way on the English muffin. Homemade pepperoni eye sockets, cashew cheese sauce, pepper mouth, and caper teeth. What's not to love? Oh right, the fact that they will tear you limb from limb, leaving only a bloody oven mitt in the middle of the kitchen floor.

MAKE THE PEPPERONIS: Before mixing the ingredients, get your steamer ready, bringing the water to a full boil.

Have ready four square sheets of aluminum foil. In a large bowl, mash the beans until no whole ones are left. Throw all the other pepperoni ingredients together in the order listed and mix with a fork. Divide the dough into four even parts (an easy way to do this: split the dough in half and then in half again).

Place one part of the dough on a sheet of foil and mold it into a 6-inch log. Wrap the dough in the foil, like a Tootsie Roll. Don't worry too much about shaping it, as it will snap into shape while it's steaming because this recipe is awesome. Repeat with the remaining dough.

Place the wrapped sausages in the steamer and steam until firm, about 40 minutes. Remove from the steamer and let cool completely before slicing. You'll only need two of the pepperonis for this recipe.

MAKE THE WHITE SAUCE: Put all the white sauce ingredients in a blender and purée until completely smooth; this can take up to 5 minutes depending on the strength of your machine. Periodically stop the machine to keep it from overheating, and scrape down the sides of the blender jar with a rubber spatula to make sure you get everything. Refrigerate until ready to use.

Recipe Continues

SAUSAGE TIME

We use a few variations of sausage in the cookbook. The method is always the same as for the Zomberoni pepperoni here—just replace the ingredients with what you find below.

Andouille Sausage

½ cup cooked or canned navy beans, rinsed and drained

1 cup vegetable broth, purchased or homemade (page 203)

2 tablespoons tamari or soy sauce

1 tablespoon olive oil

1 tablespoon tomato paste

1 tablespoon liquid smoke

1¼ cups vital wheat gluten

¼ cup nutritional yeast flakes

1 tablespoon smoked paprika

2 teaspoons onion powder

1 teaspoon granulated garlic

½ teaspoon dried thyme

½ teaspoon crushed red pepper flakes

Lots of freshly ground black pepper

Italian Sausage

½ cup cooked or canned lentils, rinsed and drained

1 cup vegetable broth, purchased or homemade (page 203)

2 tablespoons tamari or soy sauce

1 tablespoon olive oil

1¼ cups vital wheat gluten

¼ cup nutritional yeast flakes

2 teaspoons onion powder

1½ teaspoons fennel seed, crushed, or 1 teaspoon ground fennel seed

1 teaspoon granulated garlic

1 teaspoon sweet paprika

1 teaspoon dried oregano

½ teaspoon dried thyme

½ teaspoon crushed red pepper flakes

Lots of freshly ground black pepper

Tip

It's best to use baby bell peppers for the perfect-size mouths. If you can't find any, just fashion together two rounded bell pepper slices to create the mouth. Or make it spicy with a jalapeño!

Unfortunately, the most famous brand of English muffin is not vegan. Sad face! But there are plenty of wonderful vegan varieties out there. I use a nice healthy sprouted whole-grain English muffin from Ezekiel 4:9 and it tastes faboo.

ASSEMBLE THE ZOMBERONIS (BEFORE THEY DISASSEMBLE YOU!): Preheat the oven to 350°F.

Split the English muffins in half and lay them out in front of you. Spread a few tablespoons of marinara on each muffin. Tear a basil leaf into small pieces and scatter it over the marinara for a rotting flesh effect. Spoon on some white sauce in kind of a swirly way.

Place two thinly sliced pepperonis where the eyes might be, and place two thinly sliced olives on them in a googly sort of way.

Place a thinly sliced pepper for the mouth, with a few rotting caper teeth inside.

Arrange the loaded English muffins on a baking sheet and bake for about 10 minutes. Now your zombies are complete. Proceed with caution!

SPAGHETTI *and* EYEBALLS

SERVES
8
(MAKES 16 TOFU
BALLS)

TOTAL
45 MINUTES
ACTIVE
45 MINUTES

FOR THE SPAGHETTI:

1 pound spaghetti

1 recipe Marinara Sauce (page 65)

FOR THE TOFU BALLS:

1 (14-ounce) package extra-firm tofu

1 small onion, very finely chopped

3 tablespoons tamari or soy sauce

3 tablespoons creamy natural peanut butter

3 tablespoons nutritional yeast flakes

A pinch each: dried basil, oregano, thyme

Freshly ground black pepper

½ cup bread crumbs, plus extra for rolling

Olive oil, for pan-frying

FOR DECORATIONS:

1 cup Almond Ricotta (page 299)

8 cherry tomatoes, cut in half

Your spaghetti is staring back at you, how fantastic! I am so happy to finally be using these tofu balls in a recipe! This is one of the first vegan recipes I ever made, from Louise Hagler's *Tofu Cookery,* back in the late '80s. Since then, it's become the Moskowitz Family Recipe, with a few minor tweaks along the way, but with that classic vegan charm intact. You would never think that peanut butter and soy sauce would be so brilliant in an Italian recipe, but you would be wrong.

MAKE THE SPAGHETTI: Bring a large pot of salted water to a boil over high heat and then turn it off. About 10 minutes before your meatballs are done, bring the water back to a boil and cook the spaghetti according to the package directions. Heat the marinara sauce in a saucepan and keep warm until serving time.

MAKE THE TOFU BALLS: In a large mixing bowl, mush up the tofu until it resembles ricotta cheese. Add the onion, tamari, peanut butter, nutritional yeast, dried herbs, and a few grinds of black pepper. Mix everything really well so that it holds together. Now add the bread crumbs and mix with your hands until a firm dough forms. Depending on the type of bread crumbs you are using, you may need to add more to get the mixture to firm up.

Place some bread crumbs on a dinner plate. Form the tofu mixture into golf balls and roll them in the bread crumbs to coat. You should get about 16 balls out of the mixture.

Preheat a cast iron pan over medium heat and pour in a thin layer of olive oil. In two batches, pan-fry the meatballs, using a thin metal spatula to roll the balls around on all sides for browning.

ASSEMBLE: Place a portion of spaghetti in each bowl. Cover generously with marinara. Add two tofu balls. Dollop a rounded tablespoon of ricotta on each ball and then press a cherry tomato half, cut-side down, into the ricotta, to form eyeballs. Serve warm!

 Tips   *If you can find funky-colored cherry tomatoes, like purple or dark green, that can make for even more fun eyeballs!*

If you want to cut down on ingredients or just don't want to make the almond ricotta, a pimento-stuffed olive slice will work for the eyeballs, too.

Monster Mash
SHEPHERD'S PIE

FOR THE MASHED POTATO GHOULS:

3 pounds russet potatoes, peeled and roughly chopped into 1½-inch chunks

2 cups chopped scallions, green parts only

1 cup fresh cilantro, including stems

1 cup unsweetened almond milk (or your favorite nondairy milk)

½ cup olive oil

1½ teaspoons salt

1 teaspoon ground white pepper

FOR THE LENTIL-MUSHROOM SHEPHERD GUTS:

1 tablespoon cornstarch

2 cups cold vegetable broth, purchased or homemade (page 203)

2 tablespoons tomato paste

2 tablespoons olive oil

1 yellow onion, cut into medium dice

2 medium carrots, peeled and cut into thin half-moons

1 teaspoon salt, plus a pinch

2 garlic cloves, minced

1 pound cremini mushrooms, cut into pea-size pieces

2 celery ribs, thinly sliced

3 tablespoons fresh thyme

Freshly ground black pepper

4 cups cooked or canned lentils, rinsed and drained

1 cup frozen peas, thawed

FOR THE ACCOUTREMENT:

Pimento-stuffed green olives

Radishes

Fresh thyme sprigs

This is what nightmares would be made of, if nightmares were totally delicious. A grisly green ghoul with haunted olive eyes, gaping radish fangs, and ferocious claws...of thyme? Vegan food hasn't been this scary since the '80s! But beneath all the horror, this is just a friendly old lentil-mushroom shepherd's pie with scallion-cilantro mashed potatoes. There's nothing scary about that.

MAKE THE MASHED POTATOES: Put the potatoes in a large pot and cover them with salted cold water. Cover and bring to a boil over medium-high heat. Once boiling, lower the heat and simmer until very tender, about 10 minutes.

In the meantime, combine the scallions, cilantro, and milk in a blender and puree until relatively smooth and bright ghoulish green!

Once the potatoes are tender, drain them and immediately return them to the pot. Add the oil and the blender mixture, then the salt and white pepper, and mash until smooth. Taste and adjust for salt and pepper. Cover to keep warm.

MAKE THE LENTIL-MUSHROOM LAYER: In a large measuring cup, whisk the cornstarch into the cold broth until mostly dissolved. Stir in the tomato paste and set aside.

Preheat a large pan over medium heat. Heat the oil, then sauté the onion and carrots with a pinch of salt until the onion is lightly browned, 5 to 7 minutes. Add the garlic and sauté just until fragrant, 30 seconds or so. Add the mushrooms, celery, and thyme, along with the remaining 1 teaspoon salt and a bunch of freshly ground black pepper. Let cook until the mushrooms have released a lot of moisture, about 5 minutes. Add the lentils and use your spatula to mush them up a bit right in the pan.

Add the broth mixture and mix well. Let it cook until it thickens and becomes gravy-like. Fold in the peas. Taste and adjust for salt and seasoning.

ASSEMBLE: Cut the olives into ⅛-inch-thick "eyes." Cut the radishes into ⅛-inch-thick disks, then cut those disks into half-moons. Then use a paring knife to carve out triangles for teeth. Have fun with it! Don't worry about perfection here. Strip the thyme sprigs of their leaves until you reveal their "claws."

Have ready a large zip-top bag with a ¾-inch hole snipped out of one corner. Fill the bag with some mashed potatoes. Now fill individual bowls with lentil-mushroom mixture. Take your mashed potato bag and squeeze a ghoul into existence right onto each bowl of guts.

Place the olive slices into each ghoul's eye sockets. Position the radishes as their mouths. Attach thyme stems to each ghoul's arm sockets. It's alive! Ahh!

MAKES

3

DOZEN

Little PEANUT BUTTER CUPS

TOTAL
2 HOURS
ACTIVE
1 HOUR

FOR THE FILLING:

½ cup creamy natural peanut butter

¼ cup refined coconut oil, melted

2 teaspoons pure vanilla extract

½ teaspoon salt

2 cups powdered sugar, sifted to remove any lumps

4 to 5 tablespoons unsweetened almond milk (or your favorite nondairy milk)

FOR THE CHOCOLATE SHELL:

12 ounces semisweet chocolate chips

2 tablespoons refined coconut oil

1 tablespoon agave

FOR THE DECORATION:

Chopped peanuts or chocolate sprinkles or orange sprinkles

Tip

For a sweet and salty crunch, use flaky Maldon salt to top the cups instead of or along with the peanuts.

You know when you ask someone if they want a peanut butter cup and they say, "Nah"? Of course you don't know that, because it has never happened. No one would refuse a peanut butter cup. Especially a little cutie like this that you made yourself! These are just as they should be: a cracky chocolate shell with a peanut buttery filling that is somewhere between creamy and a little crumbly. Make an extra batch or two, because it's easy to eat three dozen all by yourself in an evening.

MAKE THE FILLING: In a large mixing bowl, use an electric mixer to beat the peanut butter, coconut oil, and vanilla until relatively smooth. Add the salt. Sift in the powdered sugar a little at a time until it is stiff but well blended. Now beat in the almond milk 1 tablespoon at a time, until the filling is smooth and creamy like a thick frosting. Transfer the mixture to a pastry bag fitted with a large metal tip and set aside.

MAKE THE CHOCOLATE SHELL: In a large metal bowl set over a saucepan of simmering water, melt the chocolate chips, stirring with a rubber spatula until smooth. Mix in the coconut oil and agave and stir until smooth. Turn off the heat and keep warm on the stove until ready to use.

ASSEMBLE: Line 36 mini muffin cups with tiny liners. Drop a teaspoon of the chocolate mixture into each cup to coat the bottom. Let it harden for a few minutes, to prevent the peanut butter from dropping through to the bottom once you add it. Now top each with a scant teaspoon of the peanut butter mixture. Add another teaspoon of chocolate to cover. Sprinkle the chopped peanuts on top, or use sprinkles, or just leave them plain if you prefer. Refrigerate until firm and set. Serve!

Peanut Butter–Caramel
APPLES

6 medium-size sweet red apples (see Tip)

½ cup creamy natural peanut butter, well stirred and at room temperature

½ cup brown rice syrup, at room temperature

1 cup salted roasted peanuts, chopped well

Tip

Make sure that your apples aren't overly waxed or the coating will have trouble sticking. A few of my favorite varieties are McIntosh, Fuji, Honeycrisp, and Kiku.

Do you love to spread creamy peanut butter on crisp, sweet apples? This recipe takes that heaven and multiplies it by 10. Making caramel is an art, one you might not have time to perfect in between doling out candy to the neighborhood ghouls and crafting up your perfect angel costume. This recipe dumbs it down with a secret ingredient: brown rice syrup. Now, it may not be the cheapest ingredient out there—it costs around 6 dollars for a jar—but it pretty much guarantees your caramel will turn out perfect.

Salty roasted peanuts top off the apple, making all your ooey-gooey salty and sweet dreams come true. These caramel apples are so fun and easy you can definitely get kids involved in the process! But don't get your cats involved—trust me, it will be a disaster.

Spread a piece of parchment paper over a cutting board. Make room in your fridge for the cutting board, because you'll be chilling the whole shebang.

Remove the apple stems and stick bamboo skewers (or craft sticks) through the bottoms of the apples. Make sure the apples are secure. Set aside.

Stir the peanut butter and brown rice syrup together in a small saucepan. Gently heat over low heat, stirring constantly with a fork, just until smooth and heated through. It should fall from your fork in ribbons. If it seems stiff, turn the heat off immediately and add a little extra brown rice syrup, until it's fluid again. This happens because different peanut butters have varying amounts of moisture.

Use a spoon to spread some peanut butter caramel over one entire apple. Sprinkle with some peanuts, pressing them into the caramel to make them stick. It's okay if a few fall off. Place the apple upside down on the parchment paper and continue with the rest of the apples.

Transfer the cutting board with the apples to the fridge. Let set for at least 3 hours. Now the apples are ready to eat!

Chocolate
DIPPY
APPLES

6 sweet red apples (see Tip, preceding page)

1 pound semisweet chocolate chips or chopped chocolate

1½ cups your choice of dipping stuff:

crushed salted pretzels

roughly chopped pistachios

crushed salted peanuts

crushed chocolate cookies

chocolate or rainbow sprinkles

sugar-coated crisp rice cereal

sweetened shredded coconut

toasted coconut

Tip

Tie festive ribbons at the bottom of each stick to make your apples look even sweeter.

Chocolate and apples are great—everyone knows that. But what if I told you that you can dip those chocolate apples into other stuff and make them even greater? It's true! There ain't nothing to this recipe, so if you're looking for a low-key dessert that looks super cool and never fails to impress, try these. Just follow the directions and have ready a bowl (or three) of the yummy adornments for the most fun apples around.

First, arrange your workspace. Have space set aside for the chocolate bowl, a cereal bowl for each topping, and a large, parchment-lined cutting board. Also, make room in your fridge for the cutting board so that you can chill the apples.

Remove the apple stems and stick bamboo skewers (or craft sticks) through the bottoms of the apples. Make sure the apples are secure. Set aside.

In a large metal bowl set over a saucepan of simmering water, melt the chocolate, stirring with a rubber spatula, until smooth. Don't get it too hot: It's ready once it's warm and melted. Place the bowl in your work area.

Dip one apple in the chocolate, rolling it around to coat and leaving just a little space at the stick end. Use a spoon to coat any hard-to-get spots and let the excess chocolate drip back into the bowl. Dip the bottom of the apple into your topping bowl of choice, coating it about halfway up. Place the apple upside down on the parchment paper and continue with the rest of the apples.

Transfer the cutting board with the apples to the fridge and chill for at least an hour. Now they're ready to serve!

BETWIXT BARS

FOR THE SHORTBREAD LAYER:
¾ cup plus 2 tablespoons refined coconut oil, at room temperature

⅔ cup sugar

2½ teaspoons pure vanilla extract

2 cups all-purpose flour

⅓ cup cornstarch

½ teaspoon salt

FOR THE CARAMEL:
1 cup coconut milk from a well-stirred can

2 tablespoons refined coconut oil

1 teaspoon salt

1½ cups sugar

¼ cup light corn syrup

¼ cup water

½ teaspoon pure vanilla extract

FOR THE CHOCOLATE COATING:
2 cups semisweet chocolate chips

¼ cup refined coconut oil

Tips

Be patient! The caramel takes a while to reach 245°F, but don't turn up the heat in order to expedite the process or you'll wind up with burned bits at the bottom of the pan.

Don't stir the mixture or move the pot while the caramel is heating, as that can cause crystals to form. Use a pastry brush dipped in water to brush down any crystals that form on the sides of the pan.

Shortbread caramel bars, covered in chocolate! This recipe gets into the nitty-gritty of candy making. It's definitely a project, but the skills you'll develop are worth having. Who doesn't want to be the neighborhood homemade candy champion? You'll need to get a candy thermometer and to have watched a few YouTube videos of home caramel making before beginning this recipe.

MAKE THE SHORTBREAD LAYER: Preheat the oven to 350°F. Line a 9-by-13-inch pan with parchment, lightly grease the parchment, and set aside.

In a stand mixer fitted with a wire whisk (or in a medium bowl with a hand mixer), beat the coconut oil and sugar on medium speed until creamy, about 3 minutes. Mix in the vanilla.

In a separate large mixing bowl, sift together the flour, cornstarch, and salt. Add half of the flour mixture to the coconut oil mixture, folding it in by hand and then using the mixer to fully incorporate it.

Add the rest of the flour and mix until it's even, crumbly, and still a little moist. Spread the dough out in the pan and press down, trying to keep it level and firm. Use a fork to poke the surface all over, then bake until the edges start to get golden, 30 to 35 minutes. Remove the pan from the oven and let cool.

START ON THE CARAMEL: Combine the coconut milk, coconut oil, and salt in a small pan and cook over medium heat for a few minutes, whisking occasionally, until the coconut oil is melted and any solids have dissolved.

In a 2-quart saucepot, combine the sugar, corn syrup, and water and stir until combined. Clip a candy thermometer onto the pot and heat over medium-high heat until the thermometer reads between 280° and 300°F. Then, remove the pan from the heat, remove the thermometer, and slowly whisk in the coconut milk mixture. This can produce some hot steam, so use a whisk with a long handle so you don't burn your hand. Put the candy thermometer back in, set the pot over medium heat, and let it cook until it reaches 245°F. Remove from the heat, whisk in the vanilla, and pour the mixture over the shortbread. Once it stops steaming, refrigerate to cool for at least an hour. The caramel should be firmly set.

Lift the bars out of the pan using the parchment as "handles." Place on a counter and cut into 12 rectangles. Place the rectangles on a wire rack over the sink.

MAKE THE CHOCOLATE COATING AND ASSEMBLE: In a large metal bowl set over a saucepan of simmering water, melt the chocolate, stirring with a rubber spatula until smooth. Mix in the coconut oil and stir until smooth and melty. Pour the chocolate over the caramel on the rack, smoothing over the sides of the bars, and let cool. When the chocolate has set, they are ready to eat.

ALTON'S
CANDY CORN,
Veganized

MAKES
ABOUT 6
DOZEN

TOTAL
2 HOURS
ACTIVE
1 HOUR

1¼ cups powdered sugar, sifted to remove clumps

6½ teaspoons cornstarch

¼ teaspoon salt

½ cup granulated sugar

⅓ cup light corn syrup

2½ tablespoons water

2 tablespoons refined coconut oil, at room temperature

½ teaspoon pure vanilla extract

Yellow and orange gel food coloring

—— *Tip* ——

It's pretty awesome that Wilton, which is probably the most popular brand of food coloring, confirms that its products are not derived from animal sources. Hurrah!

I don't know why nonvegans would make their own candy corn. But Alton Brown did! And we took his recipe and veganized it, so now we have candy corn, too. Now there's no reason not to go vegan!

This candy corn contains no waxes or preservatives, so it isn't as sturdy as store-bought. That means you shouldn't leave it in your pocket or let it sit in a warm room for too long, or it will melt. Keep it cool and it will be cool. I made the directions as clear as possible, but if you run into trouble, definitely watch Alton's candy corn video on YouTube.

Line a large baking sheet with parchment paper.

Sift together the powdered sugar, cornstarch, and salt. In a 2-quart saucepot, combine the granulated sugar, corn syrup, and water and heat over medium heat for a few minutes. Clip a candy thermometer onto the side of the pan, add the coconut oil, and heat the mixture to 230°F. Remove the pan from the heat and mix in the vanilla and dry ingredients until smooth, then pour the mixture out onto the lined tray. Let cool for 15 minutes.

Lay out a sheet of parchment for the finished candies.

Once the dough is cool enough to handle, divide it into three equal parts and form into balls. Add a few drops of yellow food coloring to one of the balls and knead until the color is uniform. Do the same thing to the second ball with the orange food coloring, and leave the third ball white.

Split each dough ball into two equal parts, then roll each one with your hands into ropes about 24 inches long. You should have six ropes.

Take one yellow rope, one orange rope, and one white rope and press them together side by side. Do the same with the remaining ropes so that you have two strips of yellow, orange, white.

Cut each strip into six 4-inch sections. Now press each section into a triangular wedge shape, using a ruler to keep the edges straight. The white side should be the pointy end and the yellow should be the flat end. You should now have twelve wedges.

Using a thin, sharp blade or a pizza cutter, cut each wedge crosswise into candies that are somewhere between ¼ and ½ inch thick. You can use your fingers to reshape the pieces if they lost their form when you cut them. Lay them out on the parchment paper to harden for at least an hour. Putting them in the refrigerator will help them harden more. If you don't eat them all, store leftovers in an airtight container with parchment between the layers.

15

THANKSGIVING

In all my decades as
A VEGAN COOK, I'VE
probably been asked about
THIS HOLIDAY MORE THAN
any other.

WELL, **VEGAN THANKSGIVING** is its own thing. For some reason, more than any other holiday, vegans get together for this one. It's more important than anything. Let's forget for a minute what Thanksgiving is actually based on because that's really a bunch of BS. But let's take that BS and turn it into something real. A day to give thanks. A day to celebrate friends and family. And a day to care about animals, even more than you usually do.

If you're simply looking at this section trying to find some good recipes for your vegan loved ones, thank you! And sorry about the political rant if you do truly believe that the Pilgrims gave the Indians a fair shake and everyone ended up happy.

But really, this holiday is about being together, whatever your political choices may be. It's a time to swallow your opinions and plenty of stuffing to go along with them. Then wash it all down with some pumpkin pie.

Cream of PORCINI MUSHROOM SOUP

1 ounce dried porcini mushrooms

1 cup raw cashews, soaked in water for at least 2 hours and drained

5½ cups vegetable broth, purchased or homemade (page 203)

1 tablespoon cornstarch

1 tablespoon olive oil

1 medium yellow onion, finely chopped

¾ teaspoon salt, plus a pinch

3 garlic cloves, minced

½ teaspoon dried thyme

8 ounces cremini mushrooms, cut into ¼-inch slices

¾ cup dry white wine

Freshly ground black pepper

Chopped fresh parsley or chives, for garnish (optional)

Oyster crackers, for serving

This is such a great start to a Thanksgiving meal—it tastes like an autumnal walk through the forest. It's a real trick of a recipe, too, because the dried porcini powder makes the soup sooo fancy and flavorful, but then the regular old sliced creminis make it affordable.

Put the porcinis in a blender and blend on high into a fine powder. This usually takes about a minute. Add the cashews, along with 3 cups of the vegetable broth and the cornstarch. Puree until completely smooth; this can take up to 5 minutes depending on the strength of your machine. Periodically stop the machine to keep it from overheating, and scrape down the sides of the blender jar with a rubber spatula to make sure you get everything.

Preheat a 4-quart pot over medium heat. Heat the oil, then sauté the onion with a pinch of salt until softened, about 3 minutes. Add the garlic and thyme and sauté just until fragrant, about 30 seconds. Add the cremini mushrooms and cook, stirring often, until softened, about 5 minutes.

Add the white wine, the remaining ¾ teaspoon salt, and several grinds of black pepper. Turn the heat up to boil and reduce the liquid to about half. It should take 3 minutes or so once boiling.

Bring the heat back to medium and stir in the cashew cream mixture and the remaining 2½ cups vegetable broth. Bring to a boil, then lower the heat and cook until nicely thickened, about 7 minutes. Taste and adjust for salt and seasoning. Add a little water if it seems too thick. Garnish with parsley, if you like, and serve with oyster crackers.

Caramelized
ONION *and*
CAULIFLOWER
CASSEROLE

SERVES
8–10

TOTAL
1 HOUR 30 MINUTES
ACTIVE
30 MINUTES

2 tablespoons olive oil

1 large onion, diced medium

4 garlic cloves, minced

4 cups cauliflower florets (from about 1 medium-size head)

1 (12-ounce) package extra-firm silken tofu

1 cup vegetable broth, purchased or homemade (page 203)

½ cup tahini

¼ cup fresh lemon juice

¼ cup nutritional yeast flakes

1 tablespoon smoked paprika, plus more for sprinkling

½ teaspoon salt

Freshly ground black pepper

1 cup bread crumbs

Tip

It's totally worth it here to slowly cook the onion and coax out all that sweetness. While the onion cooks, just prep all the other veggies and measure out your ingredients. That way, not a second of time is wasted!

This is the kind of casserole you want to bring to a Thanksgiving potluck, place on the table like a mic drop, and declare "Game over." It has that deep popcorny cauliflower flavor, matched with the sweet caramel of slow-cooked onions. Silken tofu is used to make it creamy and eggy, while tahini, nutritional yeast, and lemon juice bring in a cheesy element. It's sort of like a quiche in casserole form. And it will make you completely win Thanksgiving!

Preheat a large, heavy-bottomed skillet (preferably cast iron) over low heat. Add the oil and onion, cover the pan, and cook, stirring occasionally, until the onion becomes golden and soft, about 20 minutes.

Add the garlic and cauliflower, raise the heat to medium, cover, and cook, stirring occasionally, until the cauliflower is softened, about 15 minutes. Remove the pan from the heat and set it aside.

Preheat the oven to 350°F. Lightly grease a 9-inch square pan or an 11-by-8-inch casserole dish.

In a food processor, combine the tofu, vegetable broth, tahini, and lemon juice and blend until completely smooth. Add half of the cauliflower mixture, along with the nutritional yeast, paprika, salt, and a few grinds of black pepper and pulse a few times until well combined. With the food processor turned off, stir in the bread crumbs with a spatula. (I do this just to save a dish, but you can transfer the mixture to a mixing bowl to stir in the bread crumbs if you prefer. You just don't want to process them at this point because it would make the dish gummy.)

Transfer the mixture from the food processor to the prepared baking dish and spread it out evenly. Top with the remaining cauliflower mixture and lightly press it into the bottom layer.

Bake until golden on top, about 30 minutes. Let it cool slightly, sprinkle with paprika, and serve!

SERVES
10–12

TOTAL
45 MINUTES
ACTIVE
15 MINUTES

Super
SIMPLE
CORNBREAD

2 cups unsweetened almond milk
(or your favorite nondairy milk)

2 teaspoons apple cider vinegar

2 cups cornmeal

1 cup all-purpose flour

2 teaspoons baking powder

½ teaspoon salt

⅓ cup canola oil

2 tablespoons pure maple syrup

This is a delicious basic vegan cornbread. It is moist, crunchy, and corntastic—perfect for turning into Cornbread Stuffing with Goji Berries & Fennel (facing page)! It's also just great with a dab of coconut oil and a little maple syrup. The recipe doubles well if you're looking for more cornbread.

Preheat the oven to 350°F. Lightly grease a 9-by-13-inch baking pan.

In a medium bowl, whisk together the milk and vinegar and set aside to curdle.

In a large bowl, sift together the cornmeal, flour, baking powder, and salt.

Add the oil and maple syrup to the milk mixture. Whisk vigorously until it is foamy and bubbly, about 2 minutes.

Pour the wet ingredients into the dry and use a large wooden spoon or a firm spatula to mix well. Pour the batter into the prepared baking pan and bake until a toothpick inserted into the center comes out clean, 25 to 30 minutes. Slice into squares and serve warm.

CORNBREAD STUFFING

with Goji Berries & Fennel

SERVES
8–12

TOTAL
1 HOUR 15 MINUTES
ACTIVE
20 MINUTES

2 tablespoons ground flaxseed

3½ cups vegetable broth, purchased or homemade (page 203)

2 recipes Super Simple Cornbread (facing page), cut into ¾-inch cubes

4 tablespoons olive oil

1 medium yellow onion, thinly sliced

1 teaspoon sugar

1 large fennel bulb, cut into ½-inch pieces

2 tablespoons finely chopped fresh thyme

1 tablespoon finely chopped fresh parsley

1 tablespoon finely chopped fresh sage

1 teaspoon salt

Freshly ground black pepper

1 cup dried goji berries

Wanna shake things up at the Thanksgiving table? Try this weirdo stuffing! Okay, it's not *that* weird. But it is a bit of a departure from traditional stuffing. Goji berries and fennel make it really festive and offer a break from the ubiquitous cranberry.

Preheat the oven to 325°F. Line two rimmed baking sheets with parchment.

Combine the ground flaxseed and ½ cup of the vegetable broth in a small dish. Stir well and place in the refrigerator to thicken.

Scatter the cornbread cubes onto the lined baking sheets in a single layer. Bake until dried and lightly toasted, 25 to 30 minutes. Remove from the oven and cool completely. You can make these up to a day in advance and store them in an airtight container.

When you're ready to make the stuffing, preheat the oven to 400°F. Lightly grease a 9-by-13-inch casserole dish.

Preheat a 4-quart pot over medium-low heat. Heat 2 tablespoons of the oil, then sauté the onion until translucent, about 5 minutes. Add the sugar and cook until the onions have turned a dark caramel color, 20 to 30 minutes. If the onions are starting to stick, lower the heat and add a little bit of water to keep them from burning.

Once the onions look beautiful and caramelized, raise the heat to medium-high and add the remaining 2 tablespoons oil. Add the fennel and cook, stirring frequently, until soft, 8 to 10 minutes. Remove from the heat and add the thyme, parsley, sage, salt, and a few grinds of black pepper. Stir to combine.

In a large mixing bowl, combine the toasted cornbread, caramelized onion mixture, and dried goji berries and toss gently. Add the remaining 3 cups vegetable broth and the flax mixture. Mix carefully with a rubber spatula until it all holds together. Transfer to the prepared casserole and cover with aluminum foil.

Bake for 30 minutes. Remove the foil and continue baking until the top starts to lightly brown, another 15 minutes or so. Let cool slightly before serving.

PUMPKIN CORNBREAD

SERVES
8–10

TOTAL
1 HOUR
ACTIVE
20 MINUTES

1 cup unsweetened almond milk (or your favorite nondairy milk)

1 tablespoon apple cider vinegar

1 cup pumpkin puree (homemade or from a can—but not pumpkin pie filling)

½ cup pure maple syrup

¼ cup refined coconut oil, melted

1¼ cups cornmeal

1 cup all-purpose flour

2 teaspoons baking powder

2 teaspoons pumpkin pie spice

½ teaspoon salt

Plain old cornbread...sure, people love it. But pumpkin cornbread is next-level awesome, with its beautiful orange hue, moist crumb, and hint of spice. Put it out in batches so that greedy people don't snag three pieces at once. Spread on some apple butter and your heart will feel like fluttering autumn leaves.

Preheat the oven to 350°F. Lightly grease an 8-inch square baking pan.

Measure the almond milk into a liquid measuring cup and add the apple cider vinegar. Set aside to curdle.

In a large mixing bowl, mix the pumpkin puree, maple syrup, and coconut oil. Mix in the almond milk mixture and beat until well incorporated.

Sift in the cornmeal, flour, baking powder, pumpkin pie spice, and salt. Stir just until combined.

Transfer the batter to your prepared baking pan. Bake until the top is golden and firm to the touch, 30 to 35 minutes. Let cool slightly before slicing.

Super
TRADITIONAL
STUFFING

½ cup olive oil

1 large yellow onion, diced medium

3 celery ribs, thinly sliced

½ cup thinly sliced peeled carrot

2 teaspoons salt, plus a pinch

2 teaspoons onion powder

1 teaspoon dried sage

½ teaspoon dried thyme

Freshly ground black pepper

12 cups country white bread, cut into 1-inch cubes (see Tip)

1½ to 2 cups vegetable broth, purchased or homemade (page 203)

Tip

The best bread for this stuffing is a nice, big loaf of country white bread that you dice yourself. Sliced sandwich bread tends to be sliced too thin. It's also best if the bread is a few days old and relatively dry. If it seems fresh and springy, toast the bread cubes for 5 minutes in a 325°F oven before proceeding with the recipe.

Tell me you wouldn't be just fine if absolutely everything else about Thanksgiving was canceled except for the stuffing. In fact, imagine it's just you, a fireplace, a fluffy rug, some kittens, a fork (or not), and this big casserole full of perfectly seasoned, just-like-Grandma-used-to-make stuffing!

Preheat the oven to 350°F. Lightly grease a 9-by-13-inch casserole dish.

Preheat a 6-quart pot over medium heat. Heat ¼ cup of the oil, then sauté the onion, celery, and carrot with a pinch of salt until the carrot is softened and the onion is lightly browned, about 10 minutes. Stir in the onion powder, sage, thyme, remaining 2 teaspoons salt, and a few grinds of black pepper.

Transfer the vegetables to a large mixing bowl. Add the bread cubes and toss to thoroughly coat. Add the vegetable broth ½ cup at a time, stirring well in between additions of broth. The bread should be moist but not soggy, so make sure everything is not completely soaked through.

Transfer the stuffing mixture to the prepared casserole dish. Cover with aluminum foil and bake for 20 minutes. Uncover and bake until the cubes are nicely browned, about 10 minutes more. Let cool a bit before serving.

OLIVE OIL
SMASHED POTATOES

5 pounds small Yukon Gold potatoes, scrubbed and cut into 1½-inch chunks

½ cup vegetable broth, purchased or homemade (page 203), at room temperature

½ cup olive oil

1 teaspoon salt

Freshly ground black pepper

Tip

For top-notch spuds, never boil the potatoes. That will make them mushy and kind of waterlogged. Instead, once the water is boiling, lower the heat to a simmer. Drain and mash the potatoes once they are fork-tender; if they are falling apart, they have been cooking for too long.

What's the difference between smashed potatoes and mashed potatoes? Not that much, really, but smashed is for the lazier mashed potato maker in us. It yields a chunkier texture, and I like to add lots of olive oil, salt, and black pepper for your taste buds. The most important part is choosing the right potatoes: Small, thin-skinned Yukon Golds (preferably organic) give the best flavor. They're so creamy you don't need to peel them.

Put the potatoes in a pot and cover them with salted cold water by about an inch. Cover and bring to a boil over medium-high heat.

Once boiling, lower the heat to a simmer, uncover, and cook until fork-tender, about 12 minutes. Drain the potatoes, then return them to the pot. Do a preliminary mash with a potato masher, just to get them broken up. Add the broth, oil, salt, and lots of black pepper and lightly mash the potatoes, leaving lots of texture. You may want to add a bit more broth. Taste and adjust for salt and pepper and serve!

Fancy/Not Fancy
MUSHROOM
GRAVY

MAKES
6
CUPS

TOTAL
45 MINUTES
ACTIVE
20 MINUTES

½ cup all-purpose flour

4 cups vegetable broth, purchased or homemade (page 203)

2 tablespoons olive oil

1 medium yellow onion, diced small

1 pound mushrooms, thinly sliced

4 garlic cloves, minced

2 teaspoons dried thyme

1 teaspoon dried sage

½ teaspoon salt

Freshly ground black pepper

½ cup dry white wine (chardonnay is great)

2 tablespoons nutritional yeast flakes (optional)

This is mushroom lovers' gravy through and through. And you can make it as fancy or not as you like, depending on the kind of mushrooms you use. If your gravy pockets are deep this holiday season, and the farmers' market is exploding with fungi, try some porcinis or chanterelles. If you're feeling like a workaday mushroom fan, then creminis are just dandy. You can also do a mix of fancy/not fancy. The nutritional yeast isn't totally necessary, but it does give an extra umami punch.

In a small bowl, whisk the flour into about 2 cups of the vegetable broth until well dissolved. Once dissolved, stir in the remaining broth. Set aside.

Preheat a 2-quart pot over medium heat. Heat the oil, then sauté the onion until translucent, about 5 minutes. Add the mushrooms, garlic, thyme, sage, salt, and a few grinds of black pepper and sauté for 5 more minutes.

Add the wine and turn the heat up to a boil. Let the wine reduce for about 3 minutes. Add the broth-flour mix and the nutritional yeast, if using. Lower the heat to medium and cook, stirring often, for 20 minutes.

Taste and adjust for salt and pepper, transfer to a serving bowl, top with a little more pepper, and serve.

Creamy
WHIPPED
POTATOES

MAKES
4
QUARTS

TOTAL
30 MINUTES
ACTIVE
20 MINUTES

5 pounds russet potatoes, peeled and cut into 1½-inch chunks

¾ cup raw cashews, soaked in water for at least 2 hours and drained

¾ cup vegetable broth, purchased or homemade (page 203)

⅓ cup refined coconut oil, at room temperature

⅓ cup canola oil

1¼ teaspoons salt

Freshly ground black pepper

Thinly sliced fresh chives, for garnish

Cashew cream and a combo of coconut and canola oil make these potatoes sooo fluffy. They're like a floaty potato cloud, whisking you away to heaven. You whip them up with a hand mixer until they are so light and swirly it brings tears to your eyes. Don't forget the White Bean and So Sage Gravy (page 342)!

Put the potatoes in a pot and cover them with salted cold water by about an inch. Cover and bring to a boil over medium-high heat.

In the meantime, combine the cashews and broth in a blender. Puree until completely smooth; this can take up to 5 minutes depending on the strength of your machine. Periodically stop the machine to prevent it from overheating, and scrape down the sides of the blender jar with a rubber spatula to make sure you get everything.

Once the potatoes boil, lower the heat to a simmer, uncover, and cook until fork-tender, about 12 minutes. Drain the potatoes, then return them to the pot. Do a preliminary mash with a potato masher, just to get them broken up. Add half of the cashew mixture, along with the coconut and canola oils, salt, and lots of black pepper and mash until relatively smooth and no big chunks are left.

Now comes the creamiest part. Add the remaining cashew mixture, mix it in, and then use an immersion blender on high speed to whip the ever-loving life out of them. They should become very smooth, fluffy, and creamy. Taste and adjust for salt and pepper along the way, transfer to a serving bowl, garnish with chives, and serve!

WHITE BEAN *and* SO SAGE GRAVY

MAKES

4

CUPS

TOTAL
30 MINUTES
ACTIVE
30 MINUTES

2 tablespoons olive oil

1 medium yellow onion, roughly chopped

4 garlic cloves, chopped

2 teaspoons dried thyme

2 teaspoons dried sage

Freshly ground black pepper

⅔ cup all-purpose flour

3½ to 3¾ cups vegetable broth, purchased or homemade (page 203)

2 (15-ounce) cans navy beans, rinsed and drained, or 3 cups cooked navy beans

⅓ cup tamari or soy sauce

2 Italian sausages, either store-bought or homemade (page 316), torn into pea-size pieces

Salt

This is a thick, creamy, meaty number with homemade sausages and plenty of sage. It screams out for biscuits! I like to tear the sausages by hand instead of chopping, to give a more organic feel. But if you are looking for a smooth gravy (pictured with the Creamy Whipped Potatoes on page 341), just leave the sausages out.

Preheat a saucepan over medium-high heat. Heat the oil, then sauté the onion and garlic for 5 minutes. Add the thyme, sage, and lots of black pepper and cook for 3 minutes more. While that is cooking, in a small bowl, whisk the flour into 3 cups of the broth until dissolved.

If you have an immersion blender, add the beans, broth mixture, and tamari to the saucepan. Blend immediately and lower the heat to medium. Stir the gravy often for about 10 minutes while it thickens.

If you are using a countertop blender, blend the beans, broth mixture, and tamari until smooth. Transfer the onion and the other stuff from the pan to the blender. Puree again until no big chunks of onion are left. Return everything to the pot and stir often over medium heat to thicken.

Once the gravy thickens, reduce the heat to low. Now you can decide exactly how thick you want it by adding extra broth, anywhere from ½ cup to ¾ cup. Cook for about 10 more minutes to let the flavors deepen, stirring occasionally. Add the torn-up sausage pieces and heat through. Taste and adjust for salt. Keep the gravy covered and warm until ready to serve.

Curried
CANDIED
YAMS

3 pounds yams, peeled and cut into wedges about 3 inches long and 1 inch across

½ cup pure maple syrup

½ cup fresh orange juice

3 tablespoons refined coconut oil, melted

1 heaping tablespoon minced fresh ginger

2 teaspoons oriental curry powder (like S&B brand)

1 teaspoon salt

Candied yams light up the whole Thanksgiving plate. You just gotta have that sweet, caramelly, velvety bite as a counterpoint to the savory flavors. A touch of oriental curry powder gives these yams an extra-special touch that makes them memorable. The only warning I will give you is that people will expect these at every Thanksgiving going forward, so kiss your old yams good-bye.

Preheat the oven to 350°F. Lightly grease a 9-by-13-inch casserole dish.

Put the yams in the casserole. In a small bowl, whisk together the remaining ingredients. Pour the mixture over the yams and toss to coat them well.

Cover the casserole tightly with aluminum foil. Bake, tossing occasionally, until the sweet potatoes are tender and their sauce is thick and caramelly, about 1 hour. Let cool a bit before serving.

Orange-Scented
CRANBERRY
SAUCE

1 (12-ounce) bag fresh cranberries

¾ cup fresh orange juice

⅓ cup sugar

1 teaspoon grated orange zest

Pucker up for this cranberry sauce with a citrusy backdrop. It's real classic, real easy, and real delish—perfect for the purist who doesn't want a lot of "stuff" muddling up their cranberries.

Combine all the ingredients in a 4-quart pot. Cover and bring to a boil over medium-high heat. Lower the heat a bit and cook until the cranberries break down, about 5 minutes. Turn the heat off completely and let it sit. It will break down a bit more as it cools.

When completely cool, transfer to a covered container and refrigerate to chill until ready to serve.

Golden
CORN
PUDDING

2 cups coconut milk from a well-stirred can

¼ cup cornstarch

¼ cup refined coconut oil, at room temperature

9 cups frozen corn kernels, thawed

1 cup cornmeal

¼ cup pure maple syrup

2 teaspoons salt

½ teaspoon ground nutmeg

Coconut milk brings out all the lush, buttery corn flavor in this gorgeous casserole. The ingredients are minimal, except for, of course, loads and loads of corn and even some cornmeal for good measure. You can use fresh corn cut from the cobs instead of frozen—just add about a million hours of prep time. Just kidding, more like 20 minutes.

Preheat the oven to 350°F. Lightly grease a 9-by-13-inch casserole dish.

In a blender, whiz together the coconut milk and cornstarch until thoroughly combined. Add the coconut oil and puree. Add 3 cups of the corn and pulse until almost pureed. Transfer about half of that to a large mixing bowl. Add the next 3 cups of corn and puree again, leaving some texture. Transfer that to the mixing bowl as well.

Now stir in the remaining 3 cups of corn (not blended), along with the cornmeal, maple syrup, salt, and nutmeg.

Pour the batter into the prepared baking dish and bake until golden on top but still very moist inside, 40 to 45 minutes. Let cool for about 10 minutes before slicing and serving.

GREEN BEAN
CASSEROLE

1 cup raw cashews, soaked in water for at least 2 hours and drained

3 cups vegetable broth, purchased or homemade (page 203)

½ cup all-purpose flour

2 tablespoons nutritional yeast flakes

2 tablespoons olive oil

1 pound green beans, trimmed and cut into 2-inch pieces (about 4 cups)

1 small onion, finely chopped

1 teaspoon salt, plus a pinch

4 cups sliced mushrooms

1 tablespoon onion powder

Freshly ground black pepper

1 (6-ounce) can fried onions

Did your childhood Thanksgiving come out of cans and boxes? And do you kinda sorta maybe just-a-little-wittle-bit miss it? Then this casserole is right up your alley! This version has a few real ingredients, but don't let that fool you, it's still as embarrassingly good as its predecessor.

Preheat the oven to 375°F. Lightly grease a 9-by-13-inch casserole dish.

Combine the cashews, broth, flour, and nutritional yeast in a blender. Puree until completely smooth; this can take up to 5 minutes depending on the strength of your machine. Periodically stop the machine to prevent it from overheating, and scrape down the sides of the blender jar with a rubber spatula to make sure you get everything.

Meanwhile, heat a large sauté pan over medium-high heat. Heat the olive oil, then sauté the green beans and onion with a pinch of salt until the green beans are softened, about 5 minutes. Add the mushrooms and sauté 7 to 10 minutes more. The mushrooms should have released most of their moisture.

Add the blender mixture to the pan, along with the onion powder, remaining 1 teaspoon salt, and a few grinds of black pepper. Cook, stirring often, until thickened, about 10 minutes. Add half of the fried onions.

Transfer the green bean mixture to the casserole and top with the remaining fried onions. Bake until browned and bubbly, 22 to 25 minutes. Let cool for a few minutes before serving.

WINTER SQUASH
CUPS

with Wild Rice, Hazelnuts & Cherries

TOTAL
1 HOUR
ACTIVE
25 MINUTES

FOR THE SQUASH:

3 round winter squash (see Tip), halved and seeded

Olive oil, for brushing

Salt

FOR THE WILD RICE:

1 cup wild rice, rinsed

3 cups vegetable broth, purchased or homemade (page 203)

½ teaspoon salt

FOR THE FILLING:

2 tablespoons refined coconut oil

1 large yellow onion, diced medium

3 celery ribs, sliced

½ teaspoon dried thyme

¼ teaspoon dried sage

1 cup shelled hazelnuts, toasted and roughly chopped

¾ cup dried cherries

2 tablespoons brown sugar

2 tablespoons chopped fresh parsley

½ teaspoon salt

Freshly ground black pepper

Winter squash are nature's pottery! Speckled, streaked, water-colored, and splattered, no two are exactly alike. A few of my favorite varieties are carnival, dumpling, and acorn squash. A stunning mix of wild rice, hazelnuts, and cherries stuffed inside adds to the beauty and the yummy.

ROAST THE SQUASH AND MAKE THE RICE: Preheat the oven to 425°F. Line a baking sheet with parchment paper.

Lightly coat the squash with olive oil inside and out and sprinkle lightly with salt. Place the squash, cut-side down, on the lined baking sheet. Bake until the flesh is soft and can easily be pierced by a fork, about 45 minutes. Remove from the oven and let it hang out until the filling is ready.

At the same time, cook the wild rice according to the package directions, using the vegetable broth and salt.

WHEN THE SQUASH AND RICE ARE DONE, PREPARE THE FILLING: Preheat a large sauté pan over medium heat. Heat the coconut oil, then sauté the onion and celery until the onion is translucent, about 5 minutes. Add the thyme and sage. Cook for 1 more minute. Remove from the heat and toss in the cooked wild rice, hazelnuts, and dried cherries. Add the brown sugar and chopped parsley and stir to combine. Add the salt and a few grinds of black pepper and adjust to taste.

Fill each squash half with ½ to ¾ cup of the rice mixture and serve.

Tip — *Look for round squash that are a little bigger than a softball. To cut a squash in half lengthwise, start just to the right of the stem and cut on a slight diagonal, ending just to the left of the bottom nub.*

MAKES

6

BURGERS

TOTAL
1 HOUR 15 MINUTES

ACTIVE
30 MINUTES

Stuffed
THANKSGIVING BURGERS

2 tablespoons olive oil, plus more for pan-frying

1 small yellow onion, diced medium

¾ teaspoon salt, plus a pinch

8 ounces cremini mushrooms, thinly sliced

2 celery ribs, thinly sliced

2 garlic cloves, minced

1 teaspoon dried thyme

1 teaspoon dried sage

Freshly ground black pepper

4 cups (¾-inch) baguette cubes

½ to 1 cup vegetable broth, purchased or homemade (page 203)

½ cup hazelnuts

1 cup cooked or canned brown or green lentils, rinsed and drained

¼ cup dried cranberries

FOR SERVING:

6 sourdough rolls

Arugula, kale, or your preferred autumn green (see Tip)

Vegan mayo, purchased or homemade (page 67)

Tip

Kale is wonderful as the green, but rub it with a little olive oil and salt for maximum tastiness. Plain old arugula works great, too!

Get ready for an unholy carbfest: basically, stuffing that's stuffed into a roll! Lentils provide proteiny burgerness, mushrooms add earthy umaminess, and hazelnuts are deliciously festive and add great texture, too. And of course, you've got to have cranberries on Thanksgiving. Here, they are dried and studded throughout the burger like rubies, providing little bursts of tart sweetness. All the stuffing standbys—your celery, sage, and thyme—are accounted for, too. You're basically eating a Bob Ross landscape of pretty autumn foliage, in burger form. You will give thanks with every bite! Sure, you can enjoy these on Thanksgiving, but they're also great for a stand-alone pre-Thanksgiving dinner.

Preheat a large, heavy-bottomed nonstick pan (preferably cast iron) over medium-high heat. Heat 1 tablespoon of the oil, then sauté the onion with a pinch of salt until translucent, about 3 minutes. Add the mushrooms, celery, garlic, thyme, sage, and a few grinds of black pepper and sauté until the mushrooms have released most of their moisture, 7 to 10 minutes.

Add the baguette cubes to the pan and drizzle in the remaining 1 tablespoon oil. Toss the bread cubes to coat them in the mixture and cook, tossing often, to lightly brown the bread, 5 minutes or so.

Add ½ cup vegetable broth and use your spatula to really mush the bread up in the broth so that it absorbs all the liquid and resembles stuffing. Let it cook for about 3 more minutes to sop up all the flavor. If it appears to be dry or falling apart, add up to ½ cup more broth.

While everything is cooking in the pan, chop the hazelnuts with a chef's knife. Transfer the nuts to a large mixing bowl.

Put the lentils in a food processor and puree until relatively smooth. Now transfer the bread mixture from the pan to the processor and pulse 10 to 15 times. You want the mixture to hold together, but there should still be mushroom and celery bits visible. Don't make it a bread puree.

Transfer this to the mixing bowl with the hazelnuts. Add the cranberries and the remaining ¾ teaspoon salt. Combine thoroughly, using your hands if necessary, to form a firm but malleable mixture. Taste and adjust for salt and pepper. Let the mixture cool completely. Refrigerate for 15 minutes or so to firm it up and let the flavors meld.

Rinse out your cast iron pan and preheat it on medium-high. Roll the burger mixture into 6 tennis balls. Wet your hands often during this process so the burgers don't stick to your hands. Flatten the balls into 1½-inch-thick patties.

Cook the patties in a thin layer of oil for about 4 minutes on each side. Serve on buns with your choice of greens and mayo. Die of happiness!

Double Batch CHICKPEA CUTLETS

MAKES

8

CUTLETS

TOTAL
1 HOUR
ACTIVE
20 MINUTES

1 (15-ounce) can chickpeas, rinsed and drained, or 1½ cups cooked chickpeas

¼ cup olive oil, plus more for pan-frying

4 garlic cloves, pressed or grated with a Microplane

1 cup vital wheat gluten

1 cup plain bread crumbs

½ cup vegetable broth, purchased or homemade (page 203), or water

¼ cup tamari or soy sauce

1 teaspoon dried thyme

1 teaspoon paprika

½ teaspoon dried sage

1 teaspoon grated lemon zest

——— *Tip* ———

Wheat gluten can vary from brand to brand. These come out great with Arrowhead Mills or Bob's Red Mill, although I think Bob's makes them a bit firmer. Also, use store-bought bread crumbs unless you plan on tweaking the liquids in this recipe. Homemade bread crumbs tend to make the cutlet mixture too mushy.

Chickpea cutlets are a Thanksgiving classic—so classic that this recipe is modified from *Veganomicon*, the book Terry Hope Romero and I wrote over a decade ago. They come together in no time at all, taste great smothered in gravy, and put your steak knives to work. Place a big pile of these in the middle of the table or stuff them into a Thanksgiving sandwich—or, heck, just slice them up in a salad. They never go out of style.

In a mixing bowl, mash the chickpeas together with the oil until no whole chickpeas are left. Use an avocado masher or a strong fork. Alternatively, you can pulse the chickpeas in a food processor. We're not making hummus here, so be careful not to puree them, just get them mashed up. You can also sneak the garlic cloves in here instead of grating them—just pulse them up before adding the chickpeas. If you're using a food processor, transfer to a mixing bowl when done.

Add the remaining ingredients and knead together for about 3 minutes, until strings of gluten have formed.

Divide the cutlet dough into two equal pieces. Then divide each of those pieces into four separate pieces (so you'll have eight all together). To form the cutlets, knead each piece of dough in your hands for a few moments and then flatten and stretch it into a roughly 4-by-6-inch rectangle. The easiest way to do this is to form the rectangle in your hands and then place the cutlet on a clean surface to flatten and stretch it.

Preheat a large, heavy-bottomed skillet (preferably cast iron) over medium-low heat. If you have two pans and want to cook all the cutlets at once, go for it. Otherwise you'll be doing them in two batches.

Add a thin layer of olive oil to the bottom of the pan. Place the cutlets in the pan and cook on each side for 6 to 7 minutes. Add more oil, if needed, when you flip the cutlets. They're ready when lightly browned and firm to the touch. I've found that they cook more thoroughly if I cover the pan in between flips. I also use my spatula to press down on them occasionally while they're cooking, to help them cook more evenly.

Now let them rest for 10 minutes or so and serve!

ROAST
Stuffed with
LEEKS *And* SHIITAKES

SERVES
6–8

TOTAL
2 HOURS
ACTIVE
45 MINUTES

FOR THE FILLING:

2 tablespoons olive oil

6 ounces shiitake mushrooms, tough stems trimmed, thinly sliced

2 leeks, white and light green parts only, cut into thin half-moons

3 garlic cloves, minced

2 tablespoons chopped fresh thyme

½ teaspoon salt

Freshly ground black pepper

¼ cup bread crumbs

¼ cup vegetable broth, purchased or homemade (page 203)

1 tablespoon fresh lemon juice

FOR THE ROAST:

3 garlic cloves, peeled

¾ cup cooked or canned pinto beans, rinsed and drained

1½ cups vegetable broth, purchased or homemade (page 203; see Tip)

3 tablespoons tamari or soy sauce

2 tablespoons olive oil

2 cups vital wheat gluten

⅓ cup nutritional yeast flakes

1 teaspoon fennel seeds, crushed

1 teaspoon sweet paprika

1 teaspoon dried thyme, crushed with your fingers

1 teaspoon dried sage, crushed with your fingers

Freshly ground black pepper

Looking for *the* perfect, classic centerpiece for your table? This is roast perfection: succulent seitan stuffed with herbed meaty shiitakes and leeks. The seitan is mixed with pureed pinto beans to give it great, juicy texture and a hint of pink color. The stuffing is coated with bread crumbs, which keep it perfectly packed into the roast when you slice it, instead of falling out all over the place.

MAKE THE FILLING: Preheat a large pan (preferably cast iron) over medium heat. Heat the oil, then sauté the mushrooms and leeks until soft, about 10 minutes. Add the garlic, thyme, salt, and a few grinds of black pepper and cook, stirring often, for 2 more minutes.

Sprinkle in the bread crumbs and toss to coat. Cook the mixture, stirring very often, until the bread crumbs are toasty and the mixture is relatively dry. This should take about 5 minutes, and the bread crumbs should turn a few shades darker.

Drizzle in the broth and lemon juice and toss to coat until moist. If it still seems too dry to hold together, drizzle in a little extra olive oil. Set aside until ready to use.

MAKE THE ROAST: Preheat the oven to 350°F.

In a food processor, pulse the garlic until well chopped. Add the beans, broth, tamari, and olive oil and puree until mostly smooth (a few pea-size pieces of bean are okay).

In a large mixing bowl, mix the wheat gluten, nutritional yeast, and seasonings. Make a well in the center and add the bean mixture. Stir with a wooden spoon until the mixture starts coming together to form a ball of dough. Knead until everything is well incorporated.

Now you'll roll out the seitan and form the roast. Place two pieces of aluminum foil (about 18 inches long) horizontally in front of you. The sheet farther from you should overlap the closer sheet by about 6 inches—this way you have enough foil to wrap around the whole roast.

Recipe Continues

For best results, use a salty homemade vegetable broth. Salt is integral to the flavor of the seitan, so if your broth isn't seasoned, then add a teaspoon or so of salt to it. You'll also want to spoon broth over the roast before serving, to keep it from being dry. Of course you're going to be coating it in gravy, too, but the broth is a nice touch. If you're slicing and serving, ladle on spoonfuls of broth on each individual slice, too. You can't have too much juice here!

This roast reheats perfectly. Refrigerate it in its wrapper for up to 3 days beforehand. When ready to serve, preheat the oven to 350°F and cook for 20 minutes. This will dry it out a bit, so use the broth hints above for sure!

On a separate surface, use your hands or a rolling pin to flatten the seitan into a roughly 10-by-12-inch rectangle. If any pieces rip, don't worry about it—just use a pinch of dough from the ends to repair any holes.

Place the filling in the lower third of the seitan rectangle, leaving about 2 inches of space at both ends. Use your hands to form the filling into a nice, tight, compact bundle.

Now roll! Roll the bottom part of the seitan up and over the filling. Keep rolling until it's a log shape. Now pinch together the seam and pinch together the sides to seal. It doesn't have to be perfect, as it will snap into shape when baking.

Place the roll in the center of the foil and roll it up like a Tootsie Roll, making sure the ends are tightly wrapped. Transfer to a baking sheet and bake, rotating the roll every 20 minutes, for 1 hour 15 minutes. It should feel very, very firm, with little give when poked with a wooden spoon.

Remove from the oven and let cool. Unwrap, slice, and serve!

Sweet Potato
CRANBERRY BREAD

SERVES 8–12

TOTAL 1 HOUR
ACTIVE 20 MINUTES

½ cup mashed baked sweet potato (see Tip)

½ cup mashed ripe banana (see Tip)

⅓ cup brown sugar

⅓ cup granulated sugar

¾ cup unsweetened almond milk (or your favorite nondairy milk)

2 tablespoons canola oil

2 teaspoons pure vanilla extract

1½ cups all-purpose flour

1 teaspoon ground cinnamon

¾ teaspoon baking soda

¾ teaspoon salt

1 cup fresh cranberries

Who ever knew that bananas and sweet potatoes could live together so harmoniously? Little hints of each shine through this loaf to seize their moment alongside delicate wisps of cinnamon and tart cranberry bites that make you pucker! This is a reminder to my taste buds that autumn is here. A cup of chopped pecans is a nice addition, if you like.

Preheat the oven to 350°F. Lightly grease an 8-by-4-inch loaf pan.

Mash the sweet potato and banana in a large mixing bowl until relatively smooth. Spoon the mashed mixture into a measuring cup to make sure it's 1 cup, then return it to the mixing bowl. Beat in the sugars, milk, canola oil, and vanilla.

Sift in the flour, cinnamon, baking soda, and salt and gently mix just to incorporate. Fold in the cranberries. Be careful not to overmix; just make sure the cranberries are well distributed.

Transfer the batter to the prepared pan. Bake for 55 to 60 minutes. Use a butter knife to test for doneness. It shouldn't come out with batter on it, but it is a moist bread, so some streakiness is A-OK. Let cool and enjoy!

Tips

The sweet potato should be thoroughly cooked, cooled, and creamy. That way, you don't need to puree it. Just peel and mash away! You can also get away with using a can of sweet potato or pumpkin puree if you don't have any baked sweet potatoes.

The sweet potato and banana measurements don't have to be perfectly even—just make sure they come out to 1 cup total. That is usually one average-size sweet potato and two small to medium bananas.

PASTRY CRUST

FOR A SINGLE CRUST:

1½ cups all-purpose flour

½ teaspoon salt

¼ cup refined coconut oil, melted but at room temperature

¼ cup olive oil, partially frozen (see Tip)

2 to 5 tablespoons ice water

1½ teaspoons apple cider vinegar

FOR A DOUBLE CRUST:

2½ cups all-purpose flour

¾ teaspoon salt

¼ cup refined coconut oil, melted but at room temperature

⅓ cup olive oil, partially frozen (see Tip)

4 to 8 tablespoons ice water

1 tablespoon apple cider vinegar

—————— *Tip* ——————

To prepare the olive oil, about an hour before beginning the recipe, pour the olive oil into a plastic container; for best results use a thin, lightweight container, like the kind used for take-out food. Freeze until it's opaque and congealed but still somewhat soft, like the consistency of slightly melted sorbet. If it's over-frozen, that's okay—just let it thaw a bit so that you can work with it.

This is the lightest, butteriest, veganest pie crust around! A blend of frozen olive oil and melted coconut oil makes for a surprisingly flaky crust that just works.

In a large mixing bowl, sift together the flour and salt. Drizzle in the coconut oil and mix with your fingertips to form crumbs. Working quickly, add the olive oil by the tablespoonful, cutting it into the flour with your fingers or a pastry cutter, until the flour appears pebbly.

In a cup, mix the ice water (start with the smaller quantity) with the apple cider vinegar. Drizzle the liquid into the flour mixture and use a wooden spoon or rubber spatula to stir it into the dough, adding more ice water a tablespoon at a time until it holds together to form a soft ball. Take care not to overknead the dough.

If you're making a single crust, press the dough into a disk about 1 inch thick and place it between two 14-inch-long pieces of waxed paper. Use a rolling pin to roll the disk into a circle about ¼ inch thick. For a more even, uniform circle of dough, roll the pin one or two strokes outward away from you, rotate the dough a few degrees, roll a few more times, and repeat all the way around. Refrigerate the rolled dough wrapped in the waxed paper until ready to use.

If you're making a double crust, divide the dough in half. Repeat as above with both pieces of dough.

GINGER APPLE PIE

2 recipes (double) Pastry Crust (facing page)

FOR THE FILLING:

3 cups sliced (¼-inch slices) peeled Granny Smith apples (about 1½ pounds)

3 cups sliced (¼-inch slices) Honeycrisp apples (about 1½ pounds)

½ cup granulated sugar

⅓ cup brown sugar

3 tablespoons all-purpose flour

3 tablespoons grated fresh ginger

1 teaspoon ground cinnamon

⅛ teaspoon ground cloves

Pinch salt

FOR THE TOPPING:

2 tablespoons granulated sugar

½ teaspoon ground cinnamon

2 tablespoons unsweetened almond milk (or your favorite nondairy milk)

This is a really simple ingredients list that yields really special results! Using two different kinds of apples strikes just the right balance—sweetness and a pretty pink color from the Honeycrisps (I leave them unpeeled for that extra touch of color), and tartness with a sturdy shape from the Granny Smiths. Fresh ginger adds a festive spicy touch.

Preheat the oven to 425°F. Line a 9-inch pie plate with the bottom crust. Roll out the top crust and set it aside until you're ready to use it.

FOR THE FILLING: Combine all the filling ingredients in a large mixing bowl, tossing with your hands to coat the apples. Dump the filling into the pie crust. Cover with the top crust, trim the excess dough to about an inch beyond the pie plate, and crimp the edges together.

FOR THE TOPPING: In a small bowl, mix the sugar and cinnamon. Brush the top of the pie with the almond milk and then sprinkle with the cinnamon sugar. Make five slits in the middle of the pie to let steam escape (a steak knife works great for this).

Bake for 25 minutes, then lower the heat to 350°F and bake for 30 to 35 more minutes, slipping on a crust protector or aluminum foil if your edges are getting too browned. Place on a cooling rack and let cool for about 30 minutes before slicing and serving.

CHOCOLATE
PECAN PIE

1 recipe (single) Pastry Crust (page 358)

½ cup brown sugar

⅓ cup granulated sugar

¼ cup agave

3 tablespoons refined coconut oil

1 cup semisweet chocolate chips

6 ounces extra-firm silken tofu (half of a 12-ounce package)

¼ cup unsweetened almond milk (or your favorite nondairy milk), cold

2 tablespoons cornstarch

½ teaspoon salt

1 teaspoon pure vanilla extract

2 cups pecan halves

This is elbow-Great-Aunt-Dora-out-of-the-way-to-get-the-last-slice delicious! Chocolate should most certainly be represented at the Thanksgiving table, and pecans are the ideal plus-one to get it into the party. This pie is really rich and caramelly, with all that toasty pecan nuttiness studded throughout. Don't worry, once you share a bite of your slice with Great-Aunt Dora, she will totally understand all that elbowing.

Preheat the oven to 350°F. Press the pastry crust into a 9-inch pie plate and set aside.

In a 2-quart saucepan, mix the sugars and agave. Heat over medium heat, stirring often with a whisk. Once small bubbles start rapidly forming, stir constantly for about 10 minutes. The mixture should become thick and syrupy, but it shouldn't be boiling too fiercely. If it starts climbing the walls of the pan in big bubbles, lower the heat a bit.

Add the coconut oil and chocolate chips and stir to melt. Turn off the heat, transfer the mixture to a mixing bowl, and cover it to keep warm. In the meantime, prepare the rest of the filling, working quickly so that the caramel doesn't completely set.

Crumble the tofu into a blender or food processor, along with the milk, cornstarch, and salt. Puree until completely smooth, scraping down the sides of the blender to make sure you get everything.

Add the tofu mixture and the vanilla to the warm caramel in the mixing bowl and mix well. Fold in the pecans to incorporate.

Transfer the filling to the pie crust and bake for 40 minutes. The pie is going to be somewhat jiggly, but it should appear to be set.

Let cool at room temperature, then chill in the refrigerator to completely set for a few hours or overnight. Slice and serve!

PUMPKIN PIE

1 recipe (single) Pastry Crust (page 358)

3 cups cooked (or canned) pumpkin or other sweet winter squash

½ cup pure maple syrup

½ cup plain unsweetened almond milk (or your favorite nondairy milk)

4 teaspoons canola oil

2 tablespoons cornstarch

1 teaspoon agar powder

1 teaspoon ground cinnamon

1 teaspoon ground ginger

¼ teaspoon ground nutmeg

Pinch ground cloves

½ teaspoon salt

What would Thanksgiving be without pumpkin pie? This recipe first captured my heart in 2001 in Myra Kornfeld's wonderful book *The Voluptuous Vegan*. This pie was actually my first-ever attempt at a homemade vegan pumpkin pie and I have only strayed minimally from the recipe since. Why mess with perfection? It's rich and creamy and has the perfect amount of autumn spices.

Preheat the oven to 350°F. Press the pastry crust into a 9-inch pie plate and set aside.

In a blender, pulse together the pumpkin, maple syrup, milk, canola oil, cornstarch, agar powder, and spices until very smooth. Pour the filling into the pie shell and bake until the center looks semi-firm, not liquidy, 60 to 65 minutes. Check the edges of the crust after 40 minutes; if the edges appear to be browning too rapidly, carefully remove the pie and apply a crust protector or aluminum foil to the edges to keep them from getting too dark.

Transfer to a cooling rack for 30 minutes, then chill for at least 4 hours before slicing and serving.

16
HANUKKAH

It's
HANUKKAH TIME!

YEAH, THERE WILL be some dreidel spinning and maybe you'll listen to some Beastie Boys, but the main event is going to be... frying. Everything. With wild abandon. Because that oil lasted eight days and for goodness' sake we are going to celebrate it! With latkes every which way and perfectly golden jelly doughnuts every day.

Don't have a deep fryer? Don't worry! A 6-quart Dutch oven works just as well, or even your regular cast iron skillet can get the job done.

To round out your Hanukkah table so that it's not just a fry-fest, try some of the suggestions to the right, plucked from other chapters in the book.

Classic
MOSKOWITZ
LATKES

MAKES
18
LATKES

TOTAL
1 HOUR
ACTIVE
1 HOUR

2½ pounds russet potatoes, peeled

1 large yellow onion

¼ cup potato starch

1 teaspoon salt, plus extra for sprinkling

½ teaspoon freshly ground black pepper

2 cups matzoh meal

Lots of canola oil, for frying

Tip

You may want to have the oven on at 200°F to keep the latkes warm until you're ready to serve. If serving immediately, just have ready a serving plate, and tent the latkes with foil to keep them warm.

These are the latkes I've been making since forever. They're real easy because you don't have to drain the grated potatoes before you form the latkes (what a hassle!). They taste pretty much like the latkes you can get in a good Brooklyn diner, which in my view makes them the best. Potato, onion, salt, perfection. Serve with So Very Sour Cream (page 368), Caramelized Onions (page 368), and Pretty in Pink Applesauce (page 375). Honestly, if you just want to make a night out of latkes and serve nothing else, no one will complain.

If you're using a food processor, use the grating blade to shred the potatoes and the onion, and transfer to a large mixing bowl. This may be done in two or three batches, depending on the size of your machine.

If you're shredding by hand, use a box grater to shred all the potatoes. Dice the onion as finely as possible. Transfer to a large mixing bowl. Use your hands to mix the potatoes and onion with the potato starch, salt, and pepper until the potatoes have released some moisture and the starch is dissolved, about 2 minutes.

Add the matzoh meal and mix well. Set aside for about 10 minutes. The mixture should be somewhat loose but hold together if pinched. If it seems excessively wet, add a little extra matzoh meal.

In the meantime, preheat a large cast iron pan over medium-high heat. Have ready some brown paper bags or a baking sheet lined with paper towels for draining the oil from the latkes. Add about ½ inch of oil to the pan. While the oil heats, form some latkes.

With wet hands (so that the mixture doesn't stick), roll the mixture into golf balls, then flatten into thin patties. Get about six ready before you start frying.

The oil is hot enough when you drop in a pinch of batter and bubbles rapidly form around it. If it immediately smokes, then the heat is too high and you should lower it a bit. If the bubbles are really lazy, just give it a few more minutes or turn up the heat a bit.

Working in batches, fry the latkes until golden brown, about 4 minutes. Flip over and fry for another 3 minutes.

Transfer the latkes to the lined pan to drain, sprinkle with a little salt, flip, and sprinkle with salt again, then proceed with the remaining latkes. Serve warm.

SO VERY SOUR
CREAM

1 cup raw cashews, soaked in water for at least 2 hours and drained
1 (14-ounce) can coconut milk
½ cup fresh lemon juice
¼ cup refined coconut oil, melted
½ teaspoon onion powder
Big pinch salt

This is the tangiest, smoothest, sourest sour cream there is! It sets up beautifully creamy and is the perfect thing to serve with potato pancakes, pierogis, or tacos, or to dollop on top of soups. Once the sour cream has set, it's best to keep it refrigerated, because if left at room temperature for too long it will lose some of its shape.

In a blender, puree all the ingredients until completely smooth; this can take up to 5 minutes depending on the strength of your machine. Periodically stop the machine to keep it from overheating, and scrape down the sides of the blender jar with a rubber spatula to make sure you get everything.

Transfer the sour cream to a quart-size container, cover, and let set for at least a day. Dollop away!

CARAMELIZED
ONIONS

¼ cup refined coconut oil
3 pounds yellow onions, diced medium
¼ teaspoon salt

The basic idea here is to sweat the onions, which means you'll be gently cooking them over low heat, and a lot of the cooking will be done by the steam as the moisture is released. You're coaxing the sweetness out of them and locking it in. This is kind of an art, so don't rush it! It looks like a lot of onions, and it is, but everything will cook down to manageable proportions, I promise.

Preheat a heavy-bottomed pot over low heat. Add the oil and the onions and toss the onions to coat. Cover, leaving the lid slightly ajar for steam to escape, and cook for 20 minutes, stirring every 5 minutes or so with a slanted wooden spoon. The onions should turn a nice mellow amber but not burn, although a couple of darker spots are fine.

Remove the cover and turn the heat up to medium. Cook for 15 more minutes, stirring often. The onions should become a darker amber, and some of the moisture should evaporate. Stir in the salt. If you're not serving the onions immediately, let them cool and then store them in a sealed container in the refrigerator for up to 3 days.

SWEET POTATO
LATKES

1½ pounds sweet potatoes, peeled and shredded (about 4 cups)

1 cup thinly sliced scallion

½ cup all-purpose flour

¼ cup cornstarch

½ teaspoon anise seeds, chopped up a bit

¼ teaspoon ground nutmeg

½ teaspoon salt

Freshly ground black pepper

¼ cup water

Refined coconut oil, for frying

Feel like bucking tradition? Go sweet! A hint of anise and nutmeg makes these little latkes feel like winter, and frying in coconut oil gives them a butteriness that is over-the-top delicious.

In a large mixing bowl, toss together the sweet potatoes and scallion. Add the flour, cornstarch, anise, nutmeg, salt, and a few grinds of black pepper and toss to coat. Drizzle in the water and mix until everything is wet and holds together.

Preheat a large cast iron pan over medium-high heat. Have ready some brown paper bags or a baking sheet lined with paper towels for draining the oil from the latkes. Add about ¼ inch of coconut oil to the pan. While the oil heats, form the dough into golf balls and then flatten them into patties that are about ½ inch thick.

The oil is hot enough when you drop in a pinch of batter and bubbles rapidly form around it. If it immediately smokes, then the heat is too high and you should lower it a bit. If the bubbles are really lazy, just give it a few more minutes or turn up the heat a bit.

Fry the latkes until golden brown, about 4 minutes on each side, checking the underside often so that they don't burn.

Transfer to the lined pan to drain, sprinkle with a little salt, flip, and sprinkle with salt again, then proceed with the remaining latkes. Serve warm.

SAMOSA-SPICED
LATKES

2 pounds russet potatoes, peeled

2 carrots, peeled

1 large yellow onion

2 tablespoons grated fresh ginger

¼ cup potato starch

2 teaspoons curry powder

1 teaspoon ground cumin

1 teaspoon salt, plus extra for sprinkling

½ teaspoon crushed red pepper flakes

2 cups peas, fresh or frozen (mostly thawed if frozen)

2 cups matzoh meal

Lots of canola oil, for frying

1 recipe Pear Chutney (page 373)

Worlds collide! My two favorite fried finger foods combine into one sublime bite. Curry powder, carrot, and peas give these potato pancakes a samosa flair, and some pear chutney seals the deal. You've got eight days of Hanukkah, so use one of them to break from the pack and serve these fun treats.

If you're using a food processor, use the grating blade to shred the potatoes, carrots, and onion, and transfer to a large mixing bowl. This may be done in two or three batches, depending on the size of your machine.

If you're shredding by hand, use a box grater to shred the potatoes and carrots. Dice the onion as finely as possible. Transfer to a large mixing bowl.

Add the ginger, potato starch, curry, cumin, salt, and red pepper flakes to the mixing bowl. Use your hands to mix everything in with the potatoes, carrots, and onion. Keep mixing until the potatoes have released some moisture and the starch is dissolved, about 2 minutes.

Fold in the peas. Add the matzoh meal and mix well. Set aside for about 10 minutes. The mixture should be somewhat loose but hold together if pinched. If it seems excessively wet, add a little extra matzoh meal.

In the meantime, preheat a large cast iron pan over medium-high heat. Have ready some brown paper bags or a baking sheet lined with paper towels for draining the oil from the latkes. Add about ½ inch of oil to the pan. While the oil heats, form some latkes.

With wet hands (so that the mixture doesn't stick), roll the dough into golf balls, then flatten into thin patties. Get about six ready before you start frying.

The oil is hot enough when you drop in a pinch of batter and bubbles rapidly form around it. If it immediately smokes, then the heat is too high and you should lower it a bit. If the bubbles are really lazy, just give it a few more minutes or turn up the heat a bit.

Working in batches, fry the latkes until golden brown on one side, about 4 minutes. Flip over and fry for another 3 minutes.

Transfer the latkes to the lined pan to drain, sprinkle with a little salt, flip, and sprinkle with salt again, then proceed with the remaining latkes. Serve warm, with the chutney.

RÖSTI LATKES

MAKES

12

LATKES

TOTAL
1 HOUR
ACTIVE
1 HOUR

2½ pounds russet potatoes, peeled

1 large yellow onion, finely chopped

¼ cup potato starch

1 teaspoon salt, plus extra for sprinkling

½ teaspoon ground black pepper

Lots of canola oil, for frying

Tip

You need cheesecloth to be the quickest and most effective with this recipe, but a thin linen kitchen towel will work as well. Don't use one of those terrycloth towels. You can also use a lot of paper towels, but it will probably have to be done in batches that way.

A rösti is a Scandinavian potato cake, and that's what these latkes remind me of. They are more like shredded hash browns, which is a style that I've found everywhere outside of NYC. These latkes contain no flour or matzoh meal and are completely gluten-free, so that should make some of your friends happy! They go great with So Very Sour Cream (page 368) and Pretty in Pink Applesauce (page 375).

Whether you're using a food processor with a grating blade or a box grater, shred the potatoes and transfer them to the middle of the unfolded cheesecloth. Over the sink, twist the excess cloth to wring out the liquid from the potatoes. Get them as dry as possible. It can take a few minutes to really squeeze that liquid out. When done, transfer the shredded potatoes to a large mixing bowl, along with the onion.

Add the potato starch, salt, and black pepper and toss with your hands to get everything well combined. Even though you squeezed those potatoes so well, there will still be a bit of liquid left to absorb the starch.

Preheat a large cast iron pan over medium-high heat. Have ready some brown paper bags or a baking sheet lined with paper towels for draining the oil from the latkes. Add about ½ inch of oil to the pan. While the oil heats, form some latkes by pressing the potatoes into ¾-inch-thick cakes that are about 2 inches in diameter.

The oil is hot enough when you drop in a pinch of batter and bubbles rapidly form around it. If it immediately smokes, then the heat is too high and you should lower it a bit. If the bubbles are really lazy, just give it a few more minutes or turn up the heat a bit.

Fry the latkes until golden brown, about 4 minutes on each side, checking the underside often so that they don't burn.

Transfer the latkes to the lined pan to drain, sprinkle with a little salt, flip, and sprinkle with salt again, then proceed with the remaining latkes. Serve warm.

PEAR
CHUTNEY

1 tablespoon refined coconut oil

1 large yellow onion, diced small

¼ teaspoon salt

1¼ cups rice wine vinegar

1½ cups packed light brown sugar

2 tablespoons minced fresh ginger

1 teaspoon crushed red pepper
flakes

½ teaspoon ground cinnamon

2 whole star anise

4 Bosc pears, peeled and cut into
½-inch dice

¼ cup fresh lime juice

1 cup golden raisins

This recipe will make you want to start an artisanal chutney company in a formerly industrial area of Portland, Oregon! It's so full of pear flavor, with a puckery tartness and just a little heat. It goes with the Samosa-Spiced Latkes (page 370) but also, of course, with regular old Potato Samosas in Phyllo (page 103).

Preheat a 4-quart pot over medium heat. Add the coconut oil. When the oil is hot, sauté the onion with the salt just until a little softened, about 5 minutes.

Add the vinegar, brown sugar, ginger, red pepper flakes, cinnamon, and star anise and stir to combine. Stir in the pears.

Cover the pot and bring to a low boil. Lower the heat and simmer, stirring often, until the mixture is thick, about 30 minutes. The pears should still hold their shape.

Add the lime juice and raisins and cook for 5 more minutes. Let cool and remove the star anise pods. Transfer the chutney to a sealed container and refrigerate until ready to use.

Superyum
BAKED POTATO
PANCAKES

FOR THE PANCAKES:

2 pounds Yukon Gold potatoes, peeled and cut into ¾-inch chunks

1 cup thinly sliced scallions (white and light green parts only)

2 teaspoons olive oil

½ teaspoon salt

½ teaspoon freshly ground black pepper

⅓ cup plain bread crumbs

FOR THE BREADING:

1 cup plain bread crumbs

½ teaspoon salt

½ teaspoon freshly ground black pepper

2 teaspoons olive oil

Tip

These are very delicate before being baked, so handle firmly but carefully when pressing into the bread crumbs and transferring to the pan. Once in the oven they will firm up nicely.

Maybe it's day six of Hanukkah and you're like, "Please, no, not another fried thing!" Yet you'll never tire of loads and loads of potatoes. What's a girl to do? Baked latkes to the rescue! The only issue is that if they're not fried, they're not really latkes. So let's just call them potato pancakes to keep the pedants from judging. No matter what you call them, they're superyum and will fill that potato-shaped hole in your heart.

Put the potatoes in a small pot and cover with cold water. Cover and bring to a boil. Once boiling, lower the heat and simmer until tender, about 15 minutes. Drain the potatoes in a colander and run cold water over them. Let the potatoes drain and cool for about 15 minutes, giving them a stir every now again, until they are cool enough to handle.

Preheat the oven to 425°F. Line a large baking sheet with parchment paper and coat it with nonstick cooking spray.

Transfer the potatoes to a mixing bowl and add the scallions, olive oil, salt, and pepper. Use a potato masher to mash like crazy, until there aren't any big chunks of potato left. Add the bread crumbs and mix well.

Mix all the breading ingredients on a large dinner plate. Form the pancakes by rolling the dough into golf balls and then flattening them into 3-inch patties. Press the pancakes firmly and carefully into the breading mix, then transfer to the prepared baking sheet.

When you have six pancakes on the sheet and the oven is preheated, spritz the pancakes lightly with cooking spray. Bake for 12 minutes. Flip carefully, using a thin spatula, and spray the other side. Bake for 8 more minutes.

They're best when served warm!

PRETTY IN PINK
APPLESAUCE

6 pounds Granny Smith apples (about 15), peeled, cored, and cut into ½-inch dice

⅓ cup fresh lemon juice

1 cup sugar

1 teaspoon ground cinnamon

1 (2-inch) chunk peeled beet

I'm assuming that you are feeding an army of adoring latke fans, so you'll need a big ol' bucket of gorgeous pink applesauce. Everyone knows that green Granny Smiths make the best, tartest applesauce. But this is my secret: You can still have pink applesauce if you throw in a hunk of beet at the end of cooking and then pull it out before serving. It leaves behind only the beautiful color, and no beety flavor.

In a large stockpot over medium-low heat, combine the apples, lemon juice, sugar, and cinnamon. Cover the pot and cook, stirring occasionally, until the sugar is melted and the apples are a bit cooked, about 15 minutes.

Uncover and cook until the mixture is bubbly, another 30 minutes or so. The apples should be very tender and saucy but still have some shape left in them.

Add the beet chunk and cook for an additional 10 minutes. Fish out the beet and mix the applesauce. If it's pink, you can discard the beet. If it needs more color, turn off the heat so as not to overcook the apples and let the beet sit with the mixture until it's nice and pink, then remove.

Taste for sweetness and adjust if necessary. Let cool completely, then transfer to airtight containers and refrigerate until ready to serve.

FRIED PICKLES
with Ranch

16 dill pickle spears

2 tablespoons cornstarch

¾ cup unsweetened almond milk (or your favorite nondairy milk)

1 cup cornmeal

2 tablespoons nutritional yeast flakes

2 teaspoons onion powder

1 teaspoon garlic powder

1 teaspoon paprika

1½ teaspoons salt, plus more for sprinkling

Freshly ground black pepper

Canola oil, for frying

1 recipe ranch dressing (page 41)

—————— *Tip* ——————

If you can get the pickles from a deli, rather than out of a glass jar, they'll hold up a little better. But no one's going to kvetch if you use supermarket pickles, either.

I discovered the magic of eating fried pickles dipped in cool ranch on Hanukkah when I moved to the Midwest. It's not the type of thing a nice Jewish girl from Brooklyn would ever think of doing. But, boy, am I glad I did. These are welcome at my Hanukkah table anytime.

With a paper towel, blot the pickles so that they're relatively dry and ready to be breaded.

In a wide shallow dish, whisk the cornstarch into the milk until dissolved.

In another shallow dish, combine the cornmeal, nutritional yeast, onion and garlic powders, paprika, salt, and a few grinds of black pepper.

Dip each pickle into the milk mixture and use your other (dry) hand to coat it completely in the seasoned cornmeal mixture. Set the breaded pickles aside until all are coated.

Heat about ¼ inch of the canola oil in a cast iron skillet over medium heat. The oil is hot enough when you drop in a pinch of batter and bubbles rapidly form around it. If it immediately smokes, then the heat is too high and you should lower it a bit. If the bubbles are really lazy, just give it a few more minutes or turn up the heat a bit.

Fry the pickles in batches, turning occasionally, to evenly brown, about 6 minutes. Transfer to paper towels to drain, sprinkle with a little salt, and serve immediately with the ranch dressing.

ZUCCHINI
BABA GHANOUSH

4 medium zucchini or any summer squash (about 3 pounds)

2 tablespoons olive oil, plus more for coating and drizzling

Salt

2 garlic cloves, peeled

½ cup tahini

⅓ cup fresh lemon juice

Freshly ground black pepper

Ground sumac or paprika, for sprinkling (optional)

Your baba doesn't have to be limited to eggplant. The most important aspect, in my opinion, is getting that charred smoky flavor in there. The grill is the perfect device. Keep it simple: Cut the zucchini in half and let it be until it's nice and grilly. I love finishing my baba with a sprinkle of sumac, but paprika works nicely, too.

Preheat the grill to medium-high heat.

Cut the zucchini lengthwise and place on a rimmed baking sheet. Coat generously with the olive oil, and sprinkle with salt. Use your hands to massage it in.

Place the zucchini, cut-side down, on the grill and cook until dark grill marks appear, about 5 minutes. Flip the zucchini to cook the skin side until tender, 3 to 5 more minutes, depending on the size. Return the zucchini to the baking sheet to let cool a bit.

In a food processor, pulse the garlic until it's finely chopped. Add the grilled zucchini and pulse to chop it up a bit. Add the tahini, lemon juice, and 2 tablespoons olive oil and process into a creamy dip, adding a little bit of water if needed to thin.

Taste and adjust for salt, pepper, and seasoning. Transfer to a serving bowl, cover tightly, and refrigerate until ready to use. To serve, drizzle with a little olive oil and sprinkle with sumac or paprika, if you like.

GREEN FALAFEL

FOR THE FALAFEL:

1 cup dried chickpeas

3 garlic cloves, peeled

¼ cup finely chopped scallion

¼ cup finely chopped fresh parsley

¼ cup finely chopped fresh cilantro

1½ teaspoons ground cumin

1 teaspoon salt

¼ cup chickpea flour

¼ teaspoon baking powder

¼ teaspoon crushed red pepper flakes

Canola oil, for frying

FOR THE TZATZIKI:

2 garlic cloves, peeled

1 cup plain unsweetened coconut yogurt

2 tablespoons fresh lemon juice

2 tablespoons olive oil

½ teaspoon salt

1 cup chopped cucumber

¼ cup chopped fresh dill

Tip

Since the moisture in chickpeas can vary a lot, you may need to make a few adjustments to ensure that your falafel stays together and fries up beautifully. Test a mini falafel before frying all of them to make sure that it holds together. If it seems loose, add a little more chickpea flour. If it seems too dry, add a little water and retest.

This is falafel the *real* way—the green way! Crisp on the outside, soft and fluffy inside, it just ignites all your senses in the way only falafel can. **Stuff them into pitas or enjoy them on salads smothered in tahini or tzatziki—or both.**

MAKE THE FALAFEL: In a large bowl, cover the chickpeas with water by about 4 inches. Make sure there is plenty of room because the chickpeas will just about double in size. Soak for at least 24 hours.

Drain and rinse the chickpeas. Transfer them to a food processor fitted with the metal blade. Add the garlic, scallion, parsley, cilantro, cumin, and salt. Pulse into a coarse meal that resembled couscous. Make sure that there are no whole chickpeas left and that the mixture holds together when pressed, but be careful not to completely puree.

Transfer the mixture to a large mixing bowl and add the chickpea flour, baking powder, and red pepper flakes. Mix for about 2 minutes to make sure everything is well combined. Cover with plastic wrap and refrigerate for at least 2 hours, and up to overnight.

And now we fry! In a large Dutch oven, heat about 2 inches of oil over medium heat. To test the oil, toss in a little bit of dough; bubbles should quickly form around it. If the bubbles are lazy, turn up the heat a bit.

Roll the falafel into tight, walnut-size balls (see Tip). Fry in batches, using a metal spoon to turn the falafel occasionally, until gorgeously golden brown, 3 to 4 minutes. Drain on paper towels.

MAKE THE TZATZIKI: In a blender, pulse the garlic to chop. Add the yogurt, lemon juice, oil, and salt and blend until smooth. Add the cucumber and dill and pulse until the cucumber is in tiny pieces. If you need to season any further, do it in a mixing bowl so that you don't puree this into a smoothie.

Serve warm, on salads or in sandwiches, topped with the tzatziki.

KASHA
VARNISHKES

12 ounces farfalle (bow tie pasta)

2 teaspoons ground flaxseed

⅓ cup water

2 tablespoons refined coconut oil

2 large yellow onions, cut into thin half-moons

½ teaspoon salt, plus a pinch

1 cup uncooked coarse kasha

2 cups vegetable broth, purchased or homemade (page 203)

Freshly ground black pepper

3 tablespoons chopped fresh dill

1 recipe Fancy/Not Fancy Mushroom Gravy (page 339), for serving (optional)

Did you know that if you say "varnishkes" into the bathroom mirror three times fast, Mel Brooks will appear behind you? Here's what's up: Pasta and toasty buckwheat are coated with lots of buttery, caramelized onions and tossed with a little fresh dill. Simple, homey flavors—the very benchmark of Jewish cooking. You can serve with mushroom gravy, but if you're serving it with lots of other things, it's fine on its own.

Bring a pot of salted water to a boil over high heat. Cook the farfalle according to the package directions until al dente. Drain and set aside.

Meanwhile, combine the flaxseed and water in a blender. Blend until frothy and viscous, about a minute. Now you have a flax egg. Set aside until ready to use.

Preheat a large sauté pan over medium-high heat. Add the coconut oil. When the oil is hot, sauté the onions with a pinch of salt until nicely browned and caramelized, 10 to 12 minutes. Transfer to a bowl and set aside.

Add the kasha to the same pan and toss to toast and cook for about 2 minutes. Add the flax egg and cook, stirring often, until the flax egg has coated the kasha and appears relatively dry, about 5 minutes.

Add the cooked onions, broth, remaining ½ teaspoon salt, and a few grinds of black pepper. Cover the pan, lower the heat, and simmer until the kasha is cooked and the liquid is absorbed, about 12 minutes.

When the kasha is tender, add the farfalle and toss to coat. Add the fresh dill. Taste and adjust for salt and seasoning. Serve, with or without mushroom gravy, as you please.

CHOLENT
with Porcinis & Kidney Beans

SERVES
8–10

TOTAL
1 HOUR
ACTIVE
20 MINUTES

2 tablespoons olive oil

1 large onion, diced medium

3 garlic cloves, minced

1 teaspoon caraway seeds

1 teaspoon salt

Freshly ground black pepper

½ cup vegetable broth, purchased or homemade (page 203)

1 cup peeled sliced carrots (about ½ inch thick)

½ cup French lentils, rinsed

1 ounce dried porcini mushrooms, cut into ½-inch pieces if large

2 bay leaves

3 cups water

4 medium-size russet potatoes (about 1¼ pounds), peeled and cut into 1-inch chunks

1 (15-ounce) can tomato sauce

1 (25-ounce) can kidney beans, rinsed and drained, or 2¼ cups cooked kidney beans

Chopped fresh parsley, for garnish

America's got cholent! A meaty, juicy, filling, stick-to-your-vegan-ribs kind of stew. I make this every Hanukkah because it's tradition, yeah, but also because it's a nice and easy one-pot meal that can simmer up while I'm making everything else.

Preheat a 4-quart pot over medium heat. Heat the oil, then sauté the onion until lightly golden, 5 to 7 minutes. Add the garlic, caraway seeds, salt, and a few grinds of black pepper. Sauté until the garlic is fragrant, about a minute more. Deglaze the pot with the vegetable broth.

Add the carrots, lentils, mushrooms, bay leaves, and water. Cover and simmer until the carrots are tender, about 20 minutes. Add the potatoes, cover, and cook for another 15 minutes. At this point the lentils should be very tender as well. Add the tomato sauce and cook, uncovered, for another 20 minutes or so. The lentils should be very broken down, the potatoes tender, and the mushrooms soft and meaty. Stir in the kidney beans to heat through. Remove the bay leaves and serve, garnished with parsley.

JELLY DOUGHNUTS

(Sufganiyot)

2¼ teaspoons active dry yeast (one 0.75-ounce packet)

1 cup lukewarm unsweetened almond milk (or your favorite nondairy milk)

6 tablespoons water

2 tablespoons ground flaxseed

3½ cups white bread flour, plus extra for kneading

2 tablespoons sugar, plus more for coating

1 teaspoon salt

2 tablespoons refined coconut oil, melted

Vegetable oil, for deep-frying

1 cup seedless raspberry jam

—— Tip ——

Store any leftovers in a paper bag, if you can manage to not eat them all right away.

I really don't believe any of the Hanukkah stories about oil lasting for eight days. I think someone in a little village just really wanted jelly doughnuts one day, so they made up the whole thing. In any case, here we are in the 21st century with this undisputed fact: You can't have Hanukkah without jelly doughnuts! And let's just agree that there is no such thing as a "baked doughnut." These babies are deep-fried and coated in sugar, just the way our ancestors intended.

In a small bowl, whisk together the yeast and milk and set aside. In a blender, blend up the water and flaxseed for about a minute until frothy and viscous. Set aside.

In a very large mixing bowl, whisk together the flour, sugar, and salt, then make a well in the center. Pour in the yeast mixture, the flax mixture, and the coconut oil, then mix to form a dough. Add more flour a tablespoon at a time until the dough isn't sticky, then turn it out onto a floured counter to knead until the dough is smooth.

Wash out the mixing bowl, lightly coat it with nonstick cooking spray, and add the dough ball. Toss the dough ball to coat it in oil, then cover the bowl with plastic wrap. Place the bowl somewhere warm and let the dough rise until doubled in size, 1 to 2 hours.

Lightly flour the counter and a baking sheet. Turn out the dough onto the floured counter, knead it a couple of times, then roll it out until it's about ½ inch thick. Using a floured 3-inch cookie cutter (or a drinking glass), stamp out your doughnuts and place them on the floured baking sheet at least 2 inches apart. Squish the dough scraps back together and roll them out again to make more doughnuts, place them on the sheet, then cover the sheet with a clean kitchen towel or plastic wrap and let the doughnuts rise for about 20 minutes.

While the doughnuts are rising, get your fryer ready and turned to 350°F. Have ready a layer of paper towels or brown paper bags to drain. Pour some sugar into a shallow dish for coating the hot doughnuts.

Using a metal slotted spoon, lower the doughnuts into the oil, a few at a time so you don't crowd the fryer, and fry until golden brown, turning several times to keep the cooking even. Use the slotted spoon to transfer them to the paper towels or bags until cool enough to handle, then roll each one in sugar until completely covered.

Once all the doughnuts are fried and sugared, it's time to fill them! Fit a pastry bag with a large round tip and fill it with the jam. Poke the tip into the side of each doughnut, then squeeze a couple of teaspoons of jam inside! If you overfill them, the jam will leak out, but that's okay. Serve!

MAKES

4

DOZEN

TOTAL
3 HOURS
(for chilling)
ACTIVE
1 HOUR

All the
RUGELACH

FOR THE DOUGH:

2 cups all-purpose flour

¼ teaspoon salt

¾ cup refined coconut oil, at room temperature

3 tablespoons unsweetened applesauce

1 cup plain unsweetened coconut or soy yogurt

FOR THE BASIC FILLING:

½ cup sugar

1 tablespoon ground cinnamon

1 cup finely chopped walnuts

FOR THE VARIATIONS:

3 tablespoons seedless raspberry jam

¼ cup finely chopped bittersweet chocolate

¼ cup chopped raisins

Probably the most iconic of the Jewish cookies, the rugelach is the pastry that most has us pressing our faces up against the glass at the local bakery. It's rich and buttery and sweet and cinnamony and will have you drifting off in conversation with a distant cousin thrice removed whose name you can't remember in order to go grab another one. Pick your poison or make all four: classic cinnamon-walnut, raspberry, chocolate, or raisin.

PREPARE THE DOUGH: In a very large mixing bowl, sift together the flour and salt, then add the coconut oil in small clumps. Use a pastry cutter to cut the oil into the flour until pea-size crumbs have formed. Add the applesauce and yogurt and mix to form a stiff dough.

Divide the dough into four equal parts, then form them into four disks. Wrap each disk with plastic wrap and refrigerate for at least 2 hours.

FOR THE FILLING AND VARIATIONS: In a food processor, pulse together the sugar, cinnamon, and walnuts until it is in tiny crumbs.

From here you can make as many variations as you want, but these directions will be for one batch each of classic rugelach, raspberry rugelach, chocolate rugelach, and raisin rugelach. Roll the disks one at a time for best results, leaving the others in the refrigerator until their turn.

On a clean, flat surface with plenty of space, roll a disk into a 9-inch circle.

For Classic Rugelach: Sprinkle some cinnamon mixture all over the disk, leaving about ½ inch space at the edges.

For Raspberry Rugelach: Spread a thin layer of raspberry jam over the disk, leaving about ½ inch space at the edges, then sprinkle on some cinnamon mixture.

For Chocolate Rugelach: Scatter the chopped chocolate over the disk, leaving about ½ inch space at the edges, then sprinkle on some cinnamon mixture.

For Raisin Rugelach: Sprinkle some cinnamon mixture all over the disk, leaving about ½ inch space at the edges, then scatter on the chopped raisins.

Now comes the fun/tedious part. Have ready a large rimmed baking sheet lined with parchment. Use a pizza cutter to cut each round into 12 wedges, like a pizza pie. Roll each triangle from the base up to the point to form the rugelach. Place the rolled rugelach on the prepared baking sheet and put it in the refrigerator while you continue to prepare each disk.

When all the cookies are formed, let them chill for another 15 minutes in the fridge. In the meantime, preheat the oven to 375°F. Bake until lightly browned and a little puffy, 18 to 22 minutes. The sugar should appear caramelized and melty. Transfer to wire racks to cool completely.

Prune

And POPPY SEED
HAMANTASCHEN

MAKES

32

COOKIES

TOTAL
2 HOURS
ACTIVE
1 HOUR

FOR THE DOUGH:

⅔ cup refined coconut oil

1 cup sugar

1 cup unsweetened almond milk (or your favorite nondairy milk), warm

1 teaspoon grated lemon zest

4 teaspoons pure vanilla extract

3¾ cups all-purpose flour

2 tablespoons cornstarch

1 teaspoon baking powder

1 teaspoon salt

FOR THE FILLING:

8 ounces pitted prunes

¼ cup poppy seeds

¼ cup sugar

¼ cup water

¼ cup fresh orange juice

½ teaspoon grated orange zest

2 tablespoons semisweet chocolate chips

Hamantaschen are typically served at Purim, but who cares? These fabulous cookies can be enjoyed year-round! Especially during other Jewish holidays. In fact, when I was a little girl taking my yellow school bus to yeshiva kindergarten, I didn't even know that hamantaschen were holiday specific.

You can fill hamantaschen with all sorts of things, but I settled on sort of a Fig Newton filling, with crunchy, toasty poppy seeds and a few melted chocolate chips and orange for extra depth.

The dough is not quite flaky like a pastry dough. It's crisp on the exterior, but soft and cakey inside. Lemon gives the cookie just a little bit of brightness that is reminiscent of the kosher bakeries of my youth. If you grew up with these cookies, I hope they bring you back. And if you've never tried them, I hope you'll become a new fan!

PREPARE THE DOUGH: In a medium mixing bowl, use an electric hand mixer to beat together the coconut oil and sugar. It should be somewhere between creamy and crumbly. Add the milk and beat until smooth and incorporated. Mix in the lemon zest and vanilla.

Add 2 cups of the flour, along with the cornstarch, baking powder, and salt. Beat on medium until smooth. Add the remaining 1¾ cups flour, about ½ cup at a time, mixing after each addition, until the dough is stiff, smooth, and not tacky. It will probably start climbing up the beaters. That's okay!

Divide the dough in half. Roll each half into a ball and flatten a bit into a fat disk, then wrap each disk in plastic and refrigerate for about 30 minutes. In the meantime, prepare the filling.

PREPARE THE FILLING: Roughly chop the prunes and put them in a saucepot. Add the poppy seeds, sugar, water, orange juice, and orange zest. Cover and bring to a simmer over medium heat. Let the mixture cook, stirring often, until the prunes are very soft, 5 to 7 minutes. If it seems too stiff, add a little extra water, a tablespoon at a time, until it loosens up a bit. It should be the texture of a thick jam.

Recipe Continues

Transfer to a blender and add the chocolate chips. Puree the mixture while still warm so that the chips melt. If it is too thick to puree, once again add a little water until it will blend.

Once the filling is nice and smooth (although many poppy seeds will remain whole), transfer it to a bowl and set aside at room temp until you're ready to form the cookies.

MAKE THE COOKIES: Preheat the oven to 350°F. Line two large baking sheets with parchment paper.

Sprinkle a clean, dry countertop with a little flour. Take one portion of the dough and flatten it out a bit with the palm of your hand, then roll it about ⅛ inch thick, sprinkling with flour if the dough seems sticky.

Using a 3-inch cookie cutter, create 14 to 16 circles of dough, then peel away the excess dough.

In the center of each circle, place about 1 teaspoon of the filling.

Brush the circumference of one circle with water on your fingertips, to help seal. Now fold three flaps over the filling to make a triangle, leaving some of the filling still exposed in the center. Then, pinch together each corner of the triangle. Repeat until you've got a bunch of hamantaschen! Place them on one of the lined baking sheets.

Roll out the other portion of dough and repeat, filling the other baking sheet. If desired, you can roll out the excess dough and make a few more cookies.

Bake the cookies for 10 minutes, then rotate and swap the pans and bake for another 8 minutes or so. The bottoms should be golden brown.

Transfer the hamantaschen to cooling racks to cool completely. Store the cookies in a tightly sealed container at room temperature. I think they taste even better the next day.

MAKES AROUND

18

COOKIES

TOTAL
3 HOURS
ACTIVE
20 MINUTES

MANDELBROT

⅓ cup unsweetened almond milk (or your favorite nondairy milk)

2 tablespoons ground flaxseed

2 teaspoons grated orange zest

¾ cup sugar

½ cup canola oil

1 teaspoon pure vanilla extract

½ teaspoon pure almond extract

1⅔ cups all-purpose flour

2 tablespoons cornstarch

2 teaspoons baking powder

½ teaspoon salt

1 cup slivered blanched almonds, finely chopped

These translate pretty much to "almond bread," but I've always thought of them as Jewish biscotti. They're crunchy and full of (obviously) almond flavor, with hints of orange. Just like biscotti, these are perfect with a cup of coffee and some gossip.

Preheat the oven to 350°F. Line a baking sheet with parchment paper.

In a large mixing bowl, whisk together the milk and flaxseed, beating for around a minute until viscous. Mix in the orange zest, sugar, oil, and extracts. Sift in the flour, cornstarch, baking powder, and salt. Stir to combine, and just before the dough comes together, knead in the almonds. Keep kneading to form a stiff dough.

Divide the dough in two. On the lined baking sheet, form two logs about 6 inches by 3 inches. Bake until lightly puffed and browned, 20 to 22 minutes. Let cool on the baking sheet for about an hour.

Once cool, preheat the oven to 325°F. Carefully transfer one log at a time to a cutting board. With a heavy, very sharp knife, cut each log crosswise into ½-inch slices. The best way to do this is in one motion, pushing down—don't "saw" the slices off or they could crumble. Place the slices, curved-sides up, ½ inch apart on the baking sheets. Bake until dry and toasted, 18 to 22 minutes. Transfer to a cooling rack to cool completely before serving.

CHRISTMAS LIGHTS,
Christmas trees, my
SPOTIFY INDIE-ROCK
Christmas playlist—
I JUST LOVE CHRISTMAS!

SINCE I WON'T SHUT UP about it, you probably realize that I was raised Jewish, but that has never stopped me from decking the halls.

You've got your roasts and stews and all that. Plus you can pretty much use anything from the Thanksgiving chapter here, because that all makes sense. As for the rest? Cookies! No Christmas is complete without them. What would Santa eat? Kale chips? I think not!

My Christmas game plan: Make the cookie doughs a few days in advance and keep them refrigerated. Bake them off a day ahead.

To drink: There are a million wonderful vegan eggnogs on the supermarket shelves these days. Don't bother making your own. Buy a variety and have at it.

Oh, and P.S., if you're Jewish you can just use anything from the Chinese New Year section, switch on your Netflix, find a blockbuster, and you're set!

LENTIL TAMALES

with Mole Rojo

MAKES ABOUT
20
TAMALES

TOTAL
2 HOURS 30 MINUTES
ACTIVE
1 HOUR 30 MINUTES

FOR THE MOLE:

2 tablespoons olive oil

1 yellow onion, diced medium

3 garlic cloves, minced

5 teaspoons chili powder

2 teaspoons dried oregano or marjoram

1 teaspoon ground cinnamon

½ teaspoon anise seeds

1 (14-ounce) can diced tomatoes

2 cups vegetable broth, purchased or homemade (page 203)

3 tablespoons creamy natural peanut butter

¼ cup raisins

½ cup crushed tortilla chips

½ cup slivered almonds

⅓ cup semisweet chocolate chips

FOR THE DOUGH:

1 (8-ounce) package tamale corn husks

4 cups masa harina

4 cups vegetable broth, purchased or homemade (page 203)

½ cup refined coconut oil, melted

2 teaspoons baking powder

1 teaspoon salt

Everything about a tamale is Christmassy. For one, you unwrap it to eat. For another, the beautiful red mole and the green herbs are perfectly colored for the season. The hint of anise and cinnamon in the sauce just seals the deal.

MAKE THE MOLE: Preheat a 4-quart pot over medium heat. Heat the oil, then sauté the onion and garlic until the onion is translucent, 3 to 5 minutes. Add the chili powder, oregano, cinnamon, and anise and cook briefly, just till the spices become fragrant. Add the tomatoes, broth, peanut butter, and raisins and bring to a boil.

Lower the heat and stir in the tortilla chips, almonds, and chocolate chips. Once the chocolate is melted, turn off the heat and let the mole cool until it stops steaming but is still warm. Transfer in batches to a blender and blend until completely smooth. Set aside until serving time—it's great warm or at room temperature.

MAKE THE DOUGH: Put the corn husks in a large pot or bowl and cover completely with warm water. Allow the husks to soak until soft and pliable, about 20 minutes. Keep the husks in the water until you are ready to use them.

Meanwhile, in a very large bowl, combine the masa harina, broth, melted coconut oil, baking powder, and salt. With an electric hand mixer, beat until a dense, moist, fluffy dough forms and the sides of the bowl are clean. Cover the bowl with plastic wrap and set aside until ready to use.

MAKE THE FILLING: Preheat a large skillet over medium-high heat. Heat the oil, then sauté the onion and garlic with a pinch of salt until lightly browned, about 3 minutes. Add the tomato, cilantro, cumin, cayenne, and remaining 1 teaspoon salt and cook until the tomatoes are broken down, about 10 minutes.

Lower the heat to medium. Add the lentils and heat through. Use a small masher to mash the lentils a bit, until they hold together. It's perfect if there are about half of them still whole and half mashed. Add the corn and heat through. Taste and adjust for salt.

Recipe Continues

FOR THE FILLING:

2 tablespoons olive oil

1 small onion, diced small

2 garlic cloves, minced

1 teaspoon salt, plus a pinch

1 cup diced fresh tomato

¼ cup chopped fresh cilantro

1 teaspoon ground cumin

¼ teaspoon cayenne pepper

2½ cups cooked or canned lentils, rinsed and drained

2 cups corn kernels, fresh or frozen

FOR SERVING:

Chopped fresh cilantro

1 recipe Salsa Fresca (page 217)

1 recipe Super-Classic Guacamole (page 217)

MAKE THE TAMALES: Lay out one corn husk. Spread about 3 tablespoons of the tamale dough in a 3-by-4-inch rectangle down the center of the husk. Spoon 2 tablespoons of the filling down the center of the dough rectangle.

Fold the long sides of the husk snugly over the filling to enclose. Fold the bottom of the husk over the folded sides, and leave the top open. Repeat to form about 20 tamales.

In the meantime, bring your steamer to a boil. Place the tamales in the steamer with the open side up. Cover and steam until the dough is firm, about 40 minutes. This may have to be done in batches depending on the size of your steamer.

Let the tamales cool for at least 10 minutes before serving. Garnish with the cilantro and serve with the mole, salsa, and guac.

 Tip   *Use the largest tamale husks you can find. If you need to, you can overlay smaller ones to form one large one.*

BEAN
BOURGUIGNON

2 cups pearl onions

6 tablespoons olive oil

1 teaspoon salt, plus a couple pinches

1 medium yellow onion, finely diced

1 pound cremini mushrooms, sliced

4 garlic cloves, minced

3 tablespoons chopped fresh thyme, plus a few sprigs for garnish

1 tablespoon chopped fresh rosemary

Freshly ground black pepper

⅓ cup all-purpose flour

1½ cups vegetable broth, purchased or homemade (page 203)

½ cup dry red wine

2 bay leaves

1 (15-ounce) can kidney beans, rinsed and drained, or 1½ cups cooked kidney beans

1 (15-ounce) can chickpeas, rinsed and drained, or 1½ cups cooked chickpeas

The classic French dish is now 100 percent more vegan, with beautiful beans in a thick, winy stew, plus gorgeously festive roasted pearl onions. I love regular old kidney beans here, but Christmas limas are well worth seeking out! This is wonderful over either Olive Oil Smashed Potatoes (page 338) or Creamy Whipped Potatoes (page 341), but nice as just a bowl of stew, too.

Preheat the oven to 350°F. Line a large rimmed baking sheet with parchment paper.

On the baking sheet, toss the pearl onions with 2 tablespoons of the olive oil and pinch of salt. Roast for 20 minutes, until beautifully caramelized. Set aside until ready to use.

In the meantime, preheat a 4-quart pot over medium heat. Heat 2 tablespoons of the oil, then sauté the onion with a pinch of salt until softened, about 5 minutes. Add the mushrooms, garlic, thyme, rosemary, remaining 1 teaspoon salt, and a few grinds of black pepper and sauté until fragrant, 30 seconds or so.

Now we'll make the roux. Add the remaining 2 tablespoons oil and, using a slanted wooden spatula, stir constantly as you sprinkle in the flour. Keep stirring to toast the flour, adding up to another tablespoon of oil if necessary. Cook until the roux is thick and pasty and a few shades darker, about 10 minutes.

Now stream the vegetable broth into the pot, stirring constantly so that it does not clump. As soon as the mixture is smooth, add the red wine and the bay leaves. Simmer to cook out the strong wine flavor, about 15 minutes. Stir in the kidney beans and chickpeas to heat through. Taste and adjust for salt and seasoning. Add the roasted pearl onions and serve, garnished with fresh thyme sprigs.

SCALLOPED POTATOES

SERVES
8–12

TOTAL
1 HOUR 30 MINUTES
ACTIVE
20 MINUTES

1½ cups raw cashews, soaked in water for at least 2 hours and drained

3 cups vegetable broth, purchased or homemade (page 203)

3 tablespoons olive oil

1 large yellow onion, thinly sliced

5 celery ribs, thinly sliced

1 teaspoon salt, plus a pinch

⅓ cup store-bought bread crumbs (if using homemade, increase to ½ cup)

3 tablespoons fresh lemon juice

Freshly ground black pepper

3 pounds russet potatoes, peeled and very thinly sliced (about 5 large potatoes)

Chopped fresh parsley, for garnish (optional)

Tip

The key to perfectly cooked potatoes is to slice them thinly—aim for between ⅛ and ¼ inch thick. If you have a mandoline, now is the time to use it. But NBD if you don't.

Typically, scalloped potatoes are made with canned cream of celery soup, but duh, we are going the homemade route—which isn't much more difficult and is a million times yummier. Potatoes are sliced very thin and baked in a lemony cashew cream with a secret toasty ingredient (spoiler: it's bread crumbs). A while later, something gloriously golden and satisfying pops out of the oven. Even if you have a few truckloads of mashed potatoes at the Christmas table, you still need these!

Combine the cashews and vegetable broth in a blender. Puree until completely smooth; this can take up to 5 minutes depending on the strength of your machine. Periodically stop the machine to keep it from overheating, and scrape down the sides of the blender jar with a rubber spatula to make sure you get everything.

In the meantime, preheat a large pan over medium heat. Heat the oil, then sauté the onion and celery with a pinch of salt until the onion is nice and brown, about 10 minutes. Add the bread crumbs and toss to coat the onion and celery. Cook until the bread crumbs turn a few shades darker, about 3 minutes.

Now is a good time to preheat your oven to 350°F and lightly grease a 9-by-13-inch casserole dish.

Pour the cashew mixture into the pan and lower the heat a bit. Mix well. Add the lemon juice, the remaining 1 teaspoon salt, and several grinds of black pepper. Let cook for 2 minutes; it should begin to thicken. Taste and adjust for salt and seasoning.

Now we'll put this baby together!

Pour half of the sauce into the prepared casserole dish. Arrange the potatoes in the casserole, dredging them in the sauce a bit as you make slightly overlapping, fanned layers.

Pour the remaining sauce over the potatoes. They should be mostly submerged. Use a rubber spatula to spread out the sauce if needed.

Cover the dish tightly with aluminum foil and bake until the potatoes are easily pierced with a fork, about 45 minutes. Remove the foil and bake until nice and brown on top, another 15 to 20 minutes.

Garnish with chopped fresh parsley if you want, and serve!

PUMPKIN *And* CRANBERRY RISOTTO

with Chestnuts

1 (3-pound) sugar pumpkin or any winter squash (butternut, kabocha, acorn, what have you)

3 tablespoons refined coconut oil

1 small yellow onion, diced small

3 garlic cloves, minced

1 tablespoon minced fresh ginger

1½ cups Arborio rice

⅓ cup dry white wine

5 cups vegetable broth, purchased or homemade (page 203), kept warm on the stovetop

½ cup dried cranberries

1 tablespoon fresh lemon juice

½ teaspoon salt

½ teaspoon ground nutmeg (grate it fresh if you can)

¼ teaspoon ground cinnamon

¼ teaspoon crushed red pepper flakes

1 cup coconut milk from a well-stirred can

2 cups chopped peeled roasted chestnuts (fresh or from a jar)

This Christmassy risotto makes for a sweet little centerpiece, all orangey and studded with pretty cranberries, and with a nutty crunch from the chestnuts. It's even more super delish served alongside the Blood Orange Glazed Tofu (page 405).

Preheat the oven to 425°F. Lightly oil a rimmed baking sheet.

Cut the pumpkin in half with a strong chef's knife and remove the seeds and stringy bits with a tablespoon. Place the pumpkin halves on the baking sheet, cut-side down. Bake until easily pierced with a fork but not completely mushy, about 30 minutes. Once cooled, peel off the skin and chop the pumpkin into bite-size pieces.

While the pumpkin is cooling, preheat a 4-quart pot over medium heat. Heat the oil, then sauté the onion, garlic, and ginger, stirring often so you don't burn anything, until softened, about 7 minutes. Add the rice and cook, stirring to coat with oil, until lightly translucent around the edges, about 5 minutes. Add the wine to deglaze the pot, then add the first cup of vegetable broth. Use a slanted wooden spoon to stir until most of the liquid is absorbed.

Continue adding veggie broth a cup at a time, stirring very frequently and letting each cup absorb before adding the next, just until the rice is tender, 15 to 20 minutes. When you're at the last cup, add the cranberries and keep stirring. When most of the liquid has absorbed, add the lemon juice, salt, nutmeg, cinnamon, and red pepper flakes. Stir in the coconut milk. Cook for 10 more minutes, stirring occasionally. Fold in the pumpkin and chestnuts. Taste and adjust for salt. Serve!

 Tip *I recommend roasting the pumpkin a day in advance, so that it's cool, chopped, and waiting for you the day you make the risotto.*

Sorta CLASSIC POT PIE

1 recipe (double) Pastry Crust (page 358)

4 tablespoons olive oil

2 cups seitan, thinly sliced

1 medium yellow onion, diced medium

1 cup small-diced peeled carrots

1½ teaspoons salt, plus a pinch

1 cup frozen green peas (no need to thaw)

3 celery ribs, thinly sliced

1 teaspoon dried thyme

1 teaspoon dried sage

Freshly ground black pepper

⅓ cup all-purpose flour

1¾ cups vegetable broth, purchased or homemade (page 203)

⅔ cup unsweetened almond milk (or your favorite nondairy milk)

Tip

If for whatever reason you don't want to use seitan, you can substitute 2 cups cooked or canned chickpeas.

Make pretty leaf cutouts with the excess dough and bake right on top of the pie for added fall flair.

You know what to expect out of a pot pie, and this one will never in a million years disappoint. Flaky pastry, creamy béchamel, peas, carrots, and toothsome seitan. It's a downright necessity at the holiday table and, fine, I've been known to eat it for breakfast, too. So what, it's Christmas, I'm an adult, and I can do as I please.

Preheat the oven to 425°F. Line a 9-inch pie plate with the bottom crust. Roll out the top crust and put it in the fridge until you're ready to use it.

Preheat a cast iron pan over medium heat. Heat 1 tablespoon of the oil, then sauté the seitan until lightly browned, about 3 minutes. Transfer the seitan to a plate.

In the same pan, heat another 1 tablespoon oil and sauté the onion and carrots with a pinch of salt until the onion is translucent and the carrots are slightly softened, about 5 minutes. Add the peas, celery, thyme, sage, remaining 1½ teaspoons salt, and a few grinds of black pepper and sauté until the celery is softened, about 2 minutes.

Add the remaining 2 tablespoons oil and, using a slanted wooden spatula, stir constantly as you sprinkle in the flour. Keep stirring to toast the flour, adding up to another tablespoon of oil if necessary. Toast just until the flour is a shade darker, about 3 minutes.

Stream in the vegetable broth and mix until there are no clumps, then add the almond milk. Let cook until thickened, about 5 minutes.

Layer the seitan in the bottom pie crust. Pour in the filling mixture. Place the top crust over the filling and seal the edges. Make a few slits in the top crust to let steam escape.

Bake until golden brown and bubbly, about 35 minutes. Let cool for 30 minutes before slicing and serving.

EPIC
EGGPLANT LASAGNA

FOR THE EGGPLANT:

3 pounds eggplant, cut crosswise into not-quite-½-inch slices

3 tablespoons olive oil

Salt

FOR THE TOFU RICOTTA:

2 (14-ounce) packages extra-firm tofu

¼ cup nutritional yeast flakes

¼ cup olive oil

3 tablespoons fresh lemon juice

1 teaspoon salt

Freshly ground black pepper

FOR THE WHITE SAUCE:

1 cup raw cashews, soaked in water for at least 2 hours and drained

¾ cup water

2 teaspoons cornstarch

½ teaspoon salt

FOR THE LASAGNA:

3 recipes Marinara Sauce (page 65)

1 pound lasagna noodles

Fresh basil leaves

¼ cup toasted pine nuts

Tip

All lasagna noodles are "no-boil" if you seal your casserole well enough! The noodles will cook right there in the sauce, and taste way better that way because they absorb all the yummy sauce instead of plain old water.

Lasagna for Christmas: It's a thing! At least in Brooklyn it is. And if it isn't already your thing, now is a great time to make it so. This one is gorgeous and Christmassy, with the marinara and basil. And, oh, did I mention that it's epic? Layers of tofu ricotta, roasted eggplant, and perfectly cooked lasagna noodles, if you play your cards right. No one will be able to resist this centerpiece!

MAKE THE EGGPLANT: Preheat the oven to 375°F. Line two large rimmed baking sheets with parchment.

Put the eggplant slices in a large mixing bowl. Drizzle with the olive oil and sprinkle with salt, while tossing to coat. Arrange the slices in a single layer on the lined baking sheets and bake, flipping once, until tender, about 30 minutes. Set aside until ready to assemble the lasagna. Leave the oven on.

MAKE THE TOFU RICOTTA: While the eggplant is in the oven, make the ricotta. Crumble the tofu into a large bowl. Use an avocado masher to mash it up until it resembles ricotta. Add the nutritional yeast, olive oil, lemon juice, salt, and a few grinds of black pepper and continue to mash until well combined. Set aside.

MAKE THE WHITE SAUCE: Combine the cashews, water, cornstarch, and salt in a blender. Puree until completely smooth; this can take up to 5 minutes depending on the strength of your machine. Periodically stop the machine to keep it from overheating, and scrape down the sides of the blender jar with a rubber spatula to make sure you get everything. Set aside.

ASSEMBLE THE LASAGNA: Lightly grease the bottom of a 9-by-13-inch casserole dish. Ladle in a thin layer of marinara sauce, then arrange a single layer of (uncooked!) noodles over the sauce.

Ladle in another layer of sauce that is about ½ inch deep. Then arrange half of the eggplant slices over it. On top of that layer, spoon in half of the ricotta in scattered dollops.

Over the ricotta, ladle in another ½-inch layer of sauce, then repeat the noodles, eggplant, ricotta, sauce, and, finally, another layer of noodles. That will be the top layer. (You'll probably have a few lasagna noodles left over.)

Get plenty of sauce over the top layer. Tightly seal the lasagna with aluminum foil and bake for 1 hour. The noodles should be tender by this point.

Remove the foil. Drizzle the white sauce over the top with zigzagging Jackson Pollock motions, then bake, uncovered, for an additional 20 minutes.

Scatter the basil leaves and pine nuts over the top and serve!

Spinach & Pine Nut STUFFED CHEESY ROAST

SERVES
8–12

TOTAL
2 HOURS
ACTIVE
1 HOUR

FOR THE SEITAN:

3 garlic cloves, peeled

¾ cup cooked or canned pinto beans, rinsed and drained

1½ cups vegetable broth, purchased or homemade (page 203)

3 tablespoons tamari or soy sauce

2 tablespoons olive oil

2 cups vital wheat gluten

⅓ cup nutritional yeast flakes

1 teaspoon smoked paprika

1 teaspoon dried thyme

Freshly ground black pepper

FOR THE FILLING:

1 cup raw cashews, soaked in water for at least 2 hours and drained

1 cup vegetable broth, purchased or homemade (page 203)

2 tablespoons fresh lemon juice

½ cup nutritional yeast flakes

1 teaspoon smoked paprika

2 tablespoons olive oil

1 large onion, diced medium

3 garlic cloves, minced

½ teaspoon salt

Freshly ground black pepper

¼ cup bread crumbs

1 pound baby spinach

⅓ cup pine nuts, toasted

This roast is so freaking festive! It is stuffed with lots of sautéed spinach, smothered with an oozy cheese sauce, and studded with toasted pine nuts. Slice into it and watch the action happen!

PREPARE THE SEITAN: Preheat the oven to 350°F. In a food processor, pulse the garlic until well chopped. Add the beans, broth, tamari, and olive oil and puree until mostly smooth (a few pieces of bean are okay, but they should be no bigger than a pea).

In a large mixing bowl, mix the wheat gluten, nutritional yeast, paprika, thyme, and a few grinds of black pepper. Make a well in the center and add the bean mixture. Stir with a wooden spoon until the mixture starts coming together to form a ball of dough. Knead until everything is well incorporated. Set aside.

PREPARE THE FILLING: In a blender, combine the cashews, vegetable broth, lemon juice, nutritional yeast, and paprika. Puree until completely smooth; this can take up to 5 minutes depending on the strength of your machine. Periodically stop the machine to prevent it from overheating, and scrape down the sides of the blender jar with a rubber spatula to make sure you get everything.

Meanwhile, preheat a large sauté pan (preferably cast iron) over medium heat. Heat the oil, then sauté the onion until lightly browned, about 5 minutes. Add the garlic, salt, and a few grinds of black pepper and sauté for about 30 seconds.

Sprinkle in the bread crumbs and toss to coat. Cook the mixture, stirring very often, until the bread crumbs have turned a few shades darker and the mixture is relatively dry, about 5 minutes.

Add the spinach in batches to wilt. When it is just wilted, add the cashew mixture and mix well. Let the filling cook and thicken for about 5 minutes. Fold in the pine nuts.

 *Recipe Continues*

ASSEMBLE: Now we're going to roll out the seitan and form the roast. Place two pieces of aluminum foil (about 18 inches long) horizontally in front of you. The sheet farther from you should overlap the closer sheet by about 6 inches—this way you have enough foil to wrap around the whole roast.

On a separate surface, use your hands or a rolling pin to flatten the seitan into a roughly 10-by-12-inch rectangle. If any pieces rip, don't worry about it—just use a pinch of dough from the ends to repair any holes.

Place the filling in the lower third of the seitan rectangle, leaving about 2 inches of space at both ends. Use your hands to form the filling into a nice, tight, compact bundle.

Now roll! Roll the bottom part of the seitan up and over the filling. Keep rolling until it's a log shape. Now pinch together the seam and pinch together the sides to seal. It doesn't have to be perfect, as it will snap into shape when baking.

Place the roll in the center of the foil and roll it up like a Tootsie Roll, making sure the ends are tightly wrapped. Transfer to a baking sheet and bake, rotating the roll every 20 minutes, for 1 hour 15 minutes. It should feel very, very firm, with little give when poked with a wooden spoon.

Remove from the oven and let cool. Unwrap, slice, and serve!

SERVES
8

Blood Orange
GLAZED
TOFU

FOR THE MARINADE:

3 tablespoons grated fresh ginger

4 garlic cloves, minced

1 heaping tablespoon grated blood orange zest

½ cup fresh blood orange juice

¼ cup pure maple syrup

4 teaspoons tamari or soy sauce

2 teaspoons olive oil

FOR THE TOFU:

2 (14-ounce) packages extra-firm tofu, pressed

Blood orange slices, for garnish

Bring the drama with this Technicolor tofu. Blood orange is the most stunning citrus there is, and it tastes like nothing else—sweet and perfumy, almost like cotton candy, but with a bright, fresh, zingy flavor. Serve with mashed sweet potatoes, roasted butternut squash, or Pumpkin & Cranberry Risotto (page 397).

FOR THE MARINADE: Lightly grease a 9-by-13-inch baking dish. Combine all the marinade ingredients in a small bowl and whisk vigorously. Pour the marinade into the baking dish.

FOR THE TOFU: Cut each block of tofu crosswise into eight slices. Add the tofu slices to the marinade in the dish, toss to coat, and let them marinate for 1 hour.

Preheat the oven to 375°F.

Cover the baking dish with aluminum foil. Bake for 20 minutes. Remove from the oven and flip the tofu pieces over. Cook, uncovered, for 15 more minutes. To give the tofu slices more chewiness, broil them for 2 minutes on each side.

Serve immediately, garnished with blood orange slices.

SERVES
12–16

TOTAL
1 HOUR 30 MINUTES
ACTIVE
30 MINUTES

FIGGY PEAR
CRUMBLE

FOR THE FILLING:

8 cups diced peeled Anjou pears
(¾-inch dice)

1½ cups quartered Mission figs

½ cup brown sugar

½ cup granulated sugar

¼ cup all-purpose flour

1½ teaspoons ground cinnamon

1 teaspoon ground ginger

½ teaspoon ground allspice

½ teaspoon ground nutmeg

⅛ teaspoon ground cloves

Pinch salt

FOR THE TOPPING:

1 cup quick-cooking oats (not
instant)

1 cup all-purpose flour

1 cup brown sugar

½ cup finely chopped walnuts

½ teaspoon baking powder

½ teaspoon ground cinnamon

¼ teaspoon salt

⅓ cup refined coconut oil, at room
temperature

3 tablespoons unsweetened almond
milk (or your favorite nondairy
milk)

1 teaspoon pure vanilla extract

When pie takes a day off, crumbles happen—you get all the goodness of pie with about a million times less work. This one has the dressed-to-impress wintry flavors of pear and figs, bubbling up in a sugar and cinnamon streusel. It's a really great dessert for when you need to feed an army but can't be bothered to get out the rolling pins.

Preheat the oven to 350°F. Lightly grease a 9-by-13-inch baking dish.

FOR THE FILLING: In a very large mixing bowl, toss the pears and figs with all the remaining filling ingredients until the fruit is coated in the flour and spices.

FOR THE TOPPING: In a separate bowl, combine the oats, flour, brown sugar, walnuts, baking powder, cinnamon, and salt. Add the coconut oil in clumps, rubbing it into the floury mixture with your fingers. Drizzle in the milk and vanilla, tossing the crumbs to coat.

Spread out the fruit mixture in the prepared baking dish and scatter on the crumb topping. Bake until hot, bubbly, and lightly browned, about 45 minutes. Let cool for about 30 minutes before serving.

GINGERBREAD
WAFFLES

MAKES

6

WAFFLES

TOTAL
45 MINUTES
ACTIVE
15 MINUTES

2 cups unsweetened almond milk
(or your favorite nondairy milk),
at room temperature

1 teaspoon apple cider vinegar

3 tablespoons canola oil

¼ cup molasses, at room
temperature

½ cup brown sugar

1 teaspoon pure vanilla extract

3 tablespoons grated fresh ginger

2¼ cups all-purpose flour

2 teaspoons baking powder

½ teaspoon salt

1½ teaspoons ground cinnamon

¼ teaspoon ground cloves

There isn't a single minute during the holiday season that you should be without gingerbread. So, don't forget that gingerbread can come in breakfast form, too!

Measure out the milk in a measuring cup and add the apple cider vinegar. Set aside to curdle for a few minutes.

In a large bowl whisk together the canola oil and molasses. Whisk in the milk and vinegar, then the brown sugar, vanilla, and ginger. Whisk in 1 cup of the flour, along with the baking powder, salt, cinnamon, and cloves. Add the remaining 1¼ cups flour and use a spatula to mix until everything is combined.

Cook the waffles according to your waffle iron manufacturer's directions. Serve warm.

Banana
EGGNOG
PANCAKES

MAKES

8

PANCAKES

TOTAL
30 MINUTES
ACTIVE
30 MINUTES

2 very ripe medium bananas

1¼ cups eggnog

2 tablespoons canola oil

2 teaspoons apple cider vinegar

1 teaspoon pure vanilla extract

1 cup all-purpose flour

2¼ teaspoons baking powder

½ teaspoon grated fresh nutmeg, plus extra for sprinkling

¼ teaspoon salt

Refined coconut oil, for cooking

FOR SERVING:

Banana slices

Fresh or dried cranberries

Pure maple syrup

Tip

Since vegan eggnogs vary from brand to brand, your results may vary, but I can't see anything going drastically wrong from using one brand over another. Some are thinner than others, some are spicier, but you always have to play with pancake batter a little anyway, adding a tablespoon of extra flour or a splash of extra liquid to get the right consistency. Don't sweat it.

You are going to want these pancakes around throughout December the same way you are going to want to hang up vintage candy cane lights and listen to indie-rock Xmas playlists and watch *Love, Actually* over and over again. They're perfect for Christmas morning, and you won't be able to live without them. After January 1, though, put them away, let their powers recharge, and do it again next year! I've included a little extra nutmeg just to drive home the point that these are eggnog pancakes! If there still isn't enough of that woodsy perfume for you, shave a little bit more nutmeg over the top of your stack, because *yum*.

In a medium mixing bowl, mash the bananas with a small masher until they are almost pureed. Add the eggnog, canola oil, vinegar, and vanilla and set aside.

In a separate large mixing bowl, sift together the flour, baking powder, nutmeg, and salt. Make a well in the center and pour in the banana mixture. Use a fork to mix until a thick, lumpy batter forms. That should take about a minute. It doesn't need to be smooth; just make sure you get all the ingredients incorporated. Let the batter rest for 10 minutes.

Preheat a large nonstick pan (preferably cast iron) over medium-low heat. Lightly coat the pan with coconut oil. Add ⅓ cup of the batter for each pancake and cook until puffy, about 4 minutes. Flip the pancakes, adding a new coat of oil to the pan, and cook until golden brown, another 3 minutes or so.

Transfer the pancakes to a plate tented with aluminum foil while you cook the rest. Serve with sliced bananas, cranberries, and maple syrup.

CRANBERRY-ORANGE
CHEESECAKE

SERVES
8

TOTAL
4 HOURS
(to set)
ACTIVE
30 MINUTES

FOR THE CHEESECAKE:

½ cup raw cashews, soaked in water for at least 2 hours and drained

½ cup mashed ripe banana (about 2 medium-size bananas)

1 (12-ounce) package extra-firm silken tofu

⅔ cup sugar

2 tablespoons refined coconut oil, at room temperature

4 teaspoons cornstarch

¼ cup fresh orange juice

1 tablespoon grated orange zest

2 teaspoons pure vanilla extract

¼ teaspoon salt

1 recipe Graham Cracker Crust (facing page)

FOR THE CRANBERRY TOPPING:

10 ounces frozen cranberries

¼ cup water

⅓ cup sugar

½ teaspoon agar powder

½ teaspoon cornstarch

A sparkling, glowing jewel for your holiday dessert table, this cheesecake takes the, er, cake! So orangey and creamy and sweet, with a tart juicy topping.

MAKE THE CHEESECAKE: In a blender, puree all the cheesecake ingredients (except the crust!) until completely smooth; this can take up to 5 minutes depending on the strength of your machine. Periodically stop the machine to keep it from overheating, and scrape down the sides of the blender jar with a rubber spatula to make sure you get everything. Pour the batter into the crust.

MEANWHILE, MAKE THE CRANBERRY TOPPING: In a small saucepan, combine the cranberries, water, sugar, agar powder, and cornstarch. Bring the mixture to a simmer over medium heat and cook, stirring occasionally, until thickened to the consistency of melted jam, 4 to 6 minutes. Spoon the mixture on top of the cheesecake, working from the center and spreading to the edges. Let cool for 10 minutes, then move to the fridge to complete cooling, at least 3 hours or, even better, overnight. To serve, unlatch the springform pan and slice the cake with a thin, sharp knife dipped in cold water.

GRAHAM CRACKER CRUST

MAKES

1

9-INCH PIE
CRUST

TOTAL
20 MINUTES
ACTIVE
10 MINUTES

- 1¾ cups finely ground graham crackers (from 10 ounces whole graham crackers)
- 3 tablespoons sugar
- 3 tablespoons refined coconut oil, melted
- 1 tablespoon unsweetened almond milk (or your favorite nondairy milk)

Tip

If you're using a 9-inch pie plate instead of a springform pan, press the crumbs into the sides of the plate first, then work your way down to the bottom.

For all your creamy pie needs! Simple as can be.

Preheat the oven to 350°F. Lightly coat a 9-inch springform pan with nonstick cooking spray.

In a mixing bowl, combine the graham crumbs and sugar. Drizzle in the oil. Mix with your fingertips to moisten the crumbs. Drizzle in the milk and stir again to form a crumbly dough.

Pour the crumb mixture into the pan. Press the crumbs very firmly into the bottom of the pan. Bake until firm, 8 to 10 minutes. Let the crust cool before filling.

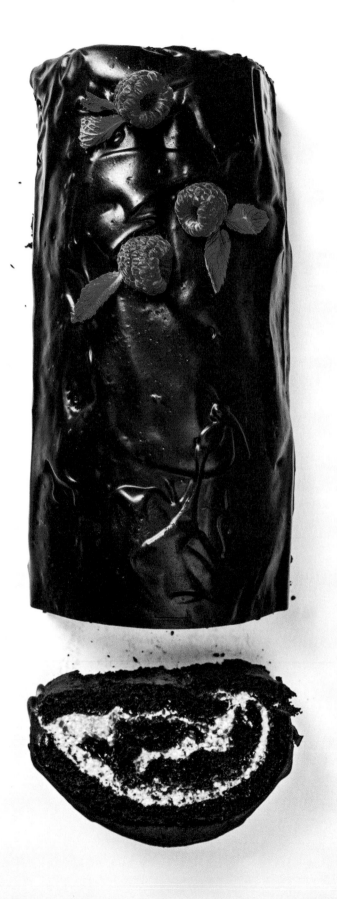

Chocolate
RASPBERRY
BÛCHE DE NOËL

SERVES
16

TOTAL
3 HOURS
ACTIVE
1 HOUR

FOR THE CAKE:

1 cup unsweetened almond milk (or your favorite nondairy milk)

1 teaspoon apple cider vinegar

¾ cup granulated sugar

⅓ cup canola oil

1 teaspoon pure vanilla extract

½ teaspoon pure almond extract

1 cup all-purpose flour

⅓ cup unsweetened cocoa powder, plus extra for dusting

¾ teaspoon baking soda

¾ teaspoon baking powder

¼ teaspoon salt

Fresh mint leaves, for decoration

FOR THE BUTTERCREAM:

1 cup fresh raspberries, plus a few more for decoration

¾ cup refined coconut oil, at room temperature

3½ cups powdered sugar, plus extra for decoration

1 teaspoon pure vanilla extract

Seedless raspberry jam

FOR THE GANACHE:

1½ cups semisweet chocolate chips

½ cup unsweetened almond milk (or your favorite nondairy milk)

2 tablespoons agave

This cake turns everyone's eyes into emoji hearts! Coated in ganache and filled with a raspberry buttercream swirl—oh, lovely little Yule log, you are so worth it. And as these things go, this one is quite easy. No need for piping skills, since raspberries and fresh mint leaves do the hard work. You definitely need a 13-by-18-inch jelly roll pan for this or the cake won't roll correctly, so that's one thing you can't improvise. But who knows? Maybe you'll become the jelly roll master all year long and that pan will pay off.

MAKE THE CAKE: Preheat the oven to 350°F. Coat a 13-by-18-inch jelly roll pan with cooking spray, line with parchment paper, spray again, and then coat in flour, tapping off the excess.

In a measuring cup, mix the milk and apple cider vinegar and set aside to curdle. In a stand mixer or in a medium bowl with a handheld electric mixer, beat the sugar, oil, and extracts on medium-high speed until fluffy.

In a separate bowl, sift together the flour, cocoa powder, baking soda, baking powder, and salt. Add the dry ingredients to the wet in two batches, scraping the bowl after each addition and mixing until no large clumps remain.

Pour the batter onto the prepared pan and spread evenly with a big rubber spatula. Bake until the top is springy, 18 to 20 minutes.

Let cool for 10 minutes or so. Now it's time to invert the cake. Dust the top with cocoa powder and cover with plastic wrap. On top of the plastic wrap place a kitchen towel, and top that with a big cutting board. Now hold that stack together tightly and flip it over so that the cutting board is on the bottom. When you lift the pan up from the top, the cake should be on the plastic on top of the towel on the cutting board. Peel off the parchment, then dust with more cocoa powder. Fold the towel over the cake and the plastic wrap a couple inches on one of the short sides, then slowly and carefully roll the cake up in the towel. Let cool completely.

Recipe Continues

WHILE THE CAKE IS COOLING, MAKE THE BUTTERCREAM: First, puree the raspberries in a food processor.

In a large mixing bowl, using an electric mixer, beat the coconut oil and gradually add the powdered sugar, scraping the bowl as you go. Beat in the vanilla and the raspberry puree until smooth and creamy.

Once the cake is cool, slowly unroll it. If it cracks a little, that's okay! The frosting will hold it together and the ganache will cover up any mistakes. Spread an even layer of buttercream over the cake and then, using the plastic wrap to help, roll the cake back up as tightly as possible. Make sure it winds up with the seam on the bottom, and put it on a serving tray, or on parchment.

MAKE THE GANACHE: In a metal bowl placed over a pot of simmering water, melt the chocolate chips with the milk and agave, stirring until completely smooth. Pour the ganache over the cake and use a rubber spatula to smooth it out everywhere, especially under the bottom curve. Put it in the fridge to set.

Very carefully transfer the cake to a serving tray, using two large thin spatulas and employing a friend. Just before serving, sift a little powdered sugar on top and decorate with fresh raspberries and mint leaves!

GINGERBREAD
PEOPLE

⅓ cup canola oil

¾ cup sugar

¼ cup molasses

¼ cup unsweetened almond milk (or your favorite nondairy milk)

2 cups whole-wheat pastry flour or all-purpose flour (or a mix of both)

½ teaspoon baking soda

½ teaspoon baking powder

½ teaspoon salt

1½ teaspoons ground ginger

½ teaspoon ground cinnamon

½ teaspoon ground nutmeg

½ teaspoon ground cloves

Whether you're going all out with your decorating or you're a part of the gingerbread minimalist movement, this recipe is a surefire winner that will have you singing Christmas carols under your breath and then looking around to make sure no one heard you. This recipe originally appeared in *Vegan Cookies Invade Your Cookie Jar,* but a Christmas chapter without gingerbread people would be pointless.

In a large bowl whisk together the oil and sugar until well blended, 3 to 5 minutes. Add the molasses and milk. The molasses and milk won't really blend with the oil, but that's okay.

Sift in all the dry ingredients, stopping to mix about halfway through. When all the dry ingredients are added, mix until a stiff dough is formed. Flatten the dough into a disk, wrap in plastic, and chill for at least 1 hour. If you chill it for longer than an hour, you may want to let it sit for 10 minutes to warm up a bit before proceeding.

Preheat the oven to 350°F. Lightly grease two rimmed baking sheets or line them with parchment paper.

On a lightly floured surface, roll out the dough to a little less than ¼ inch thick. Cut out your people with cookie cutters and use a thin spatula to gently place them on the baking sheets. If you are using them to decorate a tree or something, remember to punch a hole in their heads (!) before baking. Bake for 8 minutes.

Remove from the oven and let the cookies cool for 2 minutes on the baking sheet, then move them to a cooling rack. Wait until they are completely cool before icing.

Big, Soft CHOCOLATE CHIP COOKIES

MAKES
16
COOKIES

TOTAL
45 MINUTES
ACTIVE
20 MINUTES

½ cup brown sugar

¼ cup granulated sugar

½ cup refined coconut oil, melted

⅓ cup unsweetened applesauce

2 teaspoons cornstarch

2 teaspoons pure vanilla extract

1½ cups all-purpose flour

½ teaspoon baking soda

½ teaspoon salt

¾ cup semisweet chocolate chips

All right, you probably cut to the chase and immediately flipped to this recipe despite the hundreds of other recipes in the book. Welcome! These cookies are big, soft, and lovely, with a crisp buttery crust and a moist, yummy interior. They are the kinds of chocolate chip cookies you might find in thought bubbles over children's heads on Christmas morning.

Preheat the oven to 350°F. Line two rimmed baking sheets with parchment paper.

In a mixing bowl, mix the sugars, oil, applesauce, and cornstarch. Use a strong fork and mix really well until it resembles caramel, about 2 minutes. Mix in the vanilla.

Add 1 cup of the flour, the baking soda, and the salt. Mix until well incorporated. Mix in the remaining ½ cup flour. Fold in the chocolate chips. The dough will be a little stiff, so use your hands to really work them in.

Roll the dough into ping-pong balls. Flatten them out in your hands to about 2½ inches. Place on a baking sheet and bake, rotating and swapping the baking sheets halfway through, until they are just a little browned around the edges, about 8 minutes—no more than 9. Let cool on the baking sheets for about 5 minutes, then transfer to a cooling rack.

Lemon Drop
THUMBPRINT
COOKIES

FOR THE COOKIES:

½ cup refined coconut oil, melted

¾ cup sugar

3 tablespoons unsweetened almond milk (or your favorite nondairy milk)

1 teaspoon pure vanilla extract

2 tablespoons finely grated lemon zest

1½ cups all-purpose flour

1 teaspoon cornstarch

½ teaspoon baking powder

½ teaspoon salt

FOR THE LEMON DROP FILLING:

¾ cup water

⅓ cup fresh lemon juice

2 teaspoons finely grated lemon zest

⅓ cup sugar

1 tablespoon cornstarch

¾ teaspoon agar powder

1/16 teaspoon ground turmeric

Tip

You'll need about 8 lemons to get all of the zest and juice for this recipe. And definitely get a friend or child or the mailman to help you fill the cookies when ready, because the filling tends to set fast.

These are the cookies for the lemon lover in your life: lemon shortbread with a gorgeous, sparkling lemon gem center. They are always eye catchers on a cookie plate, and a little something different when you need a break from pumpkin and cloves.

MAKE THE COOKIES: Preheat the oven to 350°F. Line two large rimmed baking sheets with parchment paper.

In a large mixing bowl, use a fork to beat together the coconut oil and sugar for about a minute. Add the milk, vanilla, and lemon zest and beat for a minute more, until it resembles applesauce.

Add about half of the flour, plus the cornstarch, baking powder, and salt, and mix well. Add the remainder of the flour and mix until a soft dough forms.

Roll the dough into balls, about 2 tablespoons each, then flatten each ball a bit into a 2-inch disk. Place the disks on the prepared sheets about 2 inches apart. Use your thumb to create a large indentation in the center of each cookie. Bake until the bottoms are golden brown, 10 to 12 minutes. When they come out of the oven and the tops are still soft, use the rounded handle of a wooden spoon to gently press into the indentation to make sure there is plenty of room for the lemon drop filling.

Let the cookies cool on the sheets for 3 minutes or so, then transfer to cooling racks to cool the rest of the way.

MAKE THE LEMON DROP FILLING AND ASSEMBLE THE COOKIES: Don't start this until the cookies are fully cooled and ready to be filled. You need to fill them as soon as the filling is ready to make sure that it does not set before it gets to the cookies.

Stir together all the filling ingredients in a small saucepot. Bring to a boil over medium-high heat, then lower the heat and simmer for 5 minutes.

While the filling is still very hot, use a tablespoon to spoon the mixture into the indentation in each cookie. Let the filling set in a cool place at room temperature. Once it's relatively set, transfer the cookies to the refrigerator to set completely, about 30 minutes. Let the cookies come to room temperature before serving.

Peanut Butter–
CHOCOLATE CHIP
COOKIES

MAKES
24
COOKIES

TOTAL
30 MINUTES
ACTIVE
15 MINUTES

¾ cup refined coconut oil, at room temperature

¾ cup creamy natural peanut butter

½ cup granulated sugar

½ cup packed brown sugar

¼ cup unsweetened almond milk (or your favorite nondairy milk)

2 teaspoons pure vanilla extract

1½ cups all-purpose flour

1 tablespoon cornstarch

1 teaspoon baking powder

¼ teaspoon salt

1 cup semisweet chocolate chips

Peanut butter–chocolate chip has always been my comfort cookie. It takes about, oh, let's say ten, to make all my problems go away. But we don't need to worry about problems, it's Christmas! These are as peanut buttery as I could get without turning the recipe into just a big old spoonful of peanut butter. They are, not to be conceited, total perfection. The whole peanut butter package.

Preheat the oven to 350°F. Line two rimmed baking sheets with parchment paper.

In a large mixing bowl, use an electric mixer to beat together the oil and peanut butter. Beat in the sugars until fluffy. Add the milk and vanilla.

Sift in ¾ cup of the flour, along with the cornstarch, baking powder, and salt. Beat until smooth. Add the chocolate chips and use a fork to distribute them throughout. Add the remaining ¾ cup flour and mix with a fork until well combined.

Place twelve 2-tablespoon scoops of dough on each baking sheet, a few inches apart. Lightly flatten them with your hand. Bake until golden on the edges, about 10 minutes. Let the cookies cool on the baking sheets for a few minutes, then transfer to a cooling rack to cool completely.

CANDY CANE
Fudge
COOKIES

MAKES

36

COOKIES

TOTAL
45 MINUTES
ACTIVE
25 MINUTES

½ cup refined coconut oil, at room temperature

1¼ cups sugar

½ cup unsweetened applesauce, at room temperature

¼ cup unsweetened almond milk (or your favorite nondairy milk), at room temperature

2 teaspoons pure vanilla extract

2 cups all-purpose flour

⅔ cup unsweetened cocoa powder, sifted if clumpy

1 teaspoon baking soda

½ teaspoon salt

2 (3-ounce) peppermint chocolate bars, chopped up

4 crushed-up candy canes (see Tip)

Chocolate and minty chocolate with crushed candy canes. These cookies scream "CHRISTMAS" so loud that you might have to tell them to shut up! These are the cookies you bring to the office (or collective artspace) to share with everyone. They are going to be the best thing that happens to anyone this holiday season, even if they get that Cabbage Patch Kid they've been so desperately wanting.

Preheat the oven to 350°F. Lightly grease two rimmed baking sheets.

In a large bowl, cream together the oil and sugar until light and fluffy. Add the applesauce and milk and mix gently; it might make the oil clump and firm up a bit, but that's okay. Mix in the vanilla.

Add 1 cup of the flour, along with the cocoa powder, baking soda, and salt and mix well. Mix in the peppermint chocolate chunks and then add the remaining 1 cup flour and mix until it firms up. You might need to use your hands to get it fully incorporated.

Place twelve 1½-tablespoon scoops of dough on each baking sheet, a few inches apart. Flatten slightly with your hand. Place a pinch of crushed candy cane in the center of each and press gently into the surface.

Bake for 10 minutes. Remove from the oven and let cool for 5 minutes, then transfer to a cooling rack to cool completely.

Tips *You don't have to find peppermint chocolate for these, but it's pretty darn good. Chocolate chips or dark chocolate bars will work, too.*

To crush candy canes, place them in a plastic zip-top bag and pound on them with something heavy (a hammer maybe?) until they are in pieces that are no bigger than ½ inch.

Cranberry-Spice
OATMEAL COOKIES

⅓ cup refined coconut oil, at room temperature

⅓ cup packed brown sugar

⅓ cup granulated sugar

2 teaspoons pure vanilla extract

1 tablespoon cornstarch

3 tablespoons unsweetened almond milk (or your favorite nondairy milk)

½ cup all-purpose flour

½ teaspoon baking soda

1½ teaspoons pumpkin pie spice (see Tip)

½ teaspoon salt

1½ cups rolled oats

½ cup dried cranberries

½ cup chopped walnuts

——— Tip ———

If you don't have pumpkin pie spice, a combination of ¾ teaspoon ground ginger, ¾ teaspoon ground cinnamon, and a pinch of ground cloves ought to do it!

These gorgeous little clusters of oats are studded with ruby cranberries. Crispy on the edges, chewy inside, with a hint of spice. These are for the adult cookie lover. Unless the kids eat them all.

Preheat the oven to 350°F. Lightly grease two large rimmed baking sheets.

In a large mixing bowl, use a handheld electric mixer or a strong fork to cream together the oil and sugars. Mix in the vanilla. Add the cornstarch and milk and mix until the cornstarch is dissolved.

Sift in the flour, baking soda, pumpkin pie spice, and salt and mix to combine. Add the oats, cranberries, and nuts and use your hands to form a stiff dough.

Place twelve 2-tablespoon scoops of dough on each baking sheet a few inches apart. Flatten slightly with your hand. Bake until the edges are lightly browned, 10 to 12 minutes. Remove from the oven and cool for about 5 minutes, then transfer to a cooling rack to cool completely.

Acknowledgments

This book was a five-year process that could probably have its own behind-the-music-style biopic created for it. So much happened and so many people came in and out of my life that it's almost impossible to know whom to thank. But there are a few constants!

JOHN McDEVITT, for taking care of the cats while I worked like a dad in a '60s movie, never home to see his family.

TERRY ROMERO AND ABBY WOHL, for being besties. Even long distance, without getting to taste the food, you were at the table.

OMAHA CREW: Angie Anaya, for baking, testing, piping, and bringing treats! Sorry I lost your pans. Daniel Ocanto for assisting, writing ingredients down wrong, and everything. Summer Miller, for assisting, writing ingredients down meticulously. Josh Foo, for the foobulous footos. Sarah Morrison, for being the heart of Modern Love Omaha when I couldn't. Mick Ridgway, for occasional store runs.

BROOKLYN CREW: Timothy Pakron, for being my pookie boo bubble muffin. Vanessa Rees, for the gorge photos, as always. Lauren LaPenna, for stylin'. All of the interns. I forgot your names, sorry, but you're interns!

PROFESSIONAL STUFF: Mark Gerald, for agenting. Michael Szczerban at Little, Brown, for editing. And patience. Peggy Freudenthal at Little, Brown, for producing and editing. Laura Palese, for making our visions come to life! Karen Wise, for copyediting and making sense of everything.

MY RECIPE TESTERS: Nikki Benecke, Michelle Cavigliano, Panda Cookie, Stephanie Crowdis, Holly French, Paula Gross, Cara Heberling, Michelle of House Lewis, Emily Howarth, Gabrielle Pope, Dayna Rozental, Amanda Sacco, Garrick Stegner, Angela White, Liz Wyman, and everyone else!

Index

Page numbers in italics refer to photographs.

About the Author

ISA CHANDRA MOSKOWITZ
is the bestselling author or coauthor
of the hit books *Isa Does It*,
Veganomicon, *Vegan with a Vengeance*,
and many other titles. She
created the beloved website Post Punk
Kitchen, and her restaurant, Modern
Love, has locations in Omaha
and Brooklyn.